Japan's Imperial Army

Japan's Imperial Army

Its Rise and Fall, 1853–1945

Edward J. Drea

University Press of Kansas

Published by the University Press of Kansas (Lawrence, Kansas 66045),
which was organized by the Kansas Board of Regents and is operated and
funded by Emporia State University, Fort Hays State University, Kansas State
University, Pittsburg State University, the University of Kansas, and Wichita
State University

Library of Congress Cataloging-in-Publication Data

Drea, Edward J., 1944–
    Japan's Imperial Army : its rise and fall, 1853–1945 / Edward J. Drea.
        p.   cm. — (Modern war studies)
    Includes bibliographical references and index.
    ISBN 978-0-7006-1663-3 (cloth : alk. paper)
    ISBN 978-0-7006-2234-4 (pbk. : alk. paper)
    ISBN 978-0-7006-2235-1 (ebook)
    1. Japan. Rikugun—History. 2. Japan—History, Military—1868–1945.
I. Title.
    DS838.7.D74 2009
    355.00952'09034—dc22   2009007442

British Library Cataloguing-in-Publication Data is available.

Printed in the United States of America

10 9 8 7 6 5

Contents

Preface

This brief history of Japan's first modern army covers events from the 1850s through 1945. It is an introductory synthesis told mainly from secondary sources, most in the Japanese language. I made use of the many excellent English-language monographs on Japan's army but relied more heavily on Japanese-language materials because military history scholarship in Japan has become impressively sophisticated and diverse over the past twenty years. No longer do Japanese historians dismiss the old imperial army with sweeping generalizations. Instead, extensive research in primary documents, the appearance of new evidence, and fresh interpretations of the army's larger role in the context of Japanese society have revised the standard narrative of an army inherently bent on aggression. One goal, then, is to introduce the English-language readers to this new Japanese military history.

I describe major military campaigns briefly and focus on institutional issues arising from those conflicts that shaped the army's strategy, doctrine, and values. These subjects are well known to specialists of modern Japanese history, but a chronologically arranged, balanced English-language account of the army has not previously been available. Overviews of the army tend to be weighted to its twentieth-century performance, especially during World War II, creating a lopsided impression of an army with unique qualities. This narrative, generally divided by decades, gives roughly equal attention to army affairs during the 1880s and World War II. Such an approach offers a balanced perspective on the army's evolution and helps to explain the action and conduct of an institution whose major legacy is suicidal disgrace.

From an ad hoc confederation, the army became the single most powerful institution in the nation. Its leaders wrestled with describing the army's role in the newly unified nation, defining its mission, and designing its values. The intellectual foundations of the institution shifted as the army constantly reinvented itself to fulfill the changing military and cultural imperatives of a transformed Japanese society. In other words, though the outward appearances of the army of 1895 and that of 1925 were similar, the institution was substantially different.

It was not just a matter of adapting western technology or mimicking the West's pattern of modernization. Japan developed a first-class army with an efficient military schooling system, a well-organized active duty and reserve force, a professional officer corps that thought in terms of the regional threat, and tough, well-trained soldiers armed with appropriate weapons. Changing social and political ideas, personal rivalries, new concepts of warfare, evolving military doctrine, regional geography, and potential enemies and allies shaped the army's place in society. Throughout its existence the army sought its core values in real or imagined precedents and relied increasingly on an emperor-centered ideology to validate it as a special institution in the Japanese polity.

The Japanese soldier's propensity for self-immolation, the military's emphasis on intangible or spiritual factors in battle, and a fanatical determination to fight to the death became the army's hallmarks. Overemphasis of these characteristics skewed an understanding of strategy, high-level policy, and the army's evolution, especially for the period before 1941. I suggest that historical circumstances shaped Japan's first modern army and that international pressures determined the army's options, if not its fate. To deal with common danger, the army idealized traditional values, many of them imaginary but nonetheless offering a vision that a wider Japanese audience understood and shared. The formative days of the army occasionally resembled a B-grade samurai movie replete with wild sword fights in back alleys, assassinations, and murderous blood feuds over the institution's future. These sensational and sanguinary events, much like the later military coup d'états, atrocities, and suicidal banzai charges, inform our perspective of an army run amok, led by fanatics whose blind devotion to the emperor encouraged barbaric behavior. The administrative and operational expansion and development of the army, including its strategy and doctrine, did not make headlines, but this institutional process was decisive in forming the contours of the mid-1930s army, the force that fought in Asia and the Pacific.

The Japanese way of war or style of warfare evolved over seventy years. Subsequent interpretations of the immediate past layered with hoary samurai myths burnished the army's self-image. Layer upon layer of precedent and tradition formed the bedrock of the edifice by 1941. There were, of course, dramatic events that affected the army's course, but it was the accumulated past that shaped the army, narrowed its options, influenced its decisions, and made it the institution that conquered most of Asia.

I am grateful to many people in Japan and the United States for their generous assistance. Professor Akagi Kanji of Keiō University responded to my questions with celerity and accuracy. Professor Tobe Ryōichi, National Defense Academy, led me through recent Japanese military historiography; and

Professor Hata Ikuhiko, the doyen of Japanese military historians, was always helpful in explaining the fine points of Japan's prewar army. I am also indebted to the faculty and staff of the National Institute for Defense Studies, Military History Department for their sustained assistance over the years.

Dr. Robert H. Berlin, School of Advanced Military Studies, emeritus; Professor Roger Jeans, Washington and Lee University, emeritus; and Dr. Stanley L. Falk read the manuscript in its various stages. Their constructive criticism, historical expertise, and insightful comments improved the final draft and spared me from numerous errors. Professor Mark R. Peattie, the Walter H. Shorenstein Institute Asia-Pacific Research Center at Stanford University, refereed my draft and made helpful suggestions. David Rennie's cartographic and computer talents created the maps.

My thanks to Ariane De Pree-Kajfez of Stanford University Press for permission to use material that will appear in the forthcoming publication *The Battle for China: Essays on the Military History of the Sino-Japanese War*. I must also acknowledge the staff at the Pentagon Library in Washington, D.C., for their unfailing assistance and friendliness. Kathleen Heincer, Linda McGuire, Yolanda Miller, John Mills, Debbie Reed, and Barbara Risser all contributed to the research behind this book.

Finally I must thank Michael Briggs, general editor of the University of Kansas Press, for his constant encouragement and Job-like patience. When we first discussed this project several years ago, I foolishly remarked that I could complete it in three years' time. It soon became plain to me that the volume of new research, the appearance of fresh sources, and the evolving historiography in Japan and the United States would make this a more daunting effort than I imagined. My thanks also extend to the editorial staff for their first-rate editorial assistance.

Japan's Imperial Army

1

Prelude to Imperial Restoration

The arrival of Commodore Matthew Perry's black ships in 1853 shattered Japan's self-imposed isolation. The *bakufu* (shogunate)—the military government under the Tokugawa shogun or generalissimo that ruled Japan—was unable to deal effectively with the foreign intrusion, and despite violent internal opposition, within five years it concluded a commercial treaty that opened eight ports to trade, unilaterally set tariffs, and established extraterritoriality. By exposing its weakness, the *bakufu* emboldened its enemies. In an effort to rally support, the shogun's chief councilor broke tradition and sought approval for the treaty from Emperor Kōmei in Kyoto.[1] Kōmei's refusal to sanction the treaty split the *bakufu* and the court and began ten years of intrigue, violence, terror, and negotiation that culminated in the shogunate's collapse. During that tumultuous decade, radical loyalist warriors, usually of the middle- or lower-ranking samurai class, were in the forefront of efforts to overthrow the Tokugawa regime. Many were xenophobic, but the military might of the Europeans and Americans sobered upstart samurai and shogunate authorities alike.

Aware of the devastation wreaked by the Anglo-French attack on Peking in 1860 and concerned about Russian probes toward Tsushima Island, the *bakufu* established arsenals to manufacture bronze cannon, ordered a steam-driven warship from Holland, imported tens of thousands of small arms, and sought western, mainly French, military and technical experts to organize its forces into a modern army and navy.[2] By 1862 it had revitalized its military forces and assigned priority to a navy in order to control the ports and coast, the locations most imperiled by the foreign military threat. A handful of small frigates and corvettes allowed the *bakufu* to control the inland coastal shipping lanes and move troops quickly by sea to potential trouble spots. The shogun's reorganized army fared less well because it had to depend on samurai selected by local *han* (domain) authorities or resort to unpopular mandatory quotas to fill its ranks. In either case, a *han* would not necessarily send its best men to the shogun's army, and the shogun lacked the power to arbitrarily carry through military

1

reforms. Furthermore, many warriors scorned the new lock-step western-style drill and disdained firearms and bayonets in favor of their traditional swords and spears. Their resistance to change was the first indication that the warrior class was abandoning its monopoly on military power.[3]

Kyoto emerged as the center of national politics, where loyalists from southwestern Japan's Chōshū domain and court aristocrats who wanted to restore the emperor and expel the barbarians maneuvered against moderate *bakufu* officials, samurai from Satsuma *han* in southern Kyūshū, and some aristocrats who favored a union of court and shogunate. Pressured by radical reformers, in January 1863 Kōmei set June as the deadline for the *bakufu* to expel the western barbarians from Japan. This was easier decreed than done, particularly since the foreigners punished the offending domain, not the shogun.

Moderates among the shogunate's leaders understood that they were no match for western military technology and armaments and preferred a more passive resistance. At the southern tip of Honshū, however, in late June Chōshū extremists enforced the imperial command and attacked foreign commercial ships passing through the narrow Strait of Shimonoseki, cannonading a French warship and later damaging a Dutch merchantman. Retribution followed on July 26 when the gunboat USS *Wyoming* sank one Chōshū vessel, mauled a second, and knocked out several guns, all the while lying outside the range of the domain's ancient cannon.[4] A few days later, French warships bombarded the Chōshū forts and then sent a landing party ashore that spiked the guns, seized rifles and swords, and burned scores of nearby houses. This typical mid-nineteenth century punitive expedition foretold what was in store for those who resisted the power of the West.

About a month later, in mid-August, British warships appeared in southern Kyūshū's Kagoshima Bay to enforce demands that Satsuma pay an indemnity that the *bakufu* had agreed to and surrender one of its samurai who had murdered a British subject the previous year. The fleet's arrival coincided with a typhoon, but the flagship commander ignored the high winds and heavy rainsqualls to give battle. He unintentionally steered his ships into the Satsuma gunnery range, making them easy targets for the well-trained Japanese gunners. Ten coastal batteries (eighty-three cannon total) raked the British vessels as they maneuvered in the howling winds between the towering backdrop of Mt. Sakurajima and the castle town of Kagoshima, inflicting sixty-six casualties. Kagoshima, however, suffered the greater damage. The heavier British guns outranged the coastal batteries and demolished them. Strong winds compounded the effects of British incendiary rockets falling into the town and burned through large swaths of wooden neighborhoods.[5] The fighting ended in a draw, the British sailing away and the samurai dousing the flames.

Despite their antiforeign outbursts, individual domains like Chōshū and

Satsuma had experimented since the 1840s with western-style artillery to strengthen their military power vis-à-vis the *bakufu* and keep the West at arm's length.[6] It was not unusual then for Satsuma to react to its setback by arranging through British diplomats in Japan to hire English military advisers to reorganize and reequip its military forces. Satsuma samurai quickly adopted the new, dispersed infantry tactics taught by their foreign advisers and dropped the traditional massed assault formations. Satsuma's leaders also modified their political policies. In September 1863 they allied themselves with warriors from northeast Japan's Aizu domain and restored more moderate nobles in Kyoto to control the imperial court.

Chōshū responded to its defeat by organizing mixed warrior-commoner rifle units commanded by 24-year-old Takasugi Shinsaku, an antiforeign extremist recalled from internal exile (for setting fire to the British consulate) to fix the domain's army. In the late 1850s Takasugi had been a follower of loyalist leader and ideologue Yoshida Shōin and through him had connections with other young radical samurai like Maebara Issei (age 25), Itō Hirobumi (18), and Yamagata Aritomo (21). Takasugi's slight frame and reputation as a womanizer and heavy drinker belied a young man of unparalleled bravery with a passionate devotion to radical reform.

Takasugi was far more than a hired sword. He was intelligent, well versed in western military science, and on record that hereditary warriors were too cowardly to fight for an imperial restoration. He dramatized his contempt for his class by cutting off his top-knot, a samurai status symbol. To replace the reluctant samurai, by mid-1863 Takasugi had organized samurai, peasants, merchants—indeed, anyone willing to join him—into the *kiheitai* (extraordinary units), a name derived from Sun Tzu's injunction that the standing army fixes and distracts the enemy; the extraordinary (*ki*) forces strike when and where they are not expected.[7] *Kiheitai* militia units initially were supposed to back up Chōshū's standing samurai army. They were poorly equipped with various obsolete muskets and matchlocks and usually consigned to patrolling the domain's coastlines.

After the Satsuma-Aizu coup, Chōshū extremists, whose radicalism now alarmed the court, fled from the imperial city. But without an effective strategy to deal with the foreigners, the shogunate continued its conciliatory policy. Encouraged by the shogunate's weakness in dealing with the Westerners, in mid-August 1864 Chōshū radicals marched on Kyoto to restore the emperor. A combined Satsuma-Aizu force blocked their approach and fighting erupted at the Forbidden Gate, one of several entrances to the imperial palace grounds.

In the day-long battle, Aizu samurai's skill in traditional hand-to-hand combat and Satsuma's modern artillery soundly defeated the Chōshū insurgents, including the attached *kiheitai* units. Gunfire, explosions, and arson destroyed thousands of Kyoto dwellings as fires raged for three days. Thousands of refugees from the blackened neighborhoods huddled along the riverbanks, carrying whatever possessions they had on their backs. Sixteen Chōshū ringleaders and their lieutenants committed suicide just outside the capital. Radical court nobles fled the capital, and the court demanded that the shogun punish Chōshū.

Chōshū suffered another setback on September 4 when an allied fleet of eighteen warships carrying more than 5,000 troops and almost 300 cannon moved into the Shimonoseki Strait. In dense fog the next morning the ships unwittingly sailed within range of a *kiheitai* battery, where a young samurai named Yamagata Aritomo opened fire, damaging the flagship. Retaliation came swiftly. Around noon, about 2,000 western troops landed and scattered the Chōshū defenders. During the next two days the foreigners seized all the coastal defenses, spiked cannons, and tossed any remaining ammunition into the sea. After posing for a commemorative photograph atop an occupied coastal battery, the landing force carried off swords, armor, and samurai helmets as trophies.[8]

Meanwhile the shogun obtained an imperial command to punish the rebellious domain and in late 1864 launched the first Chōshū expedition. Rather than extensive fighting, the overpowering show of force by the 150,000-man coalition sufficed to oust Chōshū's discredited and isolated radical loyalists. The shogun replaced them with conservative bureaucrats and, after punishing senior Chōshū officials for encouraging the loyalists and enforcing other punitive measures, disbanded the military coalition in mid-January 1865.

After being driven from the capital, Chōshū's younger reformers concluded that inferior weaponry, not the *kiheitai* concept, was to blame for Chōshū's setback at Kyoto's Forbidden Gate. They resisted the newly installed Chōshū authorities' attempts to disband the *kiheitai* and denounced the domain's moderate leaders for suppressing the radical cause and submitting to the *bakufu's* humiliating demands. They also scorned warriors who insisted on fighting in traditional fashion and encouraged more mixed commoner-warrior volunteer units using modern western tactics and weaponry.

Loyalists marked time while Takasugi expanded the *kiheitai* peasant militias and rifle units and armed them with modern weapons purchased from British arms dealers in Shanghai by Satsuma agents and covertly delivered to Chōshū. Takasugi enforced draconian discipline, purging *kiheitai* ranks by executing dissidents and deserters. Ōmura Masujirō, another of Chōshū's young, dynamic military reformers, trained *kiheitai* rifle units in modern western skirmisher tactics. A self-taught tactician, Ōmura used translations of Dutch military manuals to develop a tactical doctrine for the *kiheitai* to fight as guerrillas or *franciers* in support of regular forces.[9] In early 1865 Takasugi's *kiheitai* units raided the domain capital at Shimonoseki, throwing Chōshū into civil war.

The mixed warrior-and-commoner *kiheitai* units displayed great tactical skill in employing their new weaponry and soon became the armed vanguard of reform. By March 1865 Takasugi controlled Shimonoseki and had routed government troops sent to oust him. He then ousted Chōshū's pro-shogunate conservatives, but by that time Takasugi was mortally ill with the consumption that eventually killed him in 1867. Because of his deteriorating physical condition, domain authorities appointed Ōmura to reorganize the army. Besides his military expertise, Ōmura was more pro-emperor than antiforeigner, which made him attractive to Chōshū's new leaders, who were trying to present a more moderate face to court and *bakufu*.

Ōmura guided army reform, sold samurai armor and helmets to raise money to buy modern small arms, and trained *kiheitai* rifle units. Recruits were armed with new Minié rifles, and close-order bayonet drills replaced traditional swordsmanship. By mid-1865 Ōmura had assembled a 4,000-man infantry force, divided equally between warriors and commoners. Word of these military initiatives alarmed the *bakufu* enough that it ordered another military expedition against Chōshū. This time, however, domains were divided over the value of such a campaign and wary of the resurgent *bakufu*. Satsuma leaders, covertly assisting Chōshū's rearmament, later concluded a secret military alliance with Chōshū. Satsuma also used its considerable influence to dilute support for another Chōshū expedition.[10]

Nevertheless, in June 1866 the *bakufu*'s weakened expeditionary army marched on Chōshū, intending to surround the domain and attack it along exterior lines. Unable to forge a strong military alliance because Satsuma refused to join the coalition, the expedition's dilatory advance gave Ōmura time to prepare his defenses. Commanding units along Chōshū's northern border, Ōmura employed flanking attacks or struck enemy forces from the rear—tactics he termed "rabbit hunting," designed to drive defenders from their warrens. Relying on such highly mobile infantry tactics, *kiheitai* units offset their inferior numbers and lack of artillery.

A *bakufu* war diary described the encounter of a government column with two ranks of *kiheitai* riflemen who fired at them from across a stream at ranges of 400 and 500 yards. The galling fire forced the densely packed *bakufu* formation to disperse and sacrifice tactical control or suffer heavy losses, either way losing operational integrity. Later that day concealed skirmishers sniped at the column from village rooftops, tree lines, or undergrowth, rarely firing more than a single round before fleeing, but still disrupting an entire column's march.[11] A combination of modern small arms and guerrilla tactics checked the *bakufu*'s advance as the *kiheitai* ambushed, outflanked, and encircled the shogun's half-hearted allies, who fought in the traditional massed formations and relied on muskets, spears, and swords. By October Ōmura had gone over to the offensive and scattered the shogun's demoralized forces.

Meanwhile, on the southern front Takasugi and his chief lieutenant, Yamagata Aritomo, led *kiheitai* units across the Shimonoseki Strait. *Kiheitai* raiding parties launched amphibious attacks against *bakufu*-held ports, burning docks and supplies. Small, nimble gunboats and launches harassed the shogunate's larger warships, which had difficulty maneuvering in the restricted waters and soon were forced to abandon the strait. Without Satsuma's military support, the *bakufu* had to throw badly armed and poorly motivated warriors from several minor fiefs into the fighting but refused to reinforce or resupply them. Troop morale cracked, and the dispirited shogunate army fled to Nagasaki.[12] Takasugi's innovative guerrilla-style ground and naval tactics had eliminated the threat on Chōshū's southern flank and given the radicals control of the Shimonoseki Strait.

The heaviest fighting against the main shogun armies raged back and forth along Chōshū's northern border, where *kiheitai* units held the mountainous high ground and ambushed the *bakufu* armies marching through passes or heavily forested areas. Peasants armed with bamboo spears or long-bladed hoes harried the shogun's troops. One *bakufu* commander was astonished at the sight of local women and children armed with bamboo spears harassing his withdrawing units. By September the *bakufu* deputy commander concluded that the inability to feed or pay his troops, coupled with their obsolete weaponry and the determination of the commoner and peasant units, made success impossible.[13] The shogun's death later that month provided the face-saving justification to end the foundering expedition.

Ōmura's *kiheitai* performance confirmed for up-and-coming Chōshū captains like Kido Kōin and Yamagata Aritomo that commoners could indeed make good soldiers. The *kiheitai* units were less effective, however, against domains like Aizu that were trained in western tactics and used artillery.[14] That experience convinced Ōmura that rifles and bayonets could not overcome well-defended breastworks; he immersed himself in studying the latest artillery tactics.

During the final campaign, Takasugi suffered a tubercular relapse. Although Yamagata had served as his chief lieutenant and displayed organizational talent, shortly before Takasugi's death in April 1867 he named Ōmura his successor. Ōmura was less politically minded and ideological than Yamagata, and his technical and tactical experience better qualified him to lead the new Chōshū army.[15] As for the *bakufu*, it tried to rebound from defeat with foreign assistance to reorganize its army. In January 1867 French military advisers had organized two modern infantry battalions and two batteries of artillery. With the shogunate and its enemies rearming and reorganizing, a military showdown was inevitable.

The Boshin Civil War

Emperor Kōmei's death in early 1867 and succession by his 14-year-old son Mutsuhito (who would become the Meiji Emperor) provided Satsuma and Chōshū the opportunity to legitimize their rebellion against the shogunate. That November the new shogun agreed to resign, hand over administrative power to the throne, and withdraw government troops from Kyoto to Osaka. Loyalist troops, including large contingents from Chōshū and Satsuma, quickly replaced them in Kyoto. The newcomers soon staged a military review. As the new emperor, shielded behind bamboo blinds in his royal box, looked on, 170 drummers paraded through the capital's streets, leading uniformed Satsuma units that performed successive demonstrations of British-style drills and tactical maneuvers.[16] The imperial presence conferred legitimacy on the new army, and the public display of pomp and military muscle was a thinly veiled warning to the *bakufu* that loyalist forces would fight.

Abetted by court radicals, leaders from Satsuma and Chōshū next obtained a rescript (memorial) from the boy emperor authorizing them to overthrow the shogun. Armed with the imperial writ, on January 3, 1868, Chōshū and Satsuma forces seized the imperial palace in Kyoto, proclaimed an imperial restoration, and ordered the shogun to surrender all his power and lands. Unwilling to accept such humiliating terms, the shogun quickly dispatched troops from Osaka to crush the rebel stronghold. Thus on the morning of January 27, about 5,000 loyalist troops, mainly from Chōshū but stiffened by Satsuma and Tosa allies, were blocking three times that many *bakufu* warriors gathered at Fushimi, a small commercial port and administrative center just south of Kyoto.[17]

Satsuma forces commanded by Saigō Takamori, a charismatic loyalist and a key domain leader, barricaded the two main roads leading from Fushimi to Kyoto. The advance echelon of a lengthy column of *bakufu* troops strung out along the Toba highway arrived at the roadblocks and demanded entry to Kyoto. Refused, they withdrew, but in late afternoon again demanded passage. The Satsuma clansmen answered with a volley of artillery fire, and the *bakufu* warriors, armed with spears and swords, rushed the well-defended barricades. Deadly artillery fire and infantry skirmisher tactics inflicted heavy losses on the massed attackers. Lacking centralized command and control, the shogun's forces fought individual skirmishes, not a coordinated battle, and eventually retreated.[18]

The cacophony of musket and cannon carried eastward to nearby Fushimi where warriors from Chōshū, Satsuma, and Tosa were blocking the shogun's columns. When pro-Tokugawa supporters from Aizu tried to force their way along the Fushimi highway, loyalist artillery and rifle fire halted the Aizu spearmen's attack and drove them back to Fushimi. Reinforced by *bakufu* supporters, the Aizu warriors fought pitched battles with loyalists in Fushimi's broad streets and narrow alleyways. Both sides torched homes and buildings to drive enemies into the streets. Cannon fire and explosions also destroyed homes and warehouses and set the large shogunate administrative complex ablaze. The fighting subsided as the Tokugawa forces withdrew after midnight under a sky reddened by flames.[19]

Meanwhile along the Toba highway, the retreating *bakufu* forces improvised a hasty defense. Fighting from behind barricades made from sake barrels, straw tatami mats, and wooden doors, they fought the pursing Satsuma troops to a standstill, inflicting heavy casualties of the attackers. The turnabout elevated *bakufu* morale, and commanders expected to rout the Satsuma army the next morning. Saigō and other key officers realized that their cause hung in the balance and prepared to spirit the young emperor to the safety of a mountain redoubt in case the loyalists were defeated. As long as the young ruler remained in their hands they could legitimately conduct a war against the government forces. Possession of the emperor, real or symbolic, was essential for the new army, which was determined to avoid the impression that the fighting was merely a personal quarrel pitting Satsuma and Chōshū against the *bakufu*.[20]

At dawn on January 28, loyalists ambushed a Tokugawa column trying to force its way up the Toba road. Formations of *bakufu* spearmen collided with one another while attempting to maneuver from march to tactical formations along the narrow dirt track, horses bolted at the sounds of cannon and gunfire, and a steady fusillade from skirmishers hidden in the undergrowth made the loyalists seem to be everywhere. Several *bakufu* commanders fell to well-aimed Minié balls, and the disorganized column fell back. They quickly regrouped, however, and charged the heavily outnumbered Satsuma defenders.

At that critical point, 21-year-old Prince Ninnaji (Yoshiaki) appeared at the head of a column of reinforcements sent from an imperial general headquarters located on Kyoto's southern fringes. Unfurling the imperial brocade banner and carrying a sword that the emperor had presented to him as commander in chief, Ninnaji personified the unity of the court and the new army. Loyalist morale soared at the sight of the imperial banner that signified their cause transcended domain interests and enjoyed the emperor's support.[21] They repulsed the assault and then pursued the retreating *bakufu* forces, harassing their flanks with artillery and rifle fire.

Little fighting had occurred near Fushimi because the greatly outnumbered Satsuma forces were reluctant to provoke a major battle and contented themselves by burning part of the town, leaving a holding force to pin down the pro-shogun units, and maneuvering to reinforce Toba. The shogunate had expected to outflank the loyalists near Fushimi and attack them from the rear. But the shogunate commander had fled two days before, and without overall leadership, piecemeal attacks soon collapsed and the dispirited government troops withdrew.

Throughout the fighting the separated *bakufu* columns had no single commander. Troops along the Toba highway fought one battle while those along a nearby parallel road fought a separate one. Each domain fought according to its idiosyncratic tactics without coordination between the two forces or with the rear guard. The shogun's army squandered its numerical superiority, left troops massed along narrow highways instead of sending them to outflank the smaller loyalist units, and frittered away warriors in a series of uncoordinated attacks that left them increasingly isolated and susceptible to ambushes. Thoroughly defeated, the *bakufu* leaders agreed to surrender Osaka castle, but during the transfer of control a fire of mysterious origin exploded the ammunition magazine and destroyed the castle.

The four days of fighting claimed about 300 Satsuma or Chōshū warriors and more than double that number of *bakufu* troops. A Satsuma shock troop unit led by Kirino Toshiaki habitually spearheaded loyalist assaults and lost twenty-eight of its forty men. During the course of the war, Satsuma and Chōshū would suffer just over 25 percent of all government army casualties.[22]

The relatively few casualties obscured the disproportionate importance of the clashes. A loyalist defeat in the opening battle would have discredited the imperial cause and diminished the emperor's role in modern Japan's history. A military stalemate with a reinvigorated *bakufu* would have delayed Japan's political unification, leaving the country more vulnerable to foreign intervention. Instead the loyalist army had defeated the shogun's forces and done so in the name of the emperor, forging an enduring bond between throne and Japan's first modern army.

2

Civil War and the New Army

The Toba-Fushimi fighting marked the opening battle of the Boshin (dragon) Civil War, named after the Chinese zodiacal cyclic character that designated the year 1868. The new army fought under makeshift arrangements with unclear channels of command and control and no reliable recruiting base. Samurai and *kiheitai* units paradoxically were fighting in the name of the throne, but they did not belong to the throne. To correct this anomaly and defend the court, which was in open rebellion against the shogunate, in early March 1868 the newly proclaimed imperial government created various administrative offices, including a military branch. The next month it organized an imperial bodyguard, about 400 or 500 warriors, composed of Satsuma and Chōshū units augmented by veterans of the Toba-Fushimi battles, yeomen, and masterless warriors from various domains, who reported directly to the court. The imperial court next notified domains to restrict the size of their local armies and contribute to the expenses of a national officers' training school in Kyoto.[1]

Within a few months, however, authorities disbanded the ineffective military branch and the imperial bodyguard, which lacked modern equipment and weapons. To replace them, in April authorities established the military affairs directorate, composed of two bureaus: one for the army, one for the navy. The directorate drafted an army organization act based on manpower contributions from each domain proportional to its respective annual rice production.[2] This conscript army (*chōheigun*) integrated samurai and commoners from the various domains into its ranks.

As the Boshin Civil War continued, the newly formed military affairs directorate had expected to raise troops from the wealthier domains. In June 1868 it fixed the organization of the army by making each fief responsible, at least in theory, for sending to Kyoto ten men per each 10,000 *koku* of rice the domain produced.[3] The policy put the government in competition with the domains to recruit troops, a contradiction not remedied until April 1869 when it banned domains from enlisting soldiers. The quota system to recruit government troops, however, never worked as intended, and the authorities abolished it the following year.

Meanwhile, in mid-March 1868 Prince Arisugawa took command of the Eastern Expeditionary Force as loyalist columns pushed along three main highways toward the shogun's capital at Edo (present-day Tokyo). Skirmishes involving a few hundred warriors on either side brushed aside *bakufu* resistance, and the columns swiftly converged on the capital. The advancing army continually proclaimed its close bond with the imperial court, first to legitimize its cause; second, to brand enemies of the government as enemies of the court and therefore traitors; and third, to gain popular support.[4]

For food, supplies, horses, and weapons, the government army established a series of logistics relay stations along the three major thoroughfares. These small depots stocked material supplied by local pro-government domains or confiscated from *bakufu* agencies, senior retainers of the old regime, and anyone opposing the government. The army routinely impressed local villagers as porters or teamsters to move supplies between the depots and the frontline units. Japan's largest merchant families also contributed money and supplies to the new army. The Mitsui branch directors in Edo, for example, donated more than 25,000 *ryō* (US$25,000) as insurance to protect their storehouses from pro-*bakufu* arsonists and probably government troops as well.[5]

Government propaganda teams accompanied the army to extol the new imperial government's virtues and to attract adherents by offering an immediate halving of taxes on rice harvests. To complement the effort, the army issued regulations governing conduct. All ranks would share the same food, accommodations, and work details; troops would immediately report anyone spreading rumors that might lower morale; quarreling and fighting in camp were forbidden; attacks against foreigners were strictly prohibited; and commanders were supposed to prevent arson, plunder, and rape from tarnishing the new government's image.[6] The results were mixed. If the populace cooperated, they were treated fairly, which meant the men might be persuaded to work as military porters or laborers, the villages to donate food, and promises made to cooperate with the government army. But the standard tactic to combat the roving bands of Tokugawa supporters who harassed government columns with hit-and-run attacks was to burn nearby homes to deny the guerrillas shelter. Suspected collaborators were summarily executed.

As the government troops pushed into *bakufu* strongholds, coercion replaced persuasion. Soldiers requisitioned food; confiscated weapons, valuables, and cash; and impressed villagers for labor details. Although government orders prohibited arson, it was an effective tactic during battle and for pacification purposes. Uncooperative villages risked being burned to the ground, likely because soldiers understood that inhabitants feared arson above all other forms of retribution. In extreme cases, such as the final northeastern campaign, government troops torched more than one-third of the homes in the Akita domain. To avoid that fate, villagers along the army's route-of-march provided commanders with food, supplies, and intelligence.[7] But this cooperation was based on little more than extortion and did not indicate a sudden shift in allegiance to the new government.

By the time the main loyalist forces reached Edo in early May, Saigō Takamori had already negotiated a peaceful surrender of the city with *bakufu* agents, the shogunate being divided internally between hard-liners and those favoring an accommodation with the new government. The 41-year-old Saigō stood almost six feet tall and weighed about 250 pounds, making him a giant by Japanese standards. After a decade as a minor provincial official, in 1854 Saigō moved to Edo to promote Satsuma policies. Four years later reactionary shogunate officials forced him to flee to Satsuma, but he was then exiled. After his pardon in 1864, Satsuma officials sent Saigō to Kyoto to handle the domain's national affairs.

There was no denying Saigō's ability, but the man was an enigma, given to lengthy silences that could be interpreted as contemplative wisdom or hopeless stupidity. His indifference to awards, honors, or material trappings, complemented by his dynamic charisma and humanism, made Saigō the most respected personality in early Meiji Japan.[8] His deal with the *bakufu*, however, had enabled more than 2,000 warriors loyal to the shogun to escape from Edo, and the guerrilla war these reactionaries were waging against the loyalists was ravaging the nearby countryside.

North of Edo pro-*bakufu* forces held Utsunomiya castle; in early June, government forces defeated the shogun's troops in a series of minor engagements between Utsunomiya and Edo. They withstood a subsequent *bakufu* counteroffensive and, strengthened with reinforcements, occupied the castle to secure the northern approaches to Edo. The vanquished *bakufu* units fled to northern Japan.

Meanwhile, loyalist troops had garrisoned the shogun's capital without opposition, but their efficiency and morale slowly disintegrated as the provincial troops settled in to the comforts and fleshpots of the big city. As martial skills eroded, Saigō worried about the diehard pro-shogun radicals who retained de facto control of the city. The most powerful of these bands was the Shōgitai (League to Demonstrate Righteousness), formed in February 1868, which eventually enrolled about 2,000 warriors, each sworn to kill a Satsuma "traitor."

Operating from its headquarters in Edo's Ueno district, Shōgitai units selectively cracked down on the roving criminal gangs that had turned the nighttime capital into a place of robbery, murder, and extortion. Besides punishing

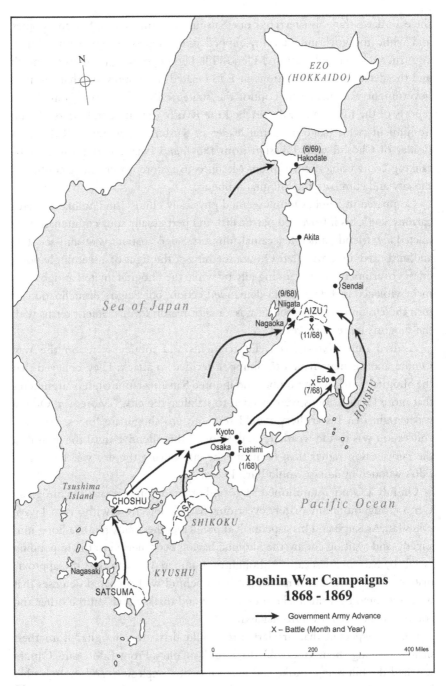

EZO
(HOKKAIDO)

(6/69)
Hakodate

Akita

Sea of Japan

Sendai

(9/68)
Niigata
Nagaoka

AIZU
X
(11/68)

HONSHU

X Edo
(7/68)

Kyoto
Osaka   Fushimi
X
(1/68)

Pacific Ocean

Tsushima
Island

CHOSHU

TOSA

SHIKOKU

Nagasaki

KYUSHU

SATSUMA

Boshin War Campaigns
1868 - 1869

→ Government Army Advance
X – Battle (Month and Year)

0   200   400 Miles

Map 1

these outlaws they also ferreted out Satsuma informers and pro-court spies, and while the government army slipped into idleness, Shōgitai units busily constructed strongholds around Ueno Hill. The ongoing fighting in the north and the deteriorating conditions in Edo created the impression that the new government was unable to control the strategically vital Edo region. When reports of the impasse in Edo reached the Kyoto government, leaders Ōkubo Toshimichi (with Saigō a central leader of Satsuma since 1864), Kido Kōin (leader of Chōshū with Takasugi from 1865), and Iwakura Tomomi (a high-ranking court noble) sent Ōmura Masujirō to restore government control in the city and eliminate the Shōgitai influence.[9]

Compared to Saigō, Ōmura seemed physically clumsy; and, unlike the gregarious Saigō, his introverted personality and perpetually sour countenance attracted few friends, much less casual admirers. Saigō's patient wait-and-see style and measured diplomacy left Ōmura seething at the sight of a seemingly powerless government army standing idly by while the Shōgitai incited antigovernment violence in Edo. Ōmura demanded action, but Saigō's disinclination to turn the city into a battleground was a major reason for his lenient terms with the shogun's representatives.

Assured from Kyoto that reinforcements and money were on the way, Ōmura and his lieutenant Etō Shimpei decided to attack. They believed that the Shōgitai were few in number and ignored Satsuma commanders' arguments that more loyalist troops were needed to stabilize the city.[10] Moreover, Ōmura was certain that his artillery would rout the pro-shogunate forces. His only concession was to the weather; he postponed the offensive until the arrival of the rainy season rather than bombard the city during the dry weather, when Edo's wooden buildings would burn like tinder.

On July 4 Ōmura summoned Saigō and ordered him to attack the Shōgitai's Ueno strongpoint immediately, overriding Saigō's objections with a casual wave of his fan. As Saigō and his captains had predicted, the attack ran headlong into a ready-and-waiting enemy, the Shōgitai having been alerted to the impending assault by Satsuma deserters. Although outnumbered two to one, the approximately 1,000 Shōgitai troops fought from behind well-prepared defenses that were anchored by a small lake on one flank and thick woods on the other and could only be taken by a frontal assault.[11]

Ōmura expected that artillery fire would drive the Shōgitai from their shelters, leaving them vulnerable to Saigō's infantry. From Edo castle, Ōmura watched the billowing smoke and heard the loud explosions and thought that his plan had succeeded. But the artillery guns soon malfunctioned, and the few that did fire were wildly inaccurate, producing noise and fireworks but few enemy casualties. Saigō's vanguard, led by Kirino Toshiaki, charged directly into the Shōgitai's barricades, losing at least 120 men killed or wounded. About twice that number of Shōgitai supporters were slain, although many more were apprehended fleeing from Ueno.[12]

The victory secured Edo for the new government, crushed one of the largest and most violent antigovernment units, restored the momentum of the imperial forces by releasing them to move north, and, by showing that the pro-Tokugawa forces could not defeat the emperor's army, calmed fears of a prolonged civil war. Despite the artillery fiasco and the heavy government casualties, Ōmura emerged as a hero, acclaimed for his grasp of modern military science, much to Saigō's chagrin, who had lost face over the incident.[13] Formidable resistance continued in northern Japan, but by controlling Edo the army had turned a corner. To signify the *bakufu*'s demise, the next month the capital moved from Kyoto to Edo, which had been the de facto political center of Japan for 250 years. On September 3 Edo was officially renamed Tokyo, and the next month Emperor Mutsuhito adopted the reign name of Meiji and henceforth was identified as the Emperor Meiji.

The Northern Campaigns

On June 10, 1868, two Aizu samurai attacked a senior Chōshū officer in a Fukushima brothel. Desperate to escape, he jumped through a second-floor window only to land face-first on a stone walkway, where he was seized by his assailants and later executed. Among the murdered official's personal effects were confidential government plans to subjugate the northern domains, including the Tokugawa stronghold of Aizu. Reacting to these threats, twenty-five pro-*bakufu* vassals in northern Honshū formed a confederation to resist the Satsuma-Chōshū government, as distinct from the imperial government.[14] To crush the league, Ōmura devised a complicated strategy to capture the city of Sendai on the Pacific (east) coast and then send converging columns southward to attack the Aizu rebel stronghold at Wakamatsu castle from the rear. Landings in Echigo Province on the Japan Sea (west) coast with probing attacks against the major passes would fix the defenders in place.

Yamagata Aritomo commanded the 12,000-man-strong government army contingent that landed along the west coast in late July and quickly captured Nagaoka castle. Then he hesitated, even though his veteran forces (leavened with about 1,000 *kiheitai* and Satsuma warriors) outnumbered the rebels three to one. Yamagata spread the entire army along a 50-mile-long defensive front, leaving him no reserve. He parceled out artillery, giving each unit a few guns but not enough firepower to blast through league fortifications. When he tried to evict rebel defenders from strategic mountain passes, the army suffered successive reverses. Thereafter the rainy season made streams and rivers impassable and restricted campaigning. By that time, Yamagata was barely on speaking terms with his second-in-command, the veteran Satsuma commander Kuroda Kiyotaka, who spent much of the campaign sulking in his tent.[15]

The opposing armies faced each other about 6 miles north of Nagaoka, with their flanks bounded on the west by a river and on the east by a large trackless swamp. Stuck in their cold, wet trenches, morale among government troops plummeted, abetted by rebels chanting Buddhist funeral sutras throughout the night. Meanwhile, battle-hardened, aggressive pro-Tokugawa commanders executed an active defense, probing and raiding government outposts and disrupting their rear supply areas.[16]

On the east coast, operations initially went smoother. The main government army moved overland from Edo on Shirokawa castle, which dominated a strategic mountain pass leading to Aizu. By mid-June government troops had taken the castle in a frontal attack coordinated with columns enveloping the town. Government artillery destroyed the prepared defenses and routed the 2,500 defenders. Several smaller domains in the league promptly capitulated. The hardcore Aizu defenders withdrew into their main defenses, which were constructed to blend into the rugged mountainous terrain. With Yamagata's western campaign stalled, there was little pressure on the Aizu rear, enabling the rebels to concentrate their forces against the eastern prong of the government offensive. The Kyoto high command sent reinforcements under Saigō's leadership to reinvigorate Yamagata's operations.[17]

Unable to break into the southern approaches to Aizu–Wakamatsu castle, government troops commanded by Itagaki Taisuke and Ichiji Masaharu maneuvered north along the main highway and in mid-October captured the northern outposts protecting Aizu's rear areas. They then pivoted west through the mountains and defeated successive Aizu contingents by concentrating artillery fire to pin down defenders while small bands of riflemen turned their flanks. When the rebels shifted troops to protect their vulnerable flanks, loyalist forces smashed through the weakened ridgeline defenses. By late October Itagaki and Ichiji were within five miles of Wakamatsu castle.

Around the same time, Saigō seized Niigata city, a major port on the Sea of Japan about forty miles north of Nagaoka castle. Capturing the port cut off rebel access to imported foreign-manufactured weapons and interdicted a major supply route running from the city to Aizu-Wakamatsu. But the day Niigata fell, rebel troops farther south capitalized on their knowledge of the local terrain to cross the supposedly impassable swamp, outflank the main government lines, and then overwhelm the small government garrison at Nagaoka castle. With government forces divided and their line of communication threatened, Yamagata fled for his life, allegedly discarding his sword and equipment in his haste. Saigō countermarched south and retook the castle five days later.

Yamagata, however, failed to cut off the withdrawing rebel forces, and the western campaign stalled again.[18]

These setbacks and the slow progress on the eastern front sowed doubt among government leaders in Kyoto that the army could finish the campaign before the region's heavy winter snows made further campaigning impossible. Satsuma troops, which formed the backbone of the army, came from southern Japan and were neither acclimated nor equipped for winter operations. Rather than risk the imperial army's carefully crafted reputation for invincibility and its best troops, Ōmura suspended eastern operations against Aizu until the following spring.[19]

Itagaki and Ijichi ignored Kyoto's orders and unilaterally assaulted the main Aizu stronghold, forcing the heavily outnumbered Aizu samurai to commit their entire reserve. One such unit, the White Tiger Brigade, consisted of a few hundred 16- and 17-year-olds and suffered severe losses. Retreating toward Wakamatsu castle, sixteen survivors mistakenly assumed that the thick black smoke and red flames rising from the adjacent castle town meant the castle had fallen. With all hope apparently lost, they committed suicide, an act of sincerity that redeemed their treason and apotheosized the White Tiger Brigade as a symbol of loyalty and selfless courage that resonated powerfully among the public.

Once the main Aizu defenses collapsed, the army overran minor strongholds in rapid succession and rebel survivors fled to Wakamatsu castle. Although the government artillery could not penetrate the thick castle walls, the defenders were unprepared for a winter siege and surrendered in early November. Losses of pro-Tokugawa forces for the entire campaign were around 2,700 killed. Sporadic fighting continued in northern Japan until mid-December, when the league finally capitulated and its leaders took responsibility for defeat by committing ritual suicide.[20]

During the Tokugawa period suicide to atone for mistakes or defeat was an accepted cultural norm among the warrior class. During the Boshin Civil War warrior customs regarding fallen enemies or prisoners likely encouraged battlefield suicides. Both armies routinely cut off the heads of dead or wounded enemies for purposes of identification or morale-enhancing displays. In one case a *bakufu* leader's severed head was brought to Kyoto for public display. The gruesome practice was widespread, and western doctors working in Japan reported that they rarely saw wounded enemy soldiers, apparently because of the criteria for head-taking and surrender.

Surrender was recognized, provided both sides agreed on terms for capitulation. During the Boshin War's early stages, potential prisoners were usually executed for suspected cowardice for surrendering (the idea of the shame of surrender) or because their wounds testified that they had resisted government troops. Suspected spies or *bakufu* agents were summarily executed. Many Shōg-itai prisoners captured at Ueno fit all categories and were promptly beheaded.[21] In the later stages of the war, the new army accepted surrenders of pro-*bakufu* troops as the government realized that reconciliation was necessary to unify the nation.

This conciliatory attitude did not carry over to the disposition of the dead. The government honored its war dead with special ceremonies that Ōmura later institutionalized by establishing the Shōkonsha (shrine for inviting spirits) in June 1869 as the official shrine to commemorate government war dead. He hoped that official memorialization of the war dead would stimulate a popular national consciousness by enshrining the concept of an official death for the sake of the nation, not merely a private death in a meaningless vendetta.

Enemy dead were regarded as traitors and ineligible for enshrinement in government shrines. Their beheaded corpses were often left where they fell, and local villagers would furtively bury the remains. Partly because the Aizu warriors had so fiercely resisted the government army and partly owing to Aizu's long-standing enmity with Chōshū, the Meiji leaders forbade even the burial of Aizu corpses and ordered them left to rot in open fields.[22]

At the end of 1868, Tokugawa supporters still controlled Ezochi (Hokkaidō). In October 1868, *bakufu* ground and naval units from Sendai had landed on Hokkaidō's south coast and overwhelmed the undermanned army garrison. The remaining government troops abandoned the island, fleeing to the safety of nearby Honshū. In the spring of 1869, reconstituted and much-strengthened government ground and naval forces returned and converged on the major rebel stronghold at Hakodate. The outnumbered pro-shogunate rebels fell back and by early May prepared for a final stand from Hakodate's pentagon-shaped fortress.

Constructed by the *bakufu* between 1857 and 1864 to protect Ezochi from the Russian threat, the first western-style fortress in Japan defended Hakodate's harbor, where the three remaining *bakufu* warships were sheltered. During naval battles on May 11, one government ship sank after a shell exploded its powder magazine, but two *bakufu* warships ran aground, and the third was previously damaged. The subsequent fighting for the fortress produced more sound and flash than bloodshed. Thousands of government artillery shells fell on the fortress, causing three casualties. Government losses were two dead and twenty-one wounded. The siege did reduce the rebels to near starvation, forcing them to surrender on May 25.

After the fall of the fortress, one company of government troops remained in Hokkaidō, but it did little more than police Hakodate city. In 1870 the colonization office responded to increasing friction with Russia over Sakhalin Island by relocating samurai families from Tokyo to Hokkaidō to create self-sufficient military communities organized around units composed of farmer-soldiers. Saigō Takamori enthusiastically backed the plan and in 1873 moved more displaced samurai to Hokkaidō to reinforce the garrison, provide jobs for otherwise unemployed warriors, and open the northern island to development.[23] An Ainu (aboriginal) uprising spurred cries for a permanent garrison, but the sparse Japanese population made it impossible to conscript enough soldiers locally to meet troop personnel requirements.

Authorities relied on the *tondenhei* system promoted by Lt. Gen. Kuroda, concurrently vice director of the colonization office. Beginning in May 1875, the government gave settlers (ex-samurai and army reservists) a small parcel of land, which became their property if they cultivated it for three years. Most of the thirty-seven *tondenhei* settlements were located along a 120-mile trace running north from Sapporo and protecting the northwest side of the island. Despite Kuroda's notions about an ideal warrior-farmer ready to take up arms to defend his home and family, Japanese warriors were not farmers, and few wanted to emigrate to faraway Hokkaidō. As late as 1905 Hokkaidō had only about 4,000 regular troops and about 1,000 reservists.[24]

An Assessment

Throughout the northern campaigns of 1868–1869, the government army outnumbered rebel forces and enjoyed overwhelming material and technological superiority. Cannons and rifles, not samurai swords and spears, decided the outcome of the Boshin Civil War. Firepower may have relegated traditional samurai weapons to the scrapheap, but paradoxically the Tokugawa forces consistently displayed superior élan and fighting spirit and atoned for their defeats with collective suicides. In short, antigovernment forces exhibited the type of battlefield behavior and morale that the government rarely saw in the new army's conscript soldiers.

The campaigns highlighted major differences between field commanders and central headquarters. Army headquarters in faraway Kyoto often proposed plans at odds with the local conditions, and as tensions increased, line officers ignored central direction in favor of unilateral action. Lacking a strong central staff capable of enforcing orders, the army was at the mercy of individual commanders for leadership and direction. Similarly, the absence of unified tactical doctrine and disputes over appropriate tactics and doctrine between line and staff left units to fight according to the tactics favored by their respective commanders. Resentment flared because the nobility and Chōshū and Satsuma samurai monopolized senior army posts. Within the ranks the composition of the new government army, especially its use of commoners, created resentment among soldiers of samurai lineage. Although the restoration wars would later take on a romantic hue filled with swashbuckling samurai, the new government's military

success in the Boshin Civil War left a residue of disgruntled warriors, marginal-
ized commoners, and a torn social fabric.[25]

Reorganizing the Army

Saigō, Ōmura, Ōkubo Toshimichi, and other military leaders of the restoration
were divided over the new army's organization. Saigō was enigmatic, leading
the new army yet retaining strong military ties to his regional base in southern
Japan. Ōmura sought a strong central government at the expense of the regional
domains and recommended a national conscription system to build a standing
army under the new government's direct control. He also proposed European-
style reforms for the new army and the abolition of traditional warrior-
class privileges such as carrying swords. Ōkubo, one of the most powerful leaders of the new regime, wanted a samurai army, and proposals that filled the
national army with commoners and peasants while they eliminated samurai
privileges repelled him.

Ōmura and Ōkubo did share a deep-rooted fear about the survival of the
imperial government that they had created. Danger seemed everywhere as
the new, unstable society seethed with sedition and treachery. In early January
1869, for example, six sword-wielding anti-foreign assassins murdered a senior
councilor in broad daylight on a major Kyoto thoroughfare. Riots and peasant uprisings underscored rural instability, disgruntled samurai were suspect,
and foreigners might overwhelm Japan as they had China. The authorities first
sought to control the reactionary warriors, who represented the immediate
armed threat to their new government, by counterposing a military organization that relied on conscription and indoctrination to inculcate soldiers' loyalty
to the government and emperor.

In order to educate junior officers, in 1868 the court and council of state (*da-
jōkan*) established a school of military science in Kyoto on the site of the former
French training ground. Enrollment was initially restricted to sons of the nobility and government officials. The following year the government converted the
former shogunate's Yokohama Foreign Language School into a French-style
military academy to train samurai from Chōshū and elsewhere for an invasion
of Korea. In July 1869, however, the government reorganized the military directorate into the military affairs ministry under the titular command of Prince
Yoshiaki. Ōmura served as vice minister of military affairs with responsibility
for training and organization.[26]

Ōmura refused to perpetuate the samurai monopoly on warfare. He first
incorporated the school of military science into the military affairs ministry
and then in September transferred the Kyoto facility to Osaka, the country's
maritime and overland transportation hub. Osaka's strategic central location
would allow government troops to move rapidly in any direction to suppress

antigovernment uprisings. The decision also shifted the military locus of power westward to check Satsuma's growing influence. Ōmura next constructed a French-style maneuver area and barracks cantonment for a battalion of Chōshū troops as well as a major arsenal. His ambitious five-year plan anticipated a revised conscription system, standardized equipment, military academies to train noncommissioned officers and educate professional officers, and a new army force structure.[27]

With institutional army reforms in progress, in September 1869 Ōmura traveled to Kyoto to inspect the new school and stayed at a nearby inn. In Kyoto's late summer twilight, assassins stormed into the two-story latticed wooden inn and mortally wounded Ōmura in a wild sword-swinging melee. His two lieutenants jumped through a paper lattice window into the alley, only to be cut down by waiting gang members. Believing that one of their bloodied victims was Ōmura, the murderers fled. Ōmura succumbed to his wounds in an Osaka hospital in early November.[28]

Twenty-four years later the army officially dedicated a statue to Ōmura during ceremonies held at the Yasukuni Shrine in 1893. Ōmura's statue, the first western-style bronze work commissioned in Japan, still rises over the entrance to Yasukuni, garbed in samurai finery and bearing two swords. The period representation, however, misrepresents the man who was determined to build an army of commoners and peasants and was a driving force in the abolition of samurai privileges, including their right to bear swords. It is faithful in one respect. Ōmura looks out at Ueno Park, scene of his greatest military victory, and one that ensured the Meiji ascendancy.

An Army in Turmoil

The attack on Ōmura shocked the fledgling Meiji government. Acting on a nationwide alert, police quickly apprehended the killers, who turned out to be reactionary samurai from northern Japan and disgruntled former *kiheitai* members.[29] Ōmura's death threw the army's leadership into turmoil with major implications for the institution's future. Maebara Issei succeeded Ōmura but soon resigned after quarreling with Kido's decision to forcibly suppress rebellious *kiheitai* units (and subsequently quit the government altogether in September 1870 for reasons described below). Itagaki Taisuke was nominated to fill the vacancy, but he did not get along with Ōkubo, who vetoed his selection. Kuroda Kiyotaka, Yamagata's nemesis during the Boshin War, was unavailable, having departed the army in 1870 to oversee Hokkaidō's development. This left Yamagata Aritomo, who had promptly returned to Japan from his European inspection tour after learning of the attack on Ōmura. In August 1870, the council of state appointed Yamagata minister of the military department, a post that had been vacant for almost one year.

Yamagata's remaining rival within the army was Maj. Gen. Yamada Akiyoshi, the deputy minister of the military department, known as the Little Napoleon because of his planning skill as the Eastern Expeditionary army's chief of staff during the Boshin War. Critics, however, dismissed him as a poseur.[30] Shortly after Yamagata took control of the army, Yamada joined the Iwakura Mission that departed Japan in November 1871 for an extended inspection tour through the United States and Europe with a delegation of Japan's most prominent statesmen.[31] Yamagata's last serious rivals, Itagaki Taisuke and Saigō Takamori, quit the government in 1873 over the Korea controversy. Itagaki became involved with the liberty and people's rights movement, and Saigō, an army general, commander of the Imperial Guard, and concurrently a senior councilor, became a magnet attracting disaffected samurai.

With his major competitors gone, Yamagata would dominate the army and cultivate a clique of Chōshū officers to consolidate his power base. Due to his patronage, by 1888 sixteen of forty-two general officers were of Chōshū lineage. With the exception of imperial family members, men from Satsuma and Chōshū would monopolize the top positions in the army until 1907. Protégés such as Katsura Tarō, Kawakami Sōroku, Kodama Gentarō, and Terauchi Masatake, among others, would lead the army's next generation and also rise to the highest civilian cabinet positions.[32] Yamagata eradicated localized loyalties that might threaten central authority while he created his personality-based regional power base.

As Yamagata consolidated his position, the same regional and individual loyalties that had provided the glue that held the government army together during the restoration wars became suspect as impediments to the new government's goal of a unified Japan. Central authorities rapidly disbanded the independent military organizations of the various domains in favor of a national army, but regionalism and factionalism dominated the selection and training of the army's future leaders.

In 1869, ostensibly for financial reasons, the government reduced the size of the quota-based conscript army that it had assembled from various domains. Government authorities questioned the conscripts' reliability, and domain leaders disliked their troops serving as long-term conscripts in a military force outside their control.[33] That December the government eliminated the Chōshū *kiheitai* and similar units as part of an army-wide reorganization.

Younger men replaced the older veterans when the army dismissed soldiers over 40 years of age or in poor physical condition. Army authorities raised officers' pay but lowered it for the more numerous rank-and-file to save money. The discarded veterans were the foot soldiers who had borne the brunt of the fighting in the restoration wars. In return they received miserly pensions and no rewards for their service. *Kiheitai* veterans, especially peasants and townsmen, vigorously protested plans to cut the 4,000-man force by half and the associated reforms.

Reactionaries played on these grievances to foment armed revolt in Chōshū. Insurgents opposed the dissolution of volunteer units, resisted westernization of weapons and equipment, and refused to obey their officers' commands. In January 1870 about 1,800 disaffected former *kiheitai* members, more than 70 percent of them peasants, attacked Yamaguchi castle, surrounded the government's administrative offices, and temporarily seized power. Peasants and merchants, aggrieved by poor harvests and runaway inflation, joined former government soldiers to raid government offices and stockpiles. Peasant revolts also broke out in nearby areas, forcing Kido, one of the government's three senior councilors (Saigō and Ōkubo were the others) to mobilize loyal units in Chōshū and elsewhere to suppress the uprising by early February 1870. About 200 men on both sides were killed or wounded in the fighting, but the government executed an additional 130 rebels. The harsh sentences were aimed less at disaffected samurai than at cowing a possible peasant uprising that Kido feared would quickly sweep across Japan.[34]

Building the New Army

Most of the new government's leaders favored some form of national conscription to create a centralized military force to maintain domestic order, but there was a fundamental question about who was qualified to serve in the army. Yamada had originally allied himself with the late Ōmura's Chōshū followers in the military department to deflect the attempts of Ōkubo, Kuroda, and other Satsuma leaders to create a professional military caste. In March 1870 the government instituted a revamped conscription system based on rice production, requiring each domain to maintain 60 troops per 10,000 *koku* of arable land production. The abolition of domains in late August 1871 simultaneously swept away the administrative infrastructure underpinning the conscription system, although a quota of five men from any class between the ages of 20 and 30 for every 10,000 *koku* of the new prefecture's harvested rice stayed in effect.[35]

Meanwhile, in March 1871, Yamagata, Iwakura, Saigō, and Kido had organized samurai from the three most powerful loyalist domains—Chōshū, Satsuma, and Tosa,—into an Imperial Guard to protect the throne and replace the diminished national army. The emperor donated 100,000 *ryō* to underwrite the new unit, which was directly subordinate to the court. The 6,200-man imperial bodyguard consisted of infantry and artillery units with a few cavalry squadrons and doubled as a national army, marking the beginning of modern Japan's military institution.[36]

More institutional changes soon followed. The military department was reorganized in July 1871, and on August 29, simultaneous with the decree abolishing the domains, the council of state ordered local lords to disband their private armies and turn over their weapons to the central government army. Though Yamagata played on the foreign threat, especially Russia's southward expansion, to justify a national army, the government's immediate perceived danger was domestic insurrection. Consequently, on August 31, with the court's approval, the military department accordingly divided the country into four military districts, each with its own garrison or *chindai*, to deal with peasant uprisings or disaffected samurai insurrections. The Imperial Guard formed the Tokyo garrison whereas conscripts filled the ranks at the Osaka, Kumamoto, and Sendai garrisons. The four garrisons marshaled about 8,000 troops—mostly infantry, but also a few hundred artillerymen and engineers. Smaller detachments guarded outposts at Kagoshima, Fushimi, Nagoya, Hiroshima, and elsewhere.[37]

By late December 1871 the military department set army modernization and coastal defense as priorities. Yamagata and his deputies devised long-range plans for an army to maintain internal security, defend strategic coastal areas, train and educate military and naval officers, and build arsenals as well as supply depots. Despite Yamagata's previous heated rhetoric about the foreign menace, little serious planning was directed against Russia.

In February 1872 the military department was abolished and separate army and navy departments were established.[38] The Imperial Guard also underwent several reorganizations, and in January 1874 Yamagata became the Guard commander and concurrently vice army minister. Although created to defend the home islands against foreign aggression, the elite unit's principal mission was to protect the throne by suppressing domestic samurai revolts, peasant uprisings, and antigovernment demonstrations.[39]

No one, however, held high hopes for a quota-based, conscript-manned garrison system. By the summer of 1871, the army had inducted about 1,500 conscripts but found 25 percent of them to be physically unfit for military service.[40] The remaining 1,100 or so were divided into various branches—infantry, cavalry, artillery, construction, and a bugle corps—collectively known as the Osaka unit.

The conscripts found themselves in a new, much more westernized world. They were forbidden to wear Japanese-style swords, although they could attach western-style bayonets to their uniform belts. New diets introduced the conscripts to meat, a change from the traditional rice and vegetable staples and one that caused indigestion and worse. In theory the conscripts received standardized uniforms, but a contemporary newspaper account described a mixed bag of conscripts, some wearing wooden clogs, others straw sandals, and a potpourri of tunics and jackets. Even more distressing, some were talking or reading books while on duty. One senior officer later recalled inspecting otherwise resplendent but bare-footed conscripts. In short, garrisons suffered from lack of weapons, money, authority, and personnel recruiting.[41]

Military Training and Education

In early 1874, under French direction, the army relocated its small-arms firing ranges to the estate of a former shogunate official. The new home of the Toyama Infantry School (founded in 1873) taught minor tactics, marksmanship, bayonet practice, and physical education designed to prepare junior officers for command assignments. The eight-month course eventually standardized infantry doctrine and officer training throughout the army.[42] The army concurrently established specialized technical schools in Tokyo for ordnance, military construction, and high explosives under the arsenal bureau's direction as well as veterinary science, farriery, and equestrian schools. Each had around sixty students, and by 1875 numerous French-designed training facilities, rifle ranges, and specialized schools were active in Tokyo.

The army invested heavily in officer and noncommissioned officer (NCO) education. The reorganized school of military science opened in January 1870 with fifty-seven students enrolled in junior officer or NCO courses. The same year the government ordered each prefecture to send cadets in numbers proportionate to their respective rice production, and thereafter classes annually averaged about 100 students. The Yokohama facility also relocated to Osaka in 1870.[43]

The Osaka school was renamed the Army Military Science School in November 1871 and moved to Tokyo in early 1872, where the army reorganized it into three provisional sections: a preparatory school with a middle school curriculum plus instruction in western languages, in effect a junior cadet school; a military academy that taught branch technical skills; and an NCO academy, which was removed from the cadet school the following year. In October 1874 the officers school formally became the military academy, and the following May the preparatory school was designated the cadet academy. The military science school was abolished. In January 1877 the cadet school was amalgamated into the military academy.[44]

Military academy classes originally enrolled two types of cadets, regular (graduates of preparatory academies or those qualified by examination) and provisional (graduates of the NCO academy or selected NCO volunteers under 27 years of age). The former had a three-year course, the latter about half that, although both received regular commissions. The curriculum covered ordnance and weapons, equestrian skills, marksmanship and physical training, foreign language (French), and records administration. Almost all of the original students were of samurai stock, with just 13 commoners versus 719 warriors enrolled in the 1872 classes. One of Yamagata's first decisions after taking over the military department, however, was to open the school of military science to commoners, and by 1881 the numbers had tilted in favor of commoners, whose 258 cadets outnumbered the 158 from warrior families.[45]

Former samurai had as much trouble with the new military discipline as peasant conscripts. When the school of military science prohibited officer candidates from wearing swords and encouraged cadets, who were overwhelmingly from the samurai class, to cut their traditional topknot, many quit. Those who stayed had to adjust to wearing western-style clothing, which was as uncomfortable for them as it was for conscripts. Pants chafed, and boots and shoes caused blisters and were generally uncomfortable.[46]

Even time changed because the military academy used the western measurements of minutes and hours to govern curriculum and schedules. Freshly commissioned officer graduates in turn drilled their conscript soldiers with the new way to measure time, and the draftees brought the concept back to their villages, factories, or offices. By the early 1870s senior officers carried pocket watches, an acknowledgment that coordination of troop movements, training schedules, and timetables made the clock a technological reality of military life.[47]

The military academy aimed to educate officers in western military science and tactics, but Japan lacked schools that taught foreign languages, western pedagogy, or natural sciences. Educational reforms of 1872 established four years of primary schooling and three of middle school, but attendance was not compulsory and most students did not graduate from primary school. Until the military preparatory schools produced their first graduates, the military academy operated on a transitional basis. During the three-year interval the provisional academy trained former samurai in French doctrine, including battalion echelon maneuver, drill, squad regulations, and the basics of field fortification.[48] In the best of circumstances, which these were not, it would take a decade to educate youths for specialized military training.

In January 1875 the relocated military academy opened at Ichigaya (a former *daimyō* residence in Tokyo) under the direct supervision of the army ministry. Altogether 158 students enrolled in either a two-year course (for the infantry and cavalry branches) or a three-year curriculum (for the more technically complex artillery and engineer branches). Upon graduation, cadets were commissioned as second lieutenants. Under the tutelage of thirteen French instructors (including eleven military officers), cadets studied French, tactics, military organization, and debate. The army adopted French army doctrine and tactics because of the availability of French military instructors in Japan (who had been employed by the shogun), Japanese officers' acquaintance with the French language through the Yokohama language school, and their familiarity with the French military system. Until 1877 the army relied exclusively on French military advisers, whose numbers reached a high of forty-three personnel in 1875.[49]

Students who enrolled in the NCO academy's twelve-month (later fifteen-month) course graduated as corporals eligible for competitive examination for entrance to the military academy. Initial confusion about the difference between the NCO academy and the cadet school led to cases of students entering both or dropping out of the NCO academy to enter the cadet school. Many selected that option, including three who later rose to the rank of full general. Others accepted NCO rank and with their academy colleagues would become the backbone and small-unit leaders of the new national army.[50]

The reorganized NCO academy offered a two-year course of instruction exclusively for noncommissioned officer candidates. Conscripts volunteered for the course and required their regimental commander's recommendation to attend. After graduation they were promoted to NCO rank. The army closed the academy in 1889 because it was attracting few volunteers, was soliciting men who had not been conscripted, and was producing lackluster graduates. The other source of NCOs was conscripts who volunteered for additional service after completing three years of active duty. Their respective regimental commanders had to endorse the application. Between 1889 and reforms in 1927, potential infantry branch NCOs learned their craft within the regiment through on-the-job training and by observing and learning from the regiment's senior NCOs.[51] Other branches had technical schools where their NCOs continued to go for training and instruction.

French instructors at the military academy relied on detailed explanations in exercises and drills, not innovation, to solve set-piece tactical problems. The order of battle rigidly divided formations into skirmishers, main force, and reserves. Officers learned their specific responsibilities within each echelon. The battalion (about 800 men) was the tactical unit for purposes of instruction, so little attention was given to large-unit operations. By stressing technical proficiency, the French advisers taught the Japanese to organize, train, and command military units from company to brigade echelon. By confining instruction to minor tactics and excluding strategy, however, they underestimated their students.[52]

The military academy organized its core curriculum around military science, mathematics, and natural sciences. Subjects included tactics, military organization, weaponry, military geography, and engineering. French was the only foreign language taught until 1883 when the curriculum introduced German, followed by Chinese the next year and English in 1894. After 1877 the government retained a handful of French advisers as language instructors and ordnance technicians.[53]

Military texts imported from the United States were popular among officers because commentators then hailed the American Civil War as the first modern war. Aspiring Japanese officers also read the French strategist Antoine Henri de Jomini, finding that his formulaic principals of warfare followed a rational progression they easily understood. Karl von Clausewitz was translated into Japanese during the late 1850s, but the Prussian strategist's theory was deemed overly complex.[54]

Under French direction the Toyama Infantry School emerged as the center for musketry, particularly after mid-1876 when Maj. Murata Tsuneyoshi, a Boshin War veteran and a Guard battalion commander, returned from his tour of Prussian and French ordnance and arsenal facilities. Murata quickly put his observations to work by designing extended firing ranges with moving and pop-up surprise targets. He also became the army's leading designer of small arms. By 1880 Murata had produced his initial rifle at the Tokyo arsenal. After redesigns that included an eight-round magazine that made loading easier and increased firepower, in 1889 the Murata rifle was issued to all active duty soldiers. It remained the standard army rifle until 1910. Reservists continued to use the older Snider rifles.[55]

The modern artillery guns used during the Franco-Prussian War (1870) impressed military observer Maj. Gen. Ōyama Iwao, who returned from Europe convinced that without an independent arms industry Japan would never be a truly sovereign nation. Acting on his advice, in July 1871 the military affairs ministry established the army artillery bureau to manage ordnance matters, including production of small arms, artillery, and ammunition. The same year an arsenal began producing obsolete French bronze mountain artillery guns to equip each garrison. In the mid-1870s the Guard imported the superior German-manufactured steel artillery piece from the Krupp factories, a practice that continued because Japan lacked iron ore and steel plants for casting. In 1879 the Osaka arsenal began manufacturing artillery guns using Italian techniques and fielded these bronze cannon army-wide in 1885.[56] Besides the arsenals, the government retained control of strategic industries such as dockyards, machine shops, and woolen mills (which produced military uniforms). The nascent strategic factories were centers for the absorption and dissemination of modern manufacturing techniques and skills that contributed to capital formation.[57]

The New Conscription Ordinance

The government's two previous attempts to introduce national conscription had failed. Its third was more ambitious, more radical, and more controversial, particularly about the size of reserve forces. No unanimity existed about a conscription system. Yamada's opinion, for example, had changed after his return from abroad, and he became an advocate of the militia system similar to those he had observed in Switzerland and the United States. Other officials wanted warriors, not commoners, to fill the ranks. Yamagata favored a Prussian conscription model. Others, including the French-trained Maj. Gen. Miura Gorō, the Tokyo garrison commander, wanted a French-style system.[58]

Yamagata, however, understood the broader implications of national conscription. He distrusted the warrior class, several members of which he regarded as clear dangers to the state, making it foolish to rely solely on samurai to defend the government. Thus, Yamagata used conscription to get rid of the samurai volunteer army, curtail the warrior class, and simultaneously inculcate a mentality of national service for the sake of the emperor and the state. To eliminate preferential treatment for the warrior volunteers, Yamagata revived ancient imperial myths and largely fanciful traditions of military service to the imperial household to promote loyalty to the emperor while curtailing samurai independence. Conscription would likewise break down the old order's feudal customs, promote the restoration's goals, and create a future pool of trained soldiers available in times of foreign crisis and able to protect their homes in times of internal disorder.[59] Furthermore, army indoctrination could translate the conscripts' regional loyalties into national allegiance and send them home as veterans to proselytize army virtues, modernization, and proto-nationalism to their communities. This in brief was the notion of "good soldiers—good citizens."

The January 10, 1873, conscription ordinance was based on the French model and provided for seven years of military service: three on active duty and the remainder in the reserves. There were liberal exemptions, including the obvious—criminals, hardship cases, and the physically unqualified—and the less obvious—heads of households or heirs, students, government bureaucrats, and teachers. A conscript could also purchase a substitute for 270 yen, an enormous sum that restricted this privilege to the wealthy.[60] Less apparent but more enduring was the emphasis on primogeniture, which though eventually abolished would exert a lasting influence on the enlisted ranks.[61] Under the new ordinance the 1873 conscript army was composed mainly of second and third sons of impoverished farmers who manned the regional garrisons while former samurai controlled the Guard and the Tokyo garrison. The long-term effect was the army's custom of discouraging first-born male conscripts from making the service a career.

Because of the army's small size and numerous exemptions, relatively few young men were actually conscripted for a three-year term on active duty. In 1873 the army numbered approximately 17,900 (from a population of 35 million); it doubled to about 33,000 in 1875.[62] The 1876 cohort of 20-year-old males numbered about 300,000 candidates, of whom the army evaluated 53,226 as suitable for active duty. Assuming a one-third turnover as three-year enlistments expired, the army needed about 13,000 draftees annually, about one-quarter of those who passed the rigorous physical examination—or approximately 4 percent of the entire cohort. Until the conscription reforms in the 1880s, the percentage of conscripts fluctuated between 3 and 6 percent of the eligible cohort, making military service highly selective (see Table 2.1).[63]

One's chances of being drafted also varied considerably by region. In 1876 the physical examination disqualified more than 85 percent of potential inductees in the Tokyo and Osaka districts. In northeastern Japan, 70 percent of inductees failed, and even among those judged physically eligible for military service, not all were called to active duty.

Regardless of how few men were actually drafted, conscription irked all classes. Former samurai opposed the draft as a class-leveling device that cost them their privileges as the armed guards of the feudal elite. Peasants equated military service with the corvée system imposed by the Tokugawa regime and resisted this latest manpower levy. Others saw it as an unwanted intrusion into their lives, and although the conscription regulations contained numerous exemptions, these applied mainly to wealthier households. Some draft-eligible young men evaded conscription by self-imposed exile, moving from their home district to faraway remote Hokkaidō or distant Okinawa (which was not subject to conscription until 1898). Publishers offered manuals on how to beat the draft. Second or third sons adopted by other families as heirs and heads of households became known as "adopted conscripts."[64] But these measures were benign compared to the large-scale violent protests against conscription that took place in 1873.

Anti-conscription riots that year joined massive popular disturbances in Fukuoka Province over inflationary rice prices and demonstrations against new excise taxes on seafood and the abolition of the ban on Christianity. In May 1873 tens of thousands of peasants rioted in Okayama Prefecture, burning the homes of the wealthy as well as torching schools and *burakumin* (the untouchable class) residences, and murdering government officials and school teachers. Rioters destroyed about 400 homes and other buildings and killed or injured more than a dozen people. Among their demands were the elimination of conscription, compulsory education, and forced hair cutting. The Osaka garrison had neither the troops nor the equipment to deal with the mass demonstrations, leaving the government to hastily enlist 300 ex-warriors to suppress the uprising.

Despite severe penalties, including the beheading of more than a dozen demonstrators and the imprisoning of several hundred others, demonstrations quickly spread to neighboring Tottori prefecture, where in mid-June 22,000 people joined five days of protests demanding an end to conscription, compulsory schooling, and the newly adopted western calendar. By the end of the

Table 2.1. Active-Duty Army Personnel during the Meiji Era

1871	14,841	1876	39,439	1881	43,419	1886	59,009
1872	17,901	1877	40,078	1882	46,363	1887	64,689
1873	17,462	1878	41,933	1883	47,504	1888	65,015
1874	32,923	1879	44,150	1884	49,642	1889	66,744
1875	33,096	1880	42,530	1885	54,124	1890	69,000

Source: Rikusen gakkai, eds., *Kindai sensōshi gaisetsu, Shiryōshū* (Rikusen gakkai, 1984), 39, table 2-1-12.

month tens of thousands of peasants rioted in Kagawa prefecture, where the authorities eventually executed several ringleaders and fined 17,000 people for joining in the disorders. Again the army needed outside help, which came this time in the form of fifty former warriors, to put down the demonstrations.[65]

Although the demonstrators opposed the "blood tax," a term to describe the conscription system that many peasants took literally, having heard wild rumors that the army would drain conscripts' blood to make wine for the westerners, at root the mass protests demanded a reduction in soaring rice prices caused by rampant inflation as well as abolition of primary schools and the western calendar. Responding to the widespread unrest, Yamada Akiyoshi pronounced national conscription premature and proposed to postpone its introduction for about a decade. During that interval the government would educate the people in the values of the new nation, which in turn would make conscription acceptable to them. Meanwhile, a citizen militia led by professional officers could protect the nation. Soon afterward Yamada left the army to pursue a career in the law; he later would become justice minister.[66] His opinions about the value of a militia system and a small standing army, however, continued to resonate with influential officers for the next two decades.

Army and Emperor

The new Meiji leaders relied heavily on the imperial institution to connect past to present when formulating national values. The army in particular stressed its links to the emperor to inculcate loyalty in the ranks. An imperial memorial issued on February 3, 1870, proclaimed the emperor a living embodiment of godhood and his throne a holy office established by the Sun Goddess and handed down in unbroken succession to the present. In 1872 the military department promulgated an imperial rescript (*tokuhō*) of eight articles that set standards of conduct for the new army by enunciating a soldier's duties based on bedrock principles of loyalty to the throne, obedience to orders, courtesy and respect for superiors, and the prohibition of various types of disruptive conduct. Thereafter, when recruits entered the barracks for the first time they were welcomed with a ceremony that included their officers reading the rescript aloud to them, a practice that continued until 1934.[67]

An 1874 photograph of a mixed bag of conscripts assembled for their preinduction physical raises questions about their quality. (Courtesy Mainichi shimbun)

Besides issuing memorials, the emperor presided over military ceremonies, beginning in February 1870 when he reviewed about 4,000 troops on the imperial grounds in conjunction with the establishment of the ordnance bureau. In October 1871, Emperor Meiji observed his newly formed imperial bodyguard conduct field training exercises in a driving rainstorm. The following year he presented the new Guard infantry regiments their unit colors, inaugurating a tradition that continued until the end of World War II. In April 1873 he attended military exercises at Tokyo and led Imperial Guard cavalry troops through field maneuvers.[68]

Emperor Meiji also presided over the military academy's first commencement, in July 1878, publicly affirming the bond between the army's officer corps and the imperial institution. To further strengthen identification with the throne, imperial family members routinely served in the military, although the court had not produced active warriors since the wars of the fourteenth century. They were exempted from conscription, preinduction physicals, and written qualification tests and were directly commissioned by an imperial order. In 1885, the year after the creation of aristocratic ranks and titles, young men from twenty-three newly ennobled families were transferred from the Peers School to the military academy, where they formed about 12 percent of the 108-man class.[69] The emperor also promoted social changes. In 1873, January 4 became Tenchōsetsu (the emperor's birthday), a national holiday. In March of that year he cut his hair in the western style, and in June he appeared in a western-style army uniform during a military exercise.

Tactics for the New Army

Until 1870, "modern" infantry tactics were found in an 1829 translation of a Dutch tactics manual. Concurrent with the new conscription system, the army adopted French tactical military doctrine, its 1873 infantry manual being a translation of the 1869 French edition. Training was conducted in squad-size groupings commanded by a corporal. Recruits received six months of basic instruction that included physical conditioning, platoon and company formations, dispersed movement, marksmanship, bayonet drill, basic sanitation, and military customs and ceremonies. Field training consisted of mandatory drills, execution of the manual of arms, rote memorization of set-piece tactical problems, and small-unit command and control. Instructors relied on strictly choreographed drill regimens, endless repetition, and iron discipline to get results. The army penal code issued in April 1873 prescribed severe punishment for disobeying superiors or conspiring against the government. In 1874 seventy soldiers were tried under the penal code; 530 were tried the following year.[70]

In October 1874 the army created the corporal's group, a squad-size unit of conscripts organized for drill and training purposes and overseen by a noncommissioned officer or junior officer. The system would eventually evolve into the squad section that regulated training, discipline, and conscripts' lives in the barracks. Squad leaders initially handled only training, but revised regulations in 1880 assigned NCOs greater administrative responsibilities for the unit's daily activities. Administration and management, however, were weak. Training regimens varied according to garrisons because of an absence of standardized training programs, frequent changes to drill manuals, irregular tables of organization, and the personalities and interests of commanders and NCOs. The army's first standardized table of organization appeared in 1877 and established the strength of an infantry company at 160 enlisted and eight NCOs, each responsible for a twenty-man section.

Monday through Friday the conscripts awakened at 5 a.m. for morning drill followed by afternoon training sessions. After Saturday morning drill, they spent the day preparing their barracks for a 4 p.m. inspection. A Saturday-night bath followed inspection, and Sunday was a free day. Although the army conscripted from all classes of society, its officers and NCOs were drawn mainly from former samurai, and the traditional hierarchical relationship of samurai and peasant endured. Former warriors who became NCOs routinely beat or physically punished the farmer conscripts to instill discipline and ensure compliance with orders. Under such conditions, desertion flourished; of fifty conscripts sent by one domain, half deserted, one of them on four different occasions.[71] It is true that the Imperial Guard received better training and equipment, but it too often relied on uncritical and uncomprehending imitation of western-style tactical drill because the army lacked a professional officer corps sophisticated enough to devise more appropriate methods.

Five years after the restoration, the new government had created a national army from scratch, fought a civil war, and imposed domestic order. It had established conscription, military schools and training facilities, and begun to standardize equipment and training. The army was small, depending on conscription as much for political reasons (to eliminate warrior influence) as social (as a leveling device) and economic (it was affordable). Significant differences about the nature of the armed institution remained unresolved; its deployment capability was haphazard at best, its personnel unproven, and its leadership divided. Standardized training and equipment were still lacking, and the effectiveness of military schools was still undetermined. The army had no popular base of support, conscription was greatly resented, and samurai bands were leading armed rebellions. On the positive side, the Meiji leaders had erected the framework for a national army that relied on the imperial symbolism of the emperor as the military leader, although they protected the army against direct imperial intervention in military affairs by establishing a system in which the emperor could rarely decide anything by himself.[72] From these shaky foundations, the new army ventured into an uncertain and dangerous future.

3

Dealing with the Samurai

During the early 1870s the government laid a foundation for a modern national army that cast the samurai class adrift. Although samurai from southwestern Japan led the restoration and became the new leaders of Japan, they distrusted their own warrior class. Authorities reduced samurai stipends in 1871, partially commuted them as lump sum payments and bonds in 1873, and in 1876 converted the stipends into government bonds. The approximately 400,000 samurai who lost their income naturally resented the parsimonious settlement. The new government was also intent on breaking the samurai monopoly on warfare. In 1871 it permitted warriors to discard their swords, the samurai status symbol, and five years later outlawed the wearing of swords. The contradiction the Meiji leaders faced was the need to eliminate feudal consciousness of the warrior class but simultaneously inculcate samurai values into the officers and men of the new army whose esprit was inferior to the warriors'.[1]

Samurai Uprisings

In late October 1873 the Council of State, after heated debate, decided against sending a military expedition to Korea to forcibly open trade relations. Pro-war advocates promptly resigned their government posts. Saigō Takamori, a senior councilor and concurrently commander of the Imperial Guard, quit on October 24. The next day Itagaki Taisuke and four senior councilors departed, leaving the government in disarray and shattering the fragile samurai coalition that had overthrown the Tokugawa shogunate. Saigō and Itagaki personified the opposite courses of antigovernment opposition; the former led disgruntled warriors who raised the specter of armed revolt, and the latter led a wider coalition of warriors and commoners who demanded a share of political authority through elected representation.[2] The political upheaval forced numerous officers and men who hailed from Satsuma and were assigned to the Guard to choose between individual and national allegiances.

An October 25 imperial rescript addressed to Imperial Guard officers acknowledged Saigō's many contributions to the restoration and then reminded them that he was but a single general in the national army that commanded their allegiance. Ignoring the memorial and two personal pleas from the emperor, several Satsuma commanders of Guard units resigned in sympathy with Saigō, and about 100 more Satsuma officers joined the walkout. Hundreds of the rank and file serving in the Guard also deserted and fled to Kagoshima. With wholesale desertions threatening the readiness of the Imperial Guard and leaving the government defenseless, army leaders hastily arranged emergency transfers of picked troops from the regional garrisons to replace the defectors. This decision was very unpopular with those selected because assignment to the Guard incurred a five-year term of service instead of the normal three-year obligation of conscripts assigned to local garrisons. Morale plummeted in the new army, already seriously understrength, at a time of growing internal turmoil and domestic disorder.[3]

In mid-January 1874 disaffected samurai attacked and wounded a senior government minister in Tokyo. A nationwide police dragnet quickly apprehended nine of the attackers, who turned out to be samurai from the former Tosa domain, including a former Guard lieutenant and his sergeants.[4] On February 4 a coalition of frustrated Korean-expedition advocates and antiforeign elements revolted in Saga Prefecture, located in northwestern Kyūshū. Saga had an unusually high samurai population and was seething with discontent because of poor harvests and resulting inflationary food prices. Etō Shimpei led the 2,500 Saga rebels.

Etō was from an impoverished samurai family and in the 1850s had concluded that overseas commerce would relieve the suffering of the countryside. His combat leadership during the Boshin Civil War led to an appointment as a senior councilor in the new government. Convinced that the dominant regional cliques in the government and military constituted a reemerging *bakufu*, he reasoned that Japanese expansion to the Asian continent would complete a popular second restoration.[5] He too had quit the government in disgust over the Korea issue.

Two days after Etō's uprising, the council of state set in motion a punitive expedition against Taiwan in a much-belated response to the November 1871 massacre of fifty-four shipwrecked Ryūkyū Island sailors by Taiwanese aborigines. The council's underlying motive was to deflect samurai energy and frustration, and army authorities deliberately organized the expedition around troops from the Kagoshima garrison in southern Kyūshū in order to neutralize Saigō's main center of support and simultaneously remove potentially rebellious sympathizers from Etō's treasonous appeals. The army then added soldiers from northern Kyūshū's Kumamoto garrison to balance the expedition and to make sure that the Kagoshima contingents followed government orders.[6]

By mid-February Etō's samurai insurgents had seized local government offices in Saga, and the insurrection seemed to be gaining momentum. Informers, however, had alerted Home Minister Ōkubo Toshimichi to the rebels' plans, and the council of state empowered Ōkubo, a civilian minister, with full military and judicial authority to crush the uprising. Ōkubo promptly ordered loyal troops from the Hiroshima and Osaka garrisons to suppress the insurrection. Unable to tap the Kagoshima garrison for troops because they were committed to the Taiwan expedition, the government had to hire more than 4,000 former samurai from nearby domains as reinforcements.

Etō's warriors captured Saga castle on February 18 but were soon surrounded. Ōkubo and Maj. Gen. Nozu Shizuo devised a campaign strategy, but the civilian Ōkubo led the army into Saga and ten days later recaptured the castle. Saga insurgents made repetitive surprise attacks designed to lure government troops into close-quarter ambushes, but the conscripts had sufficient training in minor tactics to withstand frontal assaults and then counterattack to turn rebel flanks, bypass ambushes, and force Etō's battered warriors to withdraw. The rebels relied on traditional tactics of sword and spear in close hand-to-hand combat, and few had any appreciation of the national army's small-arms firepower or understood the deadliness of government artillery. Losses amounted to about 700 men, almost evenly divided between the army and the rebels, but the much larger national army could absorb the casualties while the insurrectionists could not. Etō's decision to flee during the fighting for Saga castle rather than fight to the death with his men turned public opinion decisively against his cause. He appealed for aid to Saigō Takamori, who dismissed Etō for "being the type of man who disregarded 3,000 troops to escape."[7]

Despite the victory, the army hierarchy resented a civilian like Ōkubo commanding military forces and faulted the ad hoc command and control arrangements. The emperor had formally led the campaign from Tokyo and on February 23 had designated his military aide Second Lt. Prince Yoshiaki (Ninnaji) the titular field commander. Minister of the Army Yamagata became the imperial military adviser at the Tokyo headquarters, but he was so annoyed by civilian command that he reorganized the army ministry's sixth bureau into a small prototype general staff to exercise control over military operations. This marked the beginning of the army's assertion of its uniqueness and the independence of supreme command from civil authorities.[8] Yamagata then resigned his ministerial portfolio and appointed himself director of the revamped sixth bureau staff and concurrently commander of the Imperial Guard. He led the Guard to Saga, but by the time he arrived the major fighting was over and a manhunt for Etō was under way.

The discredited Etō was finally captured on April 13 and after an impromptu trial, presided over by Ōkubo, was beheaded. His gibbeted head went on public

display as a warning of the consequences of rebellion, and the authorities capitalized on the latest technology by posting photographs of Etō's severed head
in government offices throughout Japan. Yamagata's Guard provided a display of
overwhelming government force designed to cower other potentially rebellious
peasants, advocates of the people's rights movement, and especially Saigō and
his Satsuma bands. With Etō's short-lived rebellion crushed, Yoshiaki returned
to Tokyo, where the emperor promoted him six grades, to the rank of major
general. Yamagata resumed his duties as minister of the army in June.[9]

During the manhunt for Etō, Ōkubo appointed Saigō's younger brother
Tsugumichi to organize and command the Taiwan expedition. Several commercial ships carrying 3,000 troops departed Tokyo Bay on April 6 for Nagasaki to take on more troops and supplies. The newly appointed U.S. minister
to Japan, however, compelled Ōkubo to order a delay in the departure from
Nagasaki. Saigō Tsugumichi ignored Ōkubo's directive, claimed his writ from
the emperor took precedence, and sailed for Taiwan that night. Saigō's insubordination implied that the army's special relationship with the throne superseded
civilian control.

Campaigning in Taiwan proved tougher than anticipated. Taiwanese guerrillas in mountain strongholds held out until early June, and though Japanese
combat losses were negligible (twelve killed and seventeen wounded), an
outbreak of malaria, the effects of other tropical diseases, poor logistics, and
substandard medical support spread epidemics that resulted in more than 560
deaths. When word reached the emperor of the terrible conditions, he sent his
personal German physician to oversee medical care, a practical example of imperial benevolence that further reinforced the special bond between throne and
army. Japanese forces withdrew from Taiwan after the Chinese paid an indemnity and gave de facto recognition to Japanese claims on the Ryūkyū Islands,
which became Okinawa Prefecture in 1879.

In late March 1876, just after suppressing Etō's uprising, the government
officially outlawed the wearing of swords except for the police and military,
who carried western-style swords or sabers, not the traditional curved samurai
sword. Samurai discontent flared over this latest decree, especially in southwestern Japan. That October an uprising of about 200 xenophobic warriors erupted
in Kumamoto, where rebels mortally wounded the local garrison commander
and murdered several government officials. Troops from the Kumamoto garrison quelled the *Jimpūren* revolt while the nearby Kokura garrison crushed
another smaller disturbance. Later that month about 200 disgruntled warriors
in Hagi attacked government offices and in early November fought a four-day
pitched battle with army troops. Maebara Issei, the former senior councilor
who had temporarily controlled the army after Ōmura's assassination, led the
latest antigovernment uprising.

Maebara's motives mixed traditional samurai disdain for the conscription ordinance and frustration over the government's Korea policy. A warrior known
for simplicity, honesty, and sentimentality, Maebara's radicalism dated from his
association with Yoshida Shōin in the 1850s. But his mercurial character could
undergo sudden, unnerving mood swings and an indifference to higher orders.
After Maebara left the government, ostensibly to care for his aging parents, his
volatile personality and fanatical commitment made him a lightning rod for
samurai extremists. His followers fought with such desperate resolve that the
army needed reinforcements from the Osaka garrison to defeat them. Maebara
was captured and later executed.

The warrior revolts in southwestern Japan displayed a samurai exclusivity
with few, if any, commoners, fighting alongside of them. As warriors they were
bound by an iron-clad discipline that normally motivated them to fight against
great odds and often to the death. Fortunately for the national army, the samurai clung to their regional allegiances and antiquated tactics, and their isolated
uprisings did not coalesce into nationwide rebellions.

Besides disgruntled samurai, tens of thousands of peasants joined violent
demonstrations in central Japan to protest inflationary rice prices and higher
land taxes. With the Osaka and Nagoya garrisons overextended while suppressing the Kumamoto warrior uprisings, the government again enlisted outsiders,
hiring 1,200 former warriors that December to put down the violent peasant
outbreaks. The spontaneous and uncoordinated small-scale uprisings enabled
government troops and their hired auxiliaries to crush the outbreaks sequen-
tially.[10] The geography of rebellion also favored the national army. Peasant
uprisings were confined to central Japan whereas warrior insurrections were
centered in the southwest, where Saigō, the gravest military threat to the government, drew his greatest strength.

Since his resignation, Saigō Takamori and his lieutenants had been forging
a cadre of NCOs and junior officers trained in modern infantry tactics at his
network of private military academies (i.e., not approved by the central government) in Kagoshima City. Rifle units trained at the academies were composed
in large part of former Imperial Guard troops commanded by the same officers
who had quit the Guard in 1873. The same was true for the artillery school
students.[11] By early 1876 Saigō had mustered about 13,000 troops with battle-
hardened ex-samurai, the majority of them veterans of the restoration and
Boshin campaigns in their late 20s or early 30s, stiffening the ranks. Saigō's officers had similar battlefield pedigrees, including several who had commanded
large units during the Boshin War. This private army had stockpiled quantities
of small-arms ammunition, weapons, and equipment.

Saigō counseled patience, having already postponed his uprising scheduled
for November 3, 1876, the emperor's birthday, because of the *Jimpūren* and

Maebara uprisings. More radical officers, like Kirino Toshiaki, thought that the government was so corrupt that killing two or three ministers would cause it to collapse. A government official's coerced confession of a plot to murder Saigō and the government's decision to transfer ammunition from the Kagoshima depot provoked hot-headed academy students to attack the ammunition lockers and confiscate the ordnance. There could be no turning back.[12]

News of Saigō's academies attracted additional disgruntled samurai, and by the time he rose in revolt in early 1877 his army numbered about 30,000 men, roughly 6,000 of whom handled transport and supply duties. Although they lacked large quantities of artillery and trained ordnance specialists, they expected to seize more heavy weapons once they captured the government arsenal at Kumamoto, about 100 miles to the north. Under banners reading "Respect Virtue: Reform the Government," the advance guard marched from Kagoshima on February 15, and two days later Saigō led the rear guard and command group from the city during a heavy snowfall, whose dramatic effect endowed his expedition with the trappings of unselfishness and heroism. More recruits flocked to his cause, and at its peak Saigō commanded about 42,000 men.[13] Saigō and his followers portrayed themselves as loyal servants of the throne whose quarrel was with the emperor's evil advisers who had betrayed the restoration. This rationalization for rebellion would repeatedly serve as the army's justification for future acts of insubordination, disobedience to orders, and mutiny.

At the outbreak of the so-called Southwest War or Satsuma Rebellion the national army counted 20,000 garrison troops plus 5,000 additional men assigned to Imperial Guard units. During the fighting, the army eventually expanded to 50,000 troops, mainly by provisionally recruiting 13,000 ex-samurai, ostensibly as policemen assigned to the Tokyo Metropolitan Police. Besides these numbers, the army employed about 90,000 hastily contracted civilians on a daily basis to load, haul, and distribute military supplies. The distant battlefields of Kyūshū forced the army to operate at the end of a lengthy maritime line of communication that stretched back to Tokyo and depended on dozens of inter-coastal transports and small gunboats shuttling troops and material to southwest Japan. The absence of supply depots and a service corps compounded the logistical difficulties, as did battlefield consumption of ammunition and equipment, which far exceeded the government's projections and resupply capabilities.[14]

Reports of the Satsuma army approaching Kumamoto reached Tokyo on February 28, and the next day the emperor issued orders to suppress the rebels. Because of the recent experience with dissident samurai, Yamagata and others worried that Saigō's revolt would spread rapidly through southern and western Japan. Their greatest fear was that Itagaki's political association might join the revolt and take Shikoku into the enemy camp. Thus the army's response to rebellion was to cobble together provisional mixed brigades (then the largest maneuver unit) with a cadre from the Imperial Guard and other garrison units and quickly get them to Kyūshū. For example, an infantry battalion from the Tokyo garrison and another from Osaka, reinforced by reserve artillery and engineer units from Tokyo, formed Maj. Gen. Nozu Shizuo's 1st Brigade. These nonstandard tables of organization and equipment transfers drained troops from other units, and the frequent reorganizations aggravated already serious personnel shortages, causing the government to rely even more on former samurai.[15]

Saigō's primary objective, the vital government arsenal at Kumamoto, was defended by two infantry regiments (3,800 men) and two artillery batteries commanded by Maj. Gen. Tani Tateki. Although heavily outnumbered, the government defenders had superior firepower—most were armed with new Enfield or Snider rifles—and had been recently reinforced with a hastily recruited 400-man police unit. They were defending a strong position that Tani was determined to hold. With the Satsuma advance guard just five miles from Kumamoto, on February 19 a fire of unexplained origin broke out in a large storehouse in the adjoining town. The blaze spread rapidly and destroyed most of the town and the garrison's food supply. Luckily for Tani it did not reach his reserve stocks of ammunition.[16]

Saigō committed the bulk of his army to the Kumamoto attack while other rebel units, about 13,000 strong, moved north to control the mountain passes leading to the city. After several fierce assaults failed to overcome Kumamoto's well-armed defenders, Saigō besieged the castle. This decision sacrificed the rebels' advantages of speed and mobility of lightly armed troops in favor of positional warfare against an opponent fighting from strong defenses with more modern weaponry.[17] Saigō was waging a decisive battle without reserves and on an overextended line of communication far from his only logistic base.

During previous deliberations in Tokyo on February 12, Yamagata had recommended an amphibious landing at Kagoshima to seize the rebels' weakly held logistics base followed by the destruction of insurgent pockets throughout Kyūshū. Army leaders supported him, but Tani, facing an impending attack and having doubts about his conscripts' reliability, cabled that beleaguered Kumamoto's imminent fall would endanger all of Japan.[18] This assessment swayed court and civilian officials, who rejected Yamagata's proposal and made the relief of Kumamoto garrison the army's strategic objective.

Emperor Meiji appointed Prince Arisugawa the titular head of the expeditionary force. Yamagata, a lieutenant general, commanded the ground forces, and Vice Adm. Kawamura Sumiyoshi led the navy. They departed Tokyo on February 20 and opened their headquarters in Fukuoka six days later. The plan of campaign employed a pincer maneuver. Lt. Gen. Kuroda Kiyotaka, Yamagata's nemesis during the restoration wars and currently a government councilor,

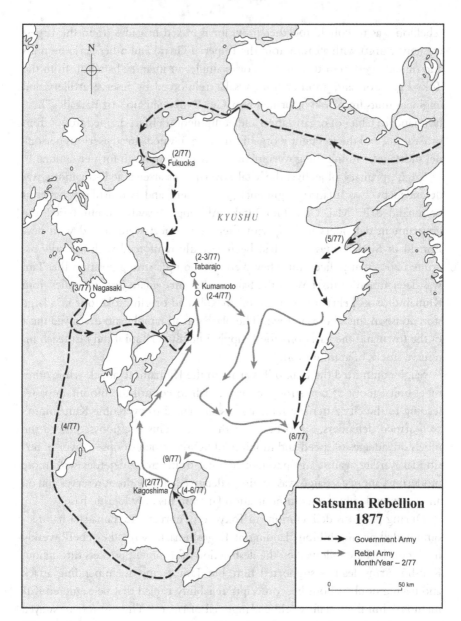

Map 2

with one corps (two brigades), and Yamagata, with another corps, would isolate Saigō's forces with a two-pronged attack and lift the siege of Kumamoto.
Kawamura would then land at Kagoshima with a third corps to cut the rebels'
line of communication. Reminiscent of the campaigns in northern Japan during the Boshin War, the national army divided its forces, established separate
field commands, and banked everything on one decisive attack.[19]

Operating in faraway Kyūshū, the army needed a unified field headquarters to coordinate the pincer movement and to adapt to unfolding demands of the campaign. Yamagata and Kuroda predictably disagreed on the overall plan of campaign; their ostensible commander, Prince Arisugawa, was not a trained professional soldier and could not control his impulsive field generals. Civilian and military leaders were also scattered across the country, which further complicated command and control arrangements. The emperor and part of the bureaucracy relocated to Kyoto accompanied by an advisory liaison body. Senior civilian ministers and the rest of the bureaucracy stayed in Tokyo as a caretaker government. The creation of a provisional field headquarters in Fukuoka relegated the general staff bureau in Tokyo to a minor advisory role, but its director relocated to the army's logistics base at Osaka and began issuing operational orders.[20]

At the operational or brigade echelon, command and control was virtually nonexistent because French training had concentrated on small-unit operations. The three corps headquarters were nominal entities that exerted very loose control over their tactical brigades and regiments. Without a higher staff to plan and coordinate operations, Yamagata and Kuroda conducted independent campaigns since neither agreed with the other's strategy and they loathed one another.

Yamagata's corps marched from Fukuoka in mid-February and cautiously advanced south, hesitating to enter the mountainous Kyūshū terrain that favored the defender. Satsuma forces took advantage of the lull to strengthen their ridgeline and hilltop field fortifications around Tabaruzaka that blocked the main passes leading to Kumamoto.

Maj. Nogi Maresuke, acting commander of the 14th Regiment, attacked Satsuma forces north of Kumamoto on February 23. Unable to dislodge the rebels, Nogi withdrew, but Satsuma troops outflanked and surrounded his regiment. During a fighting retreat, conducted in darkness and heavy rain with rebels intermingled with his troops, Nogi lost his regimental colors when the standard bearer was killed. Despite Nogi's personal bravery, his horse was shot out from under him; the loss of the colors presented by the emperor was a grave offense and tormented him throughout his career.[21]

After two brigades were mauled in the Tabaruzaka fighting, Yamagata halted to await additional reinforcements. Satsuma forces suffered heavy losses as well, about 500 killed or wounded each day during the five-day battle. There were so many wounded that field hospitals ran out of bandages and resorted to strips of clothing to dress wounds.[22] Yamagata meanwhile deployed his corps over a broad front, more or less facing the 25-mile-long Satsuma defenses, for a methodical advance much to the chagrin of the government that was urging him to relieve Kumamoto without delay.

This print conveys the ferocity of the fighting between government troops and samurai at Tabaruzaka.
(Courtesy Kumamoto Municipal Museum)

Reinforced with brigades commanded by Maj. Gen. Ōyama Iwao and Maj. Gen. Miura Gorō, Yamagata in early March attacked into the rugged mountains, promptly fell into a rebel trap, became encircled, and suffered severe losses in two weeks of fighting. With additional troops, on March 20 Yamagata again attacked. This time the government forces took advantage of a driving rainstorm to hook around the main Tabaruzaka defenses and, spearheaded by shock troops, surprise the rebels' rear area defenses. Many of the government's handpicked swordsmen were enlisted as police from Aizu. These former samurai sought to avenge their earlier defeat at Satsuma's hands during the Boshin Civil War and fought with abandon at close quarters. The Aizu contingent suffered almost 25 percent of all police casualties, although it comprised fewer than 10 percent of all mobilized police.[23] Victory left Yamagata's troops spent, and with ammunition and supplies almost exhausted Yamagata was unable to advance.

As the fighting around Tabaruzaka peaked, Kuroda departed Nagasaki by ship on March 19 and landed his troops, bolstered by a unit of recalled Boshin War veterans, about 30 miles south of Kumamoto. He immediately struck north, threatening Saigō's army from the rear. With the rebels heavily engaged by Kuroda, Yamagata refitted his corps and renewed his offensive from the north, lifting the siege of Kumamoto castle on April 14. Throughout this maneuvering, Saigō remained passive, never inspecting the front lines and relying on scouts and newspapers for intelligence.

Outnumbered two to one, the battle-seasoned Satsuma warriors were contemptuous of the army's conscripts and feared only three things: rain (which dampened the muzzle-loading primers of their older Enfield rifles, making the weapons inoperable); red hats (the Imperial Guard, which included ex-samurai sharing a common warrior ethos); and artillery (for its killing power). The national army's overwhelming superiority in artillery weapons—it enjoyed a seven-to-one advantage—was indeed decisive throughout the campaign. Mountain artillery was especially lethal because of its mobility. Two pack-horses could carry the disassembled 450-pound gun, making it easier to move over Kyūshū's dirt roads and mountainous terrain than the horse-drawn heavier field artillery gun that was often too unwieldy even to manhandle into firing position.[24]

Government troops pursued Saigō's defeated army across Kyūshū. On April 26 Kawamura landed at Kagoshima, seized the weakly defended rebel positions, and destroyed the rebels' stockpiles of arms and munitions. By early June the broken samurai army split in two, and in August Saigō, hunted and harried with only a few hundred followers left, committed suicide in a cave near Shiroyama, just north of Kagoshima. Kirino and about forty other Satsuma commanders, fighting to the last, were killed on September 24 when Maj. Gen. Soga Suke-nori's brigade overran their Shiroyama redoubt.

Losses were frightful on both sides; one in every three government troops was killed or wounded, and one of every two of Saigō's insurgents met a similar fate. All the rebellious samurai, however, did not fight to the death. Thousands surrendered after Saigō's suicide. The government subsequently executed any rebels it judged to be ringleaders of the revolt and punished more than 2,700 members of Saigō's army. But authorities eventually pardoned most of Saigō's lower-ranking officers and foot soldiers in hopes of eliminating any lingering notions of revenge while promoting a new sense of national unity in a modern military system. Saigō himself was officially rehabilitated in 1889 in recognition of his contributions to the restoration. More than 25,000 individuals contributed to a bronze statue of Saigō unveiled in Ueno Park in December 1898. Among the dignitaries in attendance was Yamagata, and one can only imagine the thoughts running through his mind during the dedication.[25]

The Satsuma Rebellion had pushed the fledgling national army beyond its limits. Fighting for the regime's survival, the army threw all its forces into the struggle, exhausting its manpower. Without an organized mobilization capability or sufficient reserves to draw upon, conscription alone could not supply the personnel needed to crush the rebellion. Furthermore, the conscript army displayed serious deficiencies.

Conscripts' battlefield performance deeply troubled the Meiji leaders, who saw that, man for man, the conscripts were no match for Saigō's samurai. With conscripts found wanting in terms of quantity and quality, the national army again had to enlist large numbers of former warriors not only as reserves to bolster the regulars but also as frontline fighters to inspire leadership and boost morale. Army leaders concluded that government troops might have better training and superior equipment, but the warriors had superior morale and the will to fight.[26]

The tenacity of Saigō's samurai convinced senior army officers that the rebels possessed special intangible qualities, and this aspect, not the national army's material superiority, was decisive. Postwar assessments determined that spiritual or intangible attributes had to be inculcated into the ranks, and authorities launched an intensive indoctrination program to instill the national army with fighting spirit.[27] Over time a reliance on intangible qualities came to mean a willingness to fight to the death regardless of the situation. Once that concept gained acceptance, death in battle became the standard by which to measure fighting spirit. No matter how bravely enlisted troops acquitted themselves in battle, their very survival could be and was interpreted by staff officers as indicative of a lack of fighting spirit that adversely affected overall performance.

Analysis of the tangible reasons for victory over Saigō's rebels led the national army to mixed conclusions. The army's material advantages, particularly in modern firepower, had overcome a stubborn and courageous foe, and the army faulted Saigō's strategy, affirming its own. It also judged propaganda extremely effective because branding Saigō's force as rebels had dampened Satsuma morale, a conclusion seemingly at odds with praise lavished on the insurgents' exceptional fighting spirit.

The government had spent more than 40 million yen (about US$38 million in 1877) on the war (almost sixty times as much as the rebels), most of it for foreign-manufactured arms, equipment, and munitions. Independent research and development of weapons technology was less important than the knowledge of foreign weapons production technology and the ability to adapt foreign-made weaponry to suit the army's needs given Japan's limited industrial capabilities. Until the military could break its near-total dependence on foreign arms suppliers, its leaders believed Japan could never be a truly sovereign nation.[28]

By eliminating the last major samurai threat, the army ensured a unified and stable state, the sine qua non for national independence. Just as the army demonstrated resiliency in a hard-fought campaign, the government displayed durability throughout the rebellion, never coming close to the collapse that Kirino had confidently predicted. Rather, traditional samurai privileges and regional challenges to a centralized state were swept away. With the army enshrined as the guarantor of a strong national government, military authorities drew on the lessons of the rebellion to shape the postwar force into a modern, professional army.

4

The Army of Meiji

On May 14, 1878, the most powerful man in Japan, Minister of Home Affairs Ōkubo, was riding alone in his unescorted carriage from his Tokyo residence to a morning appointment. Six sword-wielding former samurai surrounded his carriage in a narrow lane and hacked and stabbed him to death. The ringleader later admitted that the killers feared an Ōkubo dictatorship and had planned to murder him since they heard of Saigō's suicide. One captured assassin joked to interrogators that if life was a stage, their act might be seen as a cheap burlesque.[1]

Besides Ōkubo's brazen murder, lingering questions of loyalty and obedience to orders clouded the national army's victory over Saigō's warriors. In the aftermath of the rebellion, many units felt slighted by a government that neither recognized nor rewarded their wartime sacrifices. For example, the Imperial Guard artillery battery, despite its prominent wartime role, received belated commendations and smaller monetary awards than soldiers had expected. The parsimoniousness reflected the government's financial retrenchment policy deemed necessary to repay the enormous cost of the war, including more than 30 million yen in supplemental funding (five times the army's annual budget). In order to balance the national budget, in December 1877 the council of state ordered 20 percent across-the-board reductions to ministry budgets. The following May the army ministry reduced military pay by 5 percent and temporarily suspended work on its showcase coastal fortification construction projects.[2] These actions only added to the list of soldiers' grievances.

On the night of August 23, 1878, about 200 noncommissioned officers and enlisted men of the Guard artillery battalion garrisoned near Tokyo's Takebashi Bridge mutinied, murdered their commanding officer and the officer of the day, perfunctorily shelled the finance minister's official residence, and demanded to speak directly to the emperor. The army ministry, having been tipped off in advance, quickly crushed the insurrection. Courts-martial held in October sentenced 55 mutineers to death and punished over 300 more (including accomplices in other units) with prison terms or banishment. Unrewarded wartime service had sparked the so-called Takebashi Incident, but the trials also revealed that many of the enlisted troops were active in the nascent liberty and people's rights movement, a popular national political campaign demanding democratic rights from the Meiji government that leaders like Yamagata regarded as subversive and dangerous.

Yamagata sought to inoculate the army from the virus of mutiny by appealing to a romanticized imperial past. Fifty days after the Takebashi Incident, the army distributed his Admonition to Soldiers (*gunjin kunkai*) to all its company commanders. The instructions, aimed specifically at the officer corps, stressed that strict military discipline and unquestioning obedience to a superior's orders were the foundation of the military institution. He portrayed officers as the heirs to a glorious samurai tradition in which loyalty and valor were the "way of the warrior" (*bushidō*).[3] Real samurai were discredited, so officers and conscripts were indoctrinated to aspire to the greatly romanticized version of idealized warriors.

Yamagata also warned that disobedience to orders led to military involvement in political activities and spread subversion among the ranks. He justified that claim with another dubious assertion: that in ancient times the army had belonged to the emperor and was therefore above politics. By equating obedience to a superior's orders with compliance to a direct imperial order, Yamagata further implied that a superior's orders had to be followed unquestionably, regardless of legality.[4] In sum, Yamagata wanted an apolitical army under his control to prevent a reoccurrence of the Satsuma Rebellion or Takebashi Incident, and one means to achieve this goal was to make the military directly responsible to the emperor, thereby insuring imperial control of the army.

Institutional Reforms

In the decade following the Satsuma Rebellion, the army thoroughly reorganized. The process was gradual, but the reforms were radical. The army's fundamental institutions—a general staff, an inspector general, a general staff college, and a division force structure—evolved, but only after acrimonious debates within the army that pitted Francophile traditionalists against pro-Prussian reformers.

In the wake of rebellion, mutiny, and popular demonstrations, Yamagata feared that antigovernment politicians would restrict the army's freedom of action, or that antigovernment forces might incite the ranks to revolt and overthrow the government. These concerns justified reforms to ensure an apolitical army by removing the supreme command from the political arena. The ruling oligarchy concurred because they wanted no more Saigō Takamoris—men who held dual military-civilian appointments and might use their military power to usurp the civilian government. One possible solution was to create a general staff with direct access to the emperor that could execute imperial commands unencumbered by the agenda of civilian political leaders or military administrators.[5]

The idea was an extension of Yamagata's 1874 establishment of the sixth bureau, augmented with fresh ideas from Europe. Capt. Katsura Tarō, one of Yamagata's many Chōshū protégés, had spent the Satsuma insurrection studying at the Prussian military academy at his own expense. He returned home in 1878 convinced of the merits of a general staff that was independent of the army ministry's administrative control and enjoyed direct access to the emperor.[6] That October, apparently on Katsura's advice, Yamagata formally recommended to the council of state the separation of staff and administrative functions.

The council of state abolished the general staff bureau on December 5, 1878, and established a general staff separate from the army minister and directly responsible to the emperor, although without clearly delineating the new staff's authority. During peacetime the general staff controlled the Imperial Guard and regional garrisons, and the chief of staff, an imperial appointee, also served as the emperor's highest military adviser. During wartime the chief of staff assisted the emperor with military matters but lacked command and decision-making authority, those formally being the prerogatives of the emperor. He could, however, issue operational orders in the emperor's name. This provision institutionalized the prerogative of the independence of command (*tōsuiken*) executed in the emperor's name as supreme commander (*daigensui*).[7]

The new general staff had two bureaus divided by geographic interest. The eastern bureau was responsible for the garrisons in the Tokyo and Sendai military administrative districts as well as Hokkaidō, Siberia, and Manchuria; the western oversaw the other four regional garrisons plus Korea and China.[8] Each bureau had operational and intelligence functions, and two smaller subsections handled administration, prepared gazetteers, translated materials, and archived documents.

Within days of creating a general staff, Yamagata, who became the first chief of staff, established a superintendency on December 30 as a separate headquarters in Tokyo. It too reported directly to the emperor, coordinated army-wide training, standardized tactics and equipment, ensured that units carried out the general staff's orders, and enforced army regulations. The superintendency had no director, and the duties of its headquarters in Tokyo were limited, but its three regional superintendents enjoyed broad authority because they reported directly to the emperor, bypassing the general staff and army ministry. In peacetime each regional superintendent was responsible for the education and training at two garrisons and in wartime commanded a two-division corps formed by combining the garrisons' forces.

The three regional superintendents were superimposed on the existing garrison system, and each was of lieutenant-general rank; Tani supervised the eastern commandaries, Nozu the central, and Miura the western. Each had the
authority to enforce orders issued by the general staff with imperial approval.
This reorganization of the army's administrative system with a new inspectorate
and an independent general staff was an attempt by Yamagata and Army Minister Ōyama to consolidate their power and, by extension, the Satsuma-Chōshū
monopoly on senior army positions.[9]

The Satsuma Rebellion had exposed the need for trained staff officers to
plan and coordinate operations, formulate strategy, and remedy deficiencies in
operational planning. In 1882 the army had a total of forty-nine staff officers:
fourteen assigned to the general staff, five to the army ministry, and the remaining thirty to the various garrisons, the Imperial Guard, or the military districts.
That year the army opened the general staff college to train and educate officers
for future staff assignments. Nineteen students were selected for the three-year
course. The first year was remedial and concentrated on the study of foreign
languages (German and French), mathematics, and drafting for engineering and
map-making purposes. Officer-students studied military organization, mobilization, tactics, and road march formations in their second year; their third year
focused on the mechanics of overnight unit bivouacs, reconnaissance, strategy,
and military history. Instruction in tactics and strategy was initially limited because of a lack of qualified Japanese instructors and the continuing debate
within the army over adopting French or German doctrine. From its inception,
the staff college had a close association with the throne, personified by the emperor's personal presentation of an imperial gift to the top graduates: a telescope
in the case of the first six graduating classes, and thereafter a sword.[10]

Another manifestation of the link between emperor and army was the conversion of Ōmura's *Shōkonsha* concept of a public memorial to commemorate
those who died in the Boshin Civil War to a state-sponsored Shintō shrine to
promote imperial divinity and Japanese uniqueness. In June 1879 the *Shōkonsha*
was renamed the Yasukuni Shrine, with a status second in ranking only to the
imperial shrines. The home ministry, army, and navy administered the shrine
while the army paid for its upkeep. For purposes of army morale, the army reinterred its war dead from the Satsuma Rebellion at the Yasukuni and announced
that they had been transmogrified into spirits guarding the nation. Interment
was strictly limited to those killed in action; soldiers who died on active service
during peacetime were interred in army-designated regional cemeteries.[11]

Promulgating a New Ideology

Political agitation since the mid-1870s for a constitution and a parliament gradually matured into a campaign for freedom and people's rights, a broader-based

political movement whose origins lay in samurai discontent. By the late 1870s, peasant unrest had also increased because the government resorted to deflationary fiscal policies to repay the foreign loans that underwrote the military costs of suppressing Saigō's rebellion. Retrenchment caused a sharper decline in market prices for rice and raw silk, the cash crops of the peasantry, than in overall consumer prices. Many peasants fell into debt, borrowed money to buy seed or pay land taxes, and in some cases were unable to repay the loans. Disaffected peasants organized into groups seeking debt relief, and outbreaks of armed violence—some led by local political party branch members—erupted in central Japan during 1882.[12]

Soldiers had also been active in the people's rights movement since its inception. In January 1879 police arrested several enlisted men assigned to the Guard infantry regiment for conspiring to murder their company commander and high-ranking government officials. Sometime later they apprehended a disgruntled artillery officer who was threatening to bombard the imperial palace. Dissatisfied over the awarding of medals, troops also complained about the five-year term of active service for those assigned to the Guard, demanded special pay and allowances, and sought political redress for grievances over the living conditions of enlisted men in garrisons.[13]

Yamagata did initiate reforms that shortened the Guards' length of service and reduced pay inequalities. Conscription reforms in October 1879 extended terms of reserve duty from four to seven years by creating a first (three-year) and second reserve (four-year), halved the fee to purchase a substitute, and tightened deferments. Yamagata refused, however, to allow soldiers greater political expression, believing that it would undermine military discipline.[14] As if to underscore his fears, in 1880 a soldier stationed in Tokyo committed suicide in front of the imperial palace when the government refused to accept his petition calling for the opening of a parliament.

Internal army dissent also targeted the government and Yamagata, particularly the council of state's fire sale of the Hokkaidō Colonization Office's assets to private Mitsubishi interests allegedly to defray the retrenchment costs. Among the most vocal and persistent critics were four general officers: lieutenant generals Torio Koyata, Guard commander; Tani Tateki, commandant of the military academy and the Toyama Infantry School; Miura Gorō, superintendent of the western commandary district; and Maj. Gen. Soga Sukenori, acting superintendent of the central commandary district. The four claimed to be acting from *bushidō* principles when in September 1881 they petitioned the throne to reverse the transaction.[15]

The people's rights movement also criticized the sale, and the generals' petition forged another link in the chain of protests during the so-called crisis of 1881, which climaxed that October when the emperor canceled the sale and promised a national assembly by 1890. To prepare for the assembly, a cabinet system of government would replace the council of state in 1886 (the change actually occurred in December 1885).

Liberal members of the government resigned to join the popular rights movement in anticipation of greater political opportunity. The four generals remained on the active duty list, continued to hold important positions, and formed the conservative opposition to Yamagata's efforts to reorganize and unify the national army. The involvement of enlisted troops and senior officers in political activity stimulated army chief of staff Yamagata's fears about the military's security and reliability.

On January 4, 1882, Yamagata promulgated the imperial rescript to soldiers and sailors to remedy what he perceived as lax military discipline and military involvement in the popular rights movement. Its audience was the army rank and file, and the language was clearer and easier to understand than the highly stylized 1878 injunctions to officers. The message, however, was the same. Yamagata reemphasized respect for superiors, the spirit of courage and sacrifice, and absolute obedience because superiors' orders were direct commands from the throne. Soldiers and sailors, he wrote, should loyally serve the emperor, their commander-in-chief, "neither being led astray by current opinions or meddling in political affairs," and always recalling that "duty is heavier than a mountain while death is lighter than a feather." Yamagata again relied on hoary martial values to send a message of modernity based on loyalty to the emperor and nation, not one's former domain, and issue a caution against political involvement. The 1882 memorial would shape official popular ideology and the notion of duty and loyalty to the emperor.[16]

The army's role in controlling domestic disorders peaked in the autumn of 1884 when troops suppressed a large popular uprising in Chichibu, west of Tokyo. That October a 5,000-man-strong peasant army protesting usurious interest rates and demanding lower taxes and debt relief attacked government offices and moneylenders. In early November government troops used overwhelming force to restore order and shatter the popular rights movement, whose members disbanded rather than risk being labeled traitors for supporting insurrections.[17] By that time, the army was engaged in reorganizing its basic force structure and command and control apparatus.

The Conversion to Divisions

In January 1880 Yamagata had warned the emperor of the dangers posed by Russia's remorseless advance into East Asia and China's military modernization. Japan's lengthy coastlines left it especially vulnerable to attack from multiple directions or to a naval blockade and isolation. Yamagata would neutralize such threats by fortifying small off-shore islands as the nation's first line of defense and completing the coastal battery construction projects around Tokyo Bay that the government had suspended to pay for the Satsuma Rebellion. He voiced a recurrent theme: without a strong military, Japan could not maintain its sovereignty from the European powers—who, he claimed, built armies and navies regardless of national wealth or poverty.[18]

The army's January 1882 budget proposed a ten-year plan to field seven modern infantry divisions with supporting troops, improve coastal defenses, and upgrade weaponry, especially artillery. It reflected Yamagata's concern over the growing tension with Korea and China, which appeared to justify a larger army. Since 1877 the army had expanded slowly from around 40,000 officers and men to more than 46,000 by 1882, and its budget grew accordingly, from about 6.6 million yen (US$6 million) to 9.4 million yen (US$8.5 million), respectively. Army expansionism to counter perceived continental threats was consistent with the 1870 calls for a Korean expedition and overseas expansion. Yet it also demonstrated the government's concern that Korea under foreign (non-Japanese) influence would pose an unacceptable threat to Japan's home islands and that a larger military was necessary for self-defense against invasion.

Outbursts of anti-Japanese violence in Korea during the summer of 1882 culminated that July with the murder of the Japanese military adviser to the newly organized Korean army and an attack against the Japanese legation in Seoul. Tokyo sent two infantry companies to restore order, made demands on the Korean court, and moved large forces to Kyūshū opposite Korea during the so-called *Jingo* Incident. The Korean court promptly sought assistance from China, which dispatched 5,000 troops that eliminated pro-Japanese elements in the rebellious Korean army, installed a pro-Chinese Korean faction in power, and reasserted Chinese influence throughout the peninsula.[19]

Although the general staff had an 1880 operational plan for offensive operations in north China, it was premised on wishful thinking because Japan was too weak militarily to confront the Chinese empire. During the Korea crisis the army remained passive, fearful that China might seize Tsushima Island to use as a springboard to attack Kyūshū. If that occurred, the navy would support the Tsushima garrison by cutting the sea-lanes from China or Korea, and the army would defend strategic locations on the Kyūshū coast.[20]

The Chinese intervention unmasked the government's and the army's inability to protect Japanese interests in Korea. In August 1882 Yamagata reiterated to the throne the need for military expansion to counterbalance China's military modernization program and conduct in Korea. In his view this necessitated expanding the navy to forty-eight warships and restructuring the army into seven divisions plus a 200,000-man reserve by 1885.[21] Lt. Gen. Miura Gorō along with Lt. Gen. Soga Sukenori, both of whom had previously petitioned the emperor on the Hokkaidō sale issue, opposed a larger standing army. Much

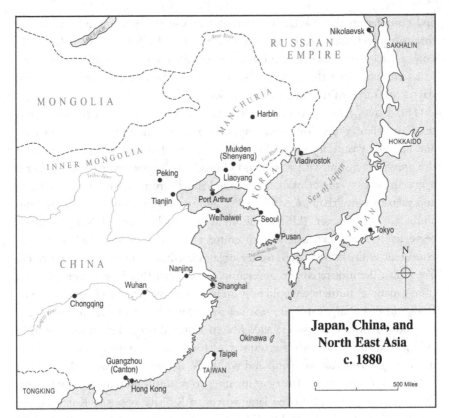

Map 3

like Yamada Akiyoshi in the 1870s, they advocated a small standing army, perhaps 30,000 men, organized as a one-division force backed by a home guard
available for duty during emergencies. Their proposal would also reduce the
current three-year active duty obligation for conscripts to a single year.

The general staff's western bureau director, Col. Katsura Tarō, however, insisted on a streamlined modern division structure because combining garrisons
during wartime created patchwork and unwieldy units with huge administrative and personnel overhead that were too large to move rapidly. Yamagata
supported Katsura and expected the finance ministry to impose new taxes on
tobacco to pay for the enlarged military and division conversion expenses. But
Finance Minister Matsukata Masayoshi cited the perilous state of Japan's finances that made additional military spending impossible. In September, Minister of the Right Iwakura Tomomi advocated an emergency tax to underwrite
military expansion and modernization. Emperor Meiji endorsed Iwakura's recommendation and in November notified prefectural governors that military
expansion was a matter of vital national security. The next month the government enacted emergency tax legislation to pay the increased personnel costs

associated with the conversion to a seven-division force structure and the improvement of coastal fortifications.[22]

About half of the additional annual tax revenue went to the army (1.2 million yen), with the remainder divided between naval shipbuilding and coastal defense construction programs spread over eight years. The National Defense Council (*kokubō kaigi*), established in March 1883, coordinated coastal defensive responsibilities between the army and the navy, establishing Japan's first line of defense on the high seas, its second along the coast, and its third, and final, on homeland soil.[23]

Advocates of a larger standing army, including Yamagata, Ōyama, Katsura, and the commander of the 2d Guard Infantry Brigade, Maj. Gen. Kawakami Sōroku, next rewrote conscription legislation to create a much larger reserve force. Reforms in 1883 created a first reserve with a four-year obligation and second reserve with five additional years of military commitment. The new legislation also eliminated paid substitutes, tightened restrictions on exemptions, and provided for volunteer one-year enlistments.[24]

Although army budgets increased substantially in 1883 and 1884 and personnel grew from 42,300 in 1880 to 54,000 by 1885,[25] division conversion lagged behind schedule because the purchase of new weapons and equipment, the coastal defense projects, and naval expansion created trade imbalances and unacceptable government deficits. These were especially sensitive issues because Foreign Minister Inoue Kaoru, hoping to impress the western powers with Japan's fiscal responsibility during renewed negotiations to secure treaty revision, rejected running a deficit to pay for military modernization.[26] At the same time, however, Inoue and imperial councilor Itō Hirobumi recognized the need for a stronger military to offset the rise of Chinese and western influence in northeast Asia. French and British naval squadrons were active around Taiwan and Korea, respectively, the Russian Vladivostok Squadron routinely operated in Korean waters, and China was modernizing its Northern Fleet to control the Yellow Sea.

Inoue would economize by cutting the army by 20,000 men, reducing terms of conscription by six months, and establishing a joint general staff. The savings would pay for limited naval expansion. Japan would rely on alliances either with England or Russia to ensure national security at a cheaper cost. Inoue drew support from big-army opponents like Miura, army Vice Chief of Staff Soga Sukenori, Minister of the Left Prince Arisugawa, and the retired but influential generals Tani and Torio. Yamagata, War Minister Ōyama, and Katsura adamantly opposed the initiative. According to Katsura, the hallmark of a first-class nation was an army capable of operating beyond its national borders, and Japan's inability to project military power overseas would relegate it to the status of a perpetual second-class power.[27]

Looking to save money, Emperor Meiji agreed with Arisugawa, Miura, and Soga, who also had the support of Prime Minister Itō. But Ōyama insisted that the volatile international situation placed Japan in such grave danger that the larger force structure was essential. When his obstinate opposition threatened to rupture Satsuma-Chōshū political hegemony, Inoue gave in to Ōyama's demands.[28]

The military share of the budget increased substantially, from about 15 million yen in 1885 to more than 20.5 million yen the next year, with the army getting an additional 2.2 million yen and the navy 3.5 million. The resulting huge deficit ruined Inoue's fiscal plans, and when serious negotiations on treaty rectification began in 1886, western insistence on certain prerogatives produced a political and popular backlash that made amendment impossible. Tani resigned his portfolio to protest the terms of the proposed treaty revision, and Miura's and Soga's unwavering opposition to the government's concessions on the emotional issue of treaty revision cost them Inoue's and Itō's backing.[29] Their fall was attributable to their loss of patronage and support from the prime minister and the foreign minister over the intertwined issues of army expansion, treaty revision, and fiscal retrenchment. The break-up of the opposition coalition of conservative generals, the court, and civilian ministers left Yamagata and Ōyama free to implement their plans. Between 1875 and 1882 the ordinary military budget ranged from about 14 to 19 percent of the national budget. Thereafter naval construction and army modernization (the conversion to divisions) steadily increased it to a 31 percent share in 1892.[30]

Construction started in late 1886 to improve Tsushima's coastal defense fortress, and the next year the emperor's personal donation of 300,000 yen to the army engineer branch launched a nationwide campaign that solicited 2.3 million more yen from wealthy individuals to employ additional laborers for work on an expanded network of fortifications.[31] The same year the army assigned division numbers to the respective garrisons; for example, the Tokyo garrison became the 1st Division. The army then projected that the conversion process would take two years, but recurrent funding shortages ultimately delayed the Guard conversion. Nevertheless, in May 1887 the army officially abolished the garrisons and adopted the division force structure. Picked officers who would lead and staff the new divisions were sent to Europe for extended study of military organization and force structure. By the time conversion was completed in 1891 the army fielded seven modern divisions and had a reserve mobilization capability of 240,000 troops.[32]

The army modeled its original 1888 division force structure on the Prussian mountain division, but with a larger peacetime establishment of about 9,000 officers and men that would double in wartime with the addition of an infantry brigade, a cavalry squadron, and various support units. The 1893-type division was organized around two infantry brigades each with two infantry regiments (a so-called square division) and had 18,500 officers and men at wartime strength as the gradual expansion of the active ranks, reform of conscription system, and volunteers provided cadre and reserves for rapid wartime expansion.[33] The modern mobile division complemented the fixed coastal fortresses already under construction by enabling troops to move rapidly and reinforce threatened points or contain enemy landings.

The phased transition to a division structure is often regarded as prima facie evidence that Japan harbored offensive continental aspirations and tailored its army for overseas deployment and aggression. No doubt some high-ranking officers dreamed of imperial expansion on the Asian continent, but not until 1900 did the general staff begin formal planning for offensive operations there.[34] In the meantime, the army continued to emphasize coastal defense against a Russian attack, and as late as 1891 the theme of the annual grand maneuvers was repelling an amphibious invasion.

It would likewise be inaccurate to say military preparations were not aimed at an external threat, but an operational offensive capability was part of a larger policy of strategic defense designed to spare Japan from foreign invasion. Rather than an indication of imminent aggressive warfare, the division force structure was a long-considered adaptation of the most up-to-date western military organization at a time when Japan was striving to master the secrets of the West's success. Rectification of the unequal treaties, rebuilding the financial and political system, and checking the Russian threat from the north were the priorities of the Meiji government.[35] In that context, the division organization was simultaneously offensive, because of the possibility of intervention in Korea due to deteriorating relations with China, and defensive, because of the emerging Russian threat in northeast Asia.

Educational Reforms and the Influence of Maj. Jakob Meckel

The growing number of critics of oligarchic rule during the mid-1880s, the violence of the people's rights movement, and the specter of antigovernment political parties in control of the promised Diet fed Yamagata's determination to isolate the army from those who would control it for political ends different from his own. One means to this end was to reorganize the army's administrative system.

Army doctrine, training, and education were haphazard well into the 1880s, relying on at least five different versions of translated French infantry manuals between 1871 and 1885. Military organization followed the French model: training a peacetime establishment in drill and ceremonies, military courtesy, and proper care of the uniform and equipment. Tactics stressed junior officer and NCO responsibilities as small-unit leaders (battalion echelon and below) but were learned by rote and consequently lacked practical application and originality. French instructors at the military academy, for example, taught cadets to prepare detailed tactical orders and rigidly apply approved formations (columns shifting to skirmisher lines) to small-unit (battalion and below) tactical problems. Senior Japanese officers believed that the overemphasis on minor tactics and technical expertise had hampered strategic planning for large-unit operations during the Satsuma Rebellion. Their hard-won experience in that conflict seemingly made foreign instruction irrelevant, and in 1879 the government terminated the French military mission's contract. But startling European advances in military science and weaponry could not long be ignored. Many officers admired the emerging Prussian doctrine, proven against the French in the Franco-Prussian War of 1870, and thought it more suited for higher-echelon operations involving brigades and divisions.[36]

In 1884 a delegation composed of four senior officers—Army Minister Lt. Gen. Ōyama; Lt. Gen. Miura, now commandant of the military academy; Col. Kawakami Sōroku, commander of the 1st Guards Infantry Regiment; and Col. Katsura conducted a year-long inspection tour of European armies. With the exception of Miura, who had been trained by the French, the delegation favored the Prussian military system, which was widely regarded as the standard for modern armies. Miura's views were well known, and he had likely been included to balance regional sensibilities; Ōyama and Kawakami were from Satsuma, and Katsura and Miura hailed from Chōshū. In any case, Ōyama overrode Miura's objections and asked Prussian War Minister Paul von Schellendorff to recommend a senior instructor for Japan's staff college. Von Schellendorff nominated Maj. Colmar von de Goltz, but the Chief of Staff, Helmut von Moltke, wanted Goltz to rebuild the Turkish army, which had been recently defeated by Russia. Moltke then nominated 43-year-old Maj. Klemens Wilhelm Jakob Meckel, a tactician, not an instructor, for the assignment.[37] The delegation returned to Japan in January 1885, and Meckel arrived in Tokyo two months later.

Tall, ramrod straight, and imposing, the bald-headed Meckel looked like the stereotypical Prussian officer martinet. Indeed, he was an exacting taskmaster and demanded the same attention to duty and detail from students. But he lacked arrogance, enjoyed drinking, and was a genial personality.[38]

Unlike the large French advisory mission, which had numbered as many as forty officers in the mid-1870s, Meckel's advisory group never numbered more than seven. The army also retained four or five French advisers into the early twentieth century as language instructors and ordnance experts. Several Italian military advisers served in Japan between 1884 and 1896, a period when the army relied on Italian-produced bronze artillery guns.[39]

Meckel and his team introduced the Prussian military education model, which switched the emphasis from technical proficiency to a more general military education, especially in the staff college, whose course was extended to three years. Meckel's dominance at the staff college changed the way Japanese officers thought about warfare, and his intellectual synthesis of modern strategy and traditional martial values held widespread appeal among the officer class. Meckel, for instance, preached that victory or defeat in battle was not simply a function of advanced weaponry. The decisive feature was élan, and he stressed the importance of the psychological dimension of warfare and offensive spirit, a philosophy of warfare that meshed nicely with the army's existing concepts of *seishin,* or fighting spirit. With the exception of foreign languages, Meckel refocused the new curriculum almost exclusively on military art and science—tactics, military history, ordnance, gunnery, fortification, communications, terrain studies, equestrian arts, and health and sanitation matters. His slighting of logistics in favor of instruction devoted to techniques of operational planning and command found a receptive audience, but it left students with a poor grasp of the planning and organization of the movement of troops, equipment, and supplies and little knowledge of the science of modern military logistics.[40]

Meckel used primary source documents and staff rides to educate officers in the application of theory on tactics and the influence of terrain on maneuver and battle, basing instruction on military history, not military theory. Lessons placed a premium on resolute decision making and glossed over intelligence gathering because that could delay action. Language was a problem because the question-translation-answer-translation format of Meckel's classroom lectures made them lengthy and boring. Written translations of the lectures were, however, widely distributed to officers throughout the army as study materials.[41]

Under Meckel's guidance the army switched to the German field manual that emphasized importance of the company echelon in tactical formations. Standardized training and procedures accompanied the shift to the new manual. Until 1887 individual regiments had determined their training tables, but that year troop training regulations standardized training army-wide. In keeping with the Prussian reforms, the army adopted the so-called family training concept, which placed the company commander in charge of conscripts' training. The army expected junior officers to both lead and teach and demanded proficiency in military art as well as the ability as instructors to inculcate the ideal of fighting spirit into the ranks. By 1889 the Prussian draft 1884 field service regulations had been translated into Japanese, and two years later the army completed the transition from the French to the Prussian training regimen and immersed recruits in training and drilling according to the new infantry manual.[42]

Rightly praised as the father of modern military education in Japan, Meckel exerted a significant and enduring influence on the army. Yet his departure from Japan was clouded, apparently because certain influential Japanese officers suspected Meckel was a German spy. He received gifts and accolades but had to insist to get the emperor's personal seal on his commendation and was awarded a lesser-grade medal. Nonetheless, Meckel took lasting pride in his accomplishments and his Japanese students.[43]

As the military education system became institutionalized, officers took competitive entrance examinations for admittance to the staff college (in 1886 the course was extended to three years). At a minimum, candidates had to be first lieutenants, be in good health, possess a good service record, and demonstrate intellectual ability. Other qualifications mandated a minimum of two years service with a troop unit, an age limit of 28 (specialists like artillerymen and engineers were eligible until age 30 because of the extra technical schooling required in those branches), and the recommendation of the candidate's commanding officer. Transportation branch officers initially were ineligible for admission because there was no logistics branch on the general staff, another indication of the army's low regard for the services of supply.

Normally it took a junior officer two or three years to prepare himself for the staff college examination. Because a candidate's admission to the staff college reflected favorably on his regiment, over time it became customary for battalion or regimental commanders to assign their most promising junior officers to light duties to enable them to study and prepare for the exam. At first, class ranking was critical, and beginning in 1887 the commandant or his deputy reported student grades to the chief of staff, who used the results to determine subsequent assignments and promotions. After the turn of the century, class ranking declined in importance as a factor in promotion, at least to the general officer ranks, and battlefield valor and practical experience with troop units were given greater consideration.[44]

The army also schooled promising officers at foreign military institutions. In 1882 there were nine student-officers in France and three in Germany; in 1898 there were three in France and twelve in Germany. Throughout its existence the army routinely assigned officers to foreign military schools, almost all in Europe, and like their navy counterparts, a high proportion of senior army officers had overseas assignments as students, attaches, or observers on their service records. Popular wisdom credits the imperial navy with producing cosmopolitan and sophisticated officers while dismissing army officers as provincial bumpkins ignorant of the West. But the army routinely dispatched its best and brightest to Europe for study and professional grooming.

Branch schools were established to educate officers and train troops in their respective military specialties. The army ministry created the transport corps bureau in 1885 and issued the transport corps field manual the next year. The army managed its own medical training school in 1871 but because of the length of medical training and the expertise demanded of instructors in 1877 abolished it and used the Tokyo University Medical School to train military doctors. After graduation they received specialized instruction in military medicine. In 1888 the army reestablished its medical school as a postgraduate center for army doctors, to offer the latest surgical techniques to reserve doctors and to train medical orderlies. In 1894 it became the army sanitary school.[45]

Prussian influence likewise changed the military academy. After 1890 cadets no longer received commissions upon graduation. Instead, using the Prussian model, before entering the academy they spent one year serving in a unit (six months if preparatory school graduates) as cadets, nineteen months at the academy, and six months after graduation as cadet aspirants with a unit. If the aspirant successfully completed his duty assignment, he received a commission as a second lieutenant. Later reforms in 1920 added a two-year preparatory course at the academy followed by six months attached to a unit as a cadet, then twenty-two months at the academy's main course, followed by two months with a unit as an aspirant.[46]

In 1896 the army adopted the Prussian system of separating the central military preparatory academy from regional preparatory academies. Thirteen-year-old boys entered the three-year course to prepare themselves for a two-year course at the central preparatory academy in Tokyo. Except for the sons of deceased soldiers or senior bureaucrats, the preparatory schools charged tuition, making it difficult for the poor to send their sons into officers' careers. After graduation, cadets spent six months with a unit before entering the military academy. Maj. Gen. Kodama Gentarō insisted on emphasizing spiritual education in the cadet academies, where it became a standard feature of the curriculum from the 1890s.[47]

The Reorganized Superintendency

In May 1885 the army ministry revised the garrison regulations. The commander of each garrison became a division commander while the superintendent controlled two divisions and became a corps commander.[48] This was the army's first step to convert the fixed garrisons to more mobile and modern infantry divisions, but it also required a more thorough overhaul of the superintendency. With Meckel serving as an adviser, recently promoted Maj. Gen. Katsura, chief of the army ministry's general affairs bureau, and other like-minded general staff officers set to work to reorganize the superintendency to accommodate the command and control requirements of the new division force structure.

Based on preliminary studies, in late 1885 Katsura recommended to Yamagata that the current superintendency be abolished as an operational headquarters and converted to the army's training command. Simultaneously, the army would introduce a centralized promotion system based on competitive examinations, not seniority, and establish age limits for active-duty service. It would also revise current regulations that made promotion to full general conditional on command of large units during wartime and subsequently on wartime command. These measures were designed to sweep away the deadwood in the officer corps and promote outstanding younger officers by competitive examination based on individual talent.[49]

With Yamagata's blessing, in March 1886 Katsura established the Provisional Committee to Study Military Systems, a nineteen-member group chaired by Col. Kodama Gentarō, to consider army reorganization. Meckel advised the committee and met with Kodama on a bi-weekly basis to discuss force structure issues and the national army's mission. Meckel also drafted position papers, including one that addressed the command and control implications of converting the fixed garrisons into mobile divisions.[50]

Meckel saw no need for a wartime corps echelon because the army would be small—only seven divisions —and its strategy defensive: to repel invasion of the home islands. Relying on mobility, individual divisions could quickly deploy to their assigned defensive sectors in wartime and, with attached artillery and technical units, conduct independent operations, much like a small corps in a European army. Thus the division became the army's operational maneuver element. If a corps echelon was superfluous, so was the current superintendency system, which functioned as a wartime corps command equivalent. According to Meckel, the superintendent could administer two divisions during peacetime, thereby providing unified training at all levels, but would have no wartime role.[51]

In line with previous studies, Meckel further recommended the creation of an inspectorate who would supervise army-wide military training and officer education and report directly to the emperor. The inspector-general would be equal in rank to the chief of staff and the war minister (which replaced the army minister under the newly installed cabinet system, discussed below). Finally, he proposed a personnel section to manage officers' promotions and assignments. War Minister Ōyama submitted Meckel's recommendations to the cabinet on July 10, 1886.[52]

Soga, Miura, and their allies adamantly opposed the abolition of the existing superintendency and its replacement by an inspector-general of military education under Yamagata's control. From their powerful positions—Miura commanded the Tokyo garrison and Soga was vice chief of the army staff—they insisted that neither the general staff nor the war ministry (which had been established in December 1885) had jurisdiction over the regional superintendents because they reported directly to the emperor, and therefore an imperial decree was needed to change their positions. They rejected reforms such as competitive examinations for promotion and drew support from officers whose professional careers were tied to the traditional seniority-based promotion system. Lt. Gen. Tani (agricultural minister at the time but still on active duty) and Chief of Staff Prince Arisugawa likewise rejected the reforms, especially placing the inspectorate functions under the war ministry, which they believed vested excessive power in the war minister's hands. According to rumors, Emperor Meiji agreed with them and hoped to appoint Miura as chief of staff. Yamagata, however, ignored the emperor's preference and schemed with Ōyama to undercut Miura by removing him from command of the Tokyo garrison.[53]

After a July 12, 1886, imperial audience with Arisugawa, Emperor Meiji temporarily postponed the initiatives to allow Prime Minister Itō time to broker a compromise. Itō got Arisugawa and Yamagata to agree that the newly established war ministry would manage infantry officer promotions and the inspectorate for all other branches. They also concurred that the general staff would control the new inspectorate based on Itō's promise that the inspectorate would be subsequently reorganized.[54] The army abolished the superintendency on July 24 and replaced it with the so-called new inspector-general, which was administratively under the war minister.

By moving the inspectorate's peacetime administrative functions to the war ministry, the army empowered the war minister with the authority to control personnel promotion policies and to issue operational orders to garrison commanders. This change diminished the authority of the regional inspector-generals by converting them from an operational headquarters that issued orders to a training one that took orders.[55] The 1886 revisions also dropped the requirement for wartime command for promotion to flag officer, made selection to full general a matter of imperial appointment, and replaced promotion by seniority with a promotion system based on competitive examination results. For their persistent opposition, Soga was transferred from vice chief of staff to the commandant of the military academy and Miura was transferred to Kumamoto. Miura resigned rather than accept the demotion. Both remained outspoken critics of the army's direction.

The settlement left unresolved the relationship between the new division force structure and the regional inspectors because the latter still reported directly to the emperor and served in wartime as corps commanders. During the transition period to divisions, the war ministry, as Itō promised, again reorganized the inspectorate. The July 1887 imperial order finally standardized army-wide training by placing it under the new inspectorate general, which was directly subordinate to the emperor and coordinated all military training and competitive examinations.[56] Yamagata, concurrently home minister, was appointed the first inspector-general but served only nine months, apparently to ensure that the new organization got off the ground. The agency was the

forerunner of the inspector-general of military education established by imperial order in January 1893 to enforce army-wide proficiency standards.

General Staff Reforms

Regulations issued in December 1885 created ten ministries in the newly organized cabinet. The war minister (formerly the army minister) continued to
manage the army's administrative functions—annual budget preparation, weapons procurement, personnel issues, and relations with the Diet—and reported
to the prime minister on such matters. The new rules allowed the chief of staff
to report directly to the throne on classified military matters without inform-
ing civilian cabinet members. Notwithstanding the chief of staff's direct access
to the throne, the war minister was encouraged to report such occurrences to
the prime minister. The chief of the council of state had previously controlled
the other ministers and held military command prerogatives; the newly designated prime minister, however, would have no say in matters of military operations or command.[57]

The new cabinet authorized a separate naval general staff under the navy
ministry. Two general staffs—one army, one navy—necessitated further reorganization, and in March 1886 the cabinet established a centralized supervisory
agency to separate operational military matters from affairs of state. The new
agency, in effect a joint general staff, was responsible for joint planning and
operational coordination. A neutral imperial family member, Prince Arisugawa,
became chief of staff to keep the lid on simmering internal service discord.
He had two vice chiefs of staff—one from the army, one from the navy—who
directed their respective staffs, and a joint staff to conduct joint planning to enable the services to react quickly to emergencies.[58] This restructuring harkened
back to the arrangement under the council of state and reflected the services'
inability to resolve roles and missions. Instead, a compromise imperial figurehead presided over two competitive general staffs that operated independently
of each other.

Arisugawa's appointment as chief of the joint staff attempted to capitalize
on the direct link between the army and the throne. The flawed organizational
arrangement proved unsatisfactory, in part because army infighting over the
nature of the joint staff's authority continued unabated, in part because the
differing expertise of army and navy officers complicated coordination, and in
part because Arisugawa, like many of his veteran contemporaries, lacked the
formal military education, specialized military knowledge, and technical expertise demanded in a rapidly changing army and navy.[59]

To remedy these deficiencies, two years later—in May 1888—the army again
reorganized the general staff, changing the name to the army and navy staff directorate, eliminating the vice chief positions, and replacing them with an army

and a navy general staff responsible to a single chief of staff for imperial forces. Arisugawa became chief of staff and served as the emperor's military adviser on matters of operational planning and national defense. Arisugawa, however, had no staff, only a deputy, and depended on the service staffs for advice.[60] In theory, the chief of staff was the ideal mechanism to coordinate joint planning and large-unit operations, but the services refused to cooperate with each other, joint planning did not materialize, and attempts at unified command again failed.

Articles eleven and twelve of the new Meiji Constitution promulgated in February 1889 formally institutionalized the military's prerogative of supreme command. Article eleven made the emperor supreme commander of the army and navy, and article twelve established the emperor's authority to set the peace-time organization of his military forces. Constitutional scholars interpreted the former to empower the general staff to assist the emperor without reference to the cabinet, effectively placing the services beyond the control of the prime minister. This was a major goal of the oligarchs—to keep the army out of politics or, phrased differently, to keep party politicians and political factions from running the army.[61]

Senior army officers also feared that under the new constitution one general officer could in theory control two separate service staffs, a situation that might impinge on imperial prerogatives of command. To prevent this possibility and to retain its dominant position in military affairs, army leaders convinced the emperor to eliminate the chief of staff and place the naval general staff under the new navy minister. The army general staff, however, would be independent of the newly created war ministry and enjoy direct access to the throne. Arisugawa became the chief of the newly reorganized general staff, and the serving army chief of staff moved to the vice chief position. This latest change made the chief of staff the de facto army chief of staff because the navy staff had to issue its orders through the navy minister, who did not enjoy direct access to the throne.[62] The arrangement left the military without an integrated joint staff to oversee operational command and control.

Diehard conservatives like Miura detested the thought of a powerful central-ized government, which had already displayed its corrupt nature by promoting regional factionalism within the army. They had devoted most of the decade of the 1880s trying to block the Satsuma-Chōshū monopoly on senior army posts and army reforms, only to see institutional reforms, a new force structure, a re-organized general staff, and a revamped administrative system that strengthened Yamagata, Ōyama, and their respective regional cliques' grips on the army.[63] Miura claimed that factionalism had led the restoration astray and that Japan's proper course should be to field a small army tailored to defend the main is-lands. Together with army Vice Chief of Staff Soga and retired generals Tani and

Torio he doggedly opposed Ōyama's and Yamagata's attempts to introduce a big army organized in a German-style military system.

Allied with Miura and Soga were an anti-mainstream group of officers, who formed a well-organized opposition centered in the Getsuyōkai, a fraternal organization of army officers established in 1881 by graduates of the military academy's initial two classes. The Getsuyōkai originally encouraged research into the latest developments in military science to improve army officers' professional expertise, contribute to national defense, and aid understanding of large-unit operations. Membership soon exceeded fifty officers. Other specialized professional associations for officers—from cavalrymen to veterinarians—proliferated throughout the army.

In 1884 the Getsuyōkai chairman, the Francophile commandant of the Toyama Infantry School, appointed Miura, Soga, Tani (now retired from active duty and director of the Peers Academy), and Torio (also retired and director of the government statistical bureau) the association's advisers. The French faction of Miura and Soga dominated the organization, using its lectures, newsletter, and later its journal, the *Getsuyōkai kiji*, to lambaste Yamagata and the army leadership, denounce the army's Prussian reforms, and promote a small-army, antiexpansionist agenda. Under Soga's direction, the journal published biting critiques of senior officers, deriding them as superannuated veterans of the wars of restoration living on their past reputations, unaware of the advances in military science, and sitting idly at their desks while real soldiers were maneuvering troops in field exercises.

Stung by charges that they were ignorant of modern military technology and doctrine, top army leaders counterattacked. Maj. Gen. Nogi, a brigade commander, and Vice Chief of Staff Kawakami Sōroku, who had recently returned from a year in Germany, publicly dismissed the critics as irresponsible tyros whose conduct was detrimental to military regulations and undermined army discipline and military order. But the Getsuyōkai would remain a thorn in the army leadership's side throughout the decade of the 1880s.

Filling the Ranks

The overwhelming majority of conscripts came from farming communities and were overrepresented in the army. Almost 80 percent of the 1888 cohort, for example, was drawn from primary industry (forestry, agriculture, and fishing) at a time when roughly 65 percent of Japanese worked in that sector. Mining, manufacturing, and construction—the second and tertiary sectors—accounted for about 35 percent of all workers but only 11 percent of conscripts in 1888.[64]

In 1887 the army adopted the Prussian system of one-year volunteers to build a reserve officer pool. Instead of facing conscription after their student deferments expired, middle school graduates could volunteer for specialized training designed to produce reserve officers.[65] Candidates volunteered for a one-year specialized active-duty service, at the end of which they were commissioned as reserve second lieutenants. They could select their branch of service, live outside the garrison confines, and were exempt from routine fatigue duties in the barracks. They wore special insignia on their uniforms and were promoted to superior private after six months. With their regimental commander's endorsement and successful completion of qualifying tests after six more months, they became reserve officers. In exchange for the privileges, the volunteers paid for their clothing, food, and equipment, which the army assessed at 60 yen (80 yen for cavalry to care for a horse). These sums were far beyond the reach of most Japanese, accounting for the tiny number (only 0.7 percent) of volunteers of the total cohort.[66]

About 100 men volunteered the first year of the program, but by 1897 more than 1,000 volunteer reserve officers were enrolled in the program, spurred in part by the 1889 conscription reforms described below.[67] Following their year on active duty, reserve officers went into the reserves for seven years, which was better than three years' active duty followed by nine years in the reserves. They were subject to annual call-ups to active duty to maintain their military proficiency.[68]

Of the more than 35,000 volunteers between 1906 and 1916, almost half chose the infantry branch, but a quarter selected transport or intendance specialties and overloaded branches the army had scant use for. Subsequent reforms created an abbreviated six-month voluntary active-duty training course designed to replace continual student deferments. As the active force gradually grew from about 65,000 in 1888 to 77,000 in 1893, the army simultaneously built a responsive reserve force capable upon mobilization of doubling the size of the force in wartime.[69]

Major changes in 1889 to conscription regulations also followed the Prussian model in order to build a large enlisted reserve that would fill out the wartime divisions. Legislation eliminated deferments and established four categories of service: active duty, first reserve, second reserve, and national militia (territorial reserve), making a clear distinction between active duty and reserve forces.[70]

The new law also delineated induction categories: graded A through E, with A and B being the source of conscripts. In 1899 the B category was subdivided into two groups, identified by minor physical differences. An annual preinduction physical rated 20-year-olds for military duty in this manner: A, fully fit; B, fit with minor deficiencies such as weaker bone and muscle structure, rashes, scars, or tattoos that did not interfere with the execution of military duties; C, those between four foot, eight inches and five feet in height, ineligible for frontline duty but placed in rear service positions; and D, those shorter than four foot, eight inches or suffering from habitual illness or deformity. The "A" candidates were conscripted, served three years on active duty, and then automatically went into the reserves for another four years, available for recall to fill out wartime augmentations. The "B" group usually was placed in the first reserve, and the "C" group went into the second reserve. The first reserve served as replacements and fillers for wartime mobilization whereas the second reserve was assigned to the transport branch to augment the expanded wartime logistics table of organization. Reservists received ninety days of basic training and thereafter were liable for one call-up per year for training, not to exceed sixty days. These remained the induction categories through 1945.[71]

Conscripts, who were forbidden by army regulations from marrying during their first three years on active duty, were separated by year-group (first-, second-, or third-year soldiers) for training purposes. Each year was subdivided into seven training periods. A recruit underwent six months of basic training (periods one through three), followed by six months of unit and field training with second- and third-year soldiers (periods four through seven). Third-year soldiers were less involved in drills and exercises, so their proficiency decreased as their longevity increased. The model stressed technical and weapons proficiency and march-discipline for rapid mobility. After 1889 the army emphasized leadership, the intangible or morale qualities of battle, and tougher discipline.

By the early 1880s, the army had adopted western (mainly French) court-martial regulations for various serious offenses such as mutiny, desertion, disobedience to orders, rape, and mistreatment of prisoners. Caning on the back or buttocks was a standard punishment. Concurrently, a system of harsh, informally administered corporal punishments to deal with minor infractions developed in the barracks. Slapping conscripts was routine, gang beatings were common, and harassment and bullying were constant. The aim was to guarantee absolute obedience to a superior's orders and instill unquestioning compliance as a reflex or habit in the tractable soldier. Henceforth, a combination of informally administered punishments and officially established courts-martial enforced Spartan discipline, linked to the notion that one's ability to endure physical hardship and suffering stoically was the essence of the Japanese spirit.[72]

Parallel with the 1889 conscription reform, the army encouraged local jurisdictions with village and city neighborhood associations to honor departing conscripts with neighborhood send-offs and conduct ceremonies to recognize returning veterans. Except for the Imperial Guard, which recruited nationwide, each division was administratively responsible for four local regimental conscription districts (one for each regiment in a division). Because each regiment recruited locally, conscripts knew each other, but more important were known to villagers, neighbors, and local authorities, increasing local peer pressure on conscripts to do well in the army.

The army's transition during the twenty-year span was remarkable. During the 1870s a hard-pressed, slapdash force had defeated samurai uprisings large and small, ending the warrior threat to the new government. It had crushed peasant uprisings and suppressed the people's rights movement, eliminating the risk of popular insurrection. By the mid-1890s the army had organized itself into a modern force structure, tested concepts in extensive field exercises, and improved communications and support functions. Its professional officer corps was well versed in tactics and operational concepts, though somewhat weaker in military strategy. A highly trained and well-disciplined NCO corps ensured order and control in the ranks. Conscription reforms in 1883 and 1889 had produced a large trained reserve force available for mobilization. The army also created a professional military bureaucracy that by 1890 had eliminated French influence in the army and introduced educational and structural reforms to ensure promotion based on merit and ability.

The institution was less successful in the formation of a general staff, which despite several reorganizations still could not coordinate joint planning, much less joint operations. Furthermore, the military's new bureaucratic processes worked well so long as the civilian and military leaders shared common objectives and respected the informal policy-making apparatus. The gradual appearance of a professional officer class, however, promoted institutionalized processes and mechanisms that undermined the unofficial personality-dependent system. Over time, the emerging military bureaucracy would prove fatal to the traditional dominance of the army's Chōshū and Satsuma officers because it rewarded professional expertise and education, not personal connections, regional affiliations, or past wartime service.

5

To Asia: The
Sino-Japanese War

An informal and passive defense strategy remained the basis of national military policy, but developments in Russia and China during the late 1880s convinced Yamagata that Japan's inability to project military power overseas would relegate the nation to a perpetual second-class power status.[1] Acutely aware of Japan's weakness, he pursued a cautious foreign policy of limited expansionist goals on the Asian mainland and reshaped Japan's army into a force capable of protecting the nation's sovereignty and interests.

In January 1888 Army Inspector-General Yamagata declared that the construction of a Panama Canal, a Trans-Siberian railway, and a Canadian-Pacific railroad would shift the thrust of western imperialism from Africa into East Asia. A clash between Britain and Russia over India was likely, and Korea was a flashpoint because of competing Chinese, Japanese, and Russian interests. He was confident that the army could repel a Russian invasion of Japan by concentrating two or three divisions against the beachhead, provided the government improved the communications infrastructure of telegraph and rail lines, finished construction of coastal fortifications, and fully funded seven infantry divisions.[2]

Retired general Soga agreed that Russia was the threat but questioned the conventional wisdom that dictated that an island nation like Japan should depend on a strong navy as its first line of defense. Rather than invest heavily in a vast naval establishment, which could not protect thousands of miles of coast anyway, Soga proposed a small standing army (90,000 regulars and 60,000 reservists) and coastal fortifications linked to the rail and road network. Even Russia, he reasoned, could transport no more than two corps (30,000 troops) by sea to Japan at one time, leaving the invaders far outnumbered by a mobilized militia and army of about 150,000 men. A small navy operating from offshore islands could harass any enemy fleet and disrupt its maritime line of communication. These joint measures would prevent any invasion.[3] Miura aired similar opinions in a series of newspaper articles written in 1889 that maintained that

Japan's topography was unsuitable for European-style, division-echelon operations. An enemy force could land anywhere along the lengthy coastline, so instead of expanding the army, the government would be better off to organize and deploy militia units at strategic locations to repulse an enemy landing.[4]

Irritated by the Getsuyōkai's directors' recurrent criticism, angered by the association's independent opinions, and displeased with the proliferation of other officer associations, in November 1887 the war ministry had ordered the consolidation of all military fraternal associations under its approved organization, the Kaikōsha. Prominent officers assigned to the war ministry and general staff left the society, urged their peers to quit, and pressured their juniors to do the same. The Getsuyōkai directors, however, refused to disband, and Soga and Miura continued their drumbeat of opposition to overseas expansion.[5] Having previously alienated their powerful civilian political backers over the issue of treaty revision, Miura and Soga were vulnerable, and army authorities seconded both to the reserves in December 1888, thereby purging the army of its last vestiges of its Francophile faction. Tani was seconded to the reserves the following year.[6]

In February 1889 five division commanders petitioned War Minister Ōyama to amalgamate the Kaikōsha and Getsuyōkai; he complied by dissolving the Getsuyōkai, disbanding all other professional officers' societies, and forbidding study groups within the army. Thereafter Kaikōsha chapters, which doubled as officers' benevolent societies (members paying a small fee that went into a relief fund to assist officers' families), promoted the army's official orthodoxy, set standards for behavior and skills, evaluated junior officers for promotion and recommendation for advanced schooling, and played a major role in determining a young officer's career progression. The implicit lesson was that the army attached little value to critical research or questioning of its prevailing orthodoxy.[7]

The inaugural imperial Diet convened in 1890. Many of the elected representatives were landowners and spent much of the session trying to cut land taxes, the main source of government revenue. As a consequence, the legislature consistently reduced or rejected the cabinet's costly budget requests for riparian and defense projects. It also steadfastly opposed the army's ambitious plans for nationwide railroad improvements because many of its members were unwilling to raise taxes to pay for the projects. Government critics such as retired general Tani Tateki, now a member of the House of Peers, unfurled the banner of fiscal responsibility to oppose expensive railway construction projects, promote Miura's less costly militia scheme, and champion investment in coastal defense construction. Now prime minister, Yamagata had to compromise to muster enough votes in the House of Peers to pass a reduced military construction bill to pay for a strategic railroad network.[8]

The government-designed rail network's major trunk lines converged at Ujina, the port of Hiroshima in western Japan, enabling the army to move units rapidly either for purposes of coastal defense or overseas deployment. Although narrow-gauge lines were easier and cheaper to build, the cabinet opted for broad-gauge rails, whose greater load capacity allowed fewer, larger cars to carry more troops. The government-stimulated construction touched off a railroad boom and increased the demand for imported steel for rails, which, added to imported steel for warships and weapons, resulted in an unfavorable balance of trade and caused severe domestic inflation. By 1893 shrewd investors cashed out and the speculation bubble of hyperinflated railroad stocks burst, adding to the nation's financial woes.[9]

Besides their shaky financial underpinnings, the new rail lines had questionable military value. Strategically the railroads often ran too close to existing coastal routes and, as Meckel had previously warned, left the tracks susceptible to interdiction by hostile naval gunfire. The general staff and the chairman of the Railroad Conference Board, Vice Chief of Staff Lt. Gen. Kawakami Sōroku, heeded the Prussian's advice and wanted the railroads relocated farther inland, but Ōyama insisted that construction through precipitous mountain ranges would be technically more difficult, more time consuming, and much more expensive than a coastal route. Besides, Japan's growing navy could protect the coasts and the coastal railroads from enemy naval bombardment and invasion. Kawakami resigned from the board in disgust.[10]

The army's quest for strategic mobility during the 1880s rapidly transformed Japan's transportation infrastructure. Army engineers completed the great military port at Ujina in 1885 and upgraded coastal batteries, military ports, naval bases, and arsenals throughout the country. The completion of a new railway line connecting Kobe and Hiroshima in mid-1894 removed the bottleneck between eastern and western Japan, and the army also improved and widened roads leading to the ports to accommodate heavy artillery caissons and divisional baggage wagons.[11] The modern transportation infrastructure opened previously isolated regions to commercial expansion as textiles, foodstuffs, and coal could be moved cheaply and easily for sale or export. It also enabled the expanding army to move troops and equipment rapidly to ports of embarkation for overseas deployments.

The Soldiers of the Sino-Japanese War

In 1893 the army had about 6,000 officers and 12,000 NCOs. Its almost 60,000 conscripts lived in garrison barracks where they trained with their respective regiments. Six months of basic training emphasized repetition in everything from military courtesies and calisthenics to small-unit formations and marksmanship. Rote memorization and constant repetition were necessary because a large percentage of the conscripts were either completely or functionally illiterate.

Although statistics are incomplete, as late as 1891, more than 60 percent of all conscripts fell into those two categories (with almost 27 percent being completely illiterate). Only 14 percent had graduated from a primary or higher school, though the army regarded 24 percent as having comparable practical or work experience. Superstitions abounded, especially among the peasant conscripts, who found themselves in a barracks amidst strange new things. A frequently cited example was the case of peasant conscripts who, having never seen a wood-burning stove, worshiped the one in their barracks as a religious idol.[12]

Between 1891 and 1903 the number of middle schools (at the time male-only) almost quadrupled, to more than 200, three-quarters of them built in rural areas. Enrollment quintupled to around 100,000 students.[13] By 1900 functional illiteracy had declined, but it was still above 30 percent (actual illiteracy 16.8 percent) and remained constant throughout the decade. Until the educational reforms in 1920 that instituted compulsory grammar school education, between 10 and 15 percent of all young men undergoing an induction physical lacked any formal schooling. Thereafter illiteracy rates became negligible—less than 1 percent—but as late as 1930 almost 40 percent of conscripts had not graduated from primary school.[14]

The army was attuned to educational changes and concentrated on indoctrinating an increasingly literate public and conscript force with themes of Japan's uniqueness by virtue of the unbroken imperial line. To spread its message, the army subsidized the publication of cheap, widely distributed commercial handbooks that explained how to organize simple public ceremonies for troops like hearty send-offs, welcome-home celebrations, or memorial observances. Army propaganda in the pamphlets explained that conscripts should be grateful the emperor wanted them for his army, underlining their soldierly duty to meet and obey imperial injunctions and reminding them, "As the cherry blossom is to flowers, the warrior is to men."[15] Military values were steadily seeping into the popular culture.

Despite the army's numerous and impressive accomplishments, the institution of the early 1890s was by no means a state-of-the-art fighting force. Its weaponry and military technology lagged far behind western standards. By the late 1880s, for example, steel-gun technology had rendered bronze weapons obsolete, but lacking the sophisticated new technology the Osaka arsenal continued to manufacture bronze field and mountain guns. This in turn retarded the artillery school's experiments with smokeless powder because the residue fouled the bronze weapons, making them unusable. Likewise, manufacturing capacity restricted shell production, and the army could not stockpile large quantities of munitions. General staff planners compensated by compiling ammunition consumption tables based on statistical data derived from the Satsuma Rebellion in expectation that a central general headquarters would carefully control the field commanders' expenditure of artillery rounds. The rebellion's legacy of light artillery was reinforced by Meckel's later pronouncement that mountain artillery hauled by packhorses was better suited for Japan's rugged landscape than heavier field artillery pulled by teams of draught horses. The army considered large-caliber guns (larger than 150 mm) defensive weapons for use in coastal fortifications. On the positive side, gunners studied direction and range findings techniques and became proficient at controlling indirect artillery fires.[16]

The Tokyo arsenal was producing Type-18 Murata rifles, a single-shot weapon. The advanced Type-38 Murata, a five-round clip-fed version, was not standard equipment in the mid-1890s, and only the Imperial Guard and the 4th Division were initially equipped with a prototype repeating rifle. Clothing and weapons were standardized. The field uniform was a black jacket and white pants complemented by a soft black kepi. In 1889 the army adopted the French-style sword. Demands to return to a Japanese samurai sword were rejected after a five-year study concluded that the samurai sword was impractical in modern warfare because both hands were needed to wield it.[17]

The army diet consisted of polished white rice, fish, poultry, pickled vegetables, and tea. Attempts by Japanese doctors to introduce white bread or a hardtack biscuit into the daily ration in the early 1890s failed, but the biscuit did become part of the emergency field ration. Soldiers received just over two pints of cooked white rice per day even though anecdotal evidence showed that cutting the rice with barley prevented beriberi, known as Japan's national disease during the Meiji period. Between 1876 and 1885 about 20 percent of enlisted troops suffered vitamin deficiencies and contracted beriberi; about 2 percent of them died. Field tests of a ration of barley mixed with rice conducted in 1885–1886 dramatically reduced beriberi cases (from almost 265 per 1,000 to just 35 per 1,000), but vitamin theory was still an unproven and contentious hypothesis. More significant, conscripts and officers alike regarded adulterated rice as penitentiary food (in fact, since 1875 it was prison fare) and considered it unfit for loyal soldiers of the emperor, a case of cultural imperatives inhibiting disease control.[18]

Geopolitics

Prime Minister Yamagata's fifteen-minute maiden address to the Diet in March 1890 outlined a geopolitical strategy based on a line of sovereignty and a line of interests to protect Japan's vital national interests. He observed that once the Trans-Siberian railway was completed, Korea would fall under the Russian shadow.[19] Accordingly, national security could no longer depend simply on a primary line of defense on Japanese shores but demanded the capability to protect a forward line of overseas interests, chiefly in Korea, where Japan had to prevent Russia from using the peninsula as a springboard to invade the home islands. The inference was that Yamagata wanted to carve out a buffer zone beyond Japan's boundaries, but his speech described a neutral Korea as the focus of Japanese interests and identified Tsushima Island as the first line of defense along his line of sovereignty.[20]

Fears of a Russian invasion had fed Japanese nightmares since the 1850s, but until the 1880s the army was too weak to do much about it. Following Meckel's guidance, the army refined counter-amphibious doctrine and tested it during a new joint grand exercise conducted in March 1890 near Nagoya. The stylized scenario had a predictable outcome (the invaders lost), but the army displayed its imagination and creativity by moving large units by rail and testing field telegraph communications to improve command and control. The emperor lent importance to the inaugural event by presiding over the maneuvers dressed in an army uniform and observing the culmination of the exercise during a driving rainstorm. Thereafter he attended special army grand maneuvers on ten occasions, always wearing his army uniform, a practice that dated from public appearances in 1880 as supreme commander.[21]

The 1890 and 1892 maneuvers field-tested the new mobile division tactics, an operational departure and a significant shift from the traditional doctrine of waterline defense. After a May 1893 mobilization exercise revealed that reserve NCOs and junior officer platoon leaders were less proficient than their regular counterparts, the war ministry redoubled efforts to improve reserve training.[22]

The same year, the ministry reorganized the *tondenhei* (the militia the authorities formed from samurai settlers in Hokkaidō in the 1870s) into an under-strength division because the available Hokkaidō cohort was still too small to fill a full division's ranks. Finally, the war minister also revamped the wartime table of organization to draw on the approximately 150,000 strong first reserves (120,000 more in the second reserve) to field a wartime division of 18,500 personnel (the Imperial Guard strength was set at 13,000). The expanded wartime division added one infantry company per battalion (twelve total), strengthened the cavalry squadron and field artillery regiment, and added two engineer companies and a transport battalion. Wartime mobilization required additional reserve officers and NCOs, and the army expanded its one-year volunteer system to train and build a larger reserve officer pool.[23]

More young men were conscripted for active service, but a rapidly growing population provided a larger available cohort, and the percentage of those conscripted remained fairly constant. Draft resistance or evasion was negligible—less than 1 percent of the cohort per year between 1882 and 1896. Each year

An unknown artist's depiction of the March 1890 Nagoya Army-Navy Grand Maneuvers. Besides the Meiji emperor, the scroll on the top left records the presence of every major army leader at the counteramphibious landing exercises. (Author's collection)

about 3,000 youths skipped the annual physical exam or appeared late for testing,[24] which suggests the system had become institutionalized and accepted by the larger society (see Table 5.1).

Training reforms instituted in 1888 devoted more time to unit exercises and field maneuvers. Company commanders were expected to display initiative and seize tactical opportunities without waiting for orders from higher headquarters, but the revised 1891 infantry regulations perpetuated Meckel's inflexible massed columns and skirmisher formations. Planners projected losses of between 25 and 50 percent during operations. In order to sustain the offensive under such conditions, officers and NCOs were expected to enforce iron discipline during the tactical advance. Army authorities relied on intensive indoctrination in the intangibles of élan and esprit to promote each soldier's sense of obligation to the nation and his unit as well as his determination to press home attacks whatever the cost.[25]

Imperial General Headquarters, Planning, and Wartime Performance

Although the services had conducted joint maneuvers, interservice cooperation and coordination faltered because the army was determined to retain its primary role in national defense. In 1886 the navy embarked on its first replenishment plan and saw the establishment of a naval general staff with a corresponding resentment among naval leaders about their service's second-class status. The admirals' push for a totally independent naval general staff was countered by

Table 5.1 Conscripts and Percentage per Cohort, 1884–1890

Year	Size	Conscripts	Cohort	Percentage
1884	49,632	19,637	320,070	6.1
1885	54,124	27,389	388,389	7.1
1886	59,009	17,963	421,278	4.3
1887	64,689	33,808	777,972	4.3
1888	65,015	19,685	427,846	4.6
1889	66,744	18,477	360,357	5.1
1890	69,000	19,119	350,369	5.5

Source: Katō, *Chōheisei*, 20.

the generals' insistence that wartime operations had to be based on peacetime plans prepared by a single authority—the army.[26] Advocates couched their arguments against the cabinet's push for joint general staff in terms of imperial prerogatives, span of control issues, and administrative requirements. The fundamental debate, however, was about the future of the army; its strategic role, its force structure, and its force design.

In January 1893 the cabinet presented the navy's proposal for an independent staff to the emperor, who harbored reservations that interservice staff rivalry might interfere with wartime performance. The army was willing to accept an independent naval general staff provided that during wartime the army chief of staff was in charge of an imperial general headquarters (IGHQ). Several days later Prince Arisugawa, the chief of the joint staff, recommended that the IGHQ chief of staff should be from the primary service—the army—and serve as the emperor's chief of staff. This would unify the services' planning and operational efforts as well as ease imperial concerns that separate staffs might create serious coordination issues.[27]

Emperor Meiji approved the establishment of a separate naval general staff on May 19, 1893, creating two parallel and independent chains of command whose chiefs reported directly to the emperor during peacetime. That same day, Meiji sanctioned regulations to organize an imperial general headquarters directly under the emperor to control wartime operations. An army general officer would fill the post of chief of the IGHQ staff to ensure that service's primary role in national defense. During wartime he had the authority to issue operational orders sanctioned by the emperor, and the army vice chief of staff and the naval chief of staff served under him.[28]

Operational Planning

Military strategy, such as it was, relied on mobile divisions to defend the homeland, a fixed defense anchored by coastal fortifications, and an offensive strategy against China in case of emergency. Col. Ogawa Mataji, the chief, second bureau, of the general staff, guided the first serious planning for offensive operations against China. His 1887 draft employed an eight-division (six regular and two reserve) expeditionary force to seize Peking. Six divisions would land near Shanhaiguan at the head of the Bohai Gulf and then advance on the capital. The remaining two divisions would land further south (along Chang-kiang coast) to prevent Chinese armies from relieving Peking. Ogawa's plan was mostly wishful thinking because the Japanese navy could neither maintain a line of communication to the continent nor transport such large numbers of troops overseas. His operational concept did serve as a strategic statement to justify the army's budget for its five-year expansion program and became a point of departure for subsequent general staff planning that influenced Vice Chief of Staff Kawakami's thinking.[29]

Officially the army continued to advocate a strategic defensive. In February 1892, for example, Kawakami submitted an operational plan to the emperor that apparently outlined a counter-amphibious campaign against an invasion. Unofficially the army had a clear awareness that it might be fighting a war on the Asian continent.[30] Since 1889 Kawakami had overseen contingency wartime planning directed against China. The army's Plan "A" for a war against China and Korea landed forces along the head of the Bohai Gulf near Shanhaiguan and then moved them west to fight a decisive battle on the Zhili (Hebei) plain. With imperial approval, Kawakami and other senior staff officers conducted a terrain reconnaissance (described as an inspection tour) in north and central China during mid-1893 to gather intelligence on Chinese forces and defenses.[31]

The team's evaluation of the state of Chinese army training, coastal defenses, and munitions factories as well as Kawakami's firsthand observations convinced him that Japan could defeat the Chinese army because the latter lacked mobilization and logistics capabilities, had no standard doctrine, and neither operated nor trained as a modern combined arms force. Army leaders excluded civilian ministers from their subsequent operational planning, justifying the action as necessary to protect the prerogative of supreme command from political interference. This military bias against civilian authorities ignored the need to integrate national political and military strategies, isolating army planning from the larger context of Japan's political and diplomatic objectives.[32]

Peasant uprisings in Korea in the early 1890s and the kingdom's growing dependence on China threatened Yamagata's strategic benchmark of a neutral Korea. In the spring of 1894 Korean peasants rebelled against the radical reforms imposed by the court, blaming the Korean elite and foreigners, especially Japanese, for their impoverishment. The Korean emperor appealed to China for help, which in turn dispatched troops to Korea to suppress the

Tonghak Rebellion. The intervention violated China's 1885 agreement with Japan whereby both countries withdrew their troops from Korea and promised advance notification to the other should they return. In these explosive circumstances, the general staff dispatched an officer to Pusan for firsthand assessment. His May 20 dispatch described an organized rebellion, led by a rebel army armed with some modern weapons and an effective command and control system that was determined to overthrow the government. Because the prospect of an anti-Japanese faction seizing power was unacceptable, he recommended sending troops to protect the more than 9,000 Japanese nationals residing in Korea.[33]

At a June 2 cabinet meeting Prime Minister Itō discussed unconfirmed reports from the army attaché in Tientsin, later proved erroneous, that 5,000 Chinese troops had moved into Korea. Despite its dubious quality, Kawakami and Foreign Minister Mutsu Munemitsu used the intelligence to justify military intervention. It was later alleged that the two conspired to conceal information from Itō that negotiations had taken a favorable turn and calm was returning to Korea.[34] Regardless of Kawakami's and Mutsu's conduct, the full cabinet likely drew the lesson based on previous Japanese setbacks in Korea in the 1880s that in order to preserve the military balance it had to commit forces before China did. With compromise impossible, war with China was inevitable.[35]

The cabinet dispatched troops to Korea the same day, and Meiji instructed his military leaders, referring to them as his *daimyōs* (military lords), to establish a mechanism to handle wartime matters. On June 4, senior officers from each service, following the emperor's guidance to cooperate, met at the war minister's residence and, after haggling most of the day over command procedures, finally agreed to establish an imperial general headquarters in accordance with the 1893 regulations. The Chief of the Combined Staff, Prince Arisugawa, received imperial approval to open imperial headquarters in the general staff building on June 5, the same day the first echelon of the 5th Division mobilized for deployment to Korea.[36]

During the almost two-month interval between the establishment of IGHQ and the declaration of war against China on August 1, the service staffs refined a two-stage operational plan. The 5th Division would prevent a Chinese advance in Korea while the navy eliminated the Chinese fleet in order to secure control of the seas. Phase two had multiple options contingent upon naval success. In the best-case scenario, the navy would defeat the Chinese fleet and secure control of the seas, which would allow the army free passage to land on Chinese soil and advance to the decisive battle on the Zhili plain. If neither navy could gain supremacy, the army would occupy Korea to exclude Chinese influence. If Japan lost control of the seas to the Chinese navy, this worst case foresaw attempts to rescue the beleaguered 5th Division in Korea while simultaneously strengthening homeland defenses to repulse a Chinese invasion. In other words, the army's contingency plans were both offensive and defensive, depending on the outcome of the naval operations.[37]

The government had initially moved cautiously. On June 2, Itō ordered the army to avoid clashes with Chinese, and Ōyama notified the 5th Division commander that his mission was to protect Japanese citizens and diplomatic outposts in Korea, not fight Chinese. Itō's resolve hardened after Mutsu provided attaché reports in mid-June that the Russian forces in northeast Asia were too few in number to intervene militarily in Korea. With Russian intervention unlikely, the army unilaterally implemented its plan to land in Bohai Gulf in anticipation of a decisive battle on the Zhili plain.[38]

Civilian ministers were not involved in the army's planning and had to rely on the military's professional expertise to prepare the nation for a possible war. Unfettered by civilian restraint, army generals likewise expected the navy to escort troop convoys to the continent, but had neither consulted with their naval counterparts beforehand nor considered the necessity of securing command of the sea before sending any transports. This haughtiness led to Captain Yamamoto Gonbei, the navy minister's secretary, to remark caustically that if army engineers built a bridge between Kyūshū and Korea the generals could probably fight the campaign all by themselves.[39]

On July 2 the full cabinet with the respective chiefs of staff present agreed on war. The first IGHQ imperial conference met in the palace on July 17 with the emperor and twelve senior officials, including the chief of the combined staff, the army vice chief of staff, the war and navy ministers, and the naval chief of staff in attendance. Privy Council Seal Yamagata was the only civilian in the room. Prime Minister Itō and Foreign Minister Mutsu then demanded the same access, and the emperor ordered the service chiefs to allow senior civilian officials to participate in IGHQ's conferences, which convened every Tuesday and Friday. The general staff presented its operational plan to the emperor on August 5, and the same day IGHQ moved onto the palace grounds.[40]

Emperor Meiji played a significant, if mostly symbolic, role in mobilizing the people for war. Despite his own reservations—allegedly remarking, "This is not my war"—he compliantly relocated along with IGHQ to Hiroshima, ostensibly to be closer to his troops fighting in Korea. Meiji always appeared in an army uniform at Hiroshima, the first time the image of the emperor as the supreme commander was consciously cultivated for the common people.[41] He lived a Spartan existence to set an example for his subjects. His quarters had no separate bedroom, and each evening orderlies cleared a chair or desk as a place for him to sleep, evidently a sign of his willingness to share the deprivations of his loyal forces.

The army acted circumspectly in June and July, carefully developing a three-month campaign in anticipation that British mediation would end any fighting by October. In mid-August, the general staff's main objective was to secure the Korean peninsula militarily before the arrival of winter weather. After China refused Japanese demands conveyed through the British, Itō resigned himself to a longer campaign and the necessity of a spring 1895 offensive. In mid-September IGHQ displaced to Hiroshima, where Itō could keep a closer eye on the field armies to ensure a unified national policy. Reminiscent of the Satsuma Rebellion, the imperial relocation hampered timely and effective liaison with the foreign ministry and the bureaucracy that remained behind in Tokyo.[42]

Kawakami's certitude in victory aside, the army hedged its bets by deploying troops overseas while simultaneously bolstering homeland garrisons and coastal defenses. Only after the September 17 naval Battle of the Yalu did IGHQ announce that the navy's victory reduced the likelihood of invasion and release homeland defense garrisons to reorganize into infantry regiments. IGHQ still retained almost 100,000 mobilized reserves in Japan throughout the conflict, most of them engaged in logistics support duties.[43]

The mobilized army grew to more than 220,000 men, including all seven regular divisions, which at wartime strength numbered about 125,000 personnel. The army relied more heavily on the reserves for its NCOs and infantrymen (40 percent of wartime NCOs and infantrymen were reservists) than for its junior officers (only 10 percent). Senior officers and division commanders were, with two exceptions, Boshin War veterans, as were most brigade commanders.[44]

The campaigns of the Sino-Japanese War (1894–1895) may be described briefly. On June 12 a brigade from the 5th Division landed at Inchon, the port of Seoul, followed throughout the month by the rest of the unit. Peking ordered its small (500-man) force in Kunsan to withdraw to Pyongyang by sea on July 15, but the Chinese commander declared that course too dangerous, refused the order, and demanded reinforcements. Eight days later three transports carrying Chinese troops and equipment sailed for Korea.

On July 25 Captain Tōgō Heihachirō, commanding the armored cruiser *Naniwa*, intercepted the third transport as it approached the Korean coast. Although the Chinese ship was sailing under British registry and Japan and China were not at war, Tōgō sank the vessel. Soon afterward, Japanese and Chinese troops clashed near Kunsan, and on August 1 Japan officially declared war on China. By mid-August IGHQ concluded that a decisive battle on the Zhili plain was infeasible before the arrival of winter. Anticipating a short war, the army found itself in a prolonged struggle and commenced planning for a spring 1895 campaign.[45]

The general staff's objective was to secure the Korean peninsula militarily

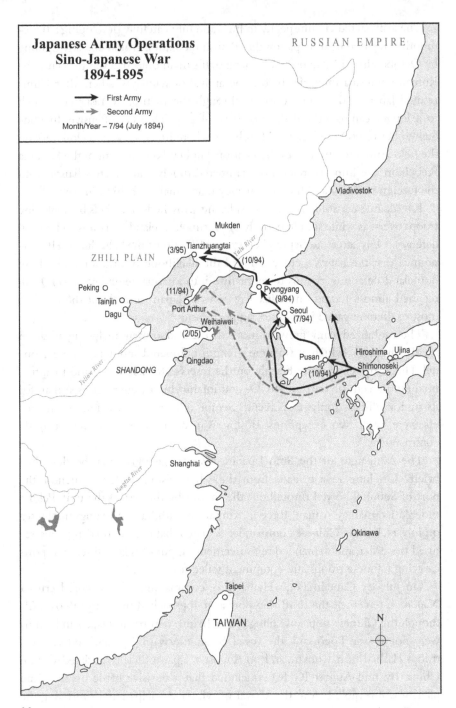

Japanese Army Operations
Sino-Japanese War
1894-1895

→ First Army

⇢ Second Army

Month/Year – 7/94 (July 1894)

RUSSIAN EMPIRE

Vladivostok

Mukden

Tianzhuangtai (3/95)

ZHILI PLAIN

(10/94)

Peking

Tainjin

Dagu

(11/94)

Port Arthur

Pyongyang (9/94)

Weihaiwei

(2/05)

Seoul (7/94)

Qingdao

SHANDONG

Yellow River

Pusan

Hiroshima Ujina

Shimonoseki

(10/94)

Shanghai

Yangtze River

Okinawa

Taipei

TAIWAN

N

Map 4

before the arrival of winter weather and then land forces near Shanhaiguan. The navy, however, was unable to bring the Chinese Northern Fleet into battle and in mid-August temporarily withdrew from the Yellow Sea to refit and replenish its warships. As a consequence, in late August the general staff ordered an overland advance on the Zhili plain via Korea and the capture of bases on the Laiodong Peninsula to prevent the Chinese forces from interfering with the drive on Peking.[46]

IGHQ activated the First Army (two divisions) under Yamagata's command on September 1, and in mid-September the First Army occupied Pyongyang as the Chinese retreated northward. The navy's stunning September 17 victory in the Battle of the Yalu surprised everyone. Yamagata wrote that although the rapid fall of Pyongyang was unexpected, it paled next to the totally unforeseen naval triumph. Japan's newly won maritime supremacy allowed Ōyama's Second Army (three divisions and one brigade) to land unopposed in mid-October on the Liaodong Peninsula, about 100 miles north of Port Arthur (Lüshun), the great Chinese fortress that controlled entry to the Bohai Gulf.[47]

Yamagata's First Army pursued the Chinese across the Yalu River in late October, but by that time attention had shifted to Ōyama's Second Army, which on November 8 occupied Dairen (Lüda). Spearheaded by Lt. Gen. Nogi's 2d Division, the Second Army next seized the fortress and harbor at Port Arthur on November 25. Farther north, Yamagata's offensive stalled, beset by supply problems and winter weather.

The western powers were caught off guard by the apparent ease of the Japanese victories, an impression the authorities in Tokyo encouraged. Foreign military observers attached to the respective armies and experts of all kinds attributed Japan's success to its modernity and westernization. The obvious advantages of standardized doctrine, weapons, and equipment complemented a well-educated professional officer corps versed in western-style modern warfare, technologically proficient, and able to maneuver division-echelon forces. Well-organized and well-trained reserves were efficiently mobilized and confidently used. Superior Japanese morale, especially after the early victories, benefited from superb fighting spirit, or esprit, under the leadership of well-trained and capable junior officers and NCOs. Finally, the Japanese soldiers had a commitment (perhaps defined as nationalism) defined by specific objectives and accepted a common ethos that subscribed to a goal greater than individual or regional interests. But these strengths, the army's hallmarks throughout its existence, masked serious structural flaws that might equally define the Japanese military institution. The most glaring shortcoming was the army's logistics system.

Logistics tables and doctrine were based on homeland defense, not overseas operations, and the general staff had conducted no detailed logistics planning during the prewar period.[48] Furthermore, in January 1894 Japan lacked

sufficient shipping to move a single division overseas. The general staff purchased ten transports from foreign companies in mid-June, but chronic shortages compelled the army to charter more than 100 commercial vessels from the
Japan Mail Line. The navy contributed twenty-three additional ships, including
armed escorts, a hospital ship, and a repair vessel.[49]

Persistent shipping bottlenecks delayed the Second Army's landing on the
Shandong Peninsula, which in turn was partly responsible for IGHQ's decision to extend the campaign into the spring of 1895. Even after occupying
Korea and the Liaodong Peninsula, the army still faced an uncertain, perhaps
precarious, future because in March 1895 some 200,000 Chinese troops were
reportedly massing on the Zhili plain. With available shipping committed to
sustaining the expeditionary armies, the general staff in desperation deployed
combat units to China with the promise that their unit equipment and supplies
would follow eventually.[50]

The army hired 153,000 civilian contractors, laborers, rickshaw men, and
coolies to sustain its war machine, many of them desperate for any work because of the economic depression afflicting Japan. These auxiliaries were neither
trained nor outfitted in military uniforms. Wearing bamboo hats, pale blue cotton jackets with tight-fitting sleeves under a *happi* coat with their unit's number
painted on it, and straw sandals, they looked like the coolies they were. Porters
carried the army's supplies on their backs, dug its fortifications, and accounted
for most of its sanitary corps personnel. Thousands perished in the cold or from
epidemics. Besides being exempt from military orders and discipline, contract
laborers received extra pay for hazardous duty, causing resentment among soldiers, who did not get a bonus.[51]

Koreans were reluctant to support the expeditionary army with labor or
goods because they, like most disinterested western observers, initially doubted
the small island nation could defeat the mighty Chinese empire. Forcibly impressed Korean coolies pilfered supply trains, by some accounts stealing 25 percent of the army's rice stockpile. Korean porters and their Japanese counterparts
deserted in droves, and in an extreme case an overwrought Japanese battalion
commander took responsibility for the delays in moving supplies forward by
committing suicide.[52]

Available maps were of poor quality and often misleading about the condition of roads and rail lines. Trusting the map, no one had reconnoitered the rail
line between Pusan and Seoul that in places was impassable, forcing bearers
to portage supplies and further delaying resupply.[53] The main road to Seoul,
shown clearly on maps, was little more than a narrow, poorly graded dirt track
that meandered through mountains and into valleys. Water-filled rice paddies
along either side reduced traffic to a single file that moved at the pace of the
slowest wagon.

When available, the wartime daily ration consisted of polished white rice, meat, vegetables, Japanese pickles, and condiments. The field ration contained dried boiled rice, tinned meat, and salt. Soldiers also foraged for food and confiscated chickens, cattle, and pigs from Chinese and Korean households. Various food combinations were tested, but none was superior to dried boiled rice and a hardtack biscuit for the emergency field ration. Paradoxically, the chaotic logistics situation determined the Japanese decision to attack Pyongyang. After reaching Seoul, the First Army was so desperate for food that troops had slaughtered the oxen that had pulled their now empty supply wagons. Officers exhorted the soldiers to capture Pyongyang with promises of mountains of Chinese rations awaiting them.[54] Besides these logistics problems, epidemic outbreaks hampered operations.

There were about 3,500 sanitary corps troops, two-thirds of them reservists, and the army had to hire large numbers of contract workers to carry litters, dig latrines, and construct field hospitals. Maintaining a potable water supply under field conditions was probably their most difficult task. Sanitary teams purified water from wells, streams, and rivers, and officers forbade troops from drinking the water in train stations or port terminals and instructed units to boil water before using it for cooking or brewing tea. Despite these efforts, there was an outbreak of cholera in the army for the first time since 1890.

On paper, each division established six field hospitals that served as treatment and collection points, but because of the shortage of sanitary troops about half that number of field hospitals were built. Military doctors and pharmacists were too scarce to treat the epidemic outbreaks. Opiates used in anesthesia were a controlled government monopoly, and the army had to negotiate with the Home Ministry to purchase 80 percent of the nation's annual supply. To relieve the burden on doctors and sanitary corps personnel, army instructors trained conscripts in field sanitation procedures and basic nursing skills.[55] The government rallied soldiers' relief organizations under the umbrella of the Japan Red Cross. Nevertheless, the scale of even a very limited war had almost overwhelmed a medical corps that had to resort to temporary emergency measures to compensate for a lack of planning, intergovernmental coordination, and proper stockpiles.

Battlefield Performance and Discipline

Japanese infantrymen fought as they had trained. Massed columns facilitated rapid mobility during the approach to the enemy. Upon contact, the columns maneuvered into a skirmish line supported by densely packed ranks of riflemen who rushed forward en masse for a short distance, threw themselves on the ground, and then repeated the maneuver. Junior officers led frontal assaults in short rushes and supported by light artillery. The tightly packed formations preserved unit integrity and fire discipline, ensured tactical command and control, and created the mass and momentum for a successful assault. The Japanese consistently took advantage of terrain to mask their movements and rushes but were willing to cross open ground to get at their objectives.

The army compiled no comprehensive analysis of its wartime campaigns to derive "lessons learned," although postwar reports by the frontline infantry units did identify deficiencies. The esprit de corps established among individual squads in an infantry company, for example, improved unit cohesion in battle, but individual companies were reluctant to sacrifice their solidity to support a neighboring unit, thus reducing overall aggressiveness and effort. The peacetime pace of the attack in training proved too rapid to be maintained in combat conditions, and when soldiers could not sustain the training tempo, their morale fell. Troop morale also wilted under heavy enemy fire, particularly when nearby comrades were killed or wounded. The revised 1898 infantry manual nevertheless validated massed formations relying on bayonet attacks because that was the only way for a company commander to control his unit. It devoted great attention to fighting spirit and morale because the army deemed these intangible qualities the keys to victory. As a consequence, postwar training became more demanding on the theory that enduring physical hardship would develop willpower that conscripts could draw upon to sustain their morale and discipline in the turmoil of battle.[56]

The army suffered 1,161 killed in action, including 44 officers and 118 NCOs.[57] With the Japanese constantly on the offensive, the retreating Chinese had little chance to take prisoners and captured just eleven Japanese, ten of them overage porters. The only soldier taken prisoner was suffering from a head wound. Officers actively discouraged the notion of surrender, warning the troops of the terrible fate that awaited them in Chinese hands. Yamagata, for instance, cautioned his officers not to allow themselves to be taken prisoner because the innately cruel Chinese would kill them.[58] Instead, it was the Japanese who committed the worst atrocity.

The *New York World* reported in late November that Japanese troops had massacred as many as 60,000 Chinese during a four-day period following the capture of Port Arthur. More conservative recent estimates are that about 2,000 Chinese were killed, apparently in retaliation for Chinese soldiers mutilating Japanese corpses. Whatever the numbers, there was no doubt that something dreadful had happened at Port Arthur, despite the Japanese government's vigorous denials.

Foreign Minister Mutsu's memoirs dismissed the reports as "exaggerated" but acknowledged that "some unnecessary bloodshed and killing did occur." He believed some provocation had occurred and that most of those killed were Chinese soldiers out of uniform. Two weeks after the incident, Ōyama admitted that in the confusion of street fighting it was difficult to avoid killing civilians who were intermingled among the Chinese soldiers.[59]

The Japanese government would later claim that numerous Chinese soldiers refused to surrender, discarded their uniforms for mufti, and were killed during mopping up operations. Yet the cabinet held no inquiries because an investigation might embarrass the army by implicating senior officers in war crimes. The cabinet's underlying fear was that a trail of responsibility might lead to Ōyama's headquarters and force his recall. If that happened, Yamagata would take command of all field forces, an outcome neither Itō nor Mutsu wanted.[60]

The government also tried to conceal the massacre because it tarnished Japan's image in world opinion as a civilized nation that the foreign ministry had burnished during ongoing negotiations for treaty revision. Commanders had issued strict orders to protect westerners, especially missionaries, for two reasons. First, they wanted to avoid provocations that might lead to western intervention; second, they wanted to demonstrate that Japan was a civilized nation that respected western standards of international law, which in turn would further the government's efforts to revise the unequal treaty system.[61]

A double standard, suffused with attitudes of racial superiority toward the Chinese, likely contributed to the massacre at Port Arthur. Expecting a rich and cultured civilization, Japanese soldiers were disillusioned when they saw firsthand the filthy conditions and hardscrabble existence of impoverished Chinese. Admiration turned to contempt and debasement. These perceptions dovetailed with notions of Japan's uniqueness and superiority to produce popular racial stereotypes of the Chinese and China as a decaying civilization.[62]

Army discipline reflected the larger society's propensity to settle disputes privately without recourse to formal courts or tribunals. Moreover, the army's concept of military discipline applied to ensuring offensive spirit and obedience to orders, not to disciplining the ranks in a formal fashion. Field courts-martial boards convened 2,000 cases during the war, more than 70 percent of which were to try civilians working for the army. About 500 soldiers, almost all conscripts, were convicted by courts-martial, mostly for petty offenses. Among the more serious charges, just six soldiers were convicted for assault on a superior officer, and eleven were convicted for desertion. Army discipline so strictly applied to punish transgressions against military regulations or commanders' orders was not invoked to control soldiers' outrages against helpless Chinese.[63] For an army that made a fetish of discipline and unquestioning obedience to orders, the incident implied that officers throughout the chain of command were either complicit in or condoned the massacre.

Newspapers scarcely mentioned the alleged massacre. At the outbreak of the war, IGHQ had accredited more than 120 reporters, artists, and photographers to cover the fighting and assigned them to army headquarters under

This 1894 Toshikata print depicts five Japanese soldiers routing 100 Chinese, reinforcing the army's superior material and intangible qualities in contrast to the decadence of China. (Author's collection)

strict guidelines. The home ministry's censorship ensured compliance, but there was little to worry about because the correspondents became cheerleaders for the war and the military. Higher literacy rates, at least in the major cities, and improved printing technology extended their influence. Newspapers published extras, evening editions, and multiple editions that romanticized and popularized the war. During the immediate postwar period, numerous published accounts—some real, most fictional—enjoyed great popularity serialized in newspapers and the newly created monthly magazines.[64]

The popular narratives of warfare suited the army's self-image and were part of a more general appeal to the literate public to support the armed institution. A credulous press abetted the army's propaganda effort, and potential critics always faced the threat of censorship or worse. Still, in an era when imperialism and nationalism were in full bloom internationally, uncritical patriotism was not only easier and safer but also more accurately reflected widely held and accepted popular opinions of Japan's place in the world.

High Command and Field Initiative

In theory the IGHQ unified civil-military functions as the place where the emperor, his military chieftains, and Prime Minister Itō devised national and military policy. In reality the central headquarters was pitted against ambitious field commanders who unilaterally tried to set military policy. Against their better judgment, Itō and army leaders bowed to Yamagata's insistence that he be appointed the First Army commander. By the time 56-year-old Yamagata arrived at Inchon on September 12, the First Army had already captured Pyongyang. A few days later he caught cold while bathing in a river, developed complications, and although chronically ill refused evacuation and participated in a minor engagement on the Yalu in late October.

By early November, Yamagata believed that the war had reached a critical stage, and he had no intention of squandering opportunities by remaining idle.[65] On November 3 he sent IGHQ three options for an active winter campaign: (1) land the Second Army at Shanhaiguan; (2) combine the First and Second armies on the Liaodong Peninsula; or (3) send the First Army to attack Mukden (Shenyang).[66] From a base at Mukden, Yamagata would reorganize his army for the spring offensive against Peking and check the resurgence of Chinese forces in the region. IGHQ rejected the recommendations and ordered the First Army into winter quarters.

In mid-November, Yamagata received intelligence that the Chinese were massing on his northern flank and again recommended an offensive. He complained that the enforced inactivity had dampened troop morale, allowed the Chinese to take advantage of the lull to improve their defenses, and conceded to the Chinese a secure rear area in Manchuria that Japan would need in order to fight the Zhili plain battle.[67] IGHQ replied ambiguously but did not reject his latest recommendations outright.

The Second Army's capture of Port Arthur in late November with fewer than 300 casualties was all the more impressive because the army had publicly implied that it would be a hard fight with heavy losses.[68] Yamagata likely realized that the striking victory had overshadowed his command, and, anxious to secure his place as a martial leader, disregarded IGHQ's operational guidance to avoid large-scale winter operations. On December 1, he unilaterally ordered the First Army to advance on Mukden, expecting to divide Chinese forces and open the way for a decisive battle the following spring. The IGHQ learned of his offensive four days later, by which time it had abandoned any plans to attack Peking because of fear of western intervention. The central headquarters, however, had not notified a frustrated and sick Yamagata of its changed thinking.[69] In short, neither the general staff nor the First Army knew what the other was doing.

Yamagata expected to draw supplies from Japanese depots at Pyongyang, but planners had calculated on sustaining the First Army in static winter quarters, where it would need fewer, not more, supplies. Furthermore, the logistics line of communication was in disarray despite the IGHQ's efforts to add thousands of supply wagons and tens of thousands more teamsters and laborers.[70] Yamagata's frail condition added another variable.

Yamagata had never recovered his health, suffered further complications from stomach trouble and diarrhea, and in November was so ill that the First Army's surgeon-general suggested that he return home to recuperate. Soon afterward several reports reached Vice War Minister and concurrently Military

Affairs Bureau Director Maj. Gen. Kodama describing Yamagata's deteriorating
physical condition and the fear that his weakened constitution might not survive the harsh winter. Prime Minister Itō was reluctant to recall Yamagata, concerned that the embarrassment might force the proud ex-samurai to commit
suicide. He thus bypassed the cabinet and had the emperor write to Yamagata
on November 29 expressing concern for his health and requesting his return
to Hiroshima to brief the court on the overall military situation. An imperial
envoy departed Hiroshima on December 5 carrying Meiji's message, but it took
him three days to reach Yamagata's headquarters.[71]

Yamagata eventually returned to Hiroshima on December 17, by which time
the First Army's offensive was well under way, pulling it farther and farther from
its supply depots. Although the initial push succeeded, by mid-December the
plunging temperatures froze Manchurian roads, making it slow and hazardous
for horse-drawn wagons to move along the slippery ice-coated surfaces. Frozen
rivers could bear the weight of a column of troops, but not the weight of their
horses and wagons. Most soldiers had no winter clothing and faced the howling
winds and blizzard conditions in their summer uniforms, tattered by months of
campaigning. Respiratory diseases reached epidemic proportions. Many troops
had not received boots and were still wearing straw sandals or low quarter shoes
that left them susceptible to frostbite.[72]

Itō's revised strategy, issued on December 14, called for the capture of the
Chinese naval base at Weihaiwei on the Shandong Peninsula to prevent surviving North Fleet warships from interfering with Japanese shipping in the Bohai
Gulf. The fortress overlooking the naval base was taken on February 2, 1895,
although Maj. Gen. Ōtera Yasuzumi, commander of the 11th Infantry Brigade,
was killed in the fighting, the only Japanese general officer lost in action during
the war.[73] The Chinese fleet, caught between Ōyama's army and the Japanese
navy's blockade, surrendered its few intact warships by mid-February. In Manchuria, the First Army, under new command, defeated Chinese forces, leading
to negotiations that produced the Treaty of Shimonoseki, signed on April 17,
1895.

The treaty compelled China to recognize Korea as an "independent state,"
pay a large indemnity, and cede to Japan control of the Liaodong Peninsula, railroad concessions rights in southern Manchuria, and Taiwan. Just six days later
Russia, Germany, and France forced Japan to return the Liaodong Peninsula.
The Tripartite Intervention shocked the Japanese public, who were still elated
by the outcome of the war, and made it painfully clear that Japan, though a regional power to be reckoned with, remained at the mercy of the West. A sense
of national humiliation was palpable, and a determination emerged, encouraged
by the government, to avenge this wrong. The immediate object of Japanese

passion was Russia, seen as the ringleader in the intervention and the inevitable future enemy.[74]

Postwar Gains and Problems

Japan's acquisition of Taiwan and Japanese special interests in Korea had serious unforeseen consequences. On May 25, 1895, indigenous Taiwanese had declared an independent republic, and an estimated 50,000 insurgents, concentrated in the southern part of the island, took up arms. Four days later the Guards Division, commanded by Maj. Gen. Prince Kitashirakawa, landed unopposed in northern Taiwan, where the Chinese governor-general and the 9,000-man Chinese garrison promptly surrendered. The Japanese opened a new governor-general headquarters in Taipei on June 2 and requested immediate reinforcements to crush the rebellion. The Guards and the 2d Division—almost 50,000 troops, supported by 26,000 civilian contractors—conducted a punitive campaign against the rebel strongholds and by the end of October declared Taiwan secure, although counterinsurgency operations continued until March 1896. About 700 Japanese troops were killed or wounded fighting the guerrillas, but epidemics claimed 20,000 more, among them Prince Kitashirakawa. Punitive expeditions to suppress armed uprisings continued until 1907, and thereafter army and police cordon operations enforced a nervous peace with the indigenous mountain tribes. Tokyo gradually reduced its military presence and formed the Taiwan Garrison, eventually reorganized in 1907 as the permanent table of organization and equipment (TO&E) formation, consisting of two infantry regiments, each with a mountain artillery company.[75]

After 1895 the Japanese government became more active in Korea, where decade-long internal power struggles had aligned court factions with Japanese, Chinese, or Russian sponsors. Tokyo attempted to solidify paramount Japanese influence in Korea through diplomacy, loans, and the creation of a Japanese-trained military force (*kunrentai*) of about 800 men to counterbalance the American- and Russian-trained palace guard. In September 1895, Miura Gorō, then a member of the House of Peers, was appointed minister to Seoul, the senior Japanese official in the country. Miura was unwilling to allow Russian predominance at Japanese expense, but his efforts backfired in early October when the Korean queen engineered a court order that dissolved the *kunrentai*.[76]

In Miura's mind this was the first step in a court-based conspiracy to assassinate pro-Japanese senior officials in the Korean government, which would likely be followed by requests for Russian intervention to restore order. Miura staged his own countercoup on October 8 when a gang of more than twenty Japanese and Korean cutthroats broke into the palace, murdered the queen, and burned her corpse in a nearby wood. Miura first notified Tokyo that no Japanese were involved in the crime, but foreign ambassadors soon revealed Japanese culpability. The foreign ministry recalled Miura and about forty other Japanese while Itō assured the western powers that Miura had acted independently without instructions from the cabinet.[77]

The queen's murder touched off an explosion of anti-Japanese violence in Korea, where local peasant militias led by Confucian-educated gentry murdered several Japanese residents. The Korean king dismissed pro-Japanese officials, executed the Korean conspirators, and requested Russian assistance. In February 1896, Russian troops entered Seoul. Around the same time, about 100 Japanese sailors went ashore to restore order on the Pusan-Seoul highway and protect the Japanese-owned telegraph lines against sabotage. A May agreement between the Japanese and the Russians allowed the stationing of small matching garrisons in Seoul and Pusan, ostensibly to protect Japanese residents and property.[78]

Ejecting China from Korea destabilized northeast Asia by exposing the military weakness of the Chinese empire and touching off a scramble among the imperialistic western powers to carve up East Asia and Pacific territories. In 1897 the United States annexed Hawaii and Germany occupied Tsingtao, China. The following year the United States moved into the Philippines. By mid-1898 Britain had leased Weihaiwei after the Japanese withdrawal as well as the New Territories. The looming Russian threat most concerned the Japanese government, which relied on diplomacy to defuse it.

The Nishi-Rosen Agreement signed in Tokyo on April 25, 1898, stipulated that neither Japan nor Russia would appoint military instructors or financial advisers to Korea without prior mutual agreement. Russia further agreed not to hinder the development of Japanese commercial and industrial relations with Korea. Russia withdrew its military and financial advisers following the agreement, but it still occupied Port Arthur, reinforced Manchuria, and expanded its financial stake in northeast Asia.[79] In 1899 Britain and Germany divided the Samoa archipelago and Germany occupied various South Seas territories, the Bismarcks, New Guinea, and the Caroline Islands. Russia continued to push deeper into Manchuria and was double-tracking the Trans-Siberian Railway, which was scheduled for completion in 1903.

Japan retained its privileged position in Korea and acquired a new colony of Taiwan. There was no dispute about the government's responsibility to protect Japanese interests in Korea against Russian encroachments. Taiwan's position, however, was ambiguous. Did the island anchor Japan's southernmost defenses, or was it a springboard for offensive expansion into China and points south? Should the empire passively defend Korea and shift resources to Taiwan for a southward expansion, or was Korea a base to move into southern Manchuria and North China? The army had to confront the new regional and strategic realities, a proposition made more difficult because the western powers now identified Japan as a serious competitor in northeast Asia. The course of Japan's expansion—north or south—plagued strategy formulation for the next fifty years and was the nation's strategic legacy from the Sino-Japanese War.

Postwar Army Plans

On April 15, 1895, two days before the signing of the Treaty of Shimonoseki, Yamagata, recently appointed war minister and concurrently inspector general, recommended to Emperor Meiji a ten-year military expansion to protect Japan's newly acquired overseas territory. Ten days previously, Yamagata had made a similar proposal to Foreign Minister Mutsu because Japan needed a larger army in order to maintain stability in East Asia.[80] Though Yamagata was a geopolitical thinker who grasped Japan's strengths and weaknesses and trusted his innate caution to guide the nation and army through its formative period, he was not a professionally educated officer. He displayed a narrow grasp of modern combined arms warfare and had little understanding of the rapid technological advances that were revolutionizing the role of field artillery in warfare. Military expansion simply meant more troops, and he wanted to double the infantry strength of each division without proportionate increases to artillery and supporting branches.[81] Put differently, Yamagata wanted bigger, not more, divisions.

The general staff likewise wanted to expand the army, but in a more balanced and professional manner. Its approved October plan called for a thirteen-division force structure, and in 1896 the general staff incorporated the thirteen-division troop basis into wartime contingency planning premised on forward offensive operations to preserve or expand overseas interests. Army expansion began in 1898, according to an amended plan to field six new divisions, two new cavalry brigades, and two new field artillery brigades. One brigade (two regiments) from each regular division formed the cadre for a new division. The two regiments of the remaining brigade were divided into cadre to create two brigades (the existing one and a newly organized one). The process took three years, incrementally adding cadre and conscripts to bring the new regiments to their full 1,800-man peacetime strength, and was operational by 1903.[82] Each regular division also organized a depot brigade responsible during wartime for garrisoning occupied territories. Depot units were usually issued obsolete weapons and equipment.

Almost doubling the force structure likewise nearly doubled the conscription rate. By 1904 the army was inducting almost 20 percent of the annual cohort and assigning double the number of those examined to the reserves (see Tables 5.2 and 5.3).

More junior officers were needed to lead the expanded ranks, and in 1897

Table 5.2. Strength of Japan's Army, 1896–1900

Year	Number of Divisions	Strength of Army (estimated)
1896	9	100,000
1897	11	120,000
1898	13	140,000
1899	13	140,000
1900	13	150,000

Source: *Kindai sensōshi gaisetsu*, 39.

the army opened six regional preparatory cadet schools to complement the army central preparatory school in Tokyo. Accepting junior cadets between 13 and 15 years of age, the preparatory schools charged six yen a month for expenses, which effectively limited the entrants to sons of middle-class families who could afford the tuition. Each school had about fifty cadets per class enrolled in a three-year preparatory course that consisted of a standard middle-school education except for the emphasis on foreign languages and overdose of instruction on military spirit. Graduates matriculated to the eighteen-month main course at the central preparatory academy. Critics maintained that the school's narrow curriculum stunted students' intellectual curiosity, fostered excessive competition and cliques, and produced martinets.[83] Because graduates from the preparatory schools also matriculated at the military academy, the average academy graduating class mushroomed from about 155 between 1890 and 1894 to 663 between 1897 and 1904. Likewise, the staff college more than doubled its annual graduating classes, from twenty to about fifty officers.[84]

Modernization accompanied the expansion. In 1897 Murata's redesign of his original rifle produced a five-shot repeating rifle with a smaller, lighter 6.5 mm round that enabled the infantry to carry more ammunition in their cartridge belts (between 150 and 180 rounds). The increased rate of fire compensated for the bullet's alleged lack of killing power and shorter effective range.[85] The general staff and war ministry wanted an artillery gun mobile enough to keep pace with a fast-paced infantry advance and capable of moving across the primitive road networks and tracks of northeast Asia. With new modifications and technological advances in artillery weapons occurring in Europe at breakneck speed, any investment in artillery was a gamble because imminent breakthroughs might soon render today's wonder weapon obsolete by tomorrow.

The case of the Type-31 artillery gun is illustrative. This 1898 model was a rapid-fire gun whose carriage absorbed the recoil. Because the gun did not move with the recoil, it did not have to be manhandled back into its original firing position after each firing, allowing for a more rapid and accurate rate of

Table 5.3. Conscription Rates, 1897 and 1904

Year	Examined	Inducted	Percentage	Reserves	Total Percentage
1897	401,952	45,791	11.4	92,158	34.3
1904	408,031	78,180	19.2	188,894	65.5

Source: Ōe, *Nichi-Rō sensō to Nihon guntai*, 103.

fire. It suffered developmental problems, forcing the army to import more than 600 semi-processed field artillery guns and their equipment (gun carriages, ammunition caissons) from German manufacturers. Within a few years, however, the superior range and higher rate of fire of the Russian 1904 field artillery gun made the German guns obsolete. In October 1904 the Japanese government had to strike a secret deal with German industrialists for 400 of their latest-model field artillery guns.[86]

Following the Sino-Japanese War the army gradually changed to a khaki uniform because the color showed fewer stains, particularly the bloodstains that had adversely affected troop morale during combat. At the time of the 1900 Boxer Rebellion soldiers still wore white trousers, but four years later everyone was outfitted in khaki. The army also adopted high boots and gaiters to prevent a recurrence of frostbite and trench foot experienced during the Sino-Japanese War. Individual soldiers were issued rain capes as well as aluminum canteens and mess kits. Blankets remained in short supply because Japan's woolen mills could not fill the demand.[87]

Postwar military budgets skyrocketed; in 1898 more than half the national budget went toward underwriting military expansion and modernization, a process made more expensive because the navy was simultaneously modernizing its fleet. The military budget of 1896 was 73 million yen—more than three times that of 1893—and in the peak year of 1900 it exceeded 100 million yen. The army invested about half its budget to pay the greatly increased personnel costs associated with additional manpower and about one-quarter to pay for weapons. The navy conversely used more than two-thirds of its budget to pay for new capital ships (almost quadrupling its tonnage by 1902) and only one-sixth in personnel because its manpower was only one-quarter that of the army. By 1903 military spending accounted for about one-third of the national budget. It remained at that level for almost the next twenty years.[88]

The cabinet funded the expansion program through a combination of reparations paid by the Chinese after the Sino-Japanese War, the sale of bonds, foreign loans, and increased consumption taxes. These measures enabled the government to reduce the land tax slightly and gain the political parties' approval for the budget. The Russian threat and the imperialist race to gobble up

Table 5.4. Total Military Budget (in millions of yen) and Individual Army and
Navy Budgets, Even Years 1894–1902

Year	Total Budget	Army Budget	Navy Budget	Percent of Total
1894	7,812	1,040	1,024	26
1896	16,855	5,323	2,000	43
1898	21,975	5,389	5,382	51
1900	29,274	6,483	5,727	42
1902	28,125	4,660	2,841	27

Source: Tobe, *Gyakusetsu no guntai*, 137.

China motivated the Diet's passage of huge military budgets, but politicians also took bribes, accepted a large pay raise for lower house members, gained access to patronage appointments, and enacted franchise reforms in exchange for their votes. Large military expenditures continued even during the financial panics of 1897–1898 and 1900–1901, in part because the government tapped into citizens' postal savings accounts when its bonds were downgraded on the world market (see Table 5.4).[89]

There was good reason to spend the money. Northeast Asia at the turn of the twentieth century was a powder keg waiting to explode. The Japanese military was in the midst of rearmament, expansion, and modernization to counter the Russian military threat in northeast Asia, but the services were divided over a north or south approach to long-term strategy. Korea was a strategic liability, its people hostile to Japan, its rulers untrustworthy, and the peninsula insecure as a rear area base. China verged on chaos as the old regime vainly struggled against internal reformers and external aggressors. Russia was a menacing presence in Manchuria and had staked out a strategic position on the Liaodong Peninsula. Japan's military goals for regional supremacy and stability in northeast Asia mirrored Russia's objectives and set the two empires on a collision course. These competing and irreconcilable versions of regional security made the war with a major western power inevitable.

6

Back to the Continent: The Russo-Japanese War

To many informed observers the advent of the new twentieth century heralded the demise of the old China. Japan's victory had exposed China's military weakness, which the western powers were quick to exploit, placing the empire in danger of dismemberment. In January 1898 Germany secured a ninety-nine-year lease on the Shandong Peninsula as a settlement for the murder of two German missionaries. Two months later Russia negotiated a long-term agreement with the Chinese court for a leasehold on the Liaodong Peninsula between Dairen and Port Arthur (where Russian warships had been anchored since the previous December). Great Britain reacted by extracting concessions in April for a naval base at Weihaiwei. France carved out a sphere of influence in southern China, and Japan sought railroad concessions in Fujian opposite its Taiwan colony.

The Boxer Expedition

Popular Chinese resentment over thirty years of foreign humiliation boiled over in 1900 as a series of violent attacks against foreigners led by the Boxers, a secret society that enjoyed covert backing from the Qing court, tapped widespread local support with its antiforeign and anti-Christian rhetoric. The murder of the German ambassador to China and the subsequent Boxer siege of the foreign legation quarter at Peking caused the western powers (Great Britain, France, Germany, Italy, Russia, and the United States) as well as Japan to send troops to north China to rescue the diplomatic missions, protect western missionaries, and punish the Boxers. The Japanese army would use the occasion to showcase its latest military reforms.

A small, hurriedly assembled allied expeditionary force under British command of about 2,000 troops, including approximately 300 Japanese, marched from Tianjin for Peking in early June. On June 12, mixed Boxer and Qing army forces halted the advance by destroying a bridge about 30 miles from the capital.

The road-bound and badly outnumbered allies withdrew to the vicinity of Tianjin, having suffered more than 300 casualties.

Aware of the worsening conditions, the general staff in Tokyo drafted ambitious contingency plans, but the cabinet, with fresh and bitter memories of the Tripartite Intervention, refused to deploy large forces unless requested by the western powers. Three days later the general staff did dispatch a 1,300-man provisional force to north China commanded by Maj. Gen. Fukushima Yasumasa, director of the second (intelligence) department, chosen because his fluent English enabled him to communicate with the British commander.[1] Fukushima's detachment landed on July 5 near Tianjin.

During the interval, a few hundred naval infantry from the Sasebo Special Landing Force had joined British, Russian, and German troops to seize the Dagu forts near Tianjin on June 17, but four days later the Qing court declared war on the foreign powers. The dangerous circumstances compelled the British, then heavily engaged in the Boer War, to ask Japan for additional reinforcements. Overriding personal doubts about supporting what many Japanese thought amounted to a religious crusade by the western powers against the Chinese, Foreign Minister Aoki Shūzō calculated that the advantages of participating in an allied coalition were too attractive to ignore. Prime Minister Yamagata thought likewise, but others in the cabinet demanded guarantees from the westerners in return for the risks and cost of reinforcements.[2] The cabinet alerted the 5th Division on July 6 for China duty but set no timetable for its deployment.

More ground troops were urgently needed to lift the Boxer siege of the foreign legations at Peking, and the Japanese had the only readily available forces in the region. As mentioned, the British army was tied down in South Africa, and it would take too much time and weaken internal security to deploy large forces from its India garrisons. On July 8, the British ambassador to Japan offered Aoki one million British pounds in exchange for more reinforcements.[3] Shortly afterward, advance units of the 5th Division departed for China, bringing Japanese strength to 3,800 personnel of the 17,000-man allied force.

This second, stronger expeditionary army stormed Tianjin on July 14 and occupied the city. The allies then consolidated and awaited the remainder of the 5th Division and other coalition reinforcements. In early August the expedition pushed toward Peking where on August 14 it lifted the Boxer siege. By that time, the 13,000-man Japanese force was the largest single contingent, about 40 percent of the approximately 33,000-man allied expedition.[4]

Japanese troops were on their best behavior throughout the campaign. The 5th Division commander (who had taken operational control from Fukushima) ordered the troops to demonstrate Japan's brand of discipline, courage, and fortitude in battle to the world. Officers at all levels enforced draconian standards of discipline. Junior officers warned troops that the army would summarily and severely deal with violence against Chinese households, arson, or theft. Rape was punishable by immediate arrest and decapitation.[5] Even minor infractions were harshly punished. Fukushima remained in China to enforce frontline discipline.

Japanese troops acquitted themselves well on all counts, although a British military observer felt their aggressiveness, densely packed formations, and willingness to attack cost them excessive and disproportionate casualties. During the Tianjin fighting, for example, they suffered more than half of the allied casualties (400 of 730) but comprised less than one-quarter of the force (3,800 of 17,000). The story was similar at Peking, where they accounted for almost two-thirds of the losses (280 of 453) but slightly less than half of the assault force. The only major lapse in discipline occurred when all ranks joined their allies in the widespread looting in Peking, apparently with the understanding that whatever the westerners did, the Japanese could do too. A British correspondent noted, however, that the Japanese plundered "so nicely that it did not seem like looting at all."[6]

As part of the September 1901 settlement with the Chinese court, the coalition powers were allowed to station troops between Tianjin and Peking to protect their nationals and maintain a secure line of communication to the sea. The war ministry activated the China Garrison Army, the designation for army units stationed in North China under terms of the Boxer Protocol. The new army was a provisional unit, not a regular one (whose troop basis was fixed by imperial decree) and drew on elements from several homeland divisions assigned to it on a temporary one-year rotating basis.[7] Other concessions included Russia's right to retain its reinforced garrisons in Manchuria, pending a phased withdrawal.

The Boxer Rebellion revealed Great Britain's growing difficulty in maintaining its influence in northeast Asia. The Boer War had drained the British army and forced diplomats to pay Japan to send troops to quell the Boxers and counterbalance Russian military intervention. The European alliance system had isolated Britain internationally, and in East Asia the combined Franco-Russian navies outnumbered the British fleet. Engaged in a naval race with Germany and wary of Russia's meddling in China and the implications of the construction of the Trans-Siberian Railroad, the British needed allies. Japan was likewise diplomatically isolated after the Tripartite Intervention and had to deal with the Russian presence in Manchuria and its potential threat to Korea. By signing the 1902 Anglo-Japanese naval alliance, the parties agreed to respect each other's interests in China, maintain strict neutrality in case one or the other became involved in a war, and to intervene if a third party entered the conflict. For Britain, the treaty restored the naval balance in East Asian waters and provided an army to check Russian expansion. For Japan, it allowed the army to address the Russian threat to Korea without fear of foreign intervention.

The treaty assumed greater significance when Russia did not withdraw the reinforcements it had sent to Manchuria to protect its railway zones and seemed intent on further expansion. Military engineers were improving the Russian naval base and fortress at Port Arthur, and the Trans-Siberian Railroad was nearing completion. Russia's greatly improved strategic mobility, particularly the potential to move large units rapidly by rail to Manchuria, alarmed Japan's leaders, and Yamagata's repeated warnings of the dangers the railroad posed to Japan's national interests seemed to be coming true.

Preparations for War

The army had regarded Russia as its traditional enemy, but the general staff only began substantive operational planning for war with Russia in 1900. Initial plans envisaged capturing Port Arthur, followed by a decisive battle near Mukden in Manchuria with secondary amphibious operations directed against Russia's Maritime Provinces. After the arrival of additional Russian reinforcements in Manchuria during July 1900 and the completion of most sections of the Trans-Siberian Railroad, the general staff revised plans in 1901 to focus on the defense of Korea.[8]

The next year Maj. Tanaka Giichi, recently returned from attaché duty in Russia, took charge of a small planning group within the general staff that worked under tight security. By August 1902 it had recast the staff's war plans into a strategy that, much like the Sino-Japanese conflict, depended on Japan's naval capabilities. If the navy could control the Yellow Sea, the army could safely deploy troops to the continent and Manchuria would be the main theater of operations. Should the navy only be able to control the Tsushima Strait, the army would land in southern Korea and defend Japanese interests on the peninsula.

For its part, the navy was dissatisfied with the arrangements for imperial headquarters, which, in case of war, would be commanded by an army general. Frustrated by playing second fiddle to the army-dominated IGHQ, naval leaders, especially Adm. Yamamoto Gombei, aggressively demanded changes to the IGHQ regulations to make the naval chief of staff coequal to his army counterpart, in effect the recognition of an independent naval general staff. Gen. Kawakami Sōroku adamantly opposed Yamamoto and insisted that wartime operations had to be based on peacetime plans prepared by a single authority—the army.[9]

After Kawakami's death in 1899, both services continually appealed to the throne for a resolution of command authority. Finally, in December 1903, with war with Russia looming, army Chief of Staff Gen. Ōyama and Prime Minister

Yamagata petitioned the emperor to allow both the chief of the naval general staff and the chief of the general staff to advise the throne on matters of national defense and military operations. This change created a wartime headquarters in which the army and navy general staffs were independent of one another, but did not resolve fundamental issues of joint planning, joint operations, or command and control.[10]

Vice Chief of Staff Maj. Gen. Tamura Iyozō was the brain behind the army's operational and mobilization concepts for the war. Having spent six years as a junior officer studying in Germany, Tamura was one of a handful of Japanese officers well versed in Clausewitz's theories of war and had matured into a first-rate if conservative strategist.[11] To keep Tamura's work secret, the army's annual report submitted to the throne continued to describe a defensive national strategy, even while the general staff rewrote its offensive contingency plans.

When Russian troops did not leave Manchuria as the Boxer Protocol stipulated, on April 21, 1903, the prime and foreign ministers met with senior statesmen at Yamagata's Kyoto villa, where they agreed to seek a diplomatic solution. If diplomacy failed, they would resort to war. Maj. Gen. Iguchi Shōgo, director of the general affairs department, a hawkish short-war proponent, pressured Tamura to notify the cabinet that the army was ready for war at a moment's notice. Tamura, however, harbored serious reservations about the army's combat readiness—the new, enlarged force structure had just become operational—and used the Russian threat to justify greater army expansion.[12]

Army Chief of Staff Field Marshal Ōyama Iwao notified the emperor that Russian meddling in East Asia would erode the overseas gains Japan had made since the restoration and that Russian domination of Korea would directly threaten national security. Immediate military preparations for war were necessary. Amidst these conflicting military assessments, an imperial conference on June 23 concluded that concessions to Russia were possible regarding Manchuria, but Korea was a vital national interest and therefore nonnegotiable.[13]

Tamura died suddenly in October 1903, having literally worked himself to death. His loss was a crushing blow to the general staff coming as it did at a critical juncture in Japanese-Russian relations that found leadership in disarray. Prime Minister Katsura Tarō was indecisive, Yamagata was depressed, and Ōyama was not psychologically ready for war. Gen. Iguchi lamented that the army and the navy were at odds over strategy, and the navy minister was placing parochial service interests above the national good. The only bright spot was Lt. Gen. Kodama Gentarō's willingness to accept a demotion in order to replace Tamura, an act that Iguchi regarded as proof that "heaven has not yet abandoned our empire."[14]

Kodama resigned two ministerial portfolios and took a two-rank demotion to serve as army vice chief of staff.[15] Under his guidance in February 1904 the general staff finalized a two-stage campaign plan that sought the destruction of the Russian field armies in Manchuria as well as the Russian Pacific Fleet. During stage one, the First Army would advance to the banks of the Yalu River to prevent a Russian invasion of northern Korea. The Second Army would establish a base of operations on the southeastern Liaodong Peninsula; then the Third Army would land, advance to Port Arthur, isolate the fortress, attack it if necessary, and support the other armies. As the First and Second armies moved north into Manchuria, the smaller Fourth Army would land between them along the northeast bank of the Bohai Gulf to secure their flanks and protect the rail line of communication.

Kodama's objective was to encircle and destroy the Russian Siberian Independent Corps and the Second Corps near Liaoyang before reinforcements from European Russia could arrive and overwhelm the Japanese with their superior numbers. Staff officers calculated that it would take about six months to move eight divisions from Europe to Manchuria, giving the army that much time to achieve Kodama's objectives. There were no specific plans for a second year of campaigning.[16]

Unable to resolve the impasse with Russia through diplomacy, the February 4, 1904, imperial conference decided on war. For several days afterward Emperor Meiji was unable to sleep or eat, dreading the possibility of having to report a defeat to his ancestors. He later told the empress that it was not his wish to fight Russia and worried about facing his subjects if Japan lost.[17] Senior army officers were also well aware that Japan could not win a protracted war. Amidst uncertainty and trepidation Japan severed diplomatic relations with Russia on February 6, and two days later, without a formal declaration of war, the navy launched a surprise attack against the Russian squadron moored in the harbor at Port Arthur.

The surprise attack aimed to destroy the Russian fleet at anchor or at least neutralize the enemy fleet by sinking obsolete Japanese transports to block the harbor entrance.[18] Maritime supremacy would then pass to the Japanese navy and permit the army to ship troops safely to Korea's west coast and the Liaodong Peninsula. Russian contempt for the Japanese led them to underestimate the seriousness of the threat and leave Port Arthur unprepared for a sudden raid. Still, the Japanese naval attack neither destroyed the Russian squadron, although it did heavily damage three capital ships, nor closed the harbor. The Russian fleet-in-being at Port Arthur remained a strategic liability for Japan that would extract a terrible toll on the emperor's army. On February 10 Meiji issued a memorial declaring war against Russia.

Imperial General Headquarters was established on the palace grounds the next day. Unlike the case during the Sino-Japanese War, the prime and foreign ministers were excluded from the headquarters and the army barred civilian ministers from officially attending IGHQ meetings, although, as will be discussed, informal networks kept civilian leaders well apprised of developments. IGHQ became the official operations center where senior staff officers reported to the emperor on strictly military matters rather than the locus of civilian-military policy formulation. Strategic decision-making occurred during the deliberations of the senior statesmen that usually preceded an imperial conference and made the meeting in the emperor's presence the highest decision-making mechanism for wartime military and foreign policy issues.[19] There was no formal apparatus to connect military and civilian policy, and the system depended on informal personal relationships cemented by years of working together in the government.

Three subsequent attempts by the navy—in late February, late March, and again in May—to seal the Port Arthur channel by sinking old transports in the mouth of the harbor also failed. The army general staff had scripted a tightly sequenced deployment schedule that depended at every stage on the navy's support, and with each disappointment, army-navy relations deteriorated. In mid-March, for example, the First Army landed safely near Pyongyang. The general staff then was shocked and dumbfounded when the navy announced that it was postponing further blockship operations against Port Arthur until mid-May. Unable to delay the Second Army's scheduled May 5 landing on the Liaodong Peninsula, the army had to risk its slow-moving troop transports to possible attack by the Port Arthur squadron in order to meet its short-war timetable.[20]

Meanwhile, the First Army moved north from Inchon and in two days of fighting over April 30 and May 1 pushed the Russians back along the Yalu River near Andong. This minor engagement had major ramifications. The Japanese, regarded by many in the West as quaint little people from an exotic land, had defeated Caucasian troops of a world-class power. Stock markets in New York and London suddenly realized Japan was a sound investment, and foreign purchases of government bonds and offers of loans buoyed the wartime economy. On the home front, however, the public was shocked and critical because the more than 900 Japanese killed or wounded exceeded total battle casualties for the Sino-Japanese War. Vice War Minister Lt. Gen. Ishimoto Shinroku defended the troops' performance to reporters by attributing the losses to modern weapons technology, not incompetent leadership.[21]

On May 25, the Second Army's three divisions attacked an entrenched Russian infantry regiment defending Nanshan on the narrow neck of the high ground that separated the northern and southern halves of the Liaodong Peninsula. Fighting began early in the day with a three-hour artillery preparation, followed by a textbook frontal assault against the still mostly intact Russian positions. By midmorning the Second Army had thrown its final reserves into the battle but still could not break the defenses. As artillery ammunition dwindled, casualties mounted, and the troops became exhausted, staff officers recommended that Gen. Oku Yasukata, the Second Army commander, withdraw and regroup. Oku instead ordered renewed attacks, regardless of losses.

Tactical doctrine depended on dense columns to build up sufficient fire superiority to carry a defensive position, but Nanshan's limited maneuver space canalized infantry attacks into direct frontal assaults. The combination of tactics and terrain left massed attackers exposed to withering Russian fire that inflicted staggering losses before the Russians finally retreated in the late afternoon. The army later described these assaults as "human-bullet attacks" and claimed for public consumption that they epitomized uniquely Japanese virtues of courage, determination, and self-sacrifice.[22] In fact, when staff officers at imperial headquarters received the first official reports of 3,817 casualties in the Nanshan fighting, their immediate reaction was that a careless cipher clerk had mistakenly added an extra digit.[23]

The army's tactical doctrine was mismatched against modern weapons technology. According to a young captain attached to the Second Army, "It's not our human-bullet tactics that throw away brave warriors' lives. It's the superior Russian fortifications and equipment and our lack of machine gun firepower that gives us no chance of winning. With machine guns extending the distance [of the killing zone], table-top tactics can no longer have any practical application." Extended lines of skirmishers soon replaced the densely packed columns, and intervals between individual soldiers increased. Some tactical commanders, such as Col. Ichiwara Shinichirō, quickly adapted. Ichiwara's nonchalant attitude had embarrassed his junior officers during peacetime maneuvers, but at Nanshan he repeatedly rallied his men, ignoring heavy Russian fire. In real fighting, he later remarked, the enemy was less cooperative than on exercises.[24]

Army Chief of Staff Yamagata, Prime Minister Katsura (concurrently an active duty general), War Minister Terauchi Masatake, Manchurian Army commander Ōyama, and his chief of staff, Kodama, gathered at Imperial General Headquarters on June 10 to set the operational direction of war. Katsura participated in IGHQ conferences in his capacity as a retired general officer but was not kept informed officially about operational matters. However, he received accurate information from the senior statesmen (Yamagata and Itō) because the army did provide them accounts of the military situation. Katsura was also a close friend and drinking companion of War Minister Terauchi, who likely passed him information. Because of the cumbersome and exclusionary bureaucratic system, informal personal relations played a crucial role in coordinating military, political, and diplomatic initiatives.[25] A brief review of operations highlights these deficiencies.

The Manchurian Campaign

The Manchurian Army, consisting of the First and Second armies, would advance along the South Manchurian Railroad to Liaoyang, where the First Army would envelop the enemy's right flank, destroy the Russian field army, and open the way to Mukden and the decisive battle before Russia could mobilize its full military strength. Simultaneously, the Third Army would attack Port Arthur and after taking the fortress rejoin the field armies near Mukden.[26] The Russian commander, however, fought a series of skillful delaying actions in June and July to buy time for reinforcements to arrive from European Russia. Port Arthur was left isolated and besieged by the recently arrived Third Army.

General staff officers had not originally considered seizing the port and were unaware of the extent of Russian improvements to the fortress's defenses. Russian military engineers had shrouded their work in tight security, and Japanese spies lacked the technical expertise to determine the strength of the improved concrete-and-steel fortifications. As a consequence, they reported that the Russians had merely extended existing trench lines, leaving the impression that Port Arthur was weakly defended as it had been during the Sino-Japanese War.[27]

On August 19 the complexion of the war changed dramatically when the Third Army commander, Lt. Gen. Nogi Marasuke's, ill-conceived frontal assault against Port Arthur cost at least 16,000 killed and wounded, a disaster compounded by his stubborn refusal to halt the futile attacks. A few days later Ōyama's armies suffered more than 23,000 casualties during the seven-day battle for Liaoyang (August 25–September 3). The First Army struck the Russian center while the Second and Fourth armies turned the enemy's eastern flank. Unable to encircle the Russians, the Japanese resorted to costly frontal attacks.

Though the army publicly glorified the efforts of the so-called human-bullets to sustain home-front morale, more responsible commanders were appalled at the needless slaughter. Junior officers blamed the "big-shot tacticians" for stubbornly applying textbook tactics that needlessly threw away soldiers' lives. Ōyama relieved three major generals, all brigade commanders, because their inflexibility caused unnecessary casualties.[28]

The combination of heavy losses and the inability to encircle and destroy the enemy field army shook Japanese regimental and division commanders' self-confidence. At the height of the Liaoyang fighting, Tokyo newspaper editorials confidently predicted another Sedan, a reference to the Prussian army's encirclement and destruction of the French army in 1870. Self-confident and certain of the outcome, the First Army's officers and men anticipated truce talks after the battle. Morale plummeted as the realization sunk in that they faced renewed

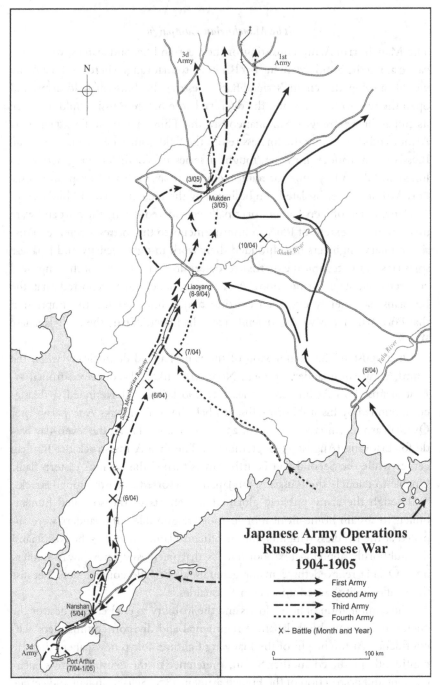

N

3d
Army

1st
Army

(3/05)

Mukden
(3/05)

(10/04)

Shahe River

Liaoyang
(8-9/04)

Yalu River

(7/04)

(5/04)

South Manchurian Railway

(6/04)

(6/04)

Nanshan
(5/04)

3d
Army

Port Arthur
(7/04-1/05)

**Japanese Army Operations
Russo-Japanese War
1904-1905**

⟶ First Army
⟶ Second Army
⟶ Third Army
⟶ Fourth Army

X – Battle (Month and Year)

0   100 km

Map 5

fighting. Replacements for Nogi's Third Army at Port Arthur lost heart when battle-toughened veterans dismissed them as cannon fodder. The commander of a Guard infantry brigade wrote to the vice chief of staff that just declaring morale was high did not necessarily make it so. Discipline suffered, and the army resorted to field gendarmes to drive reluctant troops forward, at least in one case at bayonet point.[29]

Although the army had steadily expanded from 123,000 officers and men in 1896 to 191,000 in 1903 and increased its reserves proportionately, it could not compensate for the unexpectedly high attrition during the opening engagements. These battles made clear that more troops were needed. Immediately after the Liaoyang fighting, the emperor, at IGHQ's request, on September 29 activated four new divisions, doubled the second reserve obligation to ten years, extended the age limit for the first reserve term from 32 to 37 years old, and added forty-eight infantry battalions to the second reserve. The new provisional divisions would be organized by February 1905, but they would not be trained and ready for operations until late May at the earliest. By the time the first of the new formations was activated on April 15, 1905, the major fighting was over.[30]

The Vladivostok naval squadron added to the overall sense of gloom and anxiety in Japan. On the morning of April 26, Russian warships surprised and sank a small Japanese ship carrying a 200-man infantry company. The soldiers refused surrender or rescue and went down with their sinking ship. Army authorities stoked patriotic home-front fires by portraying the act as a deliberate decision to avoid the shame of surrender and the debasement of captivity.[31] Russian raiders continued to cruise the Sea of Japan, picking off victims, spreading panic among Japanese coastal towns, and provoking public criticism of the military's incompetence.

In mid-June the Vladivostok squadron sank a large army troop transport carrying almost 2,000 soldiers and irreplaceable artillery and stores. When the admiral charged with protecting the convoy could not find the Russian warships to retaliate, angry Tokyoites stoned his house, denounced him as a Russian agent, and demanded his suicide. Wild rumors about the Vladivostok fleet terrified civilians and forced the cabinet to order an emergency reinforcement of coastal defenses in Tokyo Bay and Tsushima Island.[32]

While the Russian squadron rampaged seemingly at will and Nogi's Port Arthur offensive collapsed, the northern front stabilized around Liaoyang. By the end of September the army had committed three divisions to Port Arthur, sent eight to Liaoyang, and mobilized 65,000 replacements to fill the losses in its infantry divisions. In addition, field army commanders wanted the two divisions remaining in the homeland strategic reserve, but IGHQ insisted that they were needed for coastal defense against a possible Russian landing. Emperor Meiji intervened in the dispute between the field army and IGHQ by deciding that one homeland division would deploy to Liaoyang.[33]

In early October a Russian offensive surprised the Second Army at the Shahe River, about 45 miles northeast of Liaoyang, and in the week-long battle that followed, three Japanese armies again failed to envelop the Russian flanks. Losses were heavy: more than 41,000 Russian and 20,000 Japanese fell. By this time, sickness was ravaging the field armies as beriberi, typhoid, and dysentery incapacitated thousands more troops. Ōyama halted his armies to regroup.

While Ōyama reconstituted his battered forces, imperial headquarters, reacting to the navy's demands that Port Arthur be taken quickly, again ordered Nogi to attack the fortress. After his first setback, IGHQ had reinforced the Third Army with heavy artillery in hopes of breaching the Russian defenses. Higher headquarters grasped that artillery observers atop the dominating heights of Hill 203 could direct accurate plunging fire onto Port Arthur and its harbor, making them untenable. Nogi and his staff, however, had never been to the front lines and regarded the heights, particularly Hill 203, as secondary to the Third Army's objective of capturing the town.[34]

After a council with IGHQ liaison officers on September 5, the Third Army staff agreed to attack Hill 203. Assaults two weeks later seized outposts on Hill 203 but could not take the crest. Although Nogi had received reports from the front that parts of Port Arthur could be seen from recently captured hills, the full impact of this intelligence escaped him, and he suspended the offensive on September 22 after suffering 5,000 casualties.

The well-publicized struggle for Port Arthur captured world attention, and the western press popularized Nogi for its readers as the personification of the samurai warrior, who uncomplainingly endured hardship and suffering. Kodama and other senior commanders, however, were appalled by Nogi's incompetence, which had shifted the strategic focus of the war, cost tens of thousands of unnecessary casualties, consumed vast quantities of scarce war material, and achieved nothing. The Third Army opened its third major offensive on November 26 and the next day finally captured Hill 203. The fortress and naval base were defenseless and soon surrendered. More than 59,000 Japanese casualties paid for Nogi's victory.

In late January 1905, Russian forces tried to drive the Japanese back to Liaoyang and inflict as many casualties as possible. Fighting in bitterly cold weather near San-de-pu, the Japanese stopped the counterattack—at a cost of more than 9,000 casualties. Next followed the epic struggle from February 22 through March 10 for Mukden, a battle that pitted almost 300,000 Russians against slightly more than 200,000 Japanese. The Japanese again tried a sweeping double envelopment but could not close their pincers in time to trap the retreating

Russian armies. Despite losses of 70,000 Japanese and almost 90,000 Russians, the battle was indecisive and the ground war in Manchuria was stalemated.

Tokyo misread these results. On March 11, Katsura and Terauchi proposed new offensives to Yamagata, who in turn forwarded their recommendations to Ōyama. Responding from Manchuria a few days later, Ōyama described Mukden as indeed a great victory, but he dwelled on his heavy casualties and exhausted supplies. He needed time to rebuild his logistics network and wanted the cabinet's guidance in the form of a unified military-diplomatic policy on whether to pursue the Russians or switch to a protracted war strategy.[35]

Ōyama's sobering assessment convinced Yamagata and Terauchi that Japan had no means of forcing the Russians to capitulate, short of attacking Moscow or St. Petersburg, which of course was impossible. The Manchurian Army could not even attack Harbin some 250 miles away because of recent personnel losses, especially among officer ranks; ammunition shortages; logistics deficiencies; and transportation problems, including a requirement for extensive railroad construction to build a line for transporting supplies to forward units. Taking this into account, on March 23 Yamagata requested the cabinet end the war by diplomatic means.[36]

IGHQ recalled Kodama to Tokyo at the end of March for discussions on whether to continue a protracted war or sue for peace. Kodama's outspoken criticism of the general staff's ineptitude peaked when he called the vice chief of staff a fool for starting a fire without knowing how to put it out. At an April 8 meeting, the senior statesmen and major cabinet ministers resigned themselves to the possibility of a protracted war unless diplomatic measures could achieve satisfactory peace terms.[37]

In mid-October 1904 the Russian Baltic Fleet had sortied from its home port for an eight-month, 10,000-mile voyage via the Cape of Good Hope to reinforce the Russian Far Eastern squadrons and relieve Port Arthur. The adventure ended on May 27, 1905, in the Tsushima Strait, where Vice Adm. Tōgō Heihachirō's combined fleet sank twelve first-line Russian warships and captured four more. Antiwar demonstrations erupted in Russia, where the crew of the battleship *Potemkin* mutinied. Internal unrest, the gloomy military situation, and the czar's concern about a possible invasion of Sakhalin made the Russians amenable to negotiations. Japan's leaders, aware that their armies and resources were exhausted, were likewise anxious for talks and secretly approached U.S. President Theodore Roosevelt to mediate. After a month of discussions at Portsmouth, New Hampshire, mainly about Russian refusal to consider indemnities or territorial concessions, on September 5 the Russians grudgingly agreed to cede southern Sakhalin Island to Japan. In addition, Japan received exclusive rights in Korea and control of Russian railroad lines in southern Manchuria. But there was no indemnity.

During the lead-up to war, the army appealed to an increasingly literate public and conscript force with themes of Japan's uniqueness by virtue of the unbroken imperial line. Pamphlets subsidized by the war ministry explained in simple language that the army protected Japan from foreign threats, much like the wall around a storehouse kept wild animals or thieves from stealing treasures. Essays popularized notions that *seishin* and the intangible factors of battle were responsible for tiny Japan's victory over the enormous Chinese Empire and that Japan had to fight Russia to save China from itself and prevent a collapse of the international order.[38]

Building on that foundation, wartime propaganda had concealed Japan's military weaknesses to manufacture an unprecedented national commitment to the war across the society. The potent combination of prewar indoctrination and wartime propaganda raised popular anticipation that shared hardships would entitle everyone to benefit from the fruits of victory. With these unrealistic expectations, the Japanese people were infuriated that the treaty contained no indemnity and doled out seemingly paltry rewards for such great sacrifices. Anti-treaty rioting and popular demonstrations erupted in Tokyo as the public directed its fury against the civilian cabinet. It might better have targeted the army.

An Assessment

Despite its extensive planning, modern weaponry, and expanded force structure, the 1904 army was still an amateurish one, characterized by regional cliques, favoritism, incompetence, and nepotism. In 1901, for example, the staff college had reorganized its curriculum to prepare officers for command of large units (brigade and higher echelon) and educate them with the latest technological principles. Instruction, however, remained rooted in tactics, and the curriculum stressed individual initiative that taught officers to command by resolute action and not get bogged down in details.[39] Staff officers assigned to the respective armies in the Russo-Japanese War were expected to be decisive, but they lacked practical experience and tended toward doctrinaire staff college solutions, regardless of circumstances. An uncritical adherence to the norm pervaded the officer corps.

Many senior officers had made their rank and reputations as young soldiers in the restoration wars of the 1860s or the Satsuma Rebellion of the mid-1870s. Too many were autodidacts, ill prepared to encounter the rapid advances in early twentieth-century technology, military professionalism, and warfare. Nogi, for instance, a veteran of the restoration wars, the Satsuma Rebellion, and the Sino-Japanese War, was stumped when looking at a topographic map of the Port Arthur defenses. Unable to understand terrain contours or elevations, he concluded the shortest distance between two points was a straight line and ordered an attack into the most difficult and best-defended terrain, where his troops suffered enormous and unnecessary losses.

Nogi's selection for high command also illustrated the regional biases and web of personal connections that hampered the creation of an effective professional officer corps. The army originally recalled Nogi from retirement in February 1904 to command a reserve Guard division.[40] Two of the three serving army generals (Oku and Kuroki Tamemoto) were slated to command the First and the Second armies. The third, Sakuma Samata, had retired in October 1902 and at age 61 was judged too old to withstand the rigors of field campaigning. Yamagata then selected the 55-year-old Nogi to command the Third Army and assigned him the responsibility for Port Arthur because Nogi had captured the fortress in 1895. Nogi's Chōshū lineage and long-standing acquaintance with Yamagata made him acceptable to the Chōshū clique that dominated the army; in addition, Nogi was on friendly terms with many senior naval officers, making him a suitable liaison for a joint campaign. But Nogi was a martinet and an aesthetic who carried his notions of a samurai code to extremes and had never psychologically recovered from losing his battle standard during the Satsuma Rebellion. Yamagata and the other generals recognized his limitations, but they still agreed that Nogi could handle what was planned as a minor secondary operation to isolate Port Arthur.

The army selected Maj. Gen. Ijichi Kōsuke as Nogi's chief of staff. Ijichi was a superannuated artillery officer and former instructor at the staff college. He hailed from Satsuma, the cradle of many naval officers, making him acceptable to the navy and serving the army's desire to balance its regional cliques. He was also Ōyama's son-in-law. Though army authorities did not think much of Ijichi's abilities, they considered him at least capable of conducting a siege. Neither Ijichi nor Nogi, however, understood modern fortifications, and Nogi's lack of self-confidence allowed Ijichi to make operational decisions. Ijichi was incompetent, opinionated, but cautious, and he deferred to his overworked deputy, Lt. Col. Ōba Jirō, a Chōshū native, and a very aggressive personality.[41]

In this dysfunctional headquarters, staff officers displayed little ability or initiative, leaving Ōba, an infantry officer unacquainted with siege tactics, to handle most planning. The army's expert of fortifications and siege warfare was Maj. Gen. Uehara Yūsaku, a French-educated engineer officer. But Uehara's father-in-law was Lt. Gen. Nozu Michitsura, the 64-year-old commander of the Fourth Army, who insisted on Uehara for his chief of staff. Unfortunately Nozu's difficult personality made it all but impossible for anyone but his son-in-law to work with him.[42] Personal relationships were no better in the two main armies.

Lt. Gen. Kuroki, a 60-year-old Satsuma native, commanded the First Army. He had led a division in the Sino-Japanese War, cultivated a rude and simple lifestyle, and loved good cigars. Despite appearances, he was a bookish officer, fond of history, and not a risk-taker. His chief of staff, Maj. Gen. Fujii Shigeta, was mean-spirited, nasty, and ignorant of the working of a headquarters staff. He had been the commandant of the staff college, and after it closed for the duration of the war he was assigned to Kuroki. Fujii proved inflexible, indecisive, and continually at odds with his highly talented deputy. Vice Chief of Staff Maj. Gen. Nagaoka Gaishi regarded Fujii and Ijichi as equally dangerous incompetents whom the army would be better off without.[43]

Lt. Gen. Oku Yasukata, commander of the Second Army, was barely on speaking terms with his chief of staff, Maj. Gen. Ochiai Toyosaburō. A protégé of the late Tamura, Ochiai had headed the general staff's fifth (war history) department and served as an instructor at the staff college. He had a flair for map maneuvers and tabletop tactics, but in actual operations he proved stubborn, inflexible, and ignorant of logistics as well as rear area security requirements. Ochiai handpicked his subordinates from the ranks of staff college instructors, and, like their mentor, they were fixated on map exercises and theory, unable to adapt swiftly to rapidly changing battlefield conditions of real warfare.[44]

Intelligence collection and analysis was also personality-driven and idiosyncratic. Maj. Gen. Fukushima was the chief of the intelligence department of the general staff. Col. Matsukawa Toshitane, an infantry officer and director of the first (operations) department, however, relied on his own intelligence sources, splitting the general staff into fiercely competitive Matsukawa and Fukushima factions. The general staff's arrogance so alienated the foreign ministry that diplomats refused to share the intelligence that they gathered in the United States or Europe, leaving the army without strategic data regarding domestic unrest in Russia, manipulation of radical elements there, or the Port Arthur defenses. At the operational level, officers treated intelligence casually because the top graduates of the staff college invariably went into combat arms—infantry, artillery, cavalry—and were taught to and preferred to make their own assessments.[45]

Operational intelligence repeatedly ignored inconvenient discoveries that might disrupt planning already in progress. After the Liaoyang battle, the long-serving military attaché in London, Lt. Col. Utsunomiya Tarō, received intelligence from British sources that the Russian Second Army was about to counterattack the Japanese right flank. Imperial General Headquarters decided that the Russians could not move large formations through the rugged, mountainous terrain and did not pass on the warning.[46] Oku was thus surprised on October 5 when the Russians struck his exposed right flank to open the Battle of Shahe.

In mid-January 1905 Utsunomiya and the military attaché to Berlin, Lt. Col. Ōi Shigemoto, reported that Russians planned to attack the left flank of Ōyama's Manchurian Army along the Shahe River. Manchurian Army staff officers insisted that the bitter cold and deep snow made a major offensive impossible. When eight Russian divisions attacked in the middle of a late January snowstorm, Ōyama's headquarters dismissed the offensive as a minor reconnaissance-in-force.[47]

The displacement of IGHQ to Hiroshima a decade earlier had been disruptive because the government ministries remained in Tokyo, requiring extensive and expensive coordination that resulted in frequent delays. This time the emperor stayed in Tokyo to coordinate civil government as well as military affairs. Senior officers then complained that IGHQ was too far removed from the front lines to act as an operational headquarters, and in March 1904 Vice Chief of Staff Kodama suggested a supreme command headed by a crown prince be established in Manchuria.

Ōyama, the newly appointed commander of the field armies in Manchuria, insisted on total control of the overseas forces, including logistics and personnel matters. War Minister Terauchi rejected the general staff's proposal to grant Ōyama such sweeping authority because it would turn IGHQ into a cipher. Furthermore, Terauchi and Prime Minister Katsura—the latter acting as a general, not as the prime minister—wanted IGHQ to coordinate the joint campaign against Port Arthur directly from Tokyo. Based on Yamagata's counsel, on May 25 the emperor instructed Terauchi and Ōyama to establish a senior field headquarters to command Manchurian armies and gave Ōyama operational control of the field forces.[48]

On June 20, the war ministry activated the Manchurian Army Headquarters, appointed Ōyama as supreme commander, promoted Kodama to general, and reassigned him as Ōyama's chief of staff. Yamagata became chief of staff (rear) with control of logistics, personnel, and administrative matters at IGHQ; Nagaoka Gaishi was the vice chief of staff (rear). The brightest young officers were assigned to the Manchurian Army while recalled officers or senior statesmen staffed Imperial General Headquarters. Friction quickly developed between the Manchurian Army and IGHQ, especially over the development of the Port Arthur campaign, the deployment of strategic homeland reserves to Manchuria, and the mobilization of new divisions.[49]

Dysfunctional personalities, a cumbersome command-and-control network, and a poorly integrated imperial headquarters exacerbated the army's fundamental problem: it was essentially refighting its last war, having projected casualty rates, ammunition consumption, and logistics requirements based on its Sino-Japanese War experience.

After driving the Russians from Nanshan, IGHQ expected to systematically isolate Port Arthur, causing it to fall. As mentioned, the second department's outdated intelligence underestimated the much-improved fortress defenses that skillfully blended formidable new strong points into the hilly topography. Based on shopworn intelligence, in late February 1904 Maj. Ōba Jirō and Maj. Tanaka Giichi (both then concurrently general staff and IGHQ staff officers), among others, recommended seizing the seemingly weak fortress before reinforcements arrived from western Russia.[50] Kodama wanted to keep his armies intact and thought it better to isolate Port Arthur rather than storm it. Once the navy closed the harbor entrance, the Russians would be isolated and the Third Army could prevent the garrison from threatening the First Army's rear areas. Port Arthur would wither on the vine.[51]

Because the navy failed to close the harbor, it had to blockade Port Arthur and patrol the nearby waters to prevent the escape of the Russian naval squadron. Put differently, the Russian fleet-in-being at Port Arthur tied down a goodly part of the combined fleet. To unleash the fleet, the navy pressed IGHQ to order the army to capture the fortress, which would also neutralize the Russian fleet. Under mounting pressure from the navy, on June 24 IGHQ ordered Nogi to attack Port Arthur as soon as possible. A few weeks later, intelligence reported that the Russian Baltic fleet was making preparations to sortie. Tōgō then requested via the naval chief of staff on July 12 that the army attack Port Arthur without delay to allow the navy the time it needed to refit before arrival of the Baltic fleet. Whatever Nogi's faults—and they were many—he was the only field commander subjected to repeated operational interference by Imperial General Headquarters and the navy.[52]

IGHQ hoped to avoid a frontal attack by maneuvering the Third Army farther west to take the fortress from the rear. Nogi and his staff complained that repositioning the troops and artillery would take too much time and pull the Third Army farther from its railhead supply point. He understood his mission was to capture the city, not the defensive outposts on the high ground overlooking it, and, as mentioned, was unable to read topographic maps so chose the shortest direct route to Port Arthur.

A two-day bombardment by Nogi's light artillery did not seriously damage the concrete-and-steel–reinforced bunkers. Russian machine-gun crews secure inside their fortifications raked the massed attackers, who became snarled in barbed-wire entanglements. Faulty intelligence that the Russian line had broken prompted Nogi to renew the costly attacks. By the time he called off the assaults, the Third Army had suffered almost 16,000 casualties, including more than 5,000 killed in action. An Osaka-based regiment refused to attack after suffering heavy losses and was escorted to the rear under guard.[53]

Losses among officers were extremely heavy because tactical commanders followed their training and led from the front. The 44th Infantry Regiment, for instance, had two of its three battalion commanders killed and the third wounded; it lost all twelve of its company commanders, eight killed and four wounded; and thirty-five of forty lieutenants were killed or wounded.[54] Nogi's losses and the subsequent 23,000 casualties suffered at Liaoyang precipitated a chronic replacement crisis that was exacerbated by the lack of tactical skills and leadership ability among many replacement reserve officers and NCOs.

Government authorities tried to conceal the magnitude of Nogi's defeat through a combination of strict censorship, tight restrictions on war correspondents, and control of battlefield news releases. Army service regulations issued in January 1904 to protect military secrets complemented home ministry restrictions on newspaper articles enacted the previous year to stifle dissent. Police censors paid special attention to articles that they thought might lower the morale of soldiers' families.[55]

At the opening of the Russo-Japanese War, the government mobilized patriotic associations to organize nationwide relief campaigns to assist families of soldiers serving overseas and send troops small packages of sundries. Officials also diverted public attention from battlefield realities by publicizing real or imagined heroism and tales of glorious death in battle. Official propaganda unintentionally inflated popular expectations, working the public into a patriotic fervor that backfired when unrealistic goals could not be met. For instance, in August the government-sponsored preparations were under way nationwide to celebrate the anticipated fall of Port Arthur, but popular enthusiasm soon waned when victory was not forthcoming. After another Tokyo pro-war rally degenerated into a brawl that left thirty-nine people dead or injured, even "spontaneous" victory parades fell under greater police scrutiny.[56]

Despite government and army propaganda, Nogi too fell under a cloud of growing criticism. Irate citizens denounced him as a butcher, stoned his home, and threatened his wife. Nor could the government's upbeat official version of events conceal the grievous losses from the Japanese public. Hospital trains departed nightly from Ujina, and by mid-September the sight of caravans of wounded soldiers passing through the Tokyo streets to hospitals was commonplace. Letters from frontline soldiers and stories from replacements reached home with tales of heavy casualties, widespread illness, and war weariness. Inflation, numerous new special taxes on land and consumables to pay for the war, the continual reserve mobilizations of replacements, and rumors of terrible casualties weighed heavily on popular morale.[57]

Supplying the Army

Just three months before the outbreak of the war Col. Ōshima Ken'ichi, the director of the general staff's fourth (transport and military communications) department, and two lieutenant colonels began offering two-week crash courses for staff officers assigned as division logisticians. Each field army established an inspector-general for logistics, usually a major general or colonel with a chief of staff who reported directly to Imperial General Headquarters. Their

independence rankled army commanders who denounced logisticians and ac-
countants for dictating operational policy.[58]

The army's paucity of logisticians was directly related to its low esteem for
supply and transport duties. Top graduates of the military academy invariably
selected infantry branch while the lowest-ranking found themselves shunted
aside to the transport corps. Only 4 percent of all military academy graduates selected the transportation branch, as opposed to 63 percent entering the
infantry branch. The staff college curriculum neglected logistics, and graduates
later showed little interest in the subject.[59] In peacetime, divisions had minimal
transport and logistics personnel; wartime mobilization left the transport ranks
populated with reserve officers and enlisted fillers, who although wearing uniforms, lacked rudimentary basic training.

Nevertheless, more than 25 percent of almost 950,000 deployed troops were
involved in some kind of logistics duties, but infantrymen disparaged them,
and even the Chinese mocked them as coolie labor. The army again resorted
to auxiliary quartermaster units to move supplies, employing perhaps 700,000
Korean and Chinese porters and laborers.[60] Wagons frequently broke down
along the unimproved dirt roads, and few tools or spare parts were available for
repairs. Korean and Chinese laborers toiled at a series of depots and subdepots
that followed the wake of the advance and manhandled supplies to forward
units.

Railroads, the arteries that supplied the army's lifeblood, were few in number, and all needed major repairs. While the Manchurian Army's advance par-
alleled the South Manchurian Railway, army engineers were simultaneously
rebuilding the line, whose wide-gauge track required extensive renovation. By
July 30, 1904, the First Army had laid a light rail line from Andong to its forward positions, which eased its logistics backup. But the main rail lines needed
to support the armies did not reach as far north as Mukden until May 1905, by
which time the major fighting was over.[61]

Provisioning an army on the move was a constant struggle. Torrential rains
washed out roads and rails and forced the Second Army onto half-rations for
several weeks. An officer who had survived the Liaoyang battle wrote that malnutrition and sickness had reached a point where he doubted his regiment had
1,000 effectives from its original 3,000-man complement.[62]

Despite limited evidence that mixing rice with barley prevented beriberi,
the army issued a polished white rice ration mainly because it was easier to
transport large quantities of plain rice than rice mixed with barley. Similar
considerations ruled out a bread ration because hauling flour and the bulky
foiled baking ovens to forward areas took too many additional wagons. Besides,
soldiers could always eat dried rice, a staple of field rations, but no one could
digest a steady diet of stale bread.[63]

Troubling logistics breakdowns occurred. Japanese gunners at Nanshan fired more than 30,000 artillery rounds in a single day. This amount exceeded the army's entire artillery expenditure in the Sino-Japanese War and consumed two months' worth of shell production even though munitions factories had been working around-the-clock for two years to increase stockpiles.[64] The simultaneous offensives against Port Arthur and Liaoyang consumed ammunition stocks at unexpectedly alarming rates, and IGHQ's diversion of shells intended for the Second Army to meet Nogi's requirements worsened the shell shortage. Arsenal production expanded in August 1904, and the government purchased 450,000 artillery rounds from British and German munitions makers, but they would not be delivered until December.[65] Munitions shortages and shell malfunctions persisted because the domestic industry lacked the capacity and quality-control techniques required to mass-produce large amounts of reliable ammunition. On the eve of the decisive battle of Mukden in February 1905, Ōyama had to warn his assembled field commanders to be frugal with their artillery because there were no reserve ammunition stocks.[66] Heavy artillery was especially disappointing; observers at Port Arthur estimated that one in four of the giant 28-centimeter shells failed to explode.[67]

Yamagata's October 16, 1904, cable to Kodama detailed the precarious state of logistics and personnel shortages. It was impossible to supply sufficient artillery shells until December 1904, and no officer replacements would be available until February 1905. Hokkaidō was defenseless, and Japan had no strategic reserve. The four newly activated divisions would not be available until late May 1905. The Manchurian Army would have to wait for those reinforcements before attacking Mukden unless Nogi's Third Army could capture Port Arthur and then reinforce the northern armies.[68]

Port Arthur

By November 1, 1904, the Russian Baltic Fleet had reached the North African port of Tangiers. Japanese naval specialists estimated that the fleet could arrive at Taiwan's coast by early January 1905.[69] The fleet's progress intensified the naval general staff's demands that the army capture Port Arthur no later than December 1 to eliminate the potential threat to Tōgō's combined fleet from the rear; this move would give the admiral at least a month to refit his fleet and reinforce it with the warships currently assigned to blockade duty. Yamagata in turn notified Ōyama on November 9 that the Third Army had to take Port Arthur.[70]

Yamagata then requested the emperor replace Nogi because he was unfit for command. The emperor disagreed; he was uncertain who would replace Nogi and afraid the disgrace might drive the general to suicide. With Nogi untouchable, Manchurian Army commander Ōyama sent his chief of staff, Gen.

Kodama Gentarō, to Port Arthur to direct an assault on Hill 203, the key terrain feature. He authorized Kodama to remove Nogi, if necessary. Nogi, however, accepted the new arrangement and remained in nominal control while Kodama "borrowed" his operational authority.[71]

The Third Army attack on Hill 203 began November 26 and soon suffered heavy losses. After two days of fighting, heavy artillery finally beat down Russian fortifications on Hill 203 and a night attack by the 1st Division captured part of the critical terrain. When a Russian counterattack early the next morning threatened to retake the lost ground, Kodama took command, relegated Nogi to a deputy status, committed the Third Army's final reserves, and finally drove the Russians from the high ground on November 30.[72] Almost 17,000 Japanese troops were killed or wounded.

By early December Japanese forward observers perched atop Hill 203 were connected by telephone landlines to artillery batteries and could accurately direct plunging fire into the town and port below, making the fortress untenable. The Russian commander's offer to negotiate surrender terms on January 1, 1905, transformed Nogi into an international superstar.

Nogi's incompetence disgusted many senior officers, including one who literally wanted his freshly severed head on a platter. On New Year's Day 1905, Lt. Col. Tanaka Giichi, now assigned to Ōyama's staff, recommended Nogi's relief before the Third Army marched north toward Mukden. Kodama countered that removing the famous conqueror of Port Arthur, whose very name struck fear into Russian hearts, would destroy army morale and stain the Third Army's accomplishments. Firing Nogi, he added, would insult the spirits of the 20,000 war-dead at Port Arthur who wanted to join their commander for the decisive battle. Regardless of the rhetoric, in the end it was more important to protect the army's reputation than to relieve Nogi.[73]

Ōyama expected to use Nogi's Third Army as one arm of the massive pincer maneuver in a double envelopment that would encircle and then destroy the Russian field armies near Mukden. On the morning of February 27, while artillery fire of the First, Second, and Fourth armies diverted Russian attention, the Third Army moved north. By the time Ōyama launched his March 1 main attack, however, Nogi had positioned his army too far north to influence the action. Two days later he countermarched to link up with the Second Army and close the trap on the Russians; he moved too slowly, creating a gap that allowed the main Russian forces to escape. Nogi was not solely to blame. Senior commanders and staff officers experienced great difficulty coordinating the complex maneuvers of multiple field armies during the two-week battle. Scores of units got intermingled during the fighting, and crisscrossing supply wagons, troops, and porters congested road traffic, further impeding rapid maneuver.[74]

The inconclusive ground campaigns cost the army heavily, but precise figures are unclear. The general staff's official history acknowledged about 120,000 casualties, including 2,600 prisoners. Official statistics, however, reported only those wounded seriously enough to be invalided from service, about 58,000 personnel. Other records document more than 130,000 troops hospitalized for wounds. About 60,000 men were killed in action, most falling to small arms fire (78.6 percent, followed far behind by artillery at 12.9 percent) and 21,500 more perished from disease, with beriberi, typhoid, and amoebic dysentery accounting for 80 percent of the illness-related deaths (see Table 6.1).[75]

About four times more Japanese troops deployed to China during the Russo-Japanese War than in the earlier Sino-Japanese War and, exposed to the same indirect contact with some of the lowest classes, many concluded that all Chinese were poor, dirty, smelly, and lived in squalor. Soldiers' letters home recounted the appalling conditions, wartime diaries and postwar memoirs commented on them, and these strong impressions came home with the troops and spread throughout the community, reinforcing a prejudice among the general public about the inferiority of the Chinese.[76]

Attitudes about Death and Prisoners

The army ritualized death. Before the war, the service had popularized the concept of death before dishonor, citing ancient practices of killing oneself in accordance with the tenets of *bushidō* and *Yamato damashii* (Japanese spirit). Death in battle or suicide was preferable to capture, and catchphrases assured the public that soldiers had to avoid the shame of captivity and its accompanying stigma of cowardice. The popular imagination internalized the informal taboo against being taken captive, and repatriated prisoners of war were expected to endure vituperation and insults while they apologized for allowing themselves to be captured.[77]

Postwar military councils investigated about 2,000 repatriated prisoners of war. The ex-prisoner's parent unit conducted an initial screening, and the soldier could not be discharged until the inquiry was completed. At its simplest,

Table 6.1. Number of Japanese Soldiers Killed, Wounded, or Captured during Selected Battles of the Russo-Japanese War

Battle	Killed	Wounded	Prisoner	Total
Liaoyang	5,557	17,976	236	23,533
Port Arthur	15,390	43,914	—	59,304
Sha ho	4,099	16,398	628	20,497
Kurokodai	1,848	7,241	242	9,316
Mukden	15,683	51,247	1,581	70,028
Total	42,577	136,776	2,687	182,678

Source: Ōe, *Nichi-Ro,* table 2–4, 132–133.

the process took a couple of hours, but it could become a more complicated affair. No one was formally court-martialed, but administrative punishment could be severe. Eight officers (five army) captured when their ships were sunk were later cashiered and stripped of their rank and decorations.[78] Their names and punishments were also published in the *Official Gazette*.[79] There were also cases where some communities ostracized former prisoners, forcing them to move elsewhere.

The army's treatment of former prisoners was selective. The commander of the 28th Infantry Regiment was placed on leave in August 1906 and retired being seconded to the reserves the following February. Other captured officers, however, received medals, awards, and emoluments. Two intelligence officers operating in Manchuria were captured soon after the outbreak of the war. One was later awarded a medal for bravery and went on to become a major general. The other had the misfortune to be captured along with a supply train that offered no resistance. He had to resign. A major who was taken prisoner on a reconnaissance mission later escaped and brought back valuable intelligence. He got a medal. A second lieutenant captured on long-range reconnaissance patrol behind Russian lines received a commendation after escaping and bringing back valuable intelligence. The criterion seemed to be, "Did they do their duty to the full extent before being captured?"[80]

The distinction was lost on most of the public. Rumors spread about the shame of captivity, including one about a Diet member who was unable to bear the embarrassment of his son's captivity and committed suicide. These apocryphal stories were sufficiently widespread to convince popular opinion that captivity was shameful. Along with ideas of racial superiority, national uniqueness, and *seishin*, the myth of death before dishonor slowly permeated postwar society, incubating until the army could use it again.

Despite disparaging surrender, the army treated its almost 80,000 Russian prisoners of war decently. Those accepting parole were repatriated along with the wounded and family members, and Russian hospitals at Port Arthur continued to treat patients after the surrender. Japanese conduct toward Caucasian prisoners again demonstrated Tokyo's desire to be accepted by the West, a condition of ending the final vestiges of the unequal treaty system. After all, Japan had signed and abided by the 1899 Hague Convention on the Laws and Customs of War. At the outbreak of the war, the government had established the Prisoner of War Information Bureau in the war ministry. The bureau issued regulations regarding the treatment of prisoners who were eventually held at twenty-nine camps in Japan. After the war, the International Red Cross commended the Japanese government for its humane treatment of prisoners of war.[81]

Official and Unofficial Legacies

Strict wartime censorship played on the army's carefully cultivated prewar image as an institution that served the emperor and the nation to reinforce patriotism and obedience. In the immediate postwar era, the army created its mythology of the war with romantic and distorted tales of human bullets, whose popularity spread to the West in Lt. (later major general) Sakurai Tadayoshi's best-selling book by the same name. According to his narrative, Japanese fighting spirit overcame the enemy's advantages in men, money, and material. The offensive manifested this intangible and uniquely Japanese trait, and this belief underpinned the wholesale revision of the army's field manuals during the immediate postwar era.[82] Even the decision to die became a uniquely Japanese characteristic.

Yet the deified heroes of the war were not enlisted soldiers but two midlevel commanders, the navy's Lt. Cmdr. Hirose Takeo, killed after running his block-ship aground in the Port Arthur channel, and the army's Maj. Tachibana Shūta, killed while leading an assault that captured a key Russian redoubt at Liaoyang. Using officially sponsored mass ceremonies and public announcements, the government transmogrified both into "war gods," which was the first instance of the idea in modern Japan. The concept, interestingly enough, resonated with the larger public more because of the two officers' display of Japanese warrior spirit and virtue than for tactical success. Both officers were model commanders, respected and liked by their men, so their military prowess merely complemented their sterling characters. At a deeper level, their sacrifice stimulated a rediscovery of traditional Japanese values by ordinary citizens, many of whom felt overwhelmed and threatened by the steady encroachment of western culture on the nation. In other words, the two "war gods" exemplified the unique characteristics harbored deep in the heart of every Japanese.[83]

As would be expected, soldiers' attitudes toward death and battle depended on their proximity to the actual fighting. Survivors who witnessed the destruction and devastation described the battlefield as a cruel, tragic, or pitiful place. Professional officers generally accepted the army's idealized derivative samurai values, likely because so many of them during that era were from samurai stock. The conscripts and reserve officers, however, did not share the same values, and appeals to grandiose notions like an honorable death in battle or dying for the sake of the emperor held little attraction for them. Few aspired to become human bullets, and competent officers realized the folly of such tactics.[84]

The army and the government also suppressed inconvenient or embarrassing facts. Newspapers, for instance, published Nogi's wartime after-action report to the throne but deleted a passage critical of his performance at Mukden. Army officials later excised the offending passage from the official report on grounds of national security.[85]

Confidential internal assessments of the army's wartime performance were mixed. The army's official histories were written from the perspective of front-line commanders bragging about the spirit of the attack and the offensive. They omitted details of staff planning and coordination. Regimental histories routinely deleted references to chronic shortages of munitions that had short-circuited Japanese offensives. Bland, almost identical accounts uniformly praised the effectiveness of replacement training and the performance of reserve units.[86]

Secrecy carried beyond publications intended for general consumption. The army's multivolume official history of the war omitted detailed accounts of prewar planning, mobilization, logistics, diplomacy, reserve affairs, and ammunition and personnel shortages. A meticulous compilation dealing with those issues remained classified "top secret" and was tightly restricted even within the army. From the mid-1920s Col. Tani Hisao convened an annual special seminar of ten staff college students and used these sensitive, still highly classified documents unavailable to other officers to present a comprehensive strategic, diplomatic, and logistic appreciation of the Russo-Japanese War to the privileged elite.[87] In short, only a handful of carefully selected officers delved into the army's shortcomings during the war; the rest were left with a distorted understanding of the campaigns.

War with Russia and the postwar mythology defined modern Japan and its army. Japan's two foreign wars sharpened a popular sense of national identity and cemented national solidarity. Defeat likely would have meant permanent relegation as a second- or third-rate nation and, at worst, semicolonial status. In the public mind, victory over a major western power had achieved the Meiji leaders' goals to create a rich country and strong army, and victory parades and national interment commemorations marked the passing of an era. It also coincided with a new nationalism that reasserted mythical Japanese values in reaction to fears that the adoption of western techniques and fads brought along a social malaise that would topple traditional morality.

The concept of the Yasukuni Shrine as the final resting place for those killed in action had previously registered in a vague way in the popular imagination. After the war the shrine became a centerpiece of militarism. Both services held large public interment ceremonies at Yasukuni, and the army's grand triumphal return review there on April 30, 1906, became Army Day, a national holiday. Emperor Meiji presided over one national ceremony at Yasukuni for soldiers and sailors killed in action during the Russo-Japanese War and another one in 1907 when the army reinterred its dead from Manchurian graveyards to Yasukuni, with a concurrent special enshrinement for soldiers who had died of

A July 1905 meeting of the victors in the Russo-Japanese War in Fengtin, China. Left to right: Kuroki Tamemoto, commander First Army; Nozu Michitsura, commander Fourth Army; Yamagata Aritomo; Ōyama Iwao; Oku Yasukata, commander Second Army; Nogi Maresuke, commander Third Army; Kodama Gentarō, Chief of Staff, Manchurian Army; and Kawamura Kageaki, Yalu River Army commander. (Courtesy Japan, National Diet Library)

wounds following the war.[88] Other imperial rituals burnished Yasukuni's image. For the first time, a special imperial envoy carried word of the declaration of war against Russia to Yasukuni. Another imperial messenger announced the terms of the peace treaty to the spirits reposing there.

Just as the Yasukuni bequeathed special qualities to the war dead, victory over Russia endowed an Asian nation with world-class stature and respect, or as a brigade commander's letter to his wife more coarsely phrased it, equaled the difference between becoming a baron's wife or a back-alley whore.[89] Japan's triumph cracked the myth of white supremacy and invincibility, and the nation emerged as the premier regional military power in northeast Asia. But it also brought new, unanticipated responsibilities and commitments.

A recognized world-class navy and the Anglo-Japanese alliance removed any threat of invasion from Japan's strategic thinking. The army in turn developed an aggressive forward-based strategy and justified its special continental interests because of the price it had paid in blood and treasure to defeat the Russians in Manchuria. The war ministry kept two divisions in Manchuria to protect Japanese lives and property until 1910. Thereafter an independent garrison unit of six reserve battalions defended Japanese interests until regular units replaced them in 1916. Army Order No. 12 in 1919 activated the Headquarters, Kwantung Army to control the 10,000-man garrison. Together with the China Garrison Army, the units in Manchuria afforded the army permanent forward operating bases in China. Korea soon came completely under Japanese control, adding still another mission for the army. In response to this expanded mission, generals demanded a larger force structure to deal with the new responsibilities. Adm. Tōgō's epic victory at Tsushima elevated the navy to a coequal status with the army, and the services had to reconcile their respective differences over requirements, potential opponents, and theaters of operations with an overarching national military strategy. A new generation of army leaders had to grapple with all these issues while it ensured that the institution's prominence in state affairs would continue.

7

Institutionalizing National
Military Strategy

The Meiji ruling elite—the civilian or military oligarchs—all came from the samurai class, shared common values and national objectives, and in many cases had known each other for decades. The rise of military professionalism during the late nineteenth century altered the status quo by placing a premium on specialized knowledge, a far different criterion than the personality-based army cliques dominated by officers from the former Chōshū and Satsuma fiefs. The next generation of army leaders had to compete for power with other emerging elites, particularly the political parties, which had their own agendas. Frustrated by nepotism and determined to break the regional cliques' stranglehold on power, the army's up-and-coming leaders contested not only the political parties but also their military institution as it struggled to integrate new ideas and technologies while preserving its traditional core identity.[1]

The army's first priority was to protect Japan's recently acquired concessions. Some officers believed Russia's defeat had secured Japan's northern frontiers and that future expansion should occur in central China or the South Seas. Others insisted Russia wanted revenge and remained a threat. The government's position was equally ambiguous. When signing the Russo-Japanese commercial treaty of 1907, for example, Prime Minister Saionji Kinmochi's cabinet appended a secret protocol that placed southern Manchuria in Japan's sphere of influence, thereby committing Japan not simply to preserving the status quo in Korea but to expanding its influence northward into Manchuria. In other words, there was no consensus between cabinet and army on national defense strategy.[2]

During the immediate postwar years, army leaders repeatedly appealed to Japan's special characteristics when crafting military strategy and tactical doctrine. But planning for the army's postwar expansion threatened the consensus forged by its founders. Competing visions of a future army and future warfare divided army leaders into those who favored modern, industrial, machine warfare and those who believed that traditional combat relying on manpower and morale could overcome a materially superior opponent.

Disagreements within the army over force structure reflected the philosophical differences in styles of warfare. The army had mobilized twenty-five divisions (seventeen active and eight reserve) during the Russo-Japanese War, yet personnel shortages had still stripped the nation of its strategic reserve.[3] To prevent a reoccurrence, the ever-cautious Yamagata, convinced that Russia would seek revenge, wanted a fifty-division force structure (twenty-five active and twenty-five reserve divisions).

Army Chief of Staff Kodama insisted that equipping and sustaining that many divisions would exceed the nation's industrial capacity and would ruin the national economy. He proposed a modest two-division increase in the active forces and a thirty-eight-division force structure (nineteen active and nineteen reserve) whose modernization would improve mobility and artillery firepower. Kodama's quest for quality over quantity ended with his sudden death in July 1906, just three months after he became chief of staff. The long-serving War Minister Gen. Terauchi Masatake, a Yamagata protégé, sided with his mentor and in October submitted the fifty-division proposal with requirements for rearmament and modernization to the emperor.[4]

During the first half of 1906 Lt. Col. Tanaka Giichi, the operations branch chief, had tried to mediate the increasingly bitter dispute between Kodama and Yamagata over the postwar army's size. Tanaka hoped to avoid a repetition of the wartime interservice rivalry and divided command structure by devising an agreed-upon national defense strategy that would integrate political and military strategy, coordinate military expenditures with the economic productivity, and serve as the basis for joint operational plans to meet the rapidly changing international situation. Like Yamagata, Tanaka sought to institutionalize the army's paramount strategic offensive role on the Asian continent to justify its budget requirements. Otherwise interservice rivalry, the navy's recent wartime popularity, and the growing influence of naval theorists might interfere with army expansion.[5]

Yamagata reworked Tanaka's ideas and, in his capacity as a member of the Board of Field Marshals and Fleet Admirals, that October presented his plan to the emperor, who in turn ordered joint studies to designate a primary hypothetical enemy. Beginning in mid-December the service staffs exchanged written proposals about the operational use of forces for national defense and by mid-January 1907 had met five times to discuss four fundamental issues: (1) identifying the objective of national defense, (2) aligning military strategy with national strategy to coordinate political and military goals, (3) formulating a joint strategy, and (4) determining the appropriate force structures. Three disagreements emerged between the services; the designation of hypothetical enemies Russia for the army and the United States for the navy; the adoption of the army's continental offensive strategy versus the navy's deep water strategy; and the distribution of resources, especially budget shares.[6]

Tanaka had originally expected the services to work with the prime minister to formulate a comprehensive political-military strategy. Yamagata and other army leaders, however, invoked the prerogative of supreme command to exclude civilian participation in operational military matters. Military authorities did discuss the general outline of their draft policy with Prime Minister Saionji, but they only allowed him to see the section outlining their force structure requirements. Even that concession was made grudgingly because the cabinet would need the specific information on service expansion to justify the budget it would present to the Diet.[7]

Emperor Meiji approved imperial defense policy in April 1907 and issued it to the respective chiefs of staff as imperial guidance. The document had three sections: general military strategy, the force structure needed to execute the strategy, and the operational plans to employ the forces. Section one designated Russia as the army's primary hypothetical opponent and in deference to the navy also identified the United States as a likely opponent. It extended Japanese influence by expanding national interests in Manchuria and protecting development in Asia's southern regions. The army would conduct forward offensive operations on the Asian continent or joint operations in the Pacific. Aware of the dangers of protracted warfare, army strategists devised preemptive offensives to win the opening campaign decisively and end any conflict quickly. To win the opening battles, however, the army had to have sufficient forces immediately available to occupy strategic locations before the enemy could react.[8]

Section two set requirements for a fifty-division army (split evenly between active and reserve) and a navy with eight battleships and eight heavy cruisers by 1928. Because the services could not define a common opponent, they independently calculated their respective force structures based on differing hypothetical enemies. The number of divisions needed to win a war against Russia became the army's yardstick whereas the U.S. Navy served as the navy's standard. Neither service would compromise because of the possibility that Japan might have to fight both simultaneously.[9]

Section three assigned the navy the operational objective of destroying the enemy fleet on the high seas and the army to annihilate opposing ground forces in a series of rapidly conducted offensives. The army's theater of operations was Manchuria and the Ussuri River basin; the navy's the Pacific, although it also had to protect the line of communication to the continent and convoy army troop transports through the Yellow Sea. The navy's concession came with the caveat that a war against a coalition might make convoy escort impossible.[10]

Contrary to Tanaka's expectations, national defense policy codified strategic differences without resolving them. The services remained divided over their hypothetical enemies, their operational theaters, and their strategic objectives. Cabinet policies contradicted military ones. The army called for forward offensive ground operations on the northeast Asia continent that decoupled military strategy from the cabinet's foreign policy of promoting alliances, trade, and improved diplomatic relations to secure Japan's interests in northeast Asia. But international agreements might limit the army's freedom on the continent. Furthermore, civilian leaders saw the Anglo-Japanese alliance of 1902 as the linchpin of regional security, but the military gave primacy to unilateral action and relegated the alliance to a secondary role. Whereas civilian cabinet members identified Germany as Japan's main threat and promoted friendly relations with the United States, imperial defense policy ranked Russia and the United States as the most likely future opponents. The services' military respective strategies were also contradictory.[11]

Without a single strategic focus, the services developed plans and budgets independently, each seeking the optimum for its contingencies while dismissing the foreign ministry's holistic approach to Asia. Imperial defense policy of 1907 was at best two operational war plans—one army, one navy—that failed to address fundamental questions of common threats, available resources, and the proper integration of military strategy into a more comprehensive national strategy. These inconsistencies would never be resolved and became continual flash points between the cabinet and the military.

The army's desired force structure quickly ran into trouble. Prime Minister Saionji and Hara Kei, the leader of the Seiyūkai political party, were on record in mid-November 1906 opposing any increase in military spending for the 1907 budget because the late war had emptied the nation's coffers. Angered by the army's stubbornness during preliminary budget discussions, Saionji had threatened to resign rather than give in to the military's demands and informed the emperor that such an ambitious military expansion would bankrupt the nation. The army resentfully accepted two additional active duty divisions instead of the three it sought, and the navy agreed to refurbish captured Russian warships rather than build new ones.[12] With Japan's financial condition worsening in 1907, the cabinet adopted a retrenchment policy that forced the army to postpone its two-division increase for three additional years and the navy to suspend new ship construction for six.

The imbroglio with Saionji was only the latest in a series of clashes between the army and the political parties, which were gradually expanding their influence at the cabinet level. In 1898 Prime Minister Ōkuma Shigenobu had requested Meiji's permission to select a war minister from the inactive list because all the eligible candidates on the active list demanded a vastly increased military budget to pay for army expansion. The emperor refused, asserting that such action was beyond his purview, and the incumbents remained in office. Unable to work with the serving war minister, Ōkuma's cabinet collapsed within six months.

The new cabinet, headed by Yamagata, enacted legislation in May 1900 that restricted the war minister's portfolio to generals serving on active duty precisely to prevent the political parties from using the increasing number of retired general officers for political ends in the cabinets and to preclude dissatisfied retired generals from encroaching on the prerogative of supreme command as war ministers. The legislation institutionalized rather than altered the current informal arrangement, but it also handed the army the legal power of life and death over any cabinet.[13]

Army leaders had been wary of political parties since their inception in the 1880s, believing that parties were by nature divisive elements that invariably provoked friction and detracted from national unity.[14] Although parties had contested national elections since 1890, the struggle was for legislative control of the Diet, not executive authority in the form of a party cabinet. The oligarchs dominated the selection of cabinet ministers and the organization of the cabinets, which until 1918 were regarded, at least in theory, as nonparty entities. The parties gained influence by voting on the annual budget in the Diet. If they refused to enact the cabinet's submitted budget, by law the previous year's appropriation remained in effect. Because government expenditures, particularly for defense, increased each year, the ministers always needed more money. Regardless of the army's attitude about political parties, it had to have party support to pass the military budgets that the cabinet submitted to the legislature, and army leaders struck bargains with politicians to pay for military expansion and modernization.

In exchange for Diet votes, the cabinet and oligarchs worked a series of compromises with the political parties, including entry of party leaders into cabinets. In 1904, for example, Hara Kei and Prime Minister Katsura Tarō agreed that in exchange for the Diet's support of his wartime budget, Katsura would appoint Saionji prime minister in the postwar cabinet. This concession opened the way for party politicians to hold cabinet positions (see Table 7.1).

The violent popular demonstrations in Tokyo in 1905 against the Treaty of Portsmouth renewed Yamagata's fear of the mob and determination to curb the parties, especially the opposition Seiyūkai, which he felt bore a large measure of responsibility for the popular outbursts. For their part, Seiyūkai leaders tried to gain leverage over the army. In February 1907 the Diet enacted a law allowing the prime minister to countersign army orders submitted to the throne in peacetime (previously the army minister and vice war minister were the signatories).

Backed by Yamagata, War Minister Terauchi protested this break with custom,

Table 7.1. Military Budgets and Army-Navy Breakdowns, Selected Years, 1890–1914

Year	Budget	Military Share	Percent of Total	Army Share	Percent of Total	Navy Share	Percent of Total
1890	82,125	25,688	28.0	15,533	18.9	10,155	12.4
1893	84,584	22,822	29.3	14,721	17.4	8,101	9.6
1896	168,857	73,248	43.4	53,243	31.5	20,006	11.8
1900	292,750	133,113	45.5	74,838	26.6	58,275	19.9
1903	249,596	83,002	33.3	46,885	18.8	36,118	14.5
1907	602,401	198,316	32.9	126,044	20.9	72,272	12.0
1912	593,596	199,611	33.6	104,125	17.5	95,485	16.1
1914	648,420	170,960	26.4	87,700	13.5	83,260	12.8

Source: Tobe, *Gyakusetsu,* 109 and 137; extraordinary wartime budgets not included.

arguing that it would violate the independence of supreme command. That September newly enacted war ministry regulations excluded the prime minister from the process. The war minister alone could countersign orders or ordnances in his role as an adviser directly responsible to the emperor, and he could also present these documents directly to the throne. Saionji and senior statesman Itō Hirobumi questioned the constitutionality of military regulations that denied the emperor the advice of his senior civilian advisers, but after listening to Itō debate the point with Yamagata, the emperor authorized the revisions.[15]

Haggling also continued between the legislature and the army over force structure, aggravated by the navy's demands for a larger share of the military budget. Japan's formal annexation of Korea in 1910 revived the army's justification for two additional divisions to protect the new colony and be positioned for forward offensive operations. Simultaneously the navy wanted to increase the size of the fleet because it faced multiple threats from the combined fleets of the United States, Great Britain, and Imperial Germany.[16]

During these struggles with the Diet the army benefited from the long tenure of War Minister Terauchi, who served from March 1902 to August 1911, with a concurrent appointment as governor-general of Korea from October 1910. Terauchi, a skilled military bureaucrat, was arrogant, often browbeat opponents, and used his web of connections and knowledge of the bureaucracy to outmaneuver the legislature in his quest for the additional divisions. He also enhanced the authority of the war ministry at the expense of the general staff and blatantly favored his Chōshū clansmen, awarding them plum assignments and choice commands throughout the army.[17] In 1911 Terauchi resigned to devote his full attention to the pacification of Korea. His handpicked protégé replaced him but died a few months later, in April 1912.

The army then nominated two candidates for war minister; one was a protégé of Katsura Tarō, and the other, Lt. Gen. Uehara Yūsaku, was a Satsuma native. Saionji selected Uehara, described as "willful, egotistical, and jealous of his prerogatives." But he rejected Uehara's agenda for two additional divisions because the nation's grave financial condition necessitated increased taxes and sale of government bonds to redeem debts still outstanding from the Russo-Japanese War and to pay the heavy costs of incorporating the new colony of Korea and the Kwantung leased territory into the empire. Saionji's orders for a government-wide retrenchment program included an across-the-board 10–15 percent budget cut. Uehara promptly resigned, an act that made him a political martyr to the army and enhanced his following within the officer corps.[18]

Army leaders refused to nominate a successor, and with no active duty officer willing to accept the portfolio, Saionji's cabinet collapsed. The army, however, damaged its own case with the public by its heavy-handed maneuvering to bring down the cabinet and its attempt to manipulate the new Taishō emperor, who suffered from physical and mental disabilities, to force party leaders to form a new cabinet sympathetic to military expansion. These actions precipitated the so-called Taishō Political Crisis of 1912–1913. Nationwide popular demonstrations to protect constitutional government, fueled by the press and political party activists, forced the army into retreat. Besides its inept political performance, the military also ignored the heavy burden imperial defense was imposing on the nation's financial health. The army's political assertiveness was an embarrassment, and it had only limited success in reasserting its prominence in society into the 1920s.

When Adm. Yamamoto Gonbei organized a reform cabinet in June 1913, the army was still reeling from the aftershock of the Taishō Political Crisis and the spectacle of mobs in the street. With the arbitrary concurrence of War Minister Kigoshi Yasutsuna, Yamamoto eliminated the proviso that only active duty officers could serve as war minister and searched the inactive list for a suitable candidate. This undid Yamagata and Terauchi's earlier work and infuriated general staff officers because Kigoshi had agreed to the revision without consulting them. Indeed, the approving document's coordination column, usually red with the seals of the various army bureaus, was blank. Army leaders ostracized Kigoshi, causing his premature retirement.[19] The army further reacted to Yamamoto's decision by reorganizing its command structure to divest power from the war minister and redistribute it to the chief of staff and inspector-general of military education. Mobilization planning and operational matters were shifted from the war ministry to the general staff; personnel and doctrinal issues were decided by the ministry, staff, and inspectorate; and the inspector-general took charge of doctrine and training.

Tactical Doctrine

Postwar analysis of the army's performance in the Russo-Japanese War sought indigenous attributes to explain its victory and found them in real or imagined traditions. Army leaders officially attributed victory foremost to spiritual elitism (élan) and only secondly to the proficiency of the troops.[20] Military schools throughout the army taught this narrative of the conflict, and almost all officers studied the orthodox interpretation and lessons of the war.

Officer education stressed mobile warfare and encirclement operations and preached that a small force (like Japan's in the recent war) could defeat a superior opponent.[21] Strategists crafted plans for a classic double envelopment and fast-moving battles of annihilation that ignored the army's inability to envelop major enemy forces in any battle during the recent fighting. In part the operational concept derived from their awareness that Japan could not win a prolonged war against superior opponents; in part the short, decisive war philosophy was imbedded in newly drawn imperial defense policy.

Between 1906 and 1909, tacticians developed an aggressive offensive doctrine to complement imperial defense policy. The army had waged war against Russia according to its 1898 infantry manual, derived in large part from the 1885 German field service regulations. Both asserted that firepower secured victory in infantry combat. A lessons-learned commission established in 1906 to analyze and distill the wartime experience thought differently. Members overlooked evidence that only a handful of bayonet attacks succeeded and none had carried a fortified emplacement to conclude that the bayonet was the decisive weapon against enemy troops in hardened positions. That July the inspector-general of military education endorsed the merits of a bayonet charge and further recommended that infantrymen had to advance regardless of artillery support in order to retain the initiative and momentum of the assault.[22]

This preference for cold steel reflected the repeated frustration over the lack of infantry-artillery coordination during the war. Shell shortages, serious problems in quality control that resulted in numerous dud shells or unexploded ordnance, inappropriate guns or ordnance, and the artillery's immobility diminished confidence in the destructive power of heavy artillery to support infantry assaults. Artillery specialists pointed out that the shell shortage—a logistical problem, not an operational one—forfeited opportunities to inflict heavier casualties on the Russians or close off lines of retreat by fire. But there was a widespread loss of confidence in artillerymen, and even senior artillery officers concluded that deficient artillery doctrine had hampered combined arms interaction.[23]

Immediately after the war, Kodama had called for more firepower delivered by an artillery brigade organic to the division and a heavy field artillery brigade attached to each corps. Manufacturing, transporting, and sustaining more and heavier artillery were beyond the capability of Japan's industrial infrastructure. Heavy industries—steel making, chemical, and metallurgy—lagged far behind European and American standards and output, and until the early 1930s the majority of Japanese factory workers were employed in the textile industry. These cold production factors, internal army disputes over doctrine, and the lack of confidence in artillery ultimately caused the war ministry to reduce the number of guns per division.[24]

The army's major rationale for a fundamental shift from intensive firepower to hand-to-hand combat, however, was the supposedly unique Japanese qualities that endowed infantrymen with intangible advantages. A determined infantry attack displaying these attributes would compensate for inferior numbers and equipment. Preliminary findings in May 1907 anointed the infantry the primary combat arm, mandated that infantrymen attack even without artillery support, and elevated hand-to-hand combat to the decisive ingredient for victory. The next month an army board, echoing the inspector-general, validated the utility of the bayonet charge and instructed troops to press home attacks without waiting for artillery support.[25]

In January 1909 Maj. Gen. Nagaoka Gaishi, chief of the military affairs bureau, propounded a set of fundamental principles that with minor revisions became the bedrock of future Japanese tactical doctrine. He claimed that Japan's unique history and culture (*kokutai*), combined with national characteristics and geographical setting, determined the nature of the army. Army regulations and training would incorporate these intangibles (spiritual power, or *seishin*) to enhance technical proficiency gained from military training. Infantry was the decisive arm in combat, the spirit of the attack the basis of warfare, and hand-to-hand combat the decisive factor in battle. Nagaoka's precepts became doctrine in the revised October 1909 infantry manual.[26]

Officers and Conscripts

Since the advent of conscription, army leaders, mainly of samurai stock, questioned the fighting qualities of the enlisted ranks. Confronted by real warriors during the Satsuma Rebellion, the conscript army had performed poorly, at least in the eyes of commanders, because the troops lacked fighting spirit. Reorganized drill and training attempted to instill that intangible virtue, but the high command always suspected that the conscripted infantryman was capable of improved battlefield performance.

Examples of units that broke and ran under fire or failed to take assigned objectives because of an apparent lack of offensive spirit during the recent war disconcerted the high command and reinforced its traditional lack of confidence in the conscripts. Many senior officers felt that the rank-and-file soldiers failed to display sufficient spiritual power or morale in battle, and anecdotal observations of wartime conduct of infantry units confirmed their impressions. Improved spiritual education and training were essential to overcome the lackluster performance in combat, and after 1909 the emphasis on élan and morale became an obsession. According to the conventional army wisdom, iron discipline exemplified by unquestioning obedience to orders was the sole means to enhance spiritual power and inculcate confidence in victory.[27]

Another reason the army imposed harsher discipline was to counteract postwar societal and popular trends toward greater individual expression. An upsurge in insubordination and widespread evidence of lax discipline in the ranks in the immediate postwar period deeply troubled army leaders, who were quick to single out the baleful influence of the socialist movement for the decline of standards. Officer and NCO combat veterans were convinced that unrelenting discipline, stoical endurance, and unquestioning obedience to orders enabled them to survive on the unforgiving Manchurian battlefields, and they were determined to inculcate these virtues into their successors. To reassert these values, the army revised the 1888 squad regulations, which governed the peacetime garrison routine. Intensive physical conditioning, weapons proficiency, and demanding tactical training augmented by the spirit of the attack would enable a smaller army to defeat a larger one. Harsh physical discipline and uncompromisingly rugged training designed to make everything simple in battle became the postwar army's hallmarks.[28]

The revised squad regulations, published in 1908, extolled the army as a family whose goal was to nourish spiritual values, military discipline, and unquestioning obedience to superiors. The company commander adopted the role of the strict father, the NCOs that of the loving mother, and the enlisted troops were the children under their care and tutelage.[29] The approach romanticized enlisted life in the barracks, describing it as a place where young soldiers shared joys and sorrows together and lived and died together in the army family.

Company grade officers (captains and lieutenants) and NCOs adopted stricter oversight of daily life in barracks to enforce the regulations. NCOs took direct control and supervision of the daily life of conscripts, training them in tactics and demanding unforgiving discipline and absolute obedience to orders, whose ultimate source of authority was the emperor.[30] The direct link to the throne was layered over a tactical doctrine that placed a premium on aggressiveness, harsh training, and racial superiority. As soldiers of the emperor, they were beyond reproach and morally superior to their civilian counterparts.

Squad regulations institutionalized informally administered corporal punishment, hazing, and abuse in the barracks. The tough new regimen likely accounted for a dramatic increase in suicides in the army, which peaked in 1909 at ninety-eight cases, a rate of thirty-six per 10,000—more than two-and-a-half times the national average. Although no clear motive was apparent in more than half the suicides, army authorities attributed the remainder to confusion about spiritual training (22 percent) and remorse (12 percent).[31]

The renewed stress on discipline coincided with the army's expansion. The percentage of the eligible 20-year-old cohort conscripted rose steadily from 5 or 6 percent between 1889 and 1894 to around 10 percent in 1897 and about double that after the Russo-Japanese War, where it remained into the 1930s.[32] Expansion inevitably diluted the overall quality of the force, but the changing type of conscripts was more troubling to the army.

During the nineteenth century the army had represented modernity, especially for conscripts from rural Japan. It exposed them for the first time to, among other things, western clothing and diets, indoor stoves, electric lights, and beds. Peasant soldiers who transmitted these cultural phenomena to their villages were respected for their modernity and cosmopolitanism. As the population gravitated to the cities (by 1920 one-quarter of the population lived in urban areas), however, traditional values identified with the countryside were eclipsed as progress and modernity became centered in the cities.[33] The new conscript of the 1910s was likely drawn from an urban setting and was better educated as well as more politically conscious than his prewar comrades. Young men arrived at army depots with critical attitudes, widely differing perspectives, more spontaneous personalities, and degrees of independence that required adjustment to the training regimen.[34]

The army might regard criticism as subversive to morale and discipline, but it still had to shape the new type of conscript into a fighting soldier. The 1913 revised barracks regulations toughened the already strict discipline within the platoon in the barracks to train conscripts in *seishin* and obedience. The manual condoned informal and unofficial violence to enforce regulations and discipline within the barracks' confines as institutionalized violence eventually affirmed a soldier's aggressiveness as expressed in spontaneous mayhem.[35]

Though the army praised rural values, it preferred young men with formal education and conscripted proportionately more primary school graduates than were represented in the annual cohort. To take one example, in 1909 less than 1 percent of conscripts were semi- or totally illiterate versus 17 percent of their cohort. Furthermore, army training enabled even poorly educated conscripts to acquire technical skills and knowledge that ranked them above the standard educational levels of the general public. Evolving infantry tactics, for instance, demanded initiative and the exercise of independent judgment, technical proficiency, and some supervisory ability.[36]

A new wave of ideas from the West—initially anarchism and socialism and later democracy and communism—washed over Japan and threatened to engulf the official state orthodoxy. The government reacted by reinforcing the concept that Japan was a family in possession of unique moral attributes by virtue of each subject's connection to a divine emperor. *Kokutai*, the national structure of Japan, was the repository of special values conferred on the nation by an unbroken imperial line descended from the gods.

Before the Russo-Japanese War the army had a narrow base of popular support, and in the postwar years it attempted to enlarge and energize a constituency to advocate its ambitious expansion and rearmament plans. Veterans were a natural advocacy group, and in 1910 Col. Tanaka Giichi, military affairs section chief, created the Imperial Reservist Association to spread army ideology, organize reservists' support for army policies, and strengthen army ties with rural society. Tanaka's goal was to spread military values as widely as possible to the civilian community, and by integrating the reservist association into the existing social order, he restructured the army's societal base of support, created an activist pro-army pressure group, and expanded support at the village level.[37] The association became the umbrella organization that incorporated the thousands of local reservist groups into a centralized system.

Active-duty service was not a prerequisite for membership, although members did have to pass the army's preinduction physical, which enabled young men assigned to the reserves to join. By 1918 the IRA national headquarters supervised more than 13,000 branches, with 2.3 million members, about half of whom had neither served on active duty nor received more than cursory basic training. The association thrived in rural areas, where it served social functions in closely knit small communities. Urban branches attracted fewer members, but they tended to be more committed to the organization's political agenda and nationalistic goals.[38]

Army leaders also grasped that mandatory schooling offered the state the opportunity to inculcate patriotic, nationalistic, and military values into schoolchildren because education was a citizen's obligation and duty to the state. Formal education for most young men ended around age 14 or 15, leaving a five-year gap until they were eligible for conscription. In 1915, Tanaka, with home and education ministry cooperation, organized the Greater Japan Youth Association to fill this void by indoctrinating the youths in military, ethical, and patriotic values. Accompanying physical training and military drill under reserve officers and NCOs prepared the young men for their future military service. The association also played an important local role as a community service organization.[39] This grassroots effort to popularize the army from the bottom up coincided with a strategic reassessment that would reshape the institution from the top down.

World War I and the 1918 Revision to Imperial Defense

After the outbreak of World War I in Europe in August 1914, Japan joined the war on the side of the Entente Powers (Britain, France, Russia) but initially took minimal action against the opposing Central Powers (Germany, Austria-Hungary, Italy). The European belligerents had anticipated a short, decisive conflict, but by early November it was dreadfully apparent that their expectations had been wrong. Faced with a protracted war of attrition, British diplomats sounded out the Japanese foreign minister on the possibility of sending fifteen divisions to reinforce the western European front. The cabinet had no intention of committing the bulk of the standing army to such an overseas adventure, and army leaders hastened to add that transporting that many divisions to Europe would require two million tons of shipping, which was unavailable because of the current wartime demands. Japan instead bolstered its military position in China by seizing the German fortress at Qingdao on the Shandong Peninsula in late 1914 and in the Pacific by occupying lightly defended German colonial outposts north of the equator.[40]

The six-week Qingdao campaign cost the army approximately 1,400 casualties, including about 400 killed. Veteran commanders of the Russo-Japanese War expected rapid movement to contact and hand-to-hand combat. Instead, artillery and engineers dominated siege operations to reduce the skillfully defended fortress. The army's very limited experience with new technologies—machine guns, airplanes, and antiaircraft defenses—revealed that Japanese aircraft were inferior even to the few obsolete German planes, wireless communications were substandard, and rear area logistics were constantly teetering on the verge of collapse.[41]

The approximately 5,000 German soldiers and sailors captured during the campaign were held at more than a dozen prisoner-of-war stockades scattered throughout Japan. They received good treatment during their three years of captivity, as evidenced by a death rate of about 1 percent for the period.

The totality of the war in Europe diverted western attention, resources, and commerce from their colonial possessions and markets in Asia. Japanese merchants quickly filled the void, displacing British textiles in the Chinese and Indian markets. The fall of Qingdao extended Japan's presence in China, and in January 1915 the Ōkuma Shigenobu cabinet tried to entrench Japanese influence in China by imposing the Twenty-One Demands, whose acceptance would have reduced China to a semicolony of Japan. Western displeasure, especially from the United States, caused Tokyo to back away, and Ōkuma resigned in October.

In exchange for the political support it received from the Seiyūkai Party, the new cabinet of Marshal Terauchi Masatake (October 1915–September 1918) established the Provisional Foreign Affairs Research Committee in June 1916, with the presidents of the political parties as members. The committee was the highest national policy deliberative group during and immediately after World War I. By the time the cabinet abolished the committee in 1922, it had formulated policy for the Siberian Expedition, the Paris Peace Conference, and the Washington Conference on Naval Limitations. Indicative of Japan's ambiguous wartime role, the services did not establish an imperial general headquarters to direct the war effort.[42]

Army officers naturally took a keen professional interest in the European war, and in mid-September 1915, the war ministry established the Provisional Military Research Committee, whose broad charter included analyzing everything from grand strategy to small-unit tactics. One early observation was that Japan had to amend national defense policy because total warfare in the future would involve protracted struggles of national, not just military, endurance. As a consequence, in January 1916 the general staff authorized a military research committee to revise national military strategy and assigned Vice Chief of Staff Lt. Gen. Tanaka Giichi to chair the twenty-five-officer group.

Tanaka believed that the radically altered international situation and the interlocking system of national alliances demanded a wholesale redefinition of national defense policy.[43] His approach would preserve Japanese interests in Asia, but without the entangling military alliances that brought war to Europe (he did except the Anglo-Japanese alliance for naval reasons) or commercial treaties. Tanaka's goal was autarky, a world in which nations had to independently ensure their defense. But to achieve self-sufficiency, resource-poor Japan had to have unlimited access to China's natural resources. In other words, exploitation of China became vital to Japan's national interests.[44] The committee's various analyses and reports buttressed his sweeping proposal that identified China as vital to Japan's national interests and anticipated that Japan would simultaneously expand north and south in East Asia.

In December 1916 Tanaka approached navy leaders about a formal revision of imperial defense policy. Besides the new requirements of total protracted warfare, dramatic changes on the international scene threatened to isolate Japan in a highly unstable region. International reaction to Japan's annexation of Korea in 1910, condemnation of the Twenty-One Demands imposed on China in 1915, and apprehension about expansion into Shandong plus the seizure of German colonial possessions in the Pacific left westerners apprehensive about Japan's motives and expansion.[45] Furthermore, following the collapse of the Qing Empire in 1911, China had steadily disintegrated into warlordism, further worsening regional stability. Beyond those strategic realities lay the bottom line of military funding.

As long as the army and the navy failed to agree on a unified national defense policy, they would have to compete with each other for shares of the military budget. Service leaders worried that the political parties could turn the situation to their advantage, play the services against one another, and reduce the military's overall funding requests. To avoid the appearance of disarray, it was in the services' interests to resolve, or at least paper over, their differences in a reworked version of national defense policy that would eliminate the party threat. It took about one year to work out a new strategy agreeable to the services and acceptable to the Board of Field Marshals and Fleet Admirals as well as Yamagata.

Military strategy would still rely on forward-based offensive operations, and Tanaka initially envisaged a short, decisive conflict requiring fast-moving offensive operations.[46] Upon further reflection, however, he concluded that the age of short wars had passed and that the great powers had entered a new era of protracted warfare requiring the total mobilization of all state resources. This new awareness in theory made the nation subservient to the army because the military, not the politicians, would control national mobilization. It also made access to China's resources even more important for Japan's security.

Maj. Koiso Kuniaki, a general staff officer, reached similar conclusions in an August 1917 study compiled by the general staff's military geography section under his guidance. It addressed economic and industrial requirements of a total war state and deduced that Japan had to expand its national productivity and resource base during peacetime to prosecute a future war successfully. Koiso seconded Tanaka's assessment that unfettered access to China's natural resources was Japan's sole means to achieve these economic goals.[47]

Under Tanaka's direction these ideas merged in September 1917 when the general staff's first department synthesized Koiso's research with a May 1917 study of China's role in Japan's military preparedness into a basis for a revised national defense policy. The document acknowledged that future wars would be struggles of attrition that necessitated preparations during peacetime for a protracted conflict, not the traditional short decisive war. Japan therefore needed access to China's resources, a peacetime economic base fully convertible for wartime industrial mobilization, and personnel mobilization planning that geared the entire nation to wage total war.[48]

Also working in Tanaka's favor was Yamagata's shifting worldview. The army's elder statesman gradually grew less concerned about a Russian war of revenge and more interested in expansion into China. In October 1917 Yamagata publicly described the need for unified national power, not just the military power, and warned of an impending race war caused by western and American aggression in Asia. The Russian Revolution of 1917 and ensuing chaos further diminished Russia as a serious future opponent, and by the next year the army's strategic focus shifted to a policy of exploiting China's resources as an essential ingredient in a national effort to prepare for total war.[49]

After further discussions between army and navy staff officers, in the late spring of 1918 the army conducted a final review of the draft defense policy under the auspices of War Minister Ōshima Ken'ichi, Chief of Staff Uehara, and Prime Minister Terauchi. Terauchi's status on the active duty list allowed him to participate in military planning and made for greater unity concerning national objectives, particularly the need for the resources of China, between the government and military than had been the case in 1907.[50] After review and the Board of Field Marshals and Fleet Admirals endorsement, in June 1918 Emperor Taishō approved the revised policy.

The latest national military strategy posited Japan fighting against a coalition, likely composed of the United States, the Soviet Union, and China. It mollified the traditionalists by retaining the short-war concept of preemptive offensive operations for a quick and decisive victory, and it appealed to revisionists because early battlefield success would ensure self-sufficiency, which in turn would enable Japan to fight a protracted struggle. Some officers, like Maj. Gen. Ugaki Kazushige, noted the contradiction that peacetime preparations for short war complicated designing a national mobilization strategy to fight a protracted conflict. Others wondered why all the army's operational plans still presupposed rapid opening offensives to execute a short, decisive war since future warfare was no longer simply a matter of armies fighting one another but involved the mobilization of the state's entire war-making potential.[51]

According to the revised strategy, at the outbreak of war the army would deploy troops to defend Japanese interests and residents in China. It would seize strategic locations east of Lake Baikal and in joint operations with the navy occupy Luzon, Philippines. This required twenty-two divisions in peacetime and forty in wartime. Improved weapons and equipment would compensate for diminished manpower, making it possible to reduce the force structure. But the cost of army modernization more than offset the savings from personnel reductions.

The army would capture U.S. naval bases at Manila and Subic Bay but thereafter had no operational plan of campaign for a second stage of operations. As for the navy, one fleet would destroy U.S. Navy warships in Asian waters, another would escort army units to Luzon, and a separate third fleet, the main surface battle force, would defeat the Americans in a decisive naval engagement when they tried to retake the Philippines. Because the navy currently had two fleets, the new strategy required the enormously expensive construction of a new fleet.[52]

Increased tax revenues generated by the wartime boom had allowed the Terauchi cabinet to spend more on defense as part of a "positive economy" to promote national defense and simultaneously rebuild the domestic economy. Service budgets skyrocketed from about US$85 million, roughly divided between army and navy, in 1915 to US$324 million in 1920, with about two-thirds going to the navy for fleet expansion.[53]

Wartime prosperity soon turned to postwar bust. In October 1918 Prime Minister Hara brokered an agreement on the 1920 budget with War Minister Tanaka, Finance Minister Takahashi Korekiyo, and Navy Minister Katō Tomosaburō, who concurred that after the completion of naval expansion in 1927, the army's budget requests would receive full funding. This was the only time that the army and the navy ever agreed on a budget.[54] By 1919, however, public opinion had turned against defense spending and military expansion, an attitude subsequently reinforced by the international trend toward disarmament and Japan's 1921 financial panic.

Intervention in Siberia

During World War I, Japan had enjoyed great diplomatic and military leeway attributable to the battlefield stalemate in Europe and the Entente's need to replace its enormous casualties, which invariably brought western diplomats to Tokyo seeking military assistance. In August 1917 the French approached the Japanese ambassador in Paris about using Japanese troops on the Balkan front. A subsequent general staff study estimated that Japan would have to deploy forty divisions (a total mobilization) to exert a decisive influence on the European war. Even if this massive contribution secured recognition of Japan's wartime gains, it was not worth the investment because it would seriously weaken the nation at a time when Russia seemed in danger of disintegration and a separate German-Russian peace was likely. The disastrous Italian collapse at Caporetto in early November 1917 forced Britain to redeploy troops from the Middle East and Balkans to Italy, and London soon pressed Tokyo for troops to bolster either the Russian front or its weakened Mesopotamian theater.[55] The Americans and British were also seeking Japanese troops for a planned intervention in Russia.

Worried about postwar isolation over its aggressive China policy and under mounting allied pressure for troops, the army was unwilling to reject allied requests outright but set impossible conditions for supplying large forces. The general staff demanded an independent command, unilateral choice of its theater of operations (a decision to be determined in large part by the status of the Russian army), allied financing of Japan's operations (estimated at $1.5 billion annually), and 600,000 tons of allied shipping to move and sustain the Japanese expeditionary force. Furthermore, the allies would recognize Japan's rights in China and place the Trans-Siberian Railroad under Japanese control. The terms were intentionally outrageous because neither the army nor the cabinet wanted to gamble the fate of the nation on a far-away foreign war. Closer to home, however, the general staff was willing to take risks.

In November 1917 the Bolsheviks seized power in Russia, established the Union of Soviet Socialist Republics, and quickly negotiated an armistice with Germany. Civil war and disorder then spread throughout Russia. In December Japanese troops temporarily intervened in Vladivostok to restore order after fighting broke out between workers' soviets and local authorities. With conditions worsening, in February 1918 Vice Chief of Staff Tanaka Giichi secretly established the Military Affairs Cooperative Committee, composed of department and bureau chiefs from the war ministry and general staff, to prepare forces for Siberian operations. The committee doubled as a clandestine army headquarters and excluded political parties from interfering with its work.[56]

Tanaka at first enthusiastically supported armed intervention as a means to establish a buffer zone east of Lake Baikal and by putting additional pressure on China to exploit the natural resources of Manchuria. Uehara and the general staff saw the opportunity to rid Japan permanently of its traditional Russian enemy.[57] Yamagata and the Terauchi cabinet were more cautious, supporting involvement as part of an allied expedition to avoid a repetition of the international criticism created by Japan's unilateral and heavy-handed imposition of the Twenty-One Demands. In early March 1918 the Bolsheviks signed a formal peace treaty with Germany and then demanded that Czech army units then in Russia disarm. The Czechs, who were fighting on the Entente side, refused and occupied sections of the Trans-Siberian Railroad. Subsequent fighting between the Czechs and Bolsheviks became the pretext for allied intervention to rescue the Czech Legion.

Japanese naval infantrymen landed at Vladivostok in April, ostensibly to prevent the city's supply depots from falling into German hands and to protect Japanese nationals. Around the same time, the army was clandestinely arming anti-Bolshevik Cossacks operating from northern Manchuria. British and French preparations were under way to land forces at Murmansk in western Russia, and they requested that American and Japanese troops intervene in Siberia. The United States then proposed a combined American-Japanese expeditionary force not to exceed 7,000 personnel. The Terauchi cabinet, egged on by the general staff, approved the expedition in July, and Emperor Taishō sanctioned it in early August.

Japanese reinforcements soon exceeded the agreed personnel ceiling, alienating the Americans. The Foreign Affairs Research Committee, led by Seiyūkai chiefs Hara Kei and Makino Nobuaki, desired America's postwar cooperation and opposed additional reinforcements that might alienate the United States. Terauchi needed Hara's support for his cabinet policies and, following discussions with the Americans, agreed to limit Japanese forces to 12,000 men on condition that more reinforcements might be needed for operations beyond the immediate Vladivostok area. General staff officers used that loophole to dispatch more troops, citing the rapidly changing operational situation in Siberia to justify their action.

The 12th Division landed unopposed at Vladivostok on August 18, and the next day the division commander requested the general staff immediately dispatch reinforcements. The cabinet agreed to an emergency reinforcement of the 7th Division, then assigned to the Kwantung Army in Manchuria, and the mobilization of a third division. Hiding behind the shield of independence of supreme command, the staff thwarted the Foreign Affairs Research Committee's intentions, and soon three divisions were operating as far west as Lake Baikal. By mid-September, the 12th Division occupied Khabarovsk and continued advancing westward to the Amur River. Meanwhile, the 7th Division with Russian Cossack auxiliaries had moved from western Manchuria to seize Chita and link up with 12th Division cavalry units along the Amur. By the end of October the Japanese army's commitment had grown to 70,000 troops.[58]

The intervention soon turned sour. Army units occupied strategic nodes along the Trans-Siberian Railroad and became bogged down in a cruel guerrilla war against Soviet partisans. Alliances with notorious White Russian and Cossack gangs and consolidation of their holdings east of Baikal were crucial to the army's attempts to create an anti-Bolshevik buffer state, but they worked at cross-purposes with the western allies' objectives. The army raised further suspicions about the government's true motives by sending a large military force and expanding its zone of operations in Siberia.

In September 1918 rice riots, widespread popular outbursts against inflationary food prices, engulfed every Japanese prefecture as millions of demonstrators took to the streets and forced the government to call in the army to crush the most violent protests. Army officers who faced the demonstrations found the assignment distasteful, not for any sympathy with the mobs but because the sight of fixed bayonets confronting citizens threatened to undo a generation of public relations to develop a popular base of support for the military. Amidst worsening domestic conditions and growing labor unrest, army leaders were also keenly aware of popular complaints of the unfairness of sacrificing the nation's sons in the Siberian wastelands. Terauchi resigned, and Yamagata, frightened by the specter of the mob, agreed to support a new cabinet led by Hara Kei, leader of the Seiyūkai and an opponent of the Siberian adventure. Hara selected Tanaka Giichi, the serving vice chief of staff, for his war minister. The sight of the army mired in Siberia, American criticism of the army's excessive deployments, and growing popular disenchantment with the expedition had cooled Tanaka's earlier enthusiasm for intervention.[59]

By December the cabinet, with Tanaka's authorization, had sharply reduced the number of Japanese troops in Siberia. Uehara and Tanaka clashed over this decision and more specifically about the war minister's authority. Tanaka asserted that the expedition was not a declared war, so decisions regarding it were subject to the war minister's administrative control and the cabinet's direction. Uehara steadfastly contended that the war minister had no right to interfere in operational matters because they involved the prerogative of the general staff. Neither would budge, and the controversy left Tanaka irked by Uehara's dogmatism and Hara angered by the chief of staff's insubordination.[60]

Guerrilla warfare likewise dictated events. The 12th Division hailed from southern Kyūshū but in the 1918–1919 Siberian winter found itself fighting Bolshevik partisans around Blagoveschensk. Unacclimated and poorly equipped for a winter campaign, the troops looked more like vagabonds than soldiers. To keep warm they padded their cotton jackets with goat or dog fur, stuffed so much straw in their trousers that they bulged like pantaloons, tied strips of wool or cotton around their ears, donned hoods, and wrapped their boots in woolen cloth. In late February 1919 an infantry battalion so encumbered lost 300 men fighting Bolshevik partisans about 200 miles southeast of Blagoveschensk. Shocked by the stinging defeat, the army extracted revenge with a large-scale punitive expedition whose standing orders were to burn villages to deny the partisans shelter.[61]

In May 1919 Hara asked the western allies to recognize an anti-Bolshevik regime in Siberia backed by Japan. But the Soviet Red Army defeated the reactionary Russian forces supported by the Japanese army, and in August 1919 the anti-Communist regime collapsed. By that time the British had decided to withdraw from Russia, but the general staff in Tokyo wanted to send as many as 250,000 troops to prop up eastern Siberia. Finance Minister Takahashi Korekiyo curtly pointed out that such a deployment was unaffordable and would wreck the national economy, already under great strain. As the anti-Bolshevik front crumbled, Tanaka appealed vainly for reinforcements and Prime Minister Hara asked the Americans to supply more troops.

Instead, the United States withdrew its troops from Siberia in the spring of 1920, enabling the general staff to demand an additional division to replace the departing Americans. By this time the Czech Legion had completed its withdrawal, but the cabinet justified reinforcements because of the Soviet threat to Japanese interests in Korea and Manchuria. A subsequent massacre of Japanese civilians at Nikolaevsk in May enabled the general staff to keep troops in Siberia. By August the army began withdrawing troops from the Baikal district and northern Manchuria, but that October it launched a murderous operation to destroy the stronghold of anti-Japanese forces in northern Korea near the confluence of the Yalu and Tumen rivers. A two-month campaign marked by burning Korean villages, indiscriminate killing, and generalized violence was the last major operation of the Siberian expedition.[62]

In February 1921 Tanaka suffered a heart attack; to pave the way for his successor, Lt. Gen. Yamanashi Hanzō, he arranged for Uehara to resign so that a fresh chief of staff could work with the new war minister. In exchange, that April Uehara was promoted to field marshal and promised an appointment to the Board of Field Marshals and Fleet Admirals, conditional upon his resignation as chief of staff within a reasonable time. Yamagata, himself gravely ill, then changed the agreement and kept Uehara as the head of the general staff, leaving the ministry and staff as divided as ever over their respective powers and entrenching Uehara's traditionalist ideas in the staff.[63]

In November a publicity-seeking right-wing youth demanding reform stabbed Hara to death on a train platform at Tokyo Station. By the time the army finally withdrew troops from Siberia in late 1922, the expedition had been roundly criticized in the press and denounced in the Diet as wasteful of lives and money. The Siberian expedition and naval expansion in response to an international naval arms race drained half the national budget between 1919 and 1922, but after the conclusion of naval limitation treaties and army force structure reductions, military expenditures accounted for about one-quarter of the total budget during the 1920s. Arms reductions were the new measure of international stability and cooperation, leaving the army in a poor position to fend off critics because its Siberian misadventure cast doubt on its judgment, the traditional enemy Russia was gone, and Japan faced no threat in northeast Asia.[64] Moreover, army leaders were also divided over the implications of the revised 1918 national defense guidance.

8

Short War or Total War?

World War I's implications for warfare of the future became the source of intellectual debate and emotional controversy in Japan's postwar army. Officers grappled with the fundamental question of the military relevance of the European war for northeast Asia. Reform-minded officers believed that future conflict would be a total war and would require military, economic, and industrial mobilization on an unprecedented scale. Their more traditional-minded colleagues questioned that premise and the reformers' revised military strategy.

Traditionalists rallied around Marshal Uehara, whose long-standing support for a larger army, hard-line anti-Russian policy, and determination to preserve general staff prerogatives made him their natural champion. Uehara challenged the reformers' concept of total war on the grounds that Japan lacked the natural resources and the industrial base required for economic and industrial mobilization. He dismissed modernizers and industrial mobilization theorists because Japan's spiritual power and intangible forces compensated for any inferiority in quality and quantity of weapons. Although unable to silence the revisionists, he gradually replaced them on the general staff with officers who shared his convictions that a short decisive war could achieve national military objectives. Uehara's corollary was that Japan had to maintain its large standing army to win the critical opening battles of the next war.

Generals Tanaka Giichi and Ugaki wanted to modernize the force with new weapons, a new triangular division configuration for greater mobility, and more firepower. To pay for modernization, they would reduce personnel costs by cutting the size of the current force structure. The lines were clear; Uehara and his faction argued for the status quo and victory in the first battle based on élan and Japanese spirit while Ugaki and Tanaka advocated modernization and fewer troops.[1]

Army reformers also would replace the division as the strategic echelon with a corps organization by reorganizing the larger square divisions (two brigades and four regiments) into smaller triangular ones (one brigade and three regiments) augmented by additional artillery and logistics. A corps headquarters controlling two divisions would then handle logistical support for both and eliminate half of the current support troops. With smaller, 10,000-man triangular formations versus the 21,000-man square divisions, the army could also field more divisions and simultaneously outfit them with modern weapons and equipment. Uehara's traditionalists opposed conversion because the smaller units could neither operate independently nor sustain heavy casualties and continue to function.[2]

In June 1921 Lt. Gen. Yamanashi Hanzō replaced Tanaka as war minister as planned. Yamanashi's search for ways to save money by reducing army personnel and units reignited heated debate between traditionalists who envisaged a short, decisive war and reformers who anticipated a protracted total war. During October 1921 a special army committee met several times to calculate wartime force structure and logistics requirements.

The general staff wanted forty modernized divisions (seven against the United States, five against the USSR, twenty-two against China, and six in strategic reserve), but the war ministry believed that the weakened domestic economy and existing industrial infrastructure could support the modernization of just thirty. The operations division rejected any reductions, citing the adverse effect on army morale and concern that fewer divisions would allow the navy to claim a larger share of the military budget. A compromise would outfit twenty-one regular divisions with first-class weapons and equipment, gradually modernize eleven reserve divisions by 1933, and leave eight with obsolete weapons and equipment.[3] The agreement did not alleviate the underlying philosophical differences.

Uehara's dominant faction on the general staff advocated a short-war strategy because Japan lacked the resources either for protracted warfare or an arms race. The traditionalists made three points: (1) it would be very difficult to win a protracted war, but Japan could win a short war; (2) élan and spiritual power compensated for inferiority of weapons and numbers; and (3) it was vital to preserve the current large force structure for the first battle because victory depended on the ability to concentrate overwhelming forces to deliver a decisive opening blow. Modernization had to be accomplished without sacrificing force structure and personnel.[4]

Influential high-ranking officers like the highly opinionated Maj. Gen. Tanaka Kunishige, chief of the operations department, were unimpressed with claims for modernization because calculations of combat effectiveness had to include not only the quality of hardware (weapons) but also military élan, Japanese esprit, and the spirit of *bushidō*—the intangible ingredients for the victory over Russia in 1904–1905. Reliance on new weaponry and technology superiority was a European and American conceit, did not guarantee success, and was not easily transferable to the more primitive military and geographical conditions of Asia.[5] In fact, these multiple disparities were responsible for the distinct characteristics of the army's operational and tactical doctrine that were more appropriate against its hypothetical opponents than western ways of warfare.

In 1921 the war ministry established the Army Technical Headquarters Weapons Research and Policy Board to identify new weapons and equipment suitable for either positional or mobile warfare yet compatible with the army's current strategy and tactical doctrine. The board further evaluated the merits of animate versus mechanized transport in the rugged terrain and poor road network of the Asian continent. Following a natural tendency to distrust new, unproven technology and uncertainty about expensive, untested weapons and equipment, the board displayed little confidence in the reliability of mechanized or motorized forces operating on the primitive transportation infrastructure of northeast Asia. By using an inferior Asian standard as its baseline for designing weaponry for regional wars with backward nations, army leaders understood that they were falling behind western military trends of modernization as well as innovations in command and control and tactical doctrine.[6] It made little sense, however, to modernize ground forces to European standards when Japan would likely be fighting poorly armed Chinese warlord forces.

As these debates swirled, Yamanashi announced a two-stage reform in July 1922 that reduced personnel but not force structure. He accomplished this feat by removing one company from the peacetime table of organization of each infantry battalion and one troop from each cavalry regiment; he then eliminated 35 percent of artillery units, including three independent field artillery brigades.[7]

Many of the discarded artillery weapons were obsolete German-manufactured guns imported during the Russo-Japanese War. But Japan's preeminent artillery specialist, Lt. Col. Kobayashi Junichirō, who had been attached to the French army during World War I, lamented in 1923 that the failure to study European tactics, force structures, and the modern weaponry used during World War I might well cause the collapse of the national army. Lt. Gen. Tanaka Kunishige fired back by equating material power with defeatism and wrote to Uehara that officers like Kobayashi would destroy army morale by their excessive reliance on weaponry at the expense of elite fighting spirit.[8]

No one knew which of the many emerging new technologies might be suitable for future warfare and merit investment. Tanks, for example, had mixed results during World War I, and the postwar debate in Europe, the United States, and Japan reflected the misgivings about the proper role for the new weapon. The Japanese army worried that lack of roads and heavy load-bearing bridges in China or northeast Asia would further restrict the tank's already limited mobility. Japan's inadequate heavy industry base made it difficult to manufacture tanks, and the nation's narrow-gauge railroads made it difficult to move them. To support the army's forward operating strategy, tanks would have to be shipped from Japan to the continent. Size and weight then had to be considered in relation to a transport's loading and off-loading capacity. Balancing all these requirements, the army opted for light (10 tons or less) and medium tanks (15 tons or less).[9] One might question the decision, but it was appropriate for Japan's limited industrial base, the army's operational doctrine, and the likely future theater of operations.

Yamanashi conducted a two-stage modernization program in August 1922 and April 1923, but his concessions satisfied neither traditionalists nor reformers. Traditionalists reluctantly accepted the reduction of 62,500 troops because Yamanashi kept the twenty-one-division force structure intact. Modernizers wanted deeper personnel cuts but had to be satisfied that the resultant savings were used to create machine-gun battalions and an air squadron as well as modernize communications equipment.[10] In sum, Yamanashi's reforms did save money—an estimated 35 million yen annually—but they did not modernize the army.

The Great Tokyo Earthquake of September 1923 ended any hopes of larger military budgets because the government's priority shifted to rebuilding the capital city. The army did regain some popularity by restoring order and providing relief during the catastrophe, aligning itself as the people's protector, not their oppressor. In the aftermath of the disaster, Tanaka again took the war ministry portfolio and Lt. Gen. Ugaki Kazushige was appointed vice minister. Dissatisfied with Yamanashi's minimalist reductions, in December Tanaka Giichi appointed Ugaki to chair a committee to study army reorganization and modernization.[11]

A disgruntled youth's attempt to assassinate the imperial regent that December led to the formation of yet another new cabinet in January 1924, this one headed by Prime Minister Kiyoura Keigo. Kiyoura's choice for war minister was Gen. Fukuda Masatarō, commander of the Taiwan garrison, who came recommended by Marshal Uehara, Kiyoura's mentor and the army's senior active duty officer.[12] Uehara expected that Fukuda's appointment would reassert his waning prominence in the army.

Outgoing War Minister Tanaka blocked the selection by calling attention to Fukuda's lackluster performance as military governor during martial law imposed after the Tokyo earthquake.[13] Tanaka also enlisted the chief of staff and the inspector-general of military education, who, along with Tanaka, comprised the army's "Big Three" and were the only ones, according to Tanaka, authorized to nominate their successors. Several of Kiyoura's top advisers also opposed

Fukuda's selection, and ultimately the prime minister appointed Lt. Gen. Ugaki Kazushige war minister. Fukuda's rejection was a repudiation of Uehara and intensified his factional struggle with the Tanaka–Ugaki camp.[14]

The 1923 Revision of Imperial Defense Policy

Confronted with the postwar breakdown of the existing international order and increasing regional instability in northeast Asia, the services reexamined national defense policy. The Russian empire had disintegrated, eliminating the threat from the north. China also seemed to be breaking apart, despite international agreements to forestall such a condition. The new international system created by the Versailles Treaty (1919) and growing regional instability in northeast Asia also stimulated the army to revise national military strategy, and the Washington naval limitations agreement (1922) and the impending termination of the Anglo-Japanese alliance in 1923 exerted a similar influence on the navy. Besides these external pressures, the army was in the midst of a contentious restructuring of strategy, operational doctrine, tactics, and force structure. The best minds in the army were bitterly divided over the nature of future warfare, and their disagreements became interwoven with the army's approach to revising national military strategy.[15] The radically different concepts of national defense held by the competing factions shaped the formulation of the 1923 imperial defense policy.

Friction with the United States over the Siberian intervention, commercial rights in Manchuria, naval limitations, exclusionary immigration policies, and so forth made the Americans the services' likely common opponent. On that basis, in March 1922 representatives from the army and navy general staffs began revising defense policy.[16] The navy chief of the general staff, Adm. Katō Kanji, and his army counterpart, Gen. Uehara, were short-war proponents. Instead of thinking of ways to avoid a confrontation with the United States because of the great disparity of industrial production and untapped American potential available for a protracted total war, they believed that if Japan prepared completely beforehand, it could win a short war before the Americans brought their full power to bear. With the service chiefs of staff in general agreement, work proceeded quickly, and by November 1922, the army and navy general staffs had exchanged drafts of a revised imperial defense policy. Only in late February did the services allow the prime minister, a retired navy admiral, to see their revised force structure requirements. After discussions the same day, the cabinet meekly consented to the revisions. Six days later, on February 28, the draft was sent to the throne. The hastiness indicated a rush to justify short-term force structure, not the development of a comprehensive national military strategy.[17]

Because of the short-war operational emphasis, a large standing army was required to win the first battle just as a big navy was required to gain a decisive fleet victory. The general staff wanted a forty-division force structure; the war ministry recommended thirty divisions, with the savings put into building an air force. They compromised on twenty-one modernized regular divisions and nineteen reserve divisions armed with obsolete equipment. The navy sought nine battleships, three aircraft carriers, and forty cruisers.[18]

With these forces, the navy would engage the U.S. fleet in a decisive sea battle and the army would capture Guam and the Philippines to deny the Americans dry-dock and repair facilities in western Pacific waters. A strategy to occupy strategic bases and destroy the enemy ground forces fit perfectly with the traditionalists' short-war concept. A single sentence in the 1923 version of national defense acknowledged total-war theory but relegated it to a minor role.[19]

The general staffs concurred that the resources of East Asia were necessary for their strategic ambitions, but carving out an exclusionary zone would violate the spirit of the Washington Treaty and contradict government policy. Although the drafters recognized the likelihood of coalition warfare, they were preoccupied with the United States and left it to the politicians and diplomats to keep China and the Soviet Union neutral and prevent an alliance from waging war against Japan. With the army general staff and naval staff agreeing on these points, national defense policy shifted to a single opponent and a short-war strategy that failed to integrate national defense policy and national strategy.[20] What began as a response to a radically changed international order ended as a throwback to the original 1907 policy (see Table 8.1).

The Ugaki Reforms

Tanaka Giichi and Ugaki agreed that World War I demonstrated the necessity of preparing for a future protracted conflict. For that reason, they proposed still deeper force structure reductions so that during peacetime Japan could expand its heavy industrial base, diversify its economy, and indoctrinate the public with the philosophy of total war. During wartime, army offensive operations had to seize strategic assets at the outset of hostilities to enable Japan to fight a prolonged war. Traditionalists resurfaced their standard arguments that Japan would have difficulty fighting a protracted total war but could win a short decisive conflict; the number of regular divisions could not be reduced, and all had to be modernized to win the first battle; and spiritual power and nonmaterial factors could compensate for inferiority in the quality and quantity of weapons. Lt. Gen. Tanaka Kunishige, a division commander at the time, protested any force structure reduction because it would be a battle-axe blow to the army, lower popular awareness of national defense, and adversely affect national morale. Gen. Fukuda Masatarō, a member of the Military Board of Councilors, insisted that weapons alone did not win wars (see Table 8.2).[21]

Table 8.1. Imperial Defense Policy

	April 4, 1907	June 29, 1918	February 28, 1923
Purpose	Achieve objectives by offensive operations	Same	Offensive operations to rapidly finish situation; use diplomacy to avoid isolation and alliance to break enemy coalitions
Hypothetical Opponent(s)	Russia, then USA, Germany, France; maintain alliance with Britain	Russia, USA, China	USA primary enemy; combination of cooperation and military coercion against Russia and China
Force Structure (Army)	Peacetime: 25 divisions Wartime: 50 divisions (half reserves)	Peacetime: 21 divisions Wartime: 40 divisions	Peacetime: 21 divisions Wartime: 40 divisions
Force Structure (Navy)	First-line 8 battleships 8 armored cruisers	First-line 16 battleships 8 armored cruisers	First-line 12 capital ships (includes 3 aircraft carriers); 40 cruisers
Operational	Against Russia; offensive in Manchuria and Ussuri River regions Against others; first destroy enemy sea power, then move to next stage (planning pending)	Against Russia; occupy strategic points east of Lake Baikal Against USA; occupy Luzon; Against China; protect Japanese interests and citizens by deploying force	Preemptive offensive operations; seize Guam and Luzon Against Russia and China, same as 1918

Source: Kuwada Etsu and Maebara Toshio, eds., *Nihon no sensō zukai to dēta* [Japan's wars—maps and data] (Tokyo: Hara shobō, 1982), part 2 (appendix), table 1.

When Tanaka Giichi returned briefly as war minister in September 1923, he sought to implement his ideas on army reorganization by forming the Institutional Research Committee with his deputy Ugaki as chairman. For working purposes, the committee assumed that even when planning for a short, decisive war, Japan had to prepare for a protracted conflict. Military power became a single element that had to be integrated into national industrial, economic, and personnel mobilization for total war.[22]

Table 8.2. Competing Visions of a Future Army

Traditionalists	Revisionists
Large army	Small army
Low-tech	High-tech
Morale	Material
Short war	Long war
Bayonet	Firepower
Infantry	Combined arms
Win first battle	Endure protracted war
Military mobilization	National mobilization
Limited war	Total war
Square division	Triangular division

Ugaki became war minister in December 1923 but still kept a hand in the committee. A short war, he believed, might be possible against China, but a conflict with the Americans in the Pacific, the Soviets in the Far East, or the British and French in southwest Asia would necessarily be a drawn-out total affair. Ugaki reasoned that no matter how much planning went into a short war scenario against a single opponent the chances were good that Japan would have to fight a protracted war against a coalition. This led to the conclusion that the army had to prepare for industrial and national mobilization during peacetime by incorporating the latest advances in weapons technology and scientific applications to warfare.[23] The committee would accomplish these goals by eliminating four active divisions and the restructuring of other units. The army would invest the savings realized by the force structure and personnel reductions into modern weaponry—aircraft, tanks, antiaircraft artillery—as well as research and development.

Ugaki presented his army reorganization plan to the nine-member Military Board of Councilors in March 1925. Uehara and three others were opposed, and Gen. Fukuda raised the expected objections that Japan's industrial limitations should give added emphasis to fighting spirit and hand-to-hand combat. Ugaki, however, had previously stacked the committee by appointing five of his supporters, and they outvoted the Uehara faction five to four.[24] In May 1925 Ugaki eliminated four divisions, the Taiwan Garrison Headquarters, and two military preparatory schools (about 40,000 personnel) while he increased the numbers of radios and vehicles and established new schools to train personnel in their use. At the tactical level, he augmented the infantry battalion with more heavy machine guns and equipped platoons with a new light machine gun suitable for fast-paced mobile warfare.

Most of the savings, however, went to fund two tank units, new antiaircraft units, research and development expenses, and ten new aircraft squadrons (sixteen total), which were paired with the existing six to form eight air regiments.[25] The technical board deemed bombers less effective than artillery for ground support and only approved one light bomber regiment. The others were aerial reconnaissance and fighter units. The army turned to civilian industry to produce its aircraft and promoted competition for their design and manufacture. The Nakajima, Kawasaki, and Mitsubishi corporations, however, soon monopolized the fledgling aircraft industry.[26]

Ugaki's reforms reduced the term of conscription from three to two years in order to save more money but simultaneously build a larger reserve pool available for mobilization because conscripts would cycle through the active force quicker and then enter the reserves sooner. He placed officers from inactivated units into positions as military instructors in elementary and middle schools as drill instructors, extending the army's influence in the educational system in anticipation that the nation's schools would indoctrinate youth with accepted military values and patriotism to facilitate their transition as conscripts into the army barracks.[27]

Within two months Ugaki also forced three conservative members of the research committee to retire because of age or physical disability.[28] Uehara reacted by exposing a secret Diet slush fund established by Ugaki's patron Tanaka Giichi, but Ugaki managed to sidestep any scandal. He quickly appointed his supporters (among them Minami Jirō, Sugiyama Hajime, Koiso Kuniaki, and Tatekawa Yoshitsugu) to important posts in the war ministry and general staff but failed to eradicate Uehara's influence completely. The aging marshal rebuilt his power base around officers like Maj. Gen. Araki Sadao, operations division chief, general staff; Maj. Gen. Mazaki Jinsaburō, commandant of the military academy; and Maj. Gen. Hayashi Senjūrō, commander of the Tokyo Bay coastal defenses.

Finally, in 1926 Ugaki established the Young Men's Military Training Corps, a voluntary organization that offered civics education and military training conducted under the auspices of members of the Reservists Association to youths age 16 to 20 who had completed their formal education. Local communities organized and paid for these centers that offered 200 hours of annual instruction, half of it devoted to military drill. Regimental area commanders conducted yearly evaluations to measure military proficiency. The chief benefit of the programs was that qualified graduates who were subsequently conscripted could reduce their term of active service by six months. In exchange the army inculcated military values and virtues into large numbers of impressionistic youngsters.[29]

The Army's New Generation

During the Meiji era (1868–1912) eleven of the thirty-one officers who achieved the rank of full general came from the former Chōshū domain and

nine others were from Satsuma. Blatant pro-Chōshū bias and favoritism characterized Terauchi's nine-year tenure as war minister (1902–1911) and embedded Chōshū men in important war ministry and general staff posts. After World
War I, ambitious non-Chōshū affiliated officers were determined to break the
clique's stranglehold on senior army positions by reforming the army's personnel system and modernizing the force. Yamagata's death in 1922 weakened the
Chōshū faction, but its adherents were well entrenched, and their senior colonels and general officers regrouped themselves around War Minister Ugaki.[30]

In October 1921, Majors Nagata Tetsuzan, Okamura Yasuji, and Obata Tosh-
ishirō, three military attachés serving in Europe met at Baden-Baden, Germany,
where they proposed to eliminate army cliques by reforming the personnel system as part of a larger army reorganization. Inspired by German Gen. Eric von
Ludendorff's theories of total war and national mobilization, they envisaged
a revitalized Japanese army presiding over a nation mobilized for total war.[31]
After returning to Japan in 1923, the three, along with Maj. Tōjō Hideki, organized an informal study group of about twenty like-minded field grade officers
(colonels and majors) who were alumni of the fifteenth and sixteenth military
academy classes. Academy graduates were destined to lead the army, and they
competed fiercely for choice assignments and promotions. By the early 1920s,
many mid-career officers were dissatisfied with the army's personnel policies,
which they believed perpetuated Chōshū's institutional domination.

The informal discussions about army reform were held at a French restaurant
in Tokyo called the Futaba, and members called themselves the Futaba Club. A
separate group, members of the twenty-first through twenty-fourth academy
classes, started the Thursday Club in 1927, and its officers were soon debating
Japan's future role in Manchuria and Inner Mongolia. The two amalgamated as
the One Evening Society in May 1929, with membership restricted to officers
from the fifteenth through twenty-fifth classes who were currently assigned to
the war ministry or general staff.[32]

Nagata's group used the army's educational system to advance its agenda
by positioning members to block the admittance of Chōshū-affiliated officers
to the staff college. Only a handful of applicants passed the rigorous annual
competitive written and oral entrance examinations for admission to the staff
college. During peacetime those not selected served their careers in line units,
usually retiring as lieutenant colonels. At best they might lead battalions, but
they were ineligible for general staff assignments or large unit (regiment and
higher) command. Of course, army expansion during wartime opened promotions and command assignments to nongraduates, but staff college graduates
were destined for future high command, colonel or general rank, or high-level
staff assignments in either case. In short, selection to the staff college determined an officer's future.[33]

Several Futaba Club members became instructors at the staff college during the 1920s and 1930s, including Nagata (1923–1924) and Obata (1923–1926). Coincidentally or not, between 1922 and 1925 not a single Chōshū man qualified for admission, allegedly because the anti-Chōshū instructors failed Chōshū-affiliated candidates during the oral examinations. An exact correlation remains tentative because thirty Chōshū men did enter the staff college between 1927 and 1935, second only to the thirty-three candidates from far more populous Tokyo. Recent research suggests that Nagata played on the perception of Chōshū's domination of the army to divert careful scrutiny of his more radical ideas on army reform.[34] In any event, Nagata and other reformers also looked to younger general officers not affiliated with Chōshū for leadership and guidance and had high regard for Araki, an up-and-coming star, whom they expected to lead the army's renovation.

Large-Unit Doctrine

To remedy command and control problems exposed during the Russo-Japanese War, in 1914 the army issued *Principles of Command*. This translation of the 1910 German field manual for the command and control of large units became the doctrinal bible for corps and army-level commanders.[35] The general staff studied evolving large-unit doctrine during World War I as it related to technological advances in warfare, command and control improvements, battlefield mechanization, aircraft development, and total-war requirements. An ensuing wholesale revision of the army's field manuals formulated strategic, operational, and tactical doctrine for the first time in a comprehensive and integrated set of mutually supporting principles.

The revised 1921 *Principles of Command* acknowledged the implications of "the recent great advances in material warfare" but maintained that victory in battle ultimately still depended on intangibles like devotion to duty, patriotism, and willingness to sacrifice oneself to achieve objectives. Staff officers assumed that the next war would be short and culminate in the traditional decisive battle, but they did concede that fighting a protracted war of endurance would also require indomitable spirit. The resulting mishmash combined the contradictory strategies of rapid concentration of forces to open the war (an operational strategy designed to force a battle of annihilation) with preparations to fight a protracted war of endurance.[36]

During the postwar decade, the Japanese officers, like those in other major armies, pondered the role of firepower, mobility, and dispersion in future conflict. In the mid-1920s, the operations divisions, under Maj. Gen. Araki's guidance (May 1925–August 1927), produced the most far-reaching and influential revision of *Principles of Command*. An ideologue who believed in the intangibles of battle and a fervent anti-Communist, Araki selected like-minded younger officers as the principal authors to rewrite the manual. Lt. Col. Obata Tosh-ishirō, one of the Baden-Baden threesome, was a Soviet expert and admirer of German Gen. Alfred von Schiefflen's classic theories of wars of annihilation. He had previously served with Araki in the Guard Division and during World War I as a military observer in Russia, where the two had witnessed the 1917 Russian Revolution and were appalled at the chaos of the new Communist ideology that threatened Japan's imperial system. Maj. Suzuki Yorimichi, the top graduate of the thirtieth staff college class, who had served in France as an observer during the war, shared Araki's philosophy that spiritual or intangible values conferred special advantages in warfare.

Brilliant but arrogant, aloof, and impervious to dissenting opinions, Obata and Suzuki worked in secrecy to devise a doctrine termed by one historian as "intense spiritual training" and bayonet-led breakthroughs to compensate for inferior numbers and resources. Research on World War I campaigns, for instance, emphasized mobile warfare exemplified by the German's double en-velopment of Russian armies at Tannenburg in 1914 more than the positional warfare of attrition on the Somme or at Verdun in 1916.[37]

Unsurprisingly, the 1928 *Principles of Command* described fighting mobile battles of annihilation whose operational concept was a fast-moving, highly mobile offensive forcing a decisive battle early in the campaign. It embedded the dogma that élan and morale were the "primary causes of victory or defeat," a condition unchanged "from time immemorial," and made intangible qualities the linchpin of the army's modern doctrine.[38]

Araki's and Obata's influence also shaped the army's new combined arms handbook for the conduct of division-echelon operations designed specifically for northeast Asia operations. During the first postwar decade, the general staff sent more than 350 officers to Europe to study modern warfare. Their numer-ous reports covered topics ranging from squad tactics to large-unit operations and were the basis for the operations division's development of the combined arms manual.[39]

Araki chaired the committee that produced the original 1926 draft, and his strong feelings about the role of morale, élan, and the power of intangibles in battle pervaded the finalized 1929 manual. The fundamental premise was that an army possessing offensive spirit would defeat one relying on material. Mod-ern weapons and equipment were important, but nothing could be allowed to disparage the fighting spirit that gave soldiers total confidence in victory no matter what their material shortcomings. Commanders at every echelon would capitalize on fighting spirit to press home attacks that exploited enemy weak-nesses without waiting for approval from higher headquarters.[40]

Division and regimental commanders were expected to display initiative as they maneuvered to encircle the enemy to make possible the climactic assault with cold steel. To keep pace with a fast-moving infantry advance, the army designed light and mobile artillery. At the operational level, encirclement and night attacks were the ingredients of victory, and even outnumbered units were expected to envelop enemy flanks aggressively. Against fixed positions, units would advance under cover of darkness to avoid enemy artillery fire and position themselves for a dawn attack that combined firepower and shock action to overrun enemy positions. During a meeting engagement, commanders would maneuver to turn the opponent's flanks, surround the enemy units, and then destroy them. If temporarily forced on the defensive, commanders had to counterattack to regain the initiative. Tactical withdrawals to gain overall advantage, though not prohibited, did create a dilemma for Japanese army tacticians who could not even use the word "retreat."[41]

The ideas and concepts behind the higher-echelon doctrines were distilled into tactical form in the 1928 *Infantry Manual*. Certain World War I lessons were incorporated, especially the German infiltration tactics that appeared late in the war, but the revisions perpetuated bedrock principles of a Japanese style of warfare that exaggerated infantry tactics at the expense of combined-arms warfare. Victory, according to the manual, resulted from the combination of tangible and intangible factors found in "the magnificent tradition of Japanese arms."

Overpowering and destroying the enemy with cold steel—the soul of the offensive—would ensure a rapid victory. Attackers relied on surprise, shock, night attacks, and determination to press home assaults. Individual combat initiative was discouraged because success depended on concentrating firepower and manpower on narrow frontages to overwhelm defenders. Commanders had the responsibility to inculcate troops with a "belief in certain victory," the first appearance of that concept in any manual.[42]

Assault parties had to hold ground taken from the enemy, making a tactical withdrawal problematical. Even when the main attack faltered, soldiers had to fight to the last man, implying that surrender was impermissible. This philosophy in part accounted for Japan's refusal to ratify the 1929 Geneva Convention regarding the treatment of prisoners of war.[43] Nothing was allowed to impede the advance. Only officers could authorize soldiers to help wounded comrades, but after evacuating casualties to a clearing station they had to return immediately to the fighting or be branded cowards.[44]

The revised and new field manuals dovetailed their various components to distinguish a Japanese way of warfare characterized by the display of intangible assets inherent in national culture and tradition. By the end of the decade these concepts were embedded in the staff college curriculum and complemented an ingrained ideology of uniqueness that permeated the ranks from the highest echelon to the lowest rifle squad.

Training reinforced the certainty that intangibles would carry the day.

During field exercises, unsupported infantry units routinely penetrated the first line of Soviet defenses to depths of 1,700–2,200 yards. Maneuvers invariably revealed deficiencies in combined-arms cooperation (that was their purpose), but they always ended with an infantry breakthrough. In other words, exercises relied more on memorization of predictable tactical solutions than on imagination. Official army journals did criticize such predetermined results, and one officer reminded readers that the French army maneuvers before the Great War had likewise ignored the effects of firepower on the infantry advance and later paid a tremendous price in casualties during the real war.[45] They were dismissed as naysayers and swept away by Araki's passion for the intangibles of combat and Obata's contempt for the new Soviet Red Army as an inherently stupid military organization. These powerfully voiced opinions swayed the operations department to denigrate the Red Army's material superiority because of the Russians' supposed cultural inferiority. Obata's 1930 handbook for fighting the Soviets, for example, recommended a daredevil infantry frontal assault to break through enemy defenses. Of course not all officers were so sanguine about an offensive *a outrance*. An exchange officer with the Red Army alerted his superiors to the dangers of underestimating the Soviet military. He was in the minority. Obata dismissed the report as Soviet-phobic, and the mainstream officer corps enthusiastically adopted the unique Japanese way of war with all its intangible features.[46]

Officers, NCOs, and Conscripts

During the 1870s and 1880s, army officers were mainly from the former samurai class, but as commerce and industry expanded, the social base for officer recruitment widened to include the emerging middle classes. In 1890 about 40 percent of officers were commoners, and by 1920 that percentage had doubled. Military academy graduates included a high proportion of sons of military officers (35 percent in 1910), and these second- and third-generation soldiers were likewise overrepresented at the regional military preparatory academies.[47]

Following Ugaki's reforms, in 1927 a reserve officer system opened the way for commissions for middle-school graduates who had completed the school military training program. Officer cadets attended an eleven-month course offered at regional officer cadet schools, after which they served as cadet aspirants for four months with a regular unit. Upon successful completion of service they received commissions as reserve officers. Six years later the army abolished the provision that required volunteers to pay for their subsistence and uniforms, further expanding opportunities for commissions. Volunteers initially served four months on active duty, after which the army tested them and, depending on the results, accordingly divided them into A (officer cadets) and B (NCO cadets).[48]

Qualified graduates of the military training courses could volunteer for a reserve commission. They entered the army at a higher enlisted grade and, if they passed comprehensive tests after one year of service, matriculated to the officer cadet school for further training and commissioning as reserve second lieutenants. The officer cadet schools produced about 4,000 reserve officers annually in peacetime.[49]

The army selected its noncommissioned officers from those it allowed to reenlist and men who volunteered for active duty before being drafted. In 1927 it reestablished the NCO Preparatory School to train candidates. The school was initially restricted to the infantry branch but in 1933 expanded to include cavalry and artillery branch instruction. Other branches had their own preparatory schools or specialized training units for the purpose. By 1936 more than 14,000 young men had volunteered for NCO training, a national rate of about thirty-one applicants per 1,000 inductees, the majority from rural Japan. Volunteers spent a year training with their parent unit and a second year at the preparatory school. Upon graduation they assumed their NCO duties. Because of the Japanese respect for primogeniture, NCOs traditionally tended to be the second and third sons of farming or peasant families; during the economic downturns of the 1920s they had little prospect of employment at home and found a comfortable home and career in the army.[50]

The conscripts too were changing. Since the end of the Russo-Japanese War, the army annually inducted about 20 percent of the available 20-year-old male cohort. As Japan's population steadily migrated to the cities, the number of conscripts from farming backgrounds proportionately declined—from 75 percent of inductees in 1890 to 54 percent by 1920. Conventional army wisdom held that the city boys from the streets of Tokyo or Osaka made poor soldiers · and that their regiments suffered from low morale, lax discipline, and lackadaisical attitudes. The latest conscripts were also better educated, noticeably so after the state introduced six-year compulsory schooling in 1907. In the 1919 cohort (the last before mandatory education) more than 13 percent of those examined had not completed primary school; the next year that figure dropped to just 0.03 percent. So too did illiteracy or semiliteracy, from 30 percent in 1901 to a negligible figure by 1920.[51]

Although conscripts were better educated, the educational system had heavily indoctrinated them with state ideology that linked loyalty to the nation to filial piety and made them susceptible to further manipulation once in the barracks.[52] Draft resistance remained sporadic. Young men drank soy sauce the night before their physical examination to raise their blood pressure, others faked medical conditions, and some simply prayed to the gods for an exemption. Still, there was little outright draft evasion (between 2,500 and 3,500 cases annually among the more than 500,000 men examined), as most Japanese apparently had accepted the conscription system as a fact of life.[53]

Widespread antiwar sentiment during the postwar era, however, tarnished the military's self-image. Ideologies like communism and democracy appeared to undercut the imperial orthodoxy, which in turn diminished the army's status in society. A postwar economic depression devastated the rural communities, the source of the army's best conscripts. The Taishō emperor's physical and mental debilities and what leaders perceived as dangerous levels of lax discipline led the army to reemphasize imperial ideology.

The 1921 revision to the squad handbook sought to inoculate the barracks from the dangerous ideas and ideologies of postwar communism, democracy, and leftist philosophies. The manual first used the term *kokutai* (national polity) to accentuate the army's unique relationship with the throne along with a grassroots appeal to nationalism wrapped in contempt for other Asians. Stressing that *kokutai* and the unbroken imperial line conferred a sacred uniqueness on the army, authorities reaffirmed the army's intangible attributes of self-sacrifice, loyal service to the emperor, unselfishness, and courage to cultivate a distinctive ethos that distinguished the institution from the civilian culture. Conscripts were required to recite an abbreviated version of the imperial rescript (beginning in 1934 they had to recite the entire lengthy memorial). In an extreme, but perhaps predictable, case in 1936, a second lieutenant erred while reading the memorial to conscripts and later committed suicide to atone for his blunder. Coupling this nationalistic appeal with familial concepts that governed deportment built a powerful ideological bulwark against left-wing ideas.[54]

Authorities also enforced stricter discipline by equating the order of a superior to the direct order of the emperor that soldiers had to obey without hesitation or question. It was on that basis that an army court-martial acquitted three military policemen charged with murdering the anarchist Ōsugi Sakae in the aftermath of the 1923 Great Tokyo earthquake. Members accepted the defense's contention that the accused had no recourse except to obey a direct order from a superior and that to convict them would undermine army discipline.[55] In other words, military orders superseded the laws of the nation.

Hard-nosed training combined strict formal discipline with harsh informal punishments that hammered unquestioning obedience into recruits with fists, kicks, and hazing. As the notion of the "imperial army" and emperor cult became more pronounced, appeals to imperial symbols and imperial authority further reinforced unquestioning obedience to superiors, who were the transmitters of the imperial will. By the early 1920s, the term *kōgun* (imperial army) gained currency over *kokugun* (national army) in a conscious attempt by army authorities to link the military directly with the throne.[56] The result was a potent combination of politicized junior officers and malleable, unquestioning conscripts.

By the late 1920s the army had established on paper fundamental, integrated, and complementary doctrine for strategy, operations, tactics, and squad training. If strategy for a short war with a decisive engagement depended on forward offensive operations, then operations stressed aggressive offensive action based on tactics that stressed the attack, envelopment, and annihilation of the enemy army. The keystone tactical manual endorsed defense to the death to hold ground and sustain the attack. The squad regulations played on Japanese uniqueness to inculcate fighting spirit and absolute obedience to orders. This vertical integration of concepts permeated the army from its senior commanders to its lowliest conscript. Everyone was expected to fight to the last for an emperor who bestowed the uniqueness on Japan. Yet the army lacked a shared vision of future warfare. Reformers and traditionalists were divided over strategy—long war versus short war; over force structure and organization—large square divisions versus small triangular divisions; and over modernization—technology versus fighting spirit. Attempts by army leaders to resolve these institutional issues only accentuated fundamental disagreements and exacerbated factionalism at a time of escalating tensions with China.

9

Conspiracies, Coups, and Reshaping the Army

Convinced that control of China's resources was essential to the army's future strategic goals, senior officers were apprehensive in the spring of 1927 when Chiang Kai-shek, leader of the Guomindang and commander of China's Central Army, approached the Shandong Peninsula. Chiang's Northern Expedition had already fostered anti-foreign outbursts in central China, directed primarily against the British and Japanese residents, and army leaders blamed the foreign ministry's conciliatory policies for encouraging Chiang to take advantage of Japan's seeming weakness.

Then a financial panic following the collapse of the quasi-official Bank of Taiwan in April 1927 resulted in a change of cabinets. The new prime minister was retired general Tanaka Giichi,[1] who a decade earlier had identified access to China's natural resources as vital to Japan's national interests. Now the Seiyūkai leader and a hard-liner on China, Tanaka appointed his boyhood friend, Lt. Gen. Shirakawa Yoshinori, as war minister. Shirakawa's rise owed much to Tanaka's patronage, and the two worked closely together later that month when Tanaka, displaying his tougher stand, sent troops to Shandong to protect Japanese residents and commercial interests. After Chiang's defeat at Jinan by Manchurian warlord Zhang Zuolin, however, the Central Army forces veered away from Shandong, enabling Tokyo to recall its troops in August and end the First Shandong Expedition.

During the expedition, Tanaka had described his assertive China policy at a series of meetings, collectively known as the Far Eastern Conference (Tōhōkaigi), held in late June and early July at the foreign ministry. His new approach promoted regionalism in China to preclude the emergence of a united government capable of contesting Japan's continental ambitions and appropriate use of force to preserve Japan's special interests and to protect its citizens and concessions, especially those residing in Manchuria. Shortly afterward, at a mid-August meeting held at the Kwantung Army headquarters in Dairen, the deputy foreign minister (Tanaka was concurrently foreign minister) passed on the cabinet's willingness to interfere militarily in Chinese affairs to senior foreign ministry officials and army officers.

By the spring of 1928 Chiang had regained his traction and his armies were again advancing on Shandong. According to intelligence reports, rank-and-file Chinese soldiers, incited by inflammatory anti-Japanese propaganda, were plundering or burning Japanese-owned property and attacking Japanese residents. In mid-April Tanaka ordered the Second Shandong Expedition, expecting that a show of force near the port city of Qingdao would deter Chiang and prevent further incidents.[2]

After landing at Qingdao, however, the Japanese division commander unilaterally moved on the provincial capital at Jinan. Accepting exaggerated field reports of Chinese resistance at face value, Lt. Gen. Araki Sadao (promoted in July 1927), the director of the operations department of the general staff, and Maj. Gen. Koiso Kuniaki, the director of the general affairs department of army aviation headquarters, urged Tanaka to send reinforcements to salvage the army's reputation. Chinese and Japanese units clashed near Jinan on May 3, each side claiming self-defense. Five days later the cabinet approved reinforcements, but the same morning heavy fighting broke out near Jinan when a Japanese regimental commander arbitrarily ordered his men to fire on the Chinese. Two days of fierce fighting claimed about 3,600 Chinese casualties, most of them civilians, and Jinan fell to the Japanese.[3] Chiang again pulled out of Shandong, but a Japanese officer's intemperate action in the name of field initiative had sparked an incident that poisoned Sino-Japanese relations for years to come.

Some midlevel staff officers, including several China experts, felt Tanaka's China policy was not tough enough and that only eliminating Zhang Zuolin would resolve matters. Tanaka, however, had previously worked with Zhang, believed him amenable to fronting for Japanese interests in Manchuria, and insisted on aiding the warlord. When Chiang's reconstituted forces threatened Zhang's headquarters in Peking, Tanaka suggested the warlord withdraw to the safety of Manchuria.[4]

The Kwantung Army expected to disarm Zhang's warlord armies as they entered Manchuria and had repositioned units within its treaty-imposed railway corridor that ran from Port Arthur to Mukden. To move beyond that narrow railway zone required an imperial order, which Tanaka refused to request.[5] Alarmed by the specter of thousands of warlord soldiers streaming into Manchuria, sowing disorder, and intensifying anti-Japanese sentiment, Kwantung Army staff officers decided to kill Zhang.

The ringleader was Col. Kōmoto Daisaku, scion of a wealthy family and an experienced China hand, with service as military attaché at Peking and as the head of the China section of the general staff. With a sharp mind and a tongue to match, he cavalierly dismissed Zhang as an arrogant, ungrateful, and overbearing gangster who could be replaced by someone more favorable to Japanese interests. He decided to murder Zhang, blame Chinese bandits for the crime, and use the incident as a pretext for Japanese troops to take advantage of the disorder and overrun Manchuria. Kōmoto enjoyed tacit support from the army's highest authorities in Dairen and Tokyo as well as the sympathy of influential cabinet ministers and politicians.[6]

On June 4, 1928, an explosion along the South Manchurian Railway tore through Zhang's special railcar, mortally wounding him. The Kwantung Army disclaimed involvement, but within days Prime Minister Tanaka received a detailed account of the conspiracy. Shirakawa, having recently assured Tanaka and the foreign ministry that the army would not interfere in foreign policy, dismissed the report, but Tanaka still ordered a preliminary investigation. When the war ministry recalled Kōmoto to Tokyo in late June to testify, he officially denied any involvement but privately told several senior army officers the truth.[7]

Rumors of the army's complicity persisted, and in early September Tanaka ordered Shirakawa to open a formal investigation. Shirakawa had laundered money through the railroad minister for Kōmoto's use, and the two deflected any investigation on the grounds that it would damage the army's reputation and thereby imperil national security. Simultaneously, Prince Saionji Kinmochi, the last elder statesman or *genro*, was pressuring Tanaka to explain matters to the young new Shōwa emperor, better known in the West as Hirohito.[8] A comprehensive military police report that implicated Kōmoto as well as other Japanese officers reached Tanaka on October 8, and soon afterward a separate investigation confirmed the findings.[9]

While the investigations were in progress, the press and big business grew increasingly critical of the Shandong expedition, fearing that the inevitable Chinese backlash to the army's aggressiveness would provoke widespread boycotts of Japanese-manufactured goods. Tanaka did withdraw troops by October, but this only weakened his standing with cabinet hawks and the army. Under increasing pressure from his party, the army, and Saionji, in late December he reported to the emperor (who had been absent from the capital on official duties) about the army investigation under way and his intention to punish anyone involved severely. Hirohito agreed that harsh measures were essential to restore army discipline.[10]

By this time, Shirakawa acknowledged that Kōmoto had murdered Zhang, but he insisted that public disclosure of the crime would cause grave harm to Japan's national interests and subvert army discipline. In late March 1929 he recommended that the army handle the matter internally using administrative punishment and assured the emperor that the army's leadership backed this solution. Additional details of the plot gradually leaked to the public, and in mid-May the *Asahi* newspaper identified Kōmoto as the prime suspect.[11]

Army authorities officially continued to deny any involvement in the murder, and on June 27 Shirakawa reported their position to Tanaka. The prime minister upbraided Shirakawa, who stormed out in a rage, threatening to resign and bring down the government. Unwilling to self-destruct, the next day the cabinet endorsed the war minister's version of events. Shirakawa in turn recommended administrative punishment to Hirohito. When Tanaka went to the palace later that afternoon, Hirohito confronted him with the discrepancy between Shirakawa's plea for leniency and Tanaka's previous promises and suggested he resign.[12] Four days later Tanaka stepped down as prime minister. As for Kōmoto, on July 1 the army suspended him from active duty for misconduct, and one year later it seconded him to the reserves.

The army had placed its prestige above the law, justifying a cover-up in the name of national security. Generals had condoned a criminal conspiracy and assassination, tried to conceal evidence, and threatened to bring down the cabinet if the army did not get its way. A volatile mixture of the prerogative of field command, the decade-long emphasis on bold initiative and independent action, and an open contempt for the civilian cabinets and politicians became a familiar pattern in the army's continuing illegal attempts to achieve its domestic and international ends.

The Manchurian Incident

In October 1928 Lt. Col. Ishiwara Kanji became the operations officer on the Kwantung Army staff, due partly to Kōmoto's recommendation. After Kōmoto's relief in mid-1929, Lt. Col. Itagaki Seishirō replaced him as the senior-ranking staff officer in the headquarters. Ishiwara and Itagaki had known each other since their cadet days at the Sendai regional military preparatory academy and were the perfect combination of brilliant planner and man of action. Working with other midlevel staff officers assigned to the Kwantung Army, the two became the ringleaders of a conspiracy to seize Manchuria and create a Japanese-controlled puppet state.

Beginning in the spring of 1929, Ishiwara sponsored a series of covert reconnaissance forays to identify key facilities throughout Manchuria. He simultaneously devised new tactics to compensate for the overwhelming numerical advantage enjoyed by the forces loyal to Zhang Xueliang, the murdered Zhang's son and an implacable enemy of Japan. The centerpiece of Ishiwara's design was the rapid destruction of Zhang's Mukden headquarters and nerve center with a hard-hitting demonstration of shock and awe. Itagaki and Ishiwara coordinated with sympathetic officers assigned to the neighboring Korea Army and military authorities in Tokyo to insure their support. Col. Nagata Tetsuzan, chief of the war ministry's military affairs section, for instance, arranged for the delivery of heavy siege artillery that Ishiwara needed to destroy the Mukden barracks compound. In short, army officials at several echelons were involved in the conspiracy.[13]

There was a sense in army circles that Japan faced a national emergency demanding an extraordinary response that party politicians were incapable of providing because they were captives of narrow partisan interests.[14] A changing international order, rising Chinese nationalism, and Soviet communism threatened Japanese interests abroad while inept and timid political leadership thwarted reform at home, being unable to deal with the crushing effects of the global depression, resolve economic inequities, or forge a strong foreign policy.

Lt. Col. Hashimoto Kingorō, the Russia section chief on the general staff, appealed to these frustrations when he organized the Cherry Society (Sakurakai) in October 1930, a highly politicized group restricted to graduates of the staff college below the rank of colonel who were assigned to the war ministry or general staff. Within a year the Cherry Society had enrolled about 100 activist officers and advocated radical political reforms, by force if necessary, to establish a military-style government.

Hashimoto learned in January 1931 from the vice chief of staff that War Minister Ugaki, whose political ambitions were well known, also was receptive to a military government, and he took this revelation as a green light for a coup d'état. Hashimoto financed his coup with secret army funds that paid civilian right-wing extremists like Ōkawa Shūmei to assemble a mob to surround the Diet. When legislators summoned the army to suppress the demonstrations, the troops would instead seize the Diet. Several high-ranking army officers would enter the building, announce that the nation had lost faith in the party politicians, and demand their wholesale resignations. Ugaki would then receive an imperial command to form a government. After Hashimoto discussed the gist of the plan with several senior officers on January 13, Maj. Gen. Koiso warned him that public opinion would not tolerate a military coup and that the army would not back large-scale, disorderly demonstrations.[15]

In early February 1931 opposition Seiyūkai members assailed the ruling Minseitō Party over its proposed budget and denounced the London Naval Treaty (signed May 1930) for imperiling national security. The uproar in the Diet escalated from pushing and shoving to fistfights between rival party members as opponents hurled insults, ashtrays, and nameplates across the aisle. The spectacle confirmed Hashimoto's visceral distaste for the parties and politicians and convinced him to act.[16]

Soon afterward Ōkawa Shūmei, a right-wing ideologue and self-promoter, approached Ugaki regarding a possible coup and freely interpreted the war minister's ambiguous and evasive remarks as indicating support. Ugaki, however, realized that he could ride to the premiership legitimately as the leader of a political party and quickly lost whatever interest he may have had in a coup. Several other senior officers expressed second thoughts about the conspiracy, which collapsed by early March. Although Hashimoto's plan was melodramatic and unrealistic, senior army leaders had seriously considered an armed insurrection and went unpunished, a fact not lost on other radical officers at home or abroad.[17]

Meanwhile, Ishiwara and Itagaki demanded immediate action in Manchuria. Influential officers in Tokyo were sympathetic but wanted to postpone any action for one year to allow themselves time to prepare public opinion and the army for the takeover. During a June reconnaissance, however, Chinese warlord troops apprehended a Kwantung Army captain dressed in mufti and promptly executed him as a spy.

Lengthy newspaper editorials and sensationalized coverage of the execution and a subsequent clash between Chinese and Korean squatters near the Manchurian-Korean border brought the Manchurian issue to the forefront of public consciousness during the summer of 1931. At the annual division commander's conference held on August 4, the new war minister, Gen. Minami Jirō, created an uproar in the press when he announced his intention to resolve the Manchurian problem; the army in turn asserted that Minami had the right to voice his opinion publicly on military matters to prevent opportunistic politicians and armchair strategists from confusing its soldiers. Around this time Seiyūkai member Matsuoka Yōsuke declared in the Diet that Manchuria was Japan's lifeline, a phrase that gained widespread popular appeal.[18]

By late summer, Ishiwara's and Itagaki's sympathizers in the Kwantung Army, the war ministry, and general staff knew the outline of their plot and, in some cases, specific details. Although Tokyo advised discretion, the newly assigned commander of the Kwantung Army, Lt. Gen. Honjō Shigeru, and the commander of the Korea Army, Lt. Gen. Hayashi Senjūrō, both promised unhesitating support in case of emergency. Itagaki also developed a network of activists among South Manchurian Railroad officials and Japanese *rōnin* (civilian adventurers) in Manchuria. Early in September rumors reached the court that the Kwantung Army was up to something, and Hirohito warned Minami to pay attention to the army's tendency to resort to unilateral action to forge national policy.[19]

On September 18, 1931, a bomb planted by Japanese agents exploded on the tracks of the South Manchurian Railway just outside Mukden. The Kwantung Army blamed the attack on Chinese bandits, and well-rehearsed Japanese infantrymen quickly overran the Mukden barracks and seized the city. Provocateurs paid by Itagaki and Ishiwara fomented demonstrations in other cities to justify expanded intervention. The army leadership in Tokyo was conflicted, on the one hand refusing to dispatch reinforcements to Manchuria and on the other agreeing to bring down the cabinet if it interfered with current operations in Manchuria. The general staff ultimately rationalized the Manchurian fait accompli on the grounds that rejecting it would harm army morale and diminish public confidence in the army.[20] The Korea Army sent reinforcements on September 21 by invoking the right of field initiative to move forces across the border into Manchuria without an imperial command. Hirohito authorized the action retroactively the next day while cautioning his chief army aide-de-camp that the army had to exercise greater restraint.[21]

Couching aggression in terms of self-defense, the Kwantung Army overran most of southern and central Manchuria within two weeks, partly due to Ishiwara's innovative mobile tactics but mainly because Zhang Xueliang, following Chiang Kai-shek's orders, chose to preserve his army by not resisting the better-armed and -organized Japanese. Chiang in turn sought relief from the League of Nations to make the Japanese withdraw from Manchuria.[22]

The Manchurian Incident and the subsequent Japanese takeover of Manchuria, completed in early 1932, radically altered the military-strategic equation in northeast Asia. The conquest provoked undying Chinese hostility, increased the Soviet military presence in northeast Asia, and alienated the United States. Almost overnight the Kwantung Army had to defend an ill-defined 3,000-mile border against a militarily resurgent Soviet Red Army. It also assumed constabulary, occupation, and nation-building roles in Manchuria when it created a puppet regime; exploited natural resources; developed heavy industry; and conducted counterguerrilla operations against warlord troops, Communist insurgents, and roving bandit gangs.

Domestic emergencies and foreign crises made simplistic solutions like unilateral military action seem like attractive remedies to complex problems; the army had acted decisively, unlike the craven diplomats or partisan politicians, to resolve the Manchurian crisis, reassert Japan's continental interests, and restore Japanese pride. Within the army Ishiwara and Itagaki were heroes.

The October Incident

Lt. Col. Hashimoto had learned of the Mukden conspiracy in June 1931 when a Kwantung Army staff officer approached him for money to finance the plot. Hashimoto promised funding and a coup d'état to overthrow the cabinet should it refuse to support the army's actions. In early August he alerted several Cherry Society members that the Kwantung Army would strike in Manchuria around mid-September and that he, with the backing of the general staff, would simultaneously lead a coup d'état to install a military government.[23]

Hashimoto's sponsor was Maj. Gen. Tatekawa Yoshitsugu, newly appointed general staff first department (operations) chief, who wielded disproportionate influence because of the weakness of his two immediate superiors, an alcoholic chief of staff and a vice chief tainted by involvement in the March Incident. He encouraged Hashimoto's belief that the imminent events in Manchuria offered the chance to establish a military government.[24]

Hashimoto's latest scheme was far more violent than the March conspiracy. Army units would attack the Diet, murder the prime minister, occupy the Metropolitan Police Headquarters, and surround the war ministry and general staff offices. Gen. Araki would form a cabinet with Hashimoto as home minister controlling the police, Tatekawa the foreign minister, and Ōkawa the finance minister. Hashimoto again relied on Ōkawa to marshal civilian support, but he also used Kita Ikki, a right-wing nationalist theoretician, to solicit additional help from company-grade army officers assigned to various Tokyo units. Mid-October was the target date, but no one prepared specific plans for an uprising.

Hashimoto and his coterie boasted openly about their grandiose schemes while they partied at expensive Tokyo restaurants and geisha houses. Unsurprisingly, rumors of an army coup reached the court in early October, and word of the plot even appeared in the newspapers. General officers then rebuked Tatekawa, who in turn ordered Hashimoto on October 16 to end his plotting. Two days later the military police arrested the ringleaders. Hashimoto received twenty days confinement to quarters; the others were confined to quarters for a few days and then transferred from Tokyo.[25]

Details of the October Incident were common knowledge among junior officers stationed in Tokyo and the radicalized young officers from all over the country who had converged on the capital in anticipation of the uprising. These young lieutenants and captains, who viewed themselves as sincere patriots, were disgusted at the spectacle of Hashimoto and Ōkawa lavishing yen on geisha parties while the farming villages suffered from poverty and starvation. Disillusioned with Hashimoto, they gravitated to Kita, mesmerized by his theories of a military coup that would establish direct imperial rule and renovate Japan. They gradually established an amorphous, army-wide network of activists and sympathizers whose program would establish direct imperial rule, eliminate rapacious capitalism, and suppress dangerous left-wing ideologies.[26]

In early December 1931 the Minseitō cabinet resigned, unable to restrain the army's expansion into northern Manchuria, unprepared to deal effectively with the continuing effects of the worldwide Great Depression, and incapable of resolving deep rifts within the party. Inukai Ki, leader of the minority Seiyūkai, became prime minister and scheduled a general election for February 20, 1932. He chose the charismatic Araki for his war minister in hopes of using the popular general to curb army extremism.[27] By this time several factions within the army were competing for control of the institution and the nation.

Ugaki's followers represented the Chōshū faction whereas Araki's anti-

Chōshū group was composed of One Evening Society members. There were also diehard Cherry Society adherents and a radical contingent of junior officers. They all shared an aversion to party cabinet government, a commitment to strengthened national security, and a desire for domestic reform, as they defined these goals, respectively. They differed on the ends and means, and their internecine struggles for the soul of the army provoked murderous blood-feuds.

The First Shanghai Incident

Inukai spent his first weeks in office confronted by one international crisis after another. The previous November the Council of the League of Nations had demanded that Japanese troops withdraw from Manchuria, and on January 7, 1932, U.S. Secretary of State Henry Stimson announced that his country would not recognize any changes in Manchuria. Undeterred, in late January 1932 the Kwantung Army occupied northern Manchuria, ignoring the increasing international criticism.[28] Chinese boycotts of Japanese goods had followed the Manchurian Incident and were particularly effective in Shanghai, the center of western and Japanese trade and investment in China. Boisterous anti-Japanese demonstrations and protests complemented the ruinous boycott and played into the hands of the Kwantung Army.

In October 1931 Itagaki had summoned Maj. Tanaka Ryūkichi, the assistant military attaché at the Shanghai consulate, to Mukden and ordered him to stir up more trouble in Shanghai to distract western attention from Japanese actions in Manchuria. To incite disturbances in Shanghai, Tanaka used a secret army slush fund to hire agent provocateurs, including five Japanese members of a militant Buddhist sect. The five marched into a Chinese factory district in Shanghai on January 18, 1932, loudly chanting sutras and banging on drums. Provoked Chinese workers attacked the proselytizing procession, killing two Japanese and badly injuring the others. Hotheads in Shanghai's large Japanese community demanded revenge.[29]

Accusations, vigilantism, and anti-Japanese demonstrations that threatened to spin out of control prompted the imperial navy to put a special landing force ashore to protect Japanese lives and interests in the city. The naval infantrymen soon clashed with Chinese troops and, heavily outnumbered, called for army reinforcements on January 31. The general staff ordered a mixed brigade to Shanghai where it was surprised to encounter the highly motivated, well-disciplined, and German-trained Chinese veterans of the Nineteenth Route Army. These violently anti-Japanese soldiers from Guangzhou (Canton) in South China spearheaded the resistance to the latest Japanese aggression.[30]

The general staff estimated that the Shanghai disorders, like previous outbursts, would be settled in a few days. But the tenacious Chinese defenders took advantage of the numerous creeks and channels that intersected the area north of Shanghai to slow the Japanese attackers. To overcome the unexpectedly tough resistance, the army hurriedly deployed the 9th Division, which also anticipated a short campaign and departed without drawing its full allotment of ammunition, heavy weapons, and equipment.[31]

Contemptuous of the Chinese, the 9th Division's commander launched two bullheaded frontal assaults that failed to dislodge the well-entrenched defenders but suffered substantial casualties. One battalion commander reported that his unit was on the verge of annihilation, but his regimental commander ordered the attack to continue for the sake of the regiment's honor.[32] Artillery shells were quickly depleted, and without their standard equipment infantrymen had to jury-rig weapons to breach Chinese strongholds. In one attack, three soldiers wrapped explosive charges in bamboo matting, lit a fuse to the primer, and, carrying a live bomb, rushed the enemy position. It exploded prematurely, killing them.[33]

Eager for good news from the botched campaign, the press marketed the episode as an intentional act of self-sacrifice to achieve the unit's objectives. It was the epitome of Japanese martial valor and transmogrified the three soldiers into war gods guarding the nation. The *bakudan sanyūshi* (the three brave soldiers who became human bombs) story resonated with the Japanese public. Fueled by sensational and incessant press coverage, it stirred nationalism and patriotism and launched a spontaneous flow of donations to the soldiers' families. Newspaper descriptions of the human bombs recalled their famous human-bullet ancestors during the Russo-Japanese War to conjure up powerful images that connected glorious tradition with current operations. The two largest national newspapers sponsored poetry contests to commemorate the heroes and received more than 200,000 entries.[34] It seemed that the public was spellbound by the three soldiers' self-sacrifice for the sake of the nation.

The emotional sensationalism shielded the army from criticism of its incompetence that had needlessly wasted soldiers' lives. Instead, army leaders capitalized on the public frenzy by announcing that the three soldiers had deliberately sacrificed themselves to enable their comrades to capture the position. (A straightforward account in the army's official history recorded that when the men reached the Chinese barbed wire there was a loud explosion and they were killed.) Furthermore, the battalion commander never ordered a suicide attack. Thirty-six soldiers volunteered for the assault and were organized into twelve assault parties. Eight were killed, but the others survived the engagement. It seems that the three soldiers' act captured the popular imagination because they were ordinary young men whose unquestioning obedience to orders demonstrated a devotion to duty previously reserved for warriors but now open to all citizens.[35]

War Minister Araki presented certificates of condolences to the bereaved mothers at a public ceremony, and spontaneous nationwide fund drives paid for statues to honor the three soldiers for creating "a spiritual preparedness for death."[36] Official propaganda spread enthusiastically by the media made self-destruction to achieve objectives laudable and set a higher standard for those who followed.

Another episode at Shanghai would more profoundly influence future standards for battlefield conduct. During a night attack, Maj. Kuga Noboru, a battalion commander, and his 200-man unit were surrounded by Chinese troops. The beleaguered unit suffered severe losses, including Kuga, who was seriously wounded by a hand grenade and left for dead. He survived, but in his weakened condition was taken prisoner.[37] Chinese newspapers publicized his captivity and, after the March truce, Kuga and another officer, a captured captain, were handed over to the Japanese consul at Nanjing.

Kuga believed that he had disgraced his regiment by violating the revised 1928 *Infantry Manual*'s injunction to hold a position to the last drop of blood. He was also subjected to merciless army peer pressure (one academy classmate urged him to be a man and kill himself). Confused, depressed, and in a susceptible state of mind, Kuga committed suicide and touched off another round of newspaper sensationalism that extolled the late major as a paragon for soldiers to emulate. At least five movies were made about him in 1932 and one play performed. (The repatriated captain also killed himself, but he was awaiting court-martial for ordering an unauthorized withdrawal and for presumably not being the role model of the officer corps that the army wanted presented to the people.) Suicide became ritualized, and informally institutionalized, in the army's ethos as a laudable goal and a testament to the unique Japanese spirit.

The distractions provided by the human bombs and Kuga's suicide diverted public attention from a lackluster campaign. The general staff activated the Shanghai Expeditionary Headquarters on February 24, and as a personal favor Hirohito requested Gen. Shirakawa, the newly appointed commander, to restrict operations and end the fighting quickly. Shirakawa's reinforcements landed about 30 miles north of Shanghai on March 1, outflanked the defenders, and within a few days drove the Chinese from Shanghai. Total Japanese casualties were about 3,000, including more than 700 killed; the Chinese suffered almost four times as many losses, most within the Nineteenth Route Army.[38] A cease-fire signed on May 5 officially ended the First Shanghai Incident.

The escalated fighting in Shanghai in early February had coincided with a general election campaign in Japan that was marred by right-wing terror. On February 9, a gunman shot former Finance Minister Inoue Junnosuke, who was on his way to speak at a rally. Police immediately arrested the young killer, who blamed Inoue's fiscal policies for the ruin of the countryside.[39] They assumed that the disgruntled youth had acted alone. The February 20 election results gave the Seiyūkai Party an overwhelming majority of 301 of the 466 seats in the Lower House, but its triumph was short-lived. On March 5, Baron Dan Takuma, director-general of the Mitsui conglomerate, was shot to death in broad daylight at a side entrance to Tokyo's Mitsui Bank. Under police questioning, the assassin revealed links to a mystic Buddhist priest and radical rightist named Inoue Nisshō, who it turned out was behind both assassinations.

Inoue was the founder of the Blood Brotherhood Association (*Ketsumeidan*), a civilian right-wing group whose avowed aim was to create a national restoration by assassinating prominent financial and political leaders because they had sacrificed the welfare of the masses for personal gain. Inoue turned himself in to authorities, ending his brief reign of terror but beginning a sensationalized trial that dragged on for more than two years.[40]

Shortly after Dan's murder, military academy cadets, led by radical junior naval officers, murdered Prime Minister Inukai during an attempted coup d'état, the so-called May 15 Incident. Extremist young army officers were not involved, in part because they had high expectations that Araki would reform the army and nation. The war minister likewise had no connection with the May 15 Incident, but Araki made known the army's opposition to political party cabinets. Despite the Seiyūkai's overwhelming election victory, after Inukai's assassination a nonpartisan, national unity cabinet, headed by retired Adm. Saitō Makoto, was established. It marked the end of party cabinets in Japan and the beginning of the army's domination of the political scene.[41] Ignoring criticism from some quarters that he should accept responsibility for the army cadets' actions and resign, Araki remained as war minister in the new national unity cabinet to carry out his ambitious, and contentious, army reforms, which divided the army's leadership along even more irreconcilable factional lines.

The Struggle within the Army

Debate over the merits of a triangular or square division had continued throughout the 1920s. Traditionalists in the operations department of the general staff favored the square configuration because its additional manpower, weaponry, and equipment enabled the division to sustain combat losses yet continue to function effectively. The larger square division could also overwhelm smaller triangular formations, permitting it to conduct independent sustained operations on extended frontages, a role European and U.S. armies normally assigned to a corps echelon (two or more divisions). For these reasons, the army retained the square divisions despite the World War I trend among European armies to smaller, more mobile triangular formations.[42] By the late 1920s, however, reformers judged the bigger division too cumbersome for modern battle because it was difficult to control and maneuver, occupied too much road space during the march to be brought to bear rapidly against the enemy, and its dense ranks rendered it especially vulnerable to the concentrated firepower of modern weapons.

When Ugaki had returned as war minister in 1929, he still intended to reduce the number of divisions and transform the army into a smaller, modern, high-quality force. His five-year proposal would reduce personnel and reinvest the savings to purchase new equipment, particularly tanks and aircraft. Chief of Staff Lt. Gen. Suzuki Sōroku rejected any troop reductions; he foresaw Japan fighting its next war against a coalition (the United States, the USSR, and China) that would vastly outnumber the army and make it impossible for Japan to win a protracted war. The only option was to strike before the coalition could bring all its military strength and industrial power to bear, a strategy that required a large standing army capable of rapid mobilization and deployment to win the decisive opening battles. Col. Obata Toshishirō, chief of the operations section, endorsed the short-war strategy and insisted that large numbers of active-duty square divisions were essential for national security.[43]

The controversy continued after Ugaki's departure in April 1931, this time between the new war minister—Gen. Minami Jirō, an Ugaki protégé—and the new chief of staff, Lt. Gen. Kanaya Hanzō, an Uehara follower. Minami advocated total-war theories and supported army modernization and the economic development of Manchuria's natural resources to fight a protracted conflict. Like Ugaki, he would eliminate divisions and personnel to pay for modernization. Kanaya wanted four additional divisions to defend Korea and Manchuria against a growing Soviet threat. Converting divisions to the smaller triangular formations would satisfy both generals; Minami could reduce personnel and Kanaya could increase divisions because fewer troops would be needed for each reorganized smaller division.

Minami proposed this solution in November as part of his seven-year plan to modernize weaponry, expand armor and air force units, and improve Tokyo's air defenses. To pay for this, he would reduce the Guard Division, eliminate the post of inspector-general of military education, and abolish the Tokyo garrison headquarters. Araki, then the incumbent inspector-general, led a formidable opposition. The nation's dire financial condition also made army modernization on the scale Minami advocated impossible, and his plans collapsed completely after the Manchurian Incident and Araki's appointment as war minister in December 1931.[44]

Nevertheless, Ugaki's supporters still exerted enough influence within the Tokyo headquarters to block Araki's choice for chief of staff—his main ally, Lt. Gen. Mazaki Jinsaburō. The factions compromised by selecting Prince Kan'in, an imperial figurehead, who filled the post for the next nine years. Mazaki became vice chief of staff and imperial aide-de-camp. As war minister, Araki quickly scrapped the ministry's plans to reorganize the army into triangular divisions. He also promoted Obata to chief of the first department because of their shared belief that the triangular division was strategically misguided and would be detrimental to army tradition and esprit.[45]

The charismatic Araki's outspoken denunciations of the evils of capitalism, complemented by calls to hone spiritual values unique to Japan, initially made him extremely popular throughout the officer corps. He was seen as a forceful leader capable of reforming and modernizing the army, but Araki spoke increasingly about cultivating morale and spiritual attributes rather than paying excessive attention to national mobilization and modernization.[46]

To emphasize spiritual factors, Araki designated things "imperial," as in imperial nation (kōkoku), imperial way (kōdō), and so forth to link army to the throne and promote intangibles to improve morale. Consequently, his followers were labeled "the imperial way faction." In a similar vein, in 1933 Araki forbade the use of the Japanese words for *retreat* and *surrender* because he deemed them detrimental to army spirit and morale.[47]

Another of Araki's attempts to boost army morale was to reintroduce in 1934 the wearing of Japanese-style swords by company-grade officers. The Meiji government had prohibited the wearing of Japanese-style swords in 1876, and since 1889 army officers were issued the French-style army sword. By the early 1930s Japan's few remaining traditional swordsmiths and craftsmen were a dying breed. Araki revitalized the near-dormant sword-making industry by encouraging the opening of a foundry on the grounds of the Yasukuni Shrine in July 1933 and the following year revised uniform regulations to mandate a return to a Kamakura-age Japanese sword. By August 1945, the foundry had produced more than 8,000 "Yasukuni" swords.[48]

The flamboyant Araki publicly implied that his critics were pacifists or Communists, promoted the use of kōgun throughout the army, and spoke of traditional Japanese warrior ideals embodied in his notions of bushidō. His public relations campaign was a component of the gradual militarization of Japanese society that began after the Manchurian Incident. The hysterical response to the bakudan sanyūshi incident, and the popularity of the Manchurian and North China adventures, which gained great amounts of new territory at relatively cheap cost (by July 1933 about 9,500 killed and wounded), conferred a new prestige on the army—which alone seemed capable of action, unlike the political parties wallowing in their own corruption.

Shortly after Araki became war minister, Obata, backed by Araki, announced that Japan had to wage a preemptive war before the Soviet Union achieved overwhelming military superiority. Araki predicted that the crisis would arrive in 1936, identifying that year as the crossover point after which the Soviet Union would grow progressively stronger and Japan steadily weaker. According to Maj.

Gen. Nagata Tetsuzan, now the chief of the war ministry's second department (mobilization and ordnance), Japan could not defeat the USSR unless the army was modernized and expanded to fight a protracted war. This in turn depended on converting Japan's industrial base to support a military economy that fed off the natural resources of North China, Mongolia, and Manchuria. Nagata's proposed first step would be to reduce personnel to pay for modernization.[49]

Obata understood that in the best of circumstances war with the Soviets would strain Japan to its limits. It made no sense to him to antagonize China, whose long-term problems could not be solved by using the army for short-term solutions. Such a course would merely drain resources needed to fight the Soviets, brand Japan an aggressor in world opinion, and likely lead Japan into full-scale war against an allied coalition. Nagata countered that without China's resources Japan could not win a war against the USSR. These fundamental disagreements between Obata and Nagata came to a head at the June 1933 army conferences that Araki convened to explain his plan for war with the Soviet Union in 1936, a policy Nagata dismissed out of hand.

That August, Araki transferred officers not affiliated with his imperial way faction, including Nagata, from Tokyo headquarters and with Mazaki's aid brazenly maneuvered imperial way supporters into key staff and ministry positions. The imperial way faction now dominated the war ministry and general staff, but Araki and his adherents proved better at slogans than practical ability to enact their programs.

When Araki subsequently presented the September 1933 five ministers conference with his sweeping plan for immediate rearmament and wartime control of the nation's finances, he failed to convince them of the imminence of the Soviet threat and was unable to implement his program or secure a bigger army budget, in part because the cabinet was underwriting a massive public works program of infrastructure improvements and construction to relieve the acute financial distress of the peasantry in northeastern Japan.[50]

Araki's inability to gain cabinet support for his budget and his clash with Nagata and his adherents over army strategy and force structure divided the officer class. Academy and staff college classmates and colleagues who had worked together for army reform since the early 1920s parted ways over the fundamental differences between Obata and Nagata. Nagata and Tōjō, dissatisfied with Araki and Mazaki, formed the control (*tōsei*) faction, bringing a likewise disillusioned Hayashi to their side as well. The control group advocated a planned national economy as the basis for a national mobilization state that would modernize the army and prepare the nation for a protracted total war. The fundamental disagreement split the army's leaders and the One Evening Society's members into two major factions, one supporting Araki's imperial way faction, the other Nagata's control group.[51]

As Araki's influence dwindled, Mazaki, who was promoted in June 1933 to the post of the inspector-general of military education, intensified his agitation of the junior army officers clique to develop a new base of support. His conduct outraged Nagata and the control faction because it spawned disobedience and disunity within the army and encouraged dangerous political ideologies among younger officers. Although the junior officers claimed no direct affiliation with Araki and Mazaki, they identified with them as opponents of the status quo and therefore natural allies. Nagata was the embodiment of "staff fascism," which they defined as senior army officers who espoused a state-controlled economy and perpetuation of the existing order that the young officers held responsible for Japan's ills. In order to destroy this malevolent influence, the young officers would eliminate the evil advisers surrounding the emperor and establish direct imperial rule.[52]

In January 1934, citing ill health, Araki resigned as war minister to become a member of the Supreme Military Council. His successor, Lt. Gen. Hayashi Senjūrō, tried to oust Mazaki for subverting military discipline. Hayashi's fears seemed realized that November when the military police arrested several junior officers and military academy cadets, allegedly for plotting a military coup. Mazaki claimed the incident was concocted to discredit him and eliminate imperial way influence from the army. There was insufficient evidence to warrant a court-martial, and besides, any proceedings would occur under the jurisdiction of a known Mazaki sympathizer who, control members feared, would manipulate the proceedings to the imperial way's advantage.[53] To avoid further embarrassment, army authorities again resorted to administrative punishment, dismissing two leading agitators of the young officers movement from the army.

Mazaki, however, refused to step down and continued to stir dissension among the young officers. Hayashi notified the emperor that Mazaki had to be curbed, or discipline within the ranks would only worsen.[54] With Araki's backing, Mazaki asserted that if he was to be removed for promoting factionalism, then Nagata should also resign because of his involvement in the March 1931 incident. To end this dangerous politicization of the army, in mid-July 1935 at a closed session of the Supreme Military Council Chief of Staff Prince Kan'in, backed by senior army officers and the emperor, reassigned Mazaki to the more ceremonial and less influential board of supreme military councilors. Gen. Watanabe Jōtarō replaced Mazaki as inspector-general.

Radical junior officers interpreted Mazaki's removal as the latest in a series of control faction conspiracies. Mazaki further inflamed the dangerous situation by leaking confidential deliberations regarding his removal; the young officers in turn published his sensational revelations of the March and October plots in a series of clandestine pamphlets to discredit Nagata and his clique.

The inflammatory tracts drove an already unbalanced Lt. Col. Aizawa Saburō, a sympathizer with the young officers, to murder. On August 12, 1935, Aizawa walked calmly into Nagata's office in the war ministry, drew his sword, and hacked the chief of the military affairs bureau to death. He then nonchalantly recounted his deed in another ministry office until the military police arrested him. Araki, disregarding his own conduct after the May 15 Incident, was quick to remind Hayashi that it was traditional in such circumstances for the war minister to resign. Hayashi did accept responsibility and was replaced by Gen. Kawashima Yoshiyuki, an unaffiliated officer, but one friendly to the imperial way group.[55]

Aizawa's public court-martial began January 28, 1936, and quickly degenerated into a media spectacle and a stage for imperial way propaganda. In the midst of the trial, for numerous reasons, among them the 1st Division's imminent transfer to Manchuria, about two dozen radicalized junior officers, including key leaders of the young officers movement, led a mutiny of the Tokyo garrisons. They assembled their NCOs on the night of February 25, explained their goals for an armed insurrection to achieve an imperial restoration, and allowed any NCO who disagreed with them to leave. Only one did.[56] By the next morning 1,400 officers and men, most from the 1st Division, had occupied snow-covered downtown Tokyo, seized the key ministries, and murdered the inspector-general of military education, the finance minister, and the prime minister's brother-in-law, mistaking the last for the minister. The so-called February 26 Incident paralyzed the capital and the army for four days.

Mutiny and murder incensed control faction members, but imperial way supporters applauded the young officers' sincere motives and publicly sympathized with the mutineers, who expected the throne to intervene on their behalf. Enjoying high-level army support, the mutinous officers initially appeared successful, but the control faction steadfastly opposed any concessions.[57] Most important, the emperor, appalled at the murder of his ministers, rejected repeated appeals from imperial way leaders for leniency. Hirohito's decisiveness checked any momentum the coup could generate, and after four tense days the mutineers peacefully returned to their barracks.

Nineteen junior officers and ten civilian activists were arrested. The military police perfunctorily questioned every enlisted man involved, asking whether the soldier knew in advance of the uprising and whether he fired his weapon. Because army regulations demanded absolute obedience to orders and the soldiers had followed the commands of their superior officers, authorities reasoned that the enlisted troops should not be punished for mutiny. Nineteen enlisted men were indicted, but only four were court-martialed—for direct participation in the attacks on the ministers. They received suspended sentences. Seventy-four NCOs were court-martialed: fifteen received prison sentences, twenty-seven

The army takes to the street as rebel troops seal off the Foreign Ministry in the heart of Tokyo during the 2-26 Incident. (Courtesy Mainichi shimbun)

got suspended sentences, and the remainder received acquittals. Nine other junior officers stationed in Tokyo were accused of collaborating with the rebels and received prison sentences ranging from four years to life; seven officer sympathizers outside of the capital, also convicted as coconspirators, received terms of up to six years' imprisonment.[58]

The young officers who had taken to the streets to lead the revolt bore the full brunt of the army's revenge. In late April they were secretly tried without benefit of defense counsel and without recourse to appeal. Thirteen officers and two civilians were executed by firing squad on July 12. In separate proceedings, civilian right-wingers Kita Ikki and his disciple Nishida Mitsugi were convicted and sentenced to death "in the interests of the state" to discourage future subversion. Along with two former junior officers who testified at their proceedings, they were shot in late August. Aizawa's political theater likewise ended abruptly. A new, secret court-martial that convened in April took just four days to find him guilty. He was executed by firing squad on July 3.

A sweeping purge of the rebels' supporters and sympathizers within the army, particularly from among its higher echelons, opened the way for a take-over of key general staff and war ministry positions by control group officers committed to innovation, modernization, and renovation of the army. Seven of the ten full general officers were removed from the active list and retired, seven other flag rank officers were later seconded to the reserves, and during the annual August personnel transfers about 3,000 officers found themselves reassigned throughout the army.[59]

Despite widespread suspicions, investigators uncovered no evidence that Mazaki had secretly conspired with the young officers, although he did try to take advantage of the uprising. Tipped off by a right-wing crony a few hours before the attempted coup, Mazaki notified a navy colleague, who in turn asked the chief of naval operations, Prince Fushimi, to declare martial law, appoint Mazaki prime minister, and institute an imperial restoration. Mazaki also encouraged the rebel officers who were occupying the war minister's residence to stand fast.[60]

Under interrogation by the military police, Mazaki dismissed all the allegations as baseless rumors and slander. A court-martial eventually acquitted him in late September 1937, even though two of the three presiding officers believed that he was guilty of fomenting mutiny. By that time, however, the army's internal personnel dynamics had completely changed and Konoe Fumimaro, the new prime minister, in the process of consolidating his power allegedly interceded on Mazaki's behalf to forge national unity for the undeclared war against China.[61]

Between 1930 and 1935, there were twenty major domestic terrorist incidents, four political assassinations, five planned assassinations, and four attempted coups, the March and October incidents of 1931, the May 15 Incident of 1932, and the great military mutiny of February 1936. Furthermore the army's continual plotting in Manchuria and North China destabilized those regions and helped to isolate Japan internationally. Military involvement to one degree or another in almost all these conspiracies undercut Japan's political process and enabled the army to gain dominant political influence.

Conversely, the army's involvement in attempted coups and assassinations may have ended Japan's brief era of political party rule, but it exerted little effect on national military policy. If anything, the radical domestic threat from below had obscured an emerging army consensus on China and the Soviet Union.

Imperial Defense Policy

Since the 1923 revision to imperial defense policy, dramatic changes had realigned Japan's international standing. With regard to diplomacy, Japan reacted to international criticism of its actions in Manchuria by walking out of the League of Nations in 1933. Concerning commerce and the economy, the worldwide Great Depression had closed markets and promoted autarky. In terms of strategy, Tokyo's decision in December 1935 to abrogate the Washington naval agreements augured for an expensive naval arms race after the treaty expired in December 1936. Militarily, the weak and disorganized Soviet Union the army had faced in the early 1920s had become a formidable threat to northeast Asia—especially on the borders of Manchuria, where the Soviets had rapidly reinforced their Far East garrisons, which by 1935 had three times as many infantry divisions and five times as many aircraft as the Kwantung Army.

When Ishiwara Kanji took over the operations section, general staff in August 1935, he learned that the imperial defense policy was a badly outdated short-war scenario whose operational guidance he found unsuited for modern warfare. Ishiwara's overriding concern was the army's unreadiness to fight the militarily resurgent Soviet Union, a condition made more alarming because of his belief the great powers were already on the path to another world war. He believed that the creation of a military-industrial complex in Manchuria would deter Soviet expansion in northeast Asia; if it could not, then the heavy industrial base could still support an army capable of defeating Soviet aggression. After Japan eliminated the threat to its north, the military could move south to secure natural resources and territory. But army modernization, new weapons and equipment, and increased heavy industrial production required large budgets at a time when the navy was simultaneously demanding additional funding to expand its fleets. Last, the increased regional tension that followed the Manchurian Incident had created the possibility that Japan might have to fight against a Chinese-Soviet coalition, but current national defense policy was based on a war with a single opponent. These broader issues involved not just the army and its operational planning, but the matters of national policy, maritime strategy, and diplomacy. Solutions, Ishiwara was convinced, required a new national strategy to align national defense with national policy and make it compatible with the demands of total, protracted warfare.[62]

With these concerns in mind, in mid-December 1935, Ishiwara approached his opposite number on the naval general staff, Capt. Fukudome Shigeru, operations section chief, about revising national defense policy. Fukudome agreed on the need for revision, but the navy distrusted Ishiwara because he had been a ringleader of the Manchurian Incident, which had furthered the army's northward strategy at the navy's expense. Ishiwara favored eliminating the Soviet threat first and then moving to the southern regions. Fukudome wanted to defend the northern flank and advance south. The services also disagreed about the main hypothetical enemy (the Soviet Union for the army and the United States for the navy), whether Japan's next war would involve a single opponent (the navy's stand) or a coalition (the army's concept), and whether a future war would be quick and decisive or protracted and exhaustive. On January 23, 1936, Fukudome rejected the army's emphasis on the Soviet Union, and in mid-February 1936 Ishiwara, resigned to the navy's position, received the vice chief of staff's permission to independently revise national defense policy.[63]

In the wake of the February uprising, Prime Minister Hirota Kōki formed a new national unity cabinet on March 9, 1936. Just ten days later, the navy organized a committee to devise a naval strategy that would protect naval funding from being subsumed by Ishiwara's plans for army rearmament and expansion. Based on input from fleet commanders, the navy's mid-April "Outline of National Policy" (*Kokusaku yōryō*) assigned priority to a southern advance, naval rearmament, improving military forces as required to check Soviet expansion, and limited development and expansion in Manchuria.[64]

A parallel effort by a joint committee of midlevel staff officers to revise national defense policy had been under way since mid-February. On April 2, they circulated proposed revisions to the respective general staffs for review. As was the practice, the services had excluded civilian cabinet ministers from the process and allowed the prime, foreign, and finance ministers to see the very generally drawn strategic objectives. Only Prime Minister Hirota reviewed the operational force levels, and there is no evidence that he discussed the proposal with any members of his cabinet. No one outside the military services was cleared to see the operational plans.[65]

In mid-May, army Chief of Staff Prince Kan'in and Chief of the Naval Staff Prince Fushimi presented the draft to the throne, but the emperor questioned, among other things, how the services would pay for such an enormous expansion of their forces and the addition of Great Britain to the list of hypothetical enemies. The military enlisted Hirota, who recommended that Hirohito approve the new policy. With all his ministers backing the revised defense policy, on June 3, 1936, the emperor sanctioned the new policy.[66]

The updated 1936 imperial defense policy assigned Japan's two main hypothetical opponents, the Soviet Union and the United States, equal priority and did not resolve a primary strategic axis of expansion. China and Great Britain were considered secondary threats. To defeat the Soviet Red Army in the opening battles, the army's force structure would expand to 50 divisions supported by 140 army air force squadrons, and the navy would build 2 new battleships (12 total), construct 7 new aircraft carriers (10 total), and add 26 new air squadrons (65 total) to execute a deepwater strategy against the United States.

Contrary to Ishiwara's expectations, the 1936 version of imperial defense described preemptive offensive operations to seize strategic objectives quickly, the traditional short-war strategy. Conventional ideas of warfare and morale dominated army doctrine, and there was great reluctance to adopt Ishiwara's philosophy when it rubbed against the grain of that operational and tactical doctrine. Put differently, many army officers whose opinions mattered were uncomfortable with Ishiwara's theoretical arguments for a protracted war.

Overall military strategy was designed to control the Asian continent and the western Pacific, separate objectives that met army and navy requirements. After winning the first battles, there was no strategy to continue, end, or resolve a war. Nor were there any specifics on how to fight a protracted war, although the document acknowledged the possibility of a lengthy conflict of attrition. Similarly, it conceded the possibility of fighting a coalition, but the services continued to measure their respective force structure requirements against different—not common—potential enemies, defining the issue in terms of their respective operational strategies, not a unified national one.[67] Rather than provoke more interservice controversy, avoiding specifics allowed the services to identify their opponents and force structures.

Hirota had expected the services to resolve their fundamental disagreements over long-range military strategy for budgetary reasons and to facilitate his formulation of foreign policy. But he had been excluded from participation in the revisions to imperial defense policy, making it impossible for the cabinet to integrate military strategy and foreign policy. Furthermore, the cost of rearmament and military expansion promised to be enormous. To further complicate cabinet affairs, in mid-May the army reinstituted the provision that only active-duty general officers might serve as war minister. This gave the service the power of life and death over the civilian cabinet because withdrawing a war minister could bring down a cabinet while refusing to nominate one made it impossible to form a new cabinet.

Attempts to produce an integrated statement of national security, national defense, and foreign policy foundered on the same rocks of interservice rivalry. The five ministers conference of June 30 agreed on the "Principles of National Policy," which endorsed the navy's mid-April concept for a southern advance and naval expansion and was more a justification for naval rearmament than a comprehensive plan for national defense.[68]

The same day the army chief of staff approved the "Fundamental Principles of National Defense and National Policy." Prepared by Ishiwara's operations section, it would modernize and reequip the army to drive Caucasian influence from East Asia. Japan would maintain friendly relations with China until it defeated the Soviet Union and then move south against the United States.[69] It became the basis for army rearmament and modernization, a plan Ishiwara submitted to the war ministry on July 23, not a joint military strategy.

On August 7 the five-member inner cabinet agreed on "Fundamentals of National Policy," a slightly revised version of their June 30 decisions.[70] This called for diplomacy to neutralize the Soviets and approved a southward advance, but it simultaneously strengthened the army in Manchuria sufficiently for it to win the opening battles of the war and expanded the navy so that it could control the seas in the western Pacific against the United States. This was mere lip-service because money and resources were lacking for simultaneous preparations by both services for war against different opponents on different fronts. That afternoon the inner cabinet (less the finance minister) approved the revised "Outline of Imperial Foreign Policy."

Officials from the foreign, war, and navy ministries had worked throughout July to produce a unified foreign policy. Its objectives were to develop Manchuria, create special zones in North China, check the spread of Soviet communism, move south peacefully, and use diplomatic overtures to secure a nonaggression pact with Moscow. In other words, the foreign ministry endorsed the army's program. The decision also reaffirmed negotiations between Tokyo and Berlin already under way that would later result in the anti-Comintern Pact, aiming to deprive China of a major foreign ally.[71]

In theory the August decisions melded imperial defense policy, the five ministers' approved national policy, and imperial foreign policy into a comprehensive and unified approach to resolve Japan's international issues. But the result was a series of flawed compromises that left the army and foreign ministry promoting efforts against the Soviet Union at the same time the prime minister and the navy were seeking to expand into the southern regions. Neither the narrower military strategy nor the broader national policy resolved the competing and contradictory objectives of the services.[72]

There was also the aggravating China question. In April 1936 Hirota had appointed a secret committee composed of officials from the army, navy, and foreign ministries to reconsider China policy. Their deliberations appeared on August 11 in two strategies, one for China and one for North China. The former envisaged an anti-Communist military pact, a Sino-Japanese military alliance, Japanese political and military advisers assisting the Chinese government, promotion of economic cooperation, and so forth. The latter anticipated the separation of North China's five provinces from Nanjing's control. The army and navy did agree that a period of stability was needed to retool their respective war machines and therefore the exploitation of North China's "special zones" would be accomplished peacefully.[73] But how could Tokyo reconcile long-term strategic goals, however unrealistic they may have been, with short-range practical interests to detach North China and create a Japanese-dominated puppet state without upsetting the status quo?

In August 1936 Ishiwara brought together the major branches of the general staff and war ministry to formulate detailed plans for the industrialization of Manchuria and preparations for a war against the Soviet Union as expressed in the "Fundamental Principles of National Defense and National Policy."

Ignoring the recently revised national defense policy, he directed a wide-ranging modernization program that shaped the war ministry's five-year rear-mament plan with a proviso for an expanded fifty-division force structure, forty of them available by 1942.[74]

That November the war ministry announced plans to convert square divisions to triangular ones that would possess substantially greater firepower, mobility, and improved communications, as well as antiaircraft, antitank, and antichemical defenses. The new configuration—one brigade with three subordinate regiments, stiffened with modern weaponry—would streamline units by reducing personnel while strengthening organic firepower and strategic mobility. The seventeen infantry regiments excess to the square divisions (one from each regular division) would become the cadre for six new triangular divisions, which would enable the army to achieve its intermediate goal of fielding twenty-three active divisions by 1940, the year the war ministry expected the outbreak of a world war.[75]

The new formations were designed for mobility. Unencumbered by a lengthy baggage train, infantry and artillery units could deploy quickly off the march formation and maneuver swiftly around enemy flanks. Army officials further compressed road march formations by eliminating the fourth artillery battery of each artillery regiment, sacrificing firepower for speed and mobility. Field artillery was light, mobile, and small caliber in order to keep pace with fast-moving meeting engagements. Heavier guns were of course also employed, but usually in set-piece battles where mobility was not at a premium. Just as Kodama had earlier sought to destroy the czar's Far Eastern armies before reinforcements could arrive from western Russia, in 1937 Ishiwara wanted to destroy Soviet military power in the Maritime Provinces before reinforcements could arrive.

With the army and navy embarked on ambitious expansion programs, in November 1936 the cabinet approved a three billion yen budget—a 31 percent increase over the previous year. Military expansion would consume about half the 1937 national budget, and the cabinet relied on traditional practices of issuing bonds and raising taxes to defray the extraordinary expenses. In late 1936 the government issued 980 million yen in bonds, and in 1937 it collected an additional 420 million yen by increasing taxes on rice wine and personal incomes. The rapid expansion of military-related heavy industry, however, relied on imported raw materials from China and Manchuria and finished goods from the United States, which worsened Japan's trade balance and added to economic uncertainty.[76]

The Diet balked at underwriting the cabinet's huge military budget and bridled at the army's schemes for a planned economy, particularly War Minister Lt. Gen. Terauchi Hisaichi's incessant demands that the government enact legislation to impose state controls on business and labor organizations. These disagreements erupted openly on January 21, 1937, during a Diet interpellation involving Terauchi and the Seiyūkai's senior representative, Hamada Kunimatsu, who elicited rounds of applause as he passionately criticized the army's high-handedness, meddling in affairs of state, and dictatorial aspirations. Flushed with anger, Terauchi demanded an apology, and Hamada dramatically offered to disembowel himself if the stenographic record showed he had slandered the army. If not, then Terauchi ought to commit ritual suicide.[77] Later that day Terauchi demanded the cabinet's resignation for the slander. Hirota's besieged cabinet resigned two days later.

Army leaders then resorted to the active-duty provision to block recommendations that Ugaki become prime minister by refusing to nominate a war minister to serve in his cabinet. Too many senior officers bore him grudges, and Ugaki carried too much baggage, from eliminating divisions to involvement in the March Incident, to regain the army's trust and support. Military police prevented Ugaki's car from proceeding to the imperial palace, and the commander of the military police told him directly that the army would not approve his nomination. Unable to secure a war minister, Ugaki could not form a cabinet and withdrew from consideration. On February 2, retired army general Hayashi Senjūrō, widely regarded as Ishiwara's puppet, became prime minister. Hayashi was unable to steer his budget through the Diet and resigned a month after an embarrassing defeat in the April 30, 1937, general election.

With the assistance of the quasi-official South Manchurian Railroad research committee, in May 1937 Ishiwara submitted an outline for a five-year expansion of heavy industry to the war ministry. In mid-June recently appointed Prime Minister Konoe Fumimaro, who had coordinated on advance drafts, approved the plan that would double or triple industrial output, expand aircraft production tenfold, and convert Japan from light to heavy industry. Manchurian heavy industry would be developed separately so that no matter what happened at home, the army would still control its own military-industrial complex in Manchuria.[78] By this time, however, Ishiwara's star was in decline. He had lost out to Lt. Gen. Umezu Yoshijirō in the selection of the war minister for Hayashi's cabinet, and during the annual March 1937 personnel assignments Umezu transferred Ishiwara's backers from Tokyo. Those who remained and supported rearmament would soon split with Ishiwara over China policy.

Although overshadowed by the murderous factional struggles occurring in the war ministry and general staff, line units stationed in Japan went about their normal peacetime routines. Between 1927 and 1937, the army gradually modernized its weapons and equipment. An advanced 75mm Type 90 field artillery piece boasting increased range and a more accurate projectile entered the forces in 1930, forming with the 105mm Type 10 howitzer and 75mm pack mountain artillery (disassembled for transport on pack animals) the standard division's artillery complement. More than tactical reasons dictated the weapons procurement. To modernize the forces, the army needed to replace about 2,000 artillery guns of all calibers. A mixed government arsenal–private sector steel company consortium produced the new artillery weapons, but because of technological and manufacturing limitations most were the lighter caliber weapons. Put simply, Japan's industrial base was incapable of manufacturing large quantities of heavy artillery. It took, for example, eight months to manufacture one 150mm Type 15 cannon and eighteen months to produce a 240mm Type 24 howitzer, and the army did not believe that it had that much time.[79]

Likewise, the supply of artillery shells was well below projected operational requirements. During 1936 government arsenals manufactured less than one-tenth of the projected wartime consumption rates. Live-fire training was rare because of munitions restrictions and consequently emphasized quality rather than quantity, with a doctrine of "one round, one hit." Training exercises lacked variety and suffered from the scarcity of suitable artillery firing ranges in crowded Japan.[80] Industrial and manufacturing backwardness similarly affected motorization and armor.

Motorization was costly, dependent on foreign supply, and of dubious value on the primitive roads of northeast Asia. Military estimates that 250,000 trucks were needed to put the army on wheels were far beyond the fledgling Japanese automobile industry's capability, which until 1933 annually manufactured fewer than 1,000 automobiles. Tanks also were in short supply. The Spanish Civil War (1936–1939) seemed to expose the tank's limited off-road mobility, and smaller tanks light enough to cross unbridged rivers on pontoons or ferries were deemed more appropriate for the North China and Manchurian terrain. Amidst this uncertainty, the army was unwilling to invest heavily in an expensive but unproven weapon. Furthermore, the decision in 1936 to expand the army's air arm and homeland air defense network shifted resources, capital, and technology to aeronautical projects. Japan's industrial base could not simultaneously mass produce aircraft, vehicles, and tanks. As late as 1939, factories were manufacturing an average of twenty-eight tanks (all models) per month.[81]

But dwelling too long on force modernization obscures the fact that the army had tailored itself to operate in East Asia. By mid-1937 the army had a well-honed tactical and operational doctrine crafted over two decades to win the opening battles of a future war quickly and decisively. It numbered approximately 247,000 officers and men arrayed in an order of battle of 17 active infantry divisions, four tank regiments, and 54 air squadrons with 549 aircraft. The China Garrison Army and Taiwan Garrison Army each had two infantry regiments, and there was a separate independent mixed brigade in Manchuria.[82] Two divisions were permanently stationed in Korea and four others assigned on a rotating basis to the Kwantung Army in Manchukuo (the puppet regime in Manchuria). The balance were in the home garrison. A large pool of reservists and partially trained replacements were available upon mobilization to fill out peacetime table of organization and equipment (TO&E) units to their wartime strength.

Although predominantly an infantry force, the army's conventional combined-arms (infantry-artillery) divisions were similar in composition to European and U.S. counterparts. The triangular division had organic field artillery for shock and firepower effect. The army had operational contingency plans to fight all its major hypothetical opponents and was embarked on an ambitious rearmament plan to refit and modernize its forces. It had popular backing, in large measure because of the state values that schools inculcated in students and the army's penetration to the grassroots level through organizations like the Imperial Reservists Association, youth training groups, and military training in schools. The army had shown its muscle in the political arena by tacitly and actively supporting illegal plots and coups overseas and at home, by openly meddling in national administrative and economic matters, and by interfering in the political process of selecting prime ministers.

Among the competing elites, the army had capitalized on the volatile international situation, domestic terrorism, internal factionalism, and political party weakness to emerge as the premier power broker in Japan. But it was never powerful enough to impose its will on the navy or for that matter entirely on the civilian cabinet. Army authorities blustered, intimidated, and demanded, but they ended up compromising with other elites. Rhetoric about national defense planning and transcendental civilian cabinets aside, in mid-1937 there was no integrated national defense strategy. There was no coherent and realistic rearmament plan. There was no joint operational planning. Nothing linked doctrine, operations, military budgets, hypothetical opponents, or future war. Still, on balance, it was a very good army, appropriately armed and equipped for limited warfare on the northeast Asia continent.

10

The Pivotal Years, 1937–1941

Since the 1911 Chinese revolution Japanese army officers had repeatedly interfered in China's internal affairs. They worked with Chinese and Manchurian warlords during the turmoil that accompanied the new Chinese republic,
served as military advisers to various Chinese factions, promoted instability,
assassinated Zhang Zuolin, and conspired to seize Manchuria. After occupying Manchuria, Japanese field armies redoubled their efforts to subvert the
authority of China's Nationalist government by promoting regional autonomy
movements in North China.[1] In reaction to Japanese aggressiveness, the Soviet Union bolstered its military forces in the Soviet Far East. By early 1936
Manchuria was a Japanese strategic liability, a salient flanked on three sides by
Soviet territory with an open western flank nominally under Chinese Nationalist control. Furthermore, the field armies' heavy-handedness unleashed latent
Chinese patriotism and nationalism against Japan and helped bring together
the warring Guomindang and insurgent Chinese Communists who were unwilling to accept Japanese domination of North China and Manchuria.

Slipping into War

Tokyo's traditional response to the outbreak of serious incidents in China was
to deploy troops from homeland garrisons, deal with the localized emergency,
and then withdraw. Faced with resurgent Chinese nationalism, the Chinese
Communist expansion north of the Yellow River in February 1936, and the
spread of anti-Japanese agitation, the army's revised contingency plans called
for occupying North China's five provinces, securing the Shanghai area by
outflanking the city's defenses with an amphibious landing, and then seizing
the Nationalists' capital at Nanjing. General staff officers sympathetic to Col.
Ishiwara viewed the hard-line approach as counterproductive because it interfered with long-term plans for rearmament and army modernization. Prime
Minister Hirota agreed and adopted a more conciliatory policy toward China,
but his initiatives soon unraveled.[2]

Since 1933 the Kwantung Army had been promoting Inner Mongolian independence to create yet another puppet regime. In January 1936, Lt. Col. Tanaka
Ryūkichi, then attached to the Kwantung Army, was advising a pro-Japanese
military faction in Inner Mongolia. In midsummer he secretly raised a puppet
army to oust Nationalist forces from neighboring Suiyuan and, with the clandestine backing of the Kwantung Army, launched an unauthorized invasion of
eastern Suiyuan in mid-November. It failed miserably, giving the Nationalists a
much-needed victory, causing elation among the Chinese press and population,
and creating still more intense Chinese hatred of Japanese aggression.[3]

Meantime, in September 1936 the general staff decided to preempt major
outbreaks in North China with a show of force. Should that fail, field commanders had orders to act decisively and rely on rapid maneuver and shock action to settle outbreaks locally as quickly as possible with the minimum forces
necessary. The army considered no other countermeasures, so armed intervention in North China, even against minor flare-ups, became an all or nothing
proposition.[4]

A minor skirmish erupted on the night of July 7, 1937, between Japanese
and Chinese forces that were stationed near the Marco Polo Bridge outside
Peking. The local Japanese commander, Col. Mutaguchi Renya, was a fire-eater
who subscribed to the theory popular among army officers that weakness only
encouraged Chinese aggressiveness. He reacted to the skirmish by unilaterally
escalating the fighting, thereby setting off the powder keg in North China.

Cabinet and military authorities in Tokyo originally adopted a nonexpansion-
ist policy, anticipating a local settlement. Four days after the incident, however,
army intelligence reported that Chiang Kai-shek was sending reinforcements
to North China, causing the general staff to reinforce the China Garrison Army
with units from Korea and Manchuria. Chief of Staff Prince Kan'in and War
Minister Gen. Sugiyama Hajime informed Hirohito that the war would be over
in a month. The less sanguine emperor wondered what would happen if the
Soviet Union attacked Manchuria while Japan was mired in China.[5]

With neither the Chinese nor the Japanese willing to back down, local clashes
soon escalated into multidivision engagements. By the end of July, Japanese
reinforcements had driven Chinese forces from Peking and Tianjin as Tokyo
mobilized upwards of 200,000 troops. On August 1, the Third Fleet evacuated
Japanese citizens from Shanghai because of rising tensions in the city.

The general staff and war ministry were divided over how to handle the latest incident. The former favored a negotiated settlement to limit the fighting
whereas the latter argued that a rapid escalation and a short, decisive campaign
would eliminate the Chinese threat to Japan's strategic western flank. As the
fighting intensified, the hawks gained prominence as more and more army
divisions sailed for China to fight an undeclared war. Massive escalation raised

questions about the need for a formal declaration of war against China, and the civilian cabinet pushed for the establishment of an imperial general headquarters in hopes of controlling military operations.

Establishing Imperial Headquarters

Memories of civilian meddling during the undeclared war in Siberia made the general staff suspicious that politicians and civilian ministers would again interfere in military affairs. Staff officers consequently opposed the formation of imperial headquarters without a formal declaration of war. Prime Minister Konoe and some officers in the war ministry also wanted a formal declaration of war, the former because it was appropriate under international law and the latter to preserve operational independence. A joint study, however, concluded that an official announcement would threaten Japan's international access to trade and raw materials, which in turn would adversely affect national security.[6] Thus the emperor opened the Imperial Diet's 72d Extraordinary Session on September 4, 1937, by describing Japanese determination to resolve the China "Incident."

That October, after major fighting had engulfed North China and spread to Shanghai, the field armies again requested a formal declaration of war to enable the army to control Chinese customs revenues, postal systems, and financial services in its zones of occupation. An official break would also encourage the formation of pro-Japanese regimes and end the general staff's restrictions on military operations. A special cabinet subcommittee chaired by the head of the Cabinet Planning Board decided the following month that the advantages of an undeclared war, particularly in international trade, outweighed any disadvantages. Separate studies by the war, navy, and foreign ministries reached the same conclusion.[7]

The undeclared war likewise complicated the activation of imperial general headquarters (IGHQ). By mid-October, Konoe was increasingly frustrated by the army's unilateral actions that routinely bypassed his cabinet and believed that an imperial headquarters could unify civil-military control of the incident. The war ministry's military affairs bureau recommended a centralized policy mechanism to enable civilian and military cabinet ministers as well as the president of the privy council to coordinate the overall war effort. The general staff believed this would only encourage excessive civilian interference in the prerogative of supreme command, and the navy, fearful that the army might use the new headquarters to overrule civilian policy, would only endorse a headquarters to coordinate, not plan, joint operations.[8]

With matters at an impasse, in mid-November the military affairs bureau director notified the war minister that an imperial headquarters was immediately needed to reassert the general staff's authority over the field commanders.

New legislation amended the statutory provision that a state of war be declared to establish the IGHQ (the new ordinance stipulated war or incident). As constituted on November 27, 1937, imperial general headquarters excluded the prime minister and civilian cabinet officials from military deliberations, leaving operational matters firmly under the services' control.

Imperial headquarters was divided into army and navy sections directed by the chiefs of the general staff for both services who were the emperor's highest advisers on operational matters. The respective staffs came from the directors and selected subordinates of the more important bureaus and departments of the war and navy ministries and the army and navy general staffs. Service leaders agreed beforehand on military policy before seeking the emperor's authorization at special imperial conferences held at IGHQ (*Daihon'ei gozen kaigi*) that included the emperor and his senior military officials and dealt exclusively with military matters. Eight such sessions were held between November 1937 and May 1943 (see Table 10.1).[9]

A liaison conference composed of the two service chiefs of staff, the two service ministers, the prime and foreign ministers and other civilian officials (*Daihon'ei seifu renraku kaigi*) followed the IGHQ conference to coordinate military and civilian policy. The members of the liaison conference could also meet in the presence of the emperor to ratify their consensus on major national policies. These meetings were imperial conferences (*gozen kaigi*), fifteen of which were held between January 1938 and August 1945. Throughout the period, however, IGHQ was the military policy-making apparatus and senior operational headquarters.[10]

Hirohito's role in operational deliberations and in policy formulation remains controversial, some claiming he rubber-stamped military policy, others that he initiated it. There is no doubt that Hirohito tried to influence policy, but he rarely displayed the type of leadership associated with strong wartime

Table 10.1. Imperial Conferences at Imperial General Headquarters, 1937–1943

Date	Event
Nov. 24, 1937	Army/navy report on operational plans to emperor
Feb. 16, 1938	Outline of China operations for summer/fall 1938
June 15, 1938	Wuhan operation approved
Jan. 13, 1939	Hainan Island occupation approved
Dec. 31, 1942	Guadalcanal withdrawal approved
March 5, 1943	1943 operational policy approved
March 26, 1943	Eighth Area Army (Rabaul) established
May 20, 1943	Aleutians withdrawal approved

Source: Yamada Akira, *Daigensui Shōwa tennō* [Generalissimo Shōwa emperor] (Tokyo: Shin Nihon shuppansha, 1994), 70–72.

leaders. Rather, he questioned details to indicate his inclinations during the policy process. A lack of information also restricted the emperor. The privy seal and courtiers were well connected and gathered information from a number of sources. But they were few in number compared to the service staffs' and civilian ministries' bureaucracies. Those agencies offered the emperor selective, and sometimes contradictory, data in order to gain imperial support for their programs. Hirohito thus often operated on incomplete or biased information, and sometimes in near isolation.[11] Perhaps a stronger leader could have brought the ministries and staffs into line, but that person would not be Hirohito.

The first imperial general headquarters conference convened on the palace grounds on November 24, 1937, attended by the service chiefs of staff, the vice chiefs of staff, the operations division directors of the respective general staffs, and the war and navy ministers. The chiefs of staff informed the emperor that the military was reestablishing security, not expanding operations, in North China; that the army was pursuing the disorganized Chinese in central China and considering the capture of Nanjing; and that naval air raids were interdicting railroads in South China. They sought no imperial decision regarding pending plans or operations, and the emperor asked no questions.[12]

Later that afternoon the first IGHQ government liaison conference met at the prime minister's official residence, where the prime minister, both service ministers, and their deputies discussed limiting operations in China because of the Soviet threat and the possibility of U.S. or British intervention. The fragmented system satisfied no one and made coordination between the civilian cabinet members and the military complex and time consuming. With the services unwilling to reveal, much less discuss, operational plans, the liaison conference was discontinued in early 1938 and replaced by a four- or five-minister conference system until Konoe revived the liaison conference as a policy-coordinating entity in late November 1940. Between then and February 1944 it convened 145 times, initially every Thursday at the prime minister's official residence.[13]

The War in China

The undeclared war in China was primarily a struggle between ground forces fought over an area equivalent in size to the United States east of the Mississippi River. The vastness of the countryside rendered a contiguous defensive line impossible, and it abetted the army's aggressive tactical and operational doctrine to sweep swiftly around or outflank Chinese strong points. But these same geographical conditions that conferred operational advantages simultaneously imposed extraordinary requirements on the army's long-neglected logistical system. Supply problems were endemic, logistics support always teetered on the edge of collapse, and operations were usually conducted on a logistical shoestring.

In strictly military terms, operational guidance and official tactical doctrine were validated but evolved in an ad hoc fashion, lurching from campaign to campaign with little if any linkage toward a strategic military goal, much less an integrated national objective. Diplomats worked to resolve the crisis while field commanders demanded greater operational autonomy to expand the war. Attempts by the cabinet and general staff to limit the fighting foundered. IGHQ's creation did not unify the command structure.

The Japanese axis of attack to secure North China raced down two parallel main rail lines—the Tianjin-Pukou route on the east, and the Peking-Wuhan route on the west. Logistics doctrine dictated that the field armies operate within a 150–180 mile radius of a railhead to ensure a reliable line of communication. Whenever units moved beyond this zone, resupply and sustainment declined, often dangerously so. The First Army drove south from Peking while the Second Army was to move south then swing west to trap Chinese forces between the two armies north of the Hutuo River in a massive double envelopment. Tokyo activated the North China Area Army (NCAA) on August 26, 1937, to control and coordinate the two armies.

In August heavy fighting erupted in Shanghai, where Chiang Kai-shek opened a second front, hoping to overwhelm the Japanese units stationed near the city. Hirohito initially wanted to send two divisions to Shanghai to show Japanese resolve, control the dangerous situation, and prevent further escalation. The general staff, however, refused to commit any reinforcements while the army was so heavily engaged in North China, fearing that dividing its forces might encourage the Soviets to enter the war. Only when Nationalist forces threatened to drive the lightly armed Japanese naval infantry from the city in mid-August did the general staff deploy three divisions to Shanghai and activate the Shanghai Expeditionary Army. The emperor then asked his chiefs of staff about the possibility of massing forces to deliver a knockout blow to end the fighting.[14] Chiang was also thinking along the same lines and poured in more reinforcements (eventually seventy divisions) for a decisive battle.

Both sides avoided combat in the city, the site of significant foreign commercial, financial, and administrative interests. Japan wanted to prevent an open clash with the western powers, and China could not afford to alienate them. As a consequence, major fighting occurred north and west of Shanghai, where reinforced army units tried to break through well-fortified Chinese positions. Unable to dislodge the determined Chinese defenders and suffering severe losses, the general staff in mid-September ordered three more divisions to Shanghai to break the stalemate. Gen. Matsui Iwane, recalled from retirement to command the much-strengthened Shanghai Expeditionary Army, massed his reinforcements for an unimaginative frontal attack that quickly broke down before the skillfully sited Chinese fortifications that took maximum advantage of numerous creeks crisscrossing the area to disrupt and destroy the attackers. Infantrymen fought desperately for a few hundred yards of ground; both sides suffered severely, and both committed more reserves and replacements, but neither could break the cycle of attrition warfare.

In early October the general staff ordered the North China Area Army to destroy Chinese forces throughout Shanxi to eliminate the threat to Japan's western flank. It also transferred two NCAA divisions to Shanghai service and activated the Tenth Army on October 20 to conduct an amphibious envelopment southwest of the city. Ten days later, the general staff created the Central China Area Army to oversee the Shanghai campaign. By early November repeated Japanese assaults had broken through China's last line of defense west of Shanghai, and on November 4 the Tenth Army landed more than three divisions south of the city, threatened to encircle the Chinese, and forced Chiang to withdraw the remnants of his badly mauled armies to avoid annihilation. Losses for the four-month Shanghai fighting were enormous: more than 40,000 Japanese and perhaps 200,000 Chinese were killed, wounded, or missing.

Casualties of this magnitude shocked the Japanese public. Tokyo police had to be called to disperse angry demonstrators surrounding the home of a regimental commander whose unit had suffered heavy losses at Shanghai. In Shikoku the widow of another regimental commander killed at Shanghai committed suicide, unable to bear the stream of vituperation directed at her late husband.[15]

As Japanese ground forces pushed southward through North China and fought their way around Shanghai, Kwantung Army units and the NCAA's strategic reserve, the 5th Division, opened a third major offensive that occupied Chahar northwest of Peking. Operations went smoothly at first as Japanese mechanized forces and aircraft opened the way for mobile infantry columns moving along the Peking-Suiyuan railroad. In mid-September, however, the 5th Division suffered a tactical setback in the mountainous terrain at Pingxingguan, where the Central Army and Chinese Communist troops bloodied the Japanese before being forced to withdraw.

Japanese columns overran much of North China but failed to destroy the Chinese armies, which withdrew inland, leaving the overextended Japanese with the prospect of still more territory to occupy. The general staff's repeated attempts to limit operations had foundered when field commanders insisted on bolder offensives to annihilate the Chinese armies. Believing that the capture of the Guomindang capital at Nanjing would force Chiang to negotiate, the Tenth Army spearheaded the 170-mile march upriver from Shanghai in mid-

November. Officers issued orders to torch buildings and homes along the way that might shelter Chinese troops and, because of the danger that mufti-clad Chinese soldiers might infiltrate their lines, to deal severely with all Chinese civilians suspected of aiding the enemy.[16] By December 10 rapidly moving Japanese infantry had reached the towering 50-foot-high brick walls that encased Nanjing.

Fighting continued in the city for the next three days as Chiang Kai-shek repeatedly changed his mind about the defense of the capital, which was not formally surrendered and added to the chaos that overtook the doomed city. When the Chinese defenders finally retreated in confusion, Japanese troops sacked the city and perpetrated one of the most notorious war crimes of the twentieth century as they pillaged, raped, and murdered Chinese prisoners of war and civilians in the notorious Rape of Nanjing. "Since our policy is not to take prisoners," the 16th Division commander wrote, "we made a point of executing them as soon as we captured them."[17] Estimates of the total numbers of Chinese deaths remain contentious; the Chinese claim upwards of 300,000 victims whereas Japanese counterparts suggest a range from a few thousand to around 100,000.[18]

Whatever the precise figures, this was more than a breakdown of discipline brought on by the heavy losses suffered during the Shanghai fighting. The 16th Division, which perpetrated some of the worst atrocities at Nanjing, did not fight in Shanghai and had suffered relatively light casualties.[19] This suggests that the army targeted the civilian population as a critical component of a total war and applied indiscriminate terror to cow the Chinese into submission.

Despite Japanese conquests, the terror at Nanjing and elsewhere, and a sustained bombing offensive, the Chinese did not submit. The Guomindang relocated its capital to Wuhan on the Yangzi River in central China, and Chiang's Central Army withdrew deeper into the vast hinterland beyond the immediate reach of Japanese military might. The fall of Nanjing had not brought an end to the China war, and the news of widespread Japanese atrocities hardened Chinese resistance. Although often outmaneuvering their foes, the army had neither enough troops nor operational mobility to seal their envelopments. Chinese armies repeatedly escaped through gaps in the attempted encirclements, and Japanese field commanders constantly pressured the general staff and the IGHQ to extend the area of operations ever deeper into China.

The Mobilized Army

By the end of 1937 the army had sixteen divisions and 600,000 men committed to China operations with no end in sight. Imperial army forces in central China were exhausted, worn down by heavy casualties, insufficient ammunition stocks, and inadequate logistic support. IGHQ temporarily stood down major operations in central China in order to reconstitute, refit, and restore discipline in the ranks. It also needed the respite to mobilize ten new divisions in the home islands by mid-1938 and convert essential industries to wartime production schedules. Hirohito sanctioned this policy at a February 16, 1938, IGHQ imperial conference. The army accordingly would avoid large-scale operations while it secured the occupied zones.[20]

To replace losses, the army almost doubled draft calls for 1938 and mobilized tens of thousands of reserves. By the late summer of 1938, mobilization had doubled the prewar seventeen-division force structure; twenty-four (eight regular, sixteen reserve) of the army's thirty-four divisions were fighting in China, eight were in Manchuria (seven of them regular), one regular division garrisoned in Korea, and the other (the Guard) remained in homeland reserve.

The recalled reservists were older men, often with wives and children, and most marched off for war in the summer of 1937 confidant that they would be back home in time to celebrate New Year's Day 1938 with their families. Instead, as of August 1, 1938, just over 11 percent of Japanese soldiers in the China Expeditionary Army were regulars, 22.6 percent were from the first reserve (aged 24–28), 45.2 percent from the second reserve (aged 29–34), and 20.9 percent from the conscript reserve, the last consisting of untrained or semi-trained personnel used as replacements mainly in transport and logistical units (see Table 10.2).[21]

This distribution occurred because the general staff insisted that the regulars be immediately available in Manchuria or in homeland reserve for anticipated future operations against the Soviet Union. In other words, the army withdrew regular divisions from China for reconstitution in late 1937 and replaced them with mobilized reserve divisions (see Table 10.3).

Table 10.2. Conscription Figures, 1937–1940

Year	1937	1938	1939	1940
"A" Class				
Examined	153,000	195,200	200,600	188,800
Conscripted	153,000	195,200	200,600	188,800
"B" Class				
Examined	470,635	410,239	412,475	402,283
Conscripted	17,000	124,800	139,400	131,200
Total Cohort*	742,422	720,761	729,852	703,670
Conscripted	170,000	320,000	340,000	320,000
% Conscripted	22.9	44.4	46.6	45.6

*Includes "C," "D," and "F" categories, which accounted for no conscripts. *Source: Kindai sensōshi gaisetsu, shiryō hen*, 35, table 2-1-8, and 36, table 2-1-9.

Table 10.3. Regulars and Reserves on Active Duty, 1937–1940

	1937	1938	1939	1940
Regulars	354,000	615,400	844,400	965,700
Reserves	595,000	514,600	395,600	384,300
Total	950,000	1,130,000	1,240,000	1,350,000

Source: *Kindai sensoshi gaisetsu, shiryo hen,* 35, table 2-1-8, and 36, table 2-1-9.

Army authorities blamed the reservists' commitments to families and jobs for weakening their spiritual power and contributing to their poor discipline and criminal misconduct in China. In fact, recalled reservists were charged with four times as many criminal offensives as regulars in the first two years of the China war, and there was a widespread perception throughout the army that ill-disciplined reserves caused too many problems. Junior officers assigned to regular divisions in China believed the reserve units suffered from poor leadership, which contributed to their disciplinary problems.[22]

As the fighting expanded and the casualty lists lengthened, the Japanese home front's expectations of the rewards of the war grew accordingly.[23] After the fall of Nanjing, the Konoe cabinet adopted a harder line on peace terms, in part because the heavy losses (much like those during the Russo-Japanese War) provoked public demands for proportionate compensation in the form of concessions and indemnities. To address this issue and to obtain the emperor's authorization to set national policy, on January 11, 1938, the first imperial conference convened on the palace grounds. Participants included military leaders and the prime and foreign ministers.

Neither the prime minister, navy minister, nor foreign minister wanted the session, but the Vice Chief of the General Staff, Lt. Gen. Tada Shun, believed imperial approval of a lenient policy would restrain the military hardliners in Tokyo and aggressive field army commanders. Following senior statesman Saionji Kinmochi's advice that the government had already decided policy and therefore he need make no inquiries, Hirohito sat silently throughout the proceedings. Rather than a conciliatory approach that Tada had expected, there emerged a confirmation of the expansionists' harshest demands, including reparations and an ultimatum to China.[24] Five days later Konoe proclaimed that Japan would no longer deal with the Chiang government, leaving no one to negotiate with to end the fighting.

Mobilization at Home

Although Japan was not officially at war, its government and army relied on extensive propaganda and so-called spiritual mobilization to energize the home front and encourage popular support for the China effort. Parades, fireworks, and mass demonstrations celebrated the initial victories of 1937. Orchestrating these events, however, was risky as it had been during the Russo-Japanese War. In December 1937 the government organized a huge torchlight parade to celebrate the capture of Nanjing but had to postpone the celebration for three days when the Chinese capital did not fall as quickly as expected. In another effort to raise national morale and wartime consciousness, Hirohito opened the 74th Imperial Diet in December 1938 dressed in an army uniform bedecked with medals, not his traditional formal wear for the occasion. The escalating war in China, however, soon sapped the civilian economy and industry.[25] The army's share of the national budget had steadily increased since 1931 to pay for operations in Manchuria and North China. Waging a full-scale war in China since mid-1937, the accompanying army expansion, and the high command's retooling of the force to fight the Soviet Union[26] took more than 70 percent of the national budget.

Attempts to pass a national general mobilization law that would give the government sweeping economic powers encountered resistance in the Diet, where members heckled Lt. Col. Satō Kenryō, chief of the domestic affairs section of the military affairs branch, during his March 3, 1938, presentation. Exasperated that politicians had the temerity to contradict him, a furious Satō shouted "Shut up!" and stormed out of the room. The next day War Minister Sugiyama apologized for Satō's behavior, but he did not reprimand the hotheaded colonel. In contrast, when a member of the opposition called on Konoe to show bolder leadership like Hitler, Mussolini, and Stalin, the Lower House promptly expelled him for the reference to the Soviet dictator. As for the mobilization legislation, Konoe ultimately conceded that its provisions would be applied only during an officially declared war and not the current incident.[27]

New Operations in China

Despite the mid-February decisions, aggressive Japanese commanders in North China sought out the enemy and routinely divided their forces to envelop and destroy the Chinese armies. In March 1938 two widely separated Japanese columns of the 5th Division moved from the north and the east against Taierzhuang, located on a rail line and transportation hub along the Grand Canal. Crack Guomindang troops defeated each column separately and forced the Japanese to retreat with heavy losses. Although Japanese reinforcements later drove out the seriously weakened Chinese, the Japanese defeat at Taierzhuang was celebrated across China as a major victory that greatly enhanced Chinese morale and further reduced the chances for downscaling field operations. The battle illustrated the dangers of overextended, smaller forces relying on aggressiveness and offensive spirit to defeat a larger, determined opponent.

On April 7, just as the fighting at Taierzhuang was drawing to a close, the IGHQ ordered a seven-division (200,000 troops) operation to envelop Xuzhou from north and south and trap at least fifty Guomindang (GMD) divisions.[28] The army again split its forces and relied on converging columns to surround the Chinese. The two-month operation captured Xuzhou and destroyed scores of Chinese divisions but could not snare the main Chinese armies, most of which took advantage of a heavy fog and mist that blanketed the area to escape the encirclement. Japanese field logistics, already dangerously overextended, collapsed in the middle of the campaign, leaving frontline units hungry and precariously low on ammunition.

Unable to eliminate the GMD's main armies, the general staff abandoned its strategy of decisive engagement in favor of occupying strategic points. They struck against Wuhan—an administrative center, a staging and logistic base for Chinese forces defending the central Yangzi region, and a rallying point for the defense of China in the summer of 1938. To forestall the Japanese thrust, in early June 1938 Chiang ordered the breaching of the Yellow River dikes at Huayuankou (Henan) in what Diana Lary has aptly labeled a "drowned earth" policy. The massive flooding isolated elements of two Japanese divisions, but 900,000 Chinese civilians perished in three badly flooded provinces, and 3.9 million more became refugees.[29] Chiang's decision prevented an immediate attack on Wuhan and allowed Chinese troops to retreat and regroup, but the IGHQ was more disquieted by the outbreak of regimental-size fighting in July and early August between Japanese and Soviet forces at Changkuofeng on the Korean-Soviet border. Uncertain whether the Soviets intended to enter the war on China's side or were merely probing Japan's defenses, the general staff suspended the Wuhan campaign.

After the Japanese takeover of Manchuria, Moscow had rapidly reinforced the Soviet Far East from eight divisions and 200 aircraft in 1932 to as many as twenty divisions and 1,200 aircraft just four years later. The possibility of spillover from the China war led to further reinforcements, and by 1938 there were an estimated twenty-four Soviet divisions (450,000 troops) and 2,000 aircraft in the region. The Japanese in turn had built up the Kwantung Army to eight divisions (about 200,000 personnel) with twelve air regiments (about 230 aircraft) plus an additional first-line division available in Korea for immediate reinforcement.[30]

Tension along the 3,000-mile unmarked and disputed border produced hundreds of minor incidents and a few major ones, such as the sinking of a Soviet gunboat on the Amur River near Blagoveshchensk in mid-1937. At that time, the Soviets had acceded to Japanese demands, which convinced the Kwantung Army that the Russians would invariably back down when confronted by military might. This certitude, along with intelligence reports that Stalin's purges were ravaging the Red Army's senior officer corps, appeared to render the Soviets a less formidable opponent.

When a small number of Soviet troops occupied the high ground near Changkuofeng in early July 1938, the Korea Army's immediate reaction was to crush the intruders by force. Chief of Staff Prince Kan'in and War Minister Lt. Gen. Itagaki Seishirō separately sought imperial approval on July 20 for the attack, but their accounts contradicted the foreign minister's version of events and so upset Hirohito that he insisted not a single soldier would move without his permission. Several days later, outposts reported that the Soviets were fortifying the heights near Changkuofeng, and the local Japanese commander unilaterally ordered a 1,500-man assault on the night of July 30/31 to retake the high ground. Assured that the officer had acted in self-defense after repeated Soviet provocations, Hirohito gave ex post facto approval the next day.[31]

But on August 1 Soviet aircraft bombed the Japanese positions, and at least three Soviet divisions, supported by tanks, aircraft, and heavy artillery, counterattacked the 7,000 or so Japanese defenders in the disputed area. For ten days the Soviets pounded the Japanese infantry, who were forbidden by the emperor and general staff to respond with aircraft or heavy artillery. Infantrymen grimly held their ground under relentless Soviet bombardment and sustained more than 1,400 casualties, including over 500 killed, although the war ministry's official communiqué halved those figures for public consumption. Soviet losses were also considerable, somewhere between the officially announced 850 and 5,000 or 6,000. An August 11 cease-fire was signed in Moscow.

The cease-fire and Soviet restraint during the fighting, demonstrated by limiting their operations to the immediate contested area, reconfirmed the army's impression that the Russians would back down when confronted by force. Staff officers derided the Red Army's plodding tactics and its amateurish deployments during the fighting, views that meshed with confidential assessments of Soviet fighting ability, largely stereotypes predicated on presumed national characteristics.[32] Lastly, the general staff was certain that the action at Changkuofeng had secured the army's rear area bases in Manchuria.

With the threat to the northern flank neutralized, on August 22 the IGHQ ordered the Eleventh Army to resume the Wuhan offensive in conjunction with the Twenty-first Army's amphibious assault against Guangzhou, a major port and supply base in southern China. The Eleventh Army moved west on Wuhan along the Yangzi River, where the midsummer high-water levels made it navigable for navy gunboats to support infantrymen advancing along both banks of the great river. A separate attack drove south through the mountains to push in Chinese defenses. Altogether, 300,000 Japanese were pitted against one million Chinese troops.

Far from their depots and railheads, Japanese logistics quickly collapsed under the strain of overextended lines of communication, poor roads, and rugged mountainous terrain. Ill-supplied units operating along the banks of the Yangzi in stifling summer heat suffered epidemic malaria, amoebic dysentery, and outbreaks of cholera. Japanese troops ultimately resorted to poison gas, euphemistically known as "special smoke," to break especially strong Chinese resistance. In south China, Guangzhou fell on October 21, and in central China Wuhan followed five days later, the culmination of a ten-month campaign that seriously weakened the Central Army but did not force its capitulation.[33] To avoid a repetition of the Nanjing massacres, Chiang had ordered a general withdrawal before the Japanese reached Wuhan and relocated his capital at Chongqing in the remote interior of Sichuan (Szechwan).

The Wuhan battles marked the limit of the Japanese army's offensive capability to conduct large-scale operations.[34] By the fall of 1938 the war guidance section's new policy depended on Chinese puppet regimes and collaborators to control occupied zones, exploit the resources of North China, and protect Japan's economic and financial interests elsewhere in China. Consolidating control of the occupied areas would enable the army over time to reduce its 800,000 troops in China by half, although the remaining units would still hold key strategic areas as part of an anticommunist front formed by Japan, Manchukuo, and China. Prime Minister Konoe announced a benign version of the plan on November 3 when he described a new order in East Asia founded on an equal partnership between Japan and China.

The second imperial conference, held November 30, 1938, authorized the war guidance section's new policy to perpetuate a divided China.[35] The China Expeditionary Army strenuously objected to any troop reductions but ultimately agreed to reduce its forces to 750,000 by the end of 1939. Unable to end the China fighting and unwilling to support the army's recurrent demands for domestic reforms, Konoe resigned in early January 1939.

Regardless of talk of consolidation, IGHQ directed further offensives in central China against Nanchang in March 1939. The Eleventh Army captured the city in late March and then held it against fierce but unsuccessful Chinese counterattacks during the next two months. In May the army launched punitive raids to disrupt newly established Chinese bases in mountainous northern Hubei, but just as they commenced, heavy fighting erupted between Japanese and Soviet forces at Nomonhan, a tiny village on the ill-defined Manchuria–Outer Mongolian border. IGHQ again had to suspend major ground combat in China.

The Nomonhan campaign was the culmination of more than thirty years of army preparations for war with Russia. Decades had been invested in doctrine formulation, tactical innovation, weapons technology, and rigorous training to win the decisive first battle by rapid encirclement and annihilation of the enemy. After the Changkuofeng battles, the Kwantung Army, relatively unscathed by the war in China, ordered local commanders to act aggressively against any Soviet or Outer Mongolian intrusions into disputed territory. Under these rules of engagement, in late May 1939 a reconnaissance unit from the 23d Division tracked down a handful of Outer Mongolian troops near the village of Nomonhan.

Attempting to pin the intruders between Nomonhan and the Khalkin River, about a dozen miles to the west, the commander's aggressiveness led his unit into a Soviet ambush sprung by combined tank and infantry units. Soviet artillery, firing from the higher ground on the river's west bank, pounded the encircled, heavily outnumbered, and badly outgunned Japanese. After losing more than 60 percent of their 200-man force, the Japanese escaped the encirclement at night, although their commander was killed during the breakout.

Stung by the repulse, the Kwantung Army headquarters committed a reinforced division to clear out the disputed zone. In early July the 23d Division executed an enveloping attack under the cover of darkness. Two tank regiments (seventy-three tanks total) attached to the division spearheaded a frontal assault to hold the Soviets in place while two infantry regiments crossed the Khalkin River north of the engagement and then drove southward, outflanking and destroying Soviet artillery on the high ground while enveloping the enemy forces trapped on the east side of the river.

The classic envelopment maneuver of closing on the enemy with cold steel ended in complete failure. The frontal assault ran headlong into dug-in Soviet infantry supported by antitank and field artillery units that inflicted severe losses on the pride of Japan's armor corps, which was quickly withdrawn from the battle. Two days of heavy fighting stalled the flanking attack along the west bank, and Soviet counterattacks by hundreds of tanks and armored cars threatened to overrun the exposed Japanese, who depended on a single bridge for supplies and reinforcements because all other army bridging equipment had been previously committed to China operations.[36] Japanese infantrymen fought desperately in their shrinking bridgehead but on July 5 finally withdrew across the river, where they dug in under the sights of the Soviet gunners who dominated the higher ground on the west bank.

A protracted battle of attrition ensued as both sides reinforced, probed, and exchanged artillery bombardments for the next three weeks. The Soviets stopped a major Japanese frontal assault on July 23–25 short of its objective, a bridge at the confluence of the Khalkin and Holsten rivers. Afterward a dreary stalemate gripped the combatants until August 20, when the Red Army commanded by Lt. Gen. Georgi Zhukov unleashed a double-envelopment spearheaded by armor and mechanized brigades that turned the 23d Division's northern and southern flanks, surrounded the division, and then destroyed it. Japanese losses were more than 17,000, about half killed in action; Soviet casualties perhaps reached 20,000. In the midst of Zhukov's offensive, with the 23d Division literally fighting for its life, Japan's reputed ally Nazi Germany concluded a nonaggression pact with the Soviet Union. This dramatic turnabout caused the fall of the cabinet in Tokyo and consternation throughout the army.

Nazi armies rolled across the Polish frontier on September 1 secure in a secret protocol that divided the hapless nation with the Soviets. Some Japanese officers reckoned that the outbreak of war in Europe would compel the Soviets to withdraw units from Siberia to western Russia to deal with the crisis. Hotheads on the Kwantung Army staff urged an immediate three-division counterattack to retrieve the Nomonhan situation. Instead, on September 3 the general staff issued an imperial order canceling offensive operations and accepted defeat.

The Nomonhan disaster was all the more traumatic because the army had employed its premier doctrine, tactics, and equipment that it specially designed to produce a lightning victory. Instead, everything from nighttime bayonet assaults to vaunted spiritual power had failed. Rather than admit the full implications of the disaster, the high command blamed the troops of the recently activated 23d Division (July 1938) and their incompetent officers for the debacle. Subsequent army investigatory committees concluded that fighting spirit still retained its absolute priority in battle, although more firepower might be necessary in future engagements.[37]

Personnel reassignments followed the defeat. Senior commanders and high-level staff officers were seconded to the reserves or posted to army training schools. Regimental officers who actually fought in the battles were branded cowards or pressured to commit suicide for unauthorized withdrawals, in two cases after extended and heroic defense of their isolated positions. The army also dealt harshly with the 159 repatriated Japanese prisoners of war.[38]

The first prisoner exchanges occurred on September 27. Three days later the war minister ordered the commanders of the Kwantung Army and the China Expeditionary Army to interrogate all returning POWs and take required disciplinary measures, including assignment to penal units. The minister's objective was to tighten army discipline, but the Kwantung Army ordered disciplinary punishment even for those not indicted by review boards. Though regulations did not officially forbid surrender, the army's informal culture and the hothouse patriotism in Japan stigmatized those taken captive.

Repatriated officers were encouraged, or ordered, to commit suicide. Two repatriated army air force officers captured when their planes were shot down far behind enemy lines were allegedly handed pistols and told to do the honorable thing. Enlisted ex-prisoners of war were segregated for interrogation and

subsequent courts-martial. Punishments ranged from several years' confinement
to a few days under house arrest. After serving their sentences, former POWs
were relocated outside of Japan at locations of the former prisoners' choosing.
None was allowed to return to his parent unit, and even after being discharged
from the army only a handful returned home to Japan.[39]

If Major Kuga's troubled suicide in 1932 outside Shanghai set the standard
for officers to seek death before surrender, then the harsh treatment of returned
enlisted prisoners sent that message throughout the army. It was another example of senior officers blaming the high command's mistakes on the rank-
and-file's lack of fighting spirit.

The Occupied Zones

Army officials took little interest in long-term occupation policies, and logistics
were so strained that imperial headquarters ordered its field armies to live off
the land, an open invitation to widespread looting and pillaging. Roving Japanese and Chinese armies foraging for food repeatedly stripped contested areas
of crops, livestock, and valuables. Banditry replaced local administration, and
widespread crime characterized entire sections of occupied China throughout
the war.

Field brothels became a feature of the occupying army. Civilian and military
authorities had established a brothel system in Shanghai during 1932 to prevent
the spread of sexually transmitted diseases among troops. After the outbreak of
full-scale war with China in 1937, however, instances of Japanese troops assault-
ing, raping, or murdering Chinese women significantly increased, and commanders sought to restore military discipline by establishing field brothels, the
so-called comfort stations, in the Japanese-occupied zones. In other words, the
health, welfare, and discipline of the troops motivated the army.

In June 1938 the chief of staff of the North China Area Army complained
that numerous instances of rape harmed the pacification effort and interfered
with overall army operations because the crimes turned local inhabitants
against the Japanese. Officially approved and inspected comfort stations not
only would maintain military discipline by offering troops an outlet for their
pent-up aggression but also prevent the spread of sexual diseases contracted in
cheap Chinese brothels. Japanese civilian brothel managers were brought to
China to administer army-approved brothels under a licensing agreement, and
army doctors regularly inspected prostitutes for sexual diseases as the system
became institutionalized in the field armies.[40]

Violence against women was so widespread in China that senior officers
issued tougher regulations as early as 1940 to prevent it, but rape apparently remained so commonplace and tolerated that the army penal code was amended
in February 1942 to provide for harsher penalties.[41]

The Endless War

IGHQ activated the China Expeditionary Army (CEA, which absorbed the Central China Expeditionary Army) on September 23, 1939, and because of the rapidly changing international situation ordered it to bring what the Japanese called the China Incident quickly to an end so that the army might begin preparations for war against another, unnamed, adversary. Field commanders on the China front had chafed at the operational limits imposed by imperial headquarters. Lt. Gen. Okamura Yasuji, the commander of the Eleventh Army, for one, saw no way out of the ground war except through further offensives to destroy the Chinese armies. Now the reins were loosened and they had their chance to win the war.[42]

Plans were under way for a spring 1940 offensive when Chiang Kai-shek launched a nationwide 70-division offensive in mid-December 1939. Okamura's hard-pressed divisions were scattered across extended frontages (some were responsible for over 100 miles of front) without defenses-in-depth or a strategic reserve. By mid-January 1940 they had regrouped, then counterattacked, and defeated Chiang's offensive, but a shaken Eleventh Army notified IGHQ that the enemy was still full of fight.[43]

Concurrently, around the end of 1939 the war ministry revised its 1937 rearmament plan to field 65 divisions and 200 air squadrons by 1942. The ministry would reduce forces in China in order to increase stockpiles and ammunition reserves for the larger force structure. The general staff balked at withdrawing units from China, and the finance ministry was unwilling to pay for the latest rearmament plan. To gain imperial approval, the war minister ultimately accepted a 5 percent cut in equipment, a one-third reduction in stockpiles, and the program's extension into 1946.

Prime Minister Abe Nobuyuki, a retired general, introduced the army bill in the Diet in late December 1939, but his four-month tenure was already mired in controversy. Abe was selected to lead the cabinet because he was not pro-German and the emperor liked him. As prime minister he tried to freeze consumer prices, but drought conditions in western Japan and Korea resulted in poor rice harvests that drove up food prices and reduced Japan's hydroelectric output. The Diet refused to endorse the army expansion legislation and considered a no-confidence vote. Alarmed that a general election might vent antiwar and antimilitary sentiment, army leaders balked at dissolving the Diet, and Abe instead resigned. Shortly afterward the China Expeditionary Army commander, Gen. Itagaki Seishirō, demanded immediate reinforcements for China, which effectively ended the rearmament proposals.[44]

In March 1940 the general staff and war ministry concluded that if Japan could not defeat China militarily during 1940, then the China Expeditionary

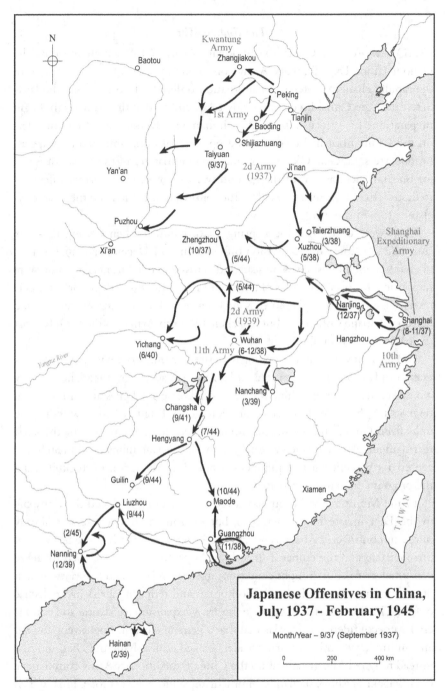

N

Kwantung
Army

Baotou

Zhangjiakou

Peking

1st Army

Tianjin

Baoding

Shijiazhuang

Taiyuan
(9/37)

2d Army
(1937)

Ji'nan

Yan'an

Puzhou

Zhengzhou
(10/37)

Taierzhuang
(3/38)

Shanghai
Expeditionary
Army

Xi'an

Xuzhou
(5/38)

(5/44)

(5/44)

2d Army
(1939)

Nanjing
(12/37)

Shanghai
(8-11/37)

Yichang
(6/40)

Yangtze River

11th Army (6-12/38)

Wuhan

Hangzhou

10th
Army

Nanchang
(3/39)

Changsha
(9/41)

Hengyang

(7/44)

Guilin
(9/44)

(10/44)

Maode

Xiamen

TAIWAN

Liuzhou
(9/44)

(2/45)

Guangzhou
(11/38)

Nanning
(12/39)

**Japanese Offensives in China,
July 1937 - February 1945**

Month/Year – 9/37 (September 1937)

0   200   400 km

Hainan
(2/39)

Map 6

Army would have to become self-sufficient because the army could no longer afford to support it and simultaneously implement the four-year rearmament plan for the anticipated war against the Soviet Union. Withdrawals from China would begin in 1941, and by 1943 the Japanese would occupy only the Shanghai delta and a triangular area in North China.

On May 1, 1940, the Eleventh Army attacked Yichang to dislodge Chinese armies in north and central Hubei, break open the doorway to Chongqing, and secure an operational air base to stage raids against the Guomindang capital. In accordance with its plan to reduce forces in China, IGHQ limited the offensive to two months' duration, after which the units would return to their original locations.[45] The general staff and war ministry agreed on May 18 that unless a combination of political, military, and covert pressure compelled Chiang to surrender by the end of 1940, the army would scale back such operations and gradually withdraw more than half of its 850,000 troops by the end of 1941.[46] The China Expeditionary Army strongly protested the proposed reductions and pressured the imperial general headquarters to retain between 700,000 and 750,000 troops in China.

The new policy's diplomatic and covert components became the *Kiri* operation when the government and army temporarily suspended the creation of a pro-Japanese regime in the occupied areas headed by Wang Jingwei and opened secret discussions with Chinese operatives in anticipation of direct cease-fire negotiations between Itagaki, now chief of staff of the CEA, and Chiang Kaishek in August 1940.[47] The stratagem collapsed over Itagaki's insistence that China recognize Manchukuo, something Chiang could never do.

As for military pressure, Japanese troops captured Yichang on June 12 and four days later withdrew as ordered. During the interval, the German blitzkrieg overran France and the stunning Nazi conquest of Western Europe appeared to usher in a new world order. German victories had isolated European colonies in Asia, where natural resources waited for Japanese picking like "fresh rice cakes off a shelf." With France defeated and Great Britain on the verge of surrender, Japan had a once-in-a-lifetime chance to isolate Chiang from western aid by severing his supply routes that ran through French Indochina and British-ruled Burma. Improved ties with Germany and Italy could prevent the United States from interfering if the army moved south into those colonies.[48] Japan's military and civilian leaders were also leery that the Germans might seek to control French Indochina and the Netherlands East Indies. Consequently, Japan had to act with celerity in order "not to miss the bus," which became a popular catchphrase during the summer of 1940 as military, political, and public opinion leaders interpreted the Axis triumph in the West as the opportunity to resolve the war in the East.

During this burst of optimism, on June 15 the emperor learned that the navy wanted Yichang as a forward operating base to stage air attacks on Chongqing. He asked Prince Kan'in, the army chief of staff, what the army was doing at Yichang. Interpreting the imperial question as an instruction, China Expeditionary Army commander Gen. Nishio Toshizō ordered the Eleventh Army to retake Yichang (which it had just abandoned) and turn it into a major air base to conduct intensified strategic bombing of Chinese cities to break Guomindang resistance. Yichang would become a springboard to move into southern China and restore the freedom of maneuver that field commanders demanded. The army simultaneously pressured France and Britain to close the military supply roads leading into China from French Indochina and Burma, respectively. The two overland routes merged at Kunming, then beyond the operational radius of the Twenty-second Army, which was headquartered in Nanning, about 360 miles to the east. Nanning, though, was 90 miles inland and difficult to resupply and defend, making it unsuitable as a staging for a major offensive campaign against Kunming. Army leaders consequently gave added importance to moving against Indochina.[49]

Succumbing to incessant Japanese diplomatic and military pressure, in late June the French allowed a forty-man Japanese team to inspect cargo destined for China for military contraband. The next month the British, under German aerial bombardment and threatened by invasion, closed the Burma route. The general staff next ordered the team in Indochina to secure garrison and air base rights for Japanese troops, actions closely tied to the army's latest strategic reappraisal caused by developments in Europe.

On June 25, 1940, the general staff and war ministry hastily drafted plans to attack western colonies in Asia. A surprise, fast-moving attack against Singapore, supported by aircraft flying from bases in French Indochina and Thailand, would open the campaign, and an invasion of the Netherlands East Indies would follow. Insofar as possible, efforts would be made to avoid war with the United States. This became the basis for the army's July 3 decision to move south against the western colonies in Asia, regardless of what happened in China. The navy agreed but insisted on simultaneous preparations for war with the United States. When Prime Minister Yonai Mitsumasa, a retired admiral, rejected such a radical policy shift, army leaders brought down his cabinet.[50]

Konoe had resigned from the Privy Council on June 18 with a call for a strong national unity cabinet to deal with the rapidly changing national and international situation. He would, of course, lead that new cabinet. A few weeks later, Prince Kan'in suggested to War Minister Lt. Gen. Hata Shunroku that he resign in favor of a stronger national unity cabinet. Hata submitted his resignation, and when the army refused to nominate a replacement, Yonai had to dissolve his cabinet. Konoe then formed his second cabinet, and his charismatic personality seemed to offer hope for a new national unity political movement to deal with the "unprecedented national and international situation."[51]

Hirohito enjoined Konoe to defend the constitution, calm the financial sector, and cooperate with the United States and Great Britain. Konoe, however, had a different agenda, and Hirohito suspected that his new prime minister was thinking about moving south to dissipate popular dissatisfaction over the lack of success in China.[52] That October Japan's political parties spontaneously dissolved as part of Konoe's plan for an imperial rule assistance association to unify the nation under his direction.

Konoe selected Lt. Gen. Tōjō Hideki as his war minister, Admiral Yoshida Zengo as navy minister, and Matsuoka Yōsuke as foreign minister. Meeting on July 19 at Konoe's residence, the four agreed that stability in East Asia required Japan to add military and economic teeth to the Axis pact, secure Soviet neutrality, and prepare militarily to move south. A clash with the United States was to be avoided, as long as the Americans did not interfere with Japan's plans for a new order in East Asia. Eight days later an imperial headquarters liaison conference, the first in more than two years, adopted a policy that neither resolved the China Incident nor avoided the risk of war with the United States. In other words, the army's thinking had shifted from (1) the necessity of ending the China war quickly so it could advance south to (2) advancing south as a means to end the China fighting.[53]

Internally the army was at odds regarding an overall strategy. The general staff would take advantage of the anticipated imminent German invasion of Britain to seize Singapore, occupy Malaya and the Netherlands East Indies, and prepare for war with the USSR or the United States, the latter being isolated and weakened by Britain's anticipated surrender. The war ministry assigned priority to ending the China Incident but was divided about the means to accomplish that goal. The navy preferred to expand peacefully into the southern area but also wanted to finalize military preparations for war.[54]

Foreign Minister Matsuoka announced in September 1940 that the new order had been expanded into a Greater East Asia Co-prosperity Sphere to include French Indochina and the Netherlands East Indies. Secure access to the region's raw materials was central to the new policy, but simply acquiring resources was meaningless unless the navy could protect merchant ships carrying oil and minerals back to Japan for processing. During recently concluded tabletop war games, Japan had occupied the Netherlands East Indies but could not keep the sea-lanes open. The navy minister ignored these results, and the services, without alternatives, continued planning for a southern advance.[55]

The war ministry and general staff were split about the value of an armed invasion of French Indochina, but the foreign ministry pressured the French to permit Japanese troops to be stationed in Indochina to seal Chinese borders from outside sources of resupply. Military muscle was added to diplomatic demands when the 5th Division massed along the northern Indochina border at the end of August. A Japanese commander unilaterally led his battalion across the border on September 6, and, although he soon withdrew, the French promptly canceled further negotiations.

Tokyo formally ordered troops into Indochina on September 22, regardless of French protests. Too weak to resist militarily, the French allowed Japanese troops to enter their colony, and a peaceful resolution of the crisis seemed near. Machinations among hawks on the general staff, regimental commanders in the 5th Division, and Maj. Gen. Tominaga Kyōji, chief of the operations department of the general staff, intentionally delayed notification of the diplomatic settlement to the 5th Division headquarters. A fabricated order, allegedly transmitted from the Twenty-second Army headquarters, instead directed the 5th Division to invade French Indochina at midnight on September 23. Fighting broke out near Lang Son, site of a French fort that the Japanese soon captured. After a hastily arranged cease-fire, negotiations continued into October before the French finally allowed Japan to station troops in northern French Indochina.[56]

Reacting to these aggressive moves, on September 28 the United States embargoed scrap iron and steel shipments to Japan and underwrote a $25 million loan to China. The British reopened the Burma Road in mid-October because the immediate threat of German invasion had eased and previous concessions to Japan seemed only to encourage extremists in Tokyo. Discarding its previous policy of appeasement, the British government also announced a loan of £10 million to China.[57]

Field commanders' insubordination, staff officers' intrigues, and the Indochina fiasco infuriated War Minister Tōjō, who resorted to wholesale personnel transfers to reassert army discipline. Unit commanders and line officers held responsible for the border incident were seconded to the reserves while their superiors on the general staff, like Tominaga, who had goaded them into action, were transferred to minor commands or sent as instructors to army schools.[58]

In an effort to reassert discipline, enhance soldiers' spiritual power, and improve morale, especially for units stationed in China, on January 8, 1941, Tōjō promulgated the "Code of Battlefield Conduct" (*Senjinkun*). Prominent academics had vetted the draft for political correctness, and the well-known author Shimazaki Tōson and the poet Satō Sōnosuke had filled it with rhetorical flourishes, including what became the notorious injunction to avoid the shame of being taken captive. Flowery passages invoked a romanticized notion of samurai values and imperial benevolence to restore discipline. Troops were expected to respect their enemies and civilians, protect enemy property, and demonstrate imperial benevolence by tempering justice with mercy for captives. In fact, such derivative samurai values were modern myths, having about as much application and appreciation to the Japanese foot soldier as the European code of chivalry might exert on his European or American counterpart.[59]

Foreign Alliances

During the Indochina crisis, Konoe tried to strengthen Japan's ties with Germany and Italy, a pillar of his diplomacy grounded in his belief that an Axis military alliance would keep the United States from interfering in Asia. Navy Minister Yoshida opposed the pact and under extreme pressure from hawks within the navy resigned in early September, claiming illness. At the September 12 four ministers' conference, which included the new navy minister, Adm. Oikawa Koshirō, the alliance was approved provided it contained no automatic war entry clause. One week later at the third imperial conference, the emperor endorsed the liaison committee's policy, accepting the possibility of a Japanese-American war but hoping it would not come to pass.[60]

A ten-year military and economic Axis alliance was signed on September 27 in Berlin. The three signatories—Japan, Germany, and Italy—promised mutual assistance if any of them became involved in a war with a power not then a belligerent (a provision aimed at the United States). The pact placed Japan squarely in the Axis camp, and within days Prince Kan'in resigned as army chief of staff. The following April, Prince Fushimi followed suit and resigned as the navy's chief of staff. Their resignations were designed to disassociate the court from the military services and shield the imperial house from any formal responsibility for decisions on war or peace.[61]

Behind the flurry of military and diplomatic activity was China, which continued to drain Japan's military and economic resources. In a dramatic shift from guerrilla to conventional warfare, in August 1940 Chinese Communist forces in North China launched the Hundred Regiments Offensive. The well-coordinated, broad series of attacks initially surprised the Japanese and their puppet troops, but by mid-September the Japanese had regained their traction and slugged it out with Communist units in set-piece battles where superior firepower and equipment drove the guerrillas into retreat. By November, Japanese units were in murderous pursuit,[62] but the scale and intensity of the Communist offensive forced the army to rethink its counterinsurgency doctrine.

Between late 1938 and the summer of 1940 the army had conducted pacification and counterguerrilla sweeps in North China, eventually to prop up Wang Jingwei's pro-Japanese regime, established on March 30, 1940, in Nanjing. It used the model of fighting irregulars in Manchuria, where in 1933 it had organized the indigenous Manchurian Army, about 70,000 personnel led by 3,000 or 4,000 Japanese military advisers, many of whom were volunteer reserve officers. Another 70,000-man strong Japanese-trained Manchurian police force, about 10 percent of whom were Japanese or Koreans, backstopped the army and provided local security. These indigenous organizations freed regular Japanese units to train for conventional warfare.[63]

In North China the Japanese army likewise depended on indigenous Chinese units to provide local security. A series of strongpoints were constructed along major roads and railroads, many manned by puppet Chinese troops, while Japanese garrison divisions—specially configured light infantry units without field artillery or motorized transport—periodically swept through the more dangerous Communist-infested areas to deny the guerrillas a safe haven. This "point and line" strategy coupled with punitive raids was somewhat effective against traditional hit-and-run guerrilla tactics.

In the aftermath of the Hundred Regiments Offensive of late 1940, the North China Area Army moved from a passive strategy of blockade to an active counterguerrilla strategy based on terror, forced relocation, and plunder. Its subordinate First Army routinely executed Chinese males between the ages of 16 and 60 with impunity on the premise that guerrillas often disguised themselves as locals. Hamlets suspected of sheltering guerrillas were burned to the ground. In July 1941 the NCAA's three-year plan to restore order and eliminate guerrillas consisted of destroying villages, forcibly relocating villagers, and confiscating crops and food for the purpose of depopulating zones to deny guerrillas sustenance.[64] The Chinese mordantly nicknamed it the "Three All" policy—"kill all, burn all, loot all"—an appropriate description of the hundreds of small punitive campaigns that brought destruction and misery to North China well into 1943. Given the upsurge in counterguerrilla operations, IGHQ's revised January 16, 1941, policy called for fewer troop reductions from China spread over a longer period, leaving at least half a million troops there for the foreseeable future.[65]

At the strategic level, IGHQ relied on a combination naval blockade and aerial bombardment of China's cities to break the Chinese Central Government's will. Limited multidivision amphibious operations in early 1941 sealed many of south China's harbors, disrupted coastal traffic, and cut overland supply routes for Chiang's armies. Army aircraft normally struck tactical targets within specific ground areas of operations. Naval land-based bombers spearheaded sustained bombing campaigns against Chongqing, Kunming, and other major cities that drove their populations into underground shelters and wrecked Nationalist efforts to construct an industrial base and arms industry. Navy planners had concluded that strategic air strikes would contribute to naval control of the China coast and inland waterways, especially the Yangzi River.

By the summer of 1941, with its strategic focus shifting to preparations for a Pacific war, the navy began withdrawing its bomber force from China, giving respite to Chongqing and other cities. The army, with a few exceptions such as the amphibious operations in south China that complemented the blockade strategy, avoided large-scale ground operations and concentrated on security operations by cleaning the occupied areas of anti-Japanese or anti–Wang Jing-wei elements.[66]

The imperial headquarters sanctioned limited ground campaigns insofar as they preempted Chinese operations and disrupted enemy troop concentrations. Invariably, the Chinese traded space for time in a series of indecisive campaigns in north and central China during the first half of 1941. Japanese troops repeatedly reconquered the same places only to withdraw after a few days, knowing that they would soon be back. In April 1941 the new commander of the Eleventh Army, Lt. Gen. Anami Korechika, frustrated by the futility of these back-and-forth forays, proposed to capture Changsha, destroy the 300,000-strong GMD armies defending the city, and seize China's granary. These blows would, he believed, end the China war.

By that time, however, international pressure compelled a reassessment of Japan's strategic goals and the means available to achieve them. In January 1941 the United States had embargoed copper and brass shipments to Japan. Tokyo's attempts to secure oil from the Netherlands East Indies had foundered as the Dutch stalled repeatedly in the negotiations. In mid-June, President Franklin D. Roosevelt had announced that domestic oil shortages compelled the United States to stop shipping oil to Japan from U.S. East Coast ports.[67]

Large segments of Japan's civilian economy had already converted from civilian to military production, and the dislocations created shortages of consumer goods. Gasoline rationing had started in March 1938, and charcoal-burning automobiles appeared that June. Leather goods were scarce because of military requirements, and government-sponsored campaigns urged citizens to avoid luxury items and buy war bonds for the family and state. The cabinet imposed price controls in September 1939, which encouraged black marketeering. It simultaneously raised prices on tobacco, a government monopoly. Matches and sugar were rationed beginning in June 1940. In April 1941 the six major cities began rationing rice.[68] In other words, belt tightening was a harsh fact of daily life as the seemingly endless China war dragged on.

Foreign Minister Matsuoka tried to end the war by enlisting the USSR in a tripartite commercial pact with Japan and Germany to form an economic bloc that would isolate the United States and also end the Soviets' considerable aid to China. During Matsuoka's late March 1941 visit to Berlin his Nazi hosts showed no interest and instead pressed him to attack Singapore immediately. Matsuoka then turned to Moscow, where he concluded a neutrality pact with Joseph Stalin. Although it was not the nonaggression pact he sought, Matsuoka accepted the hero's welcome he received in Japan. In truth, all he had accomplished was to annoy Germany, appease the Soviet Union, and displease the United States.[69] Within weeks Matsuoka's flamboyant diplomacy turned to ashes.

The mid-April 1941 neutrality pact with the USSR seemingly secured Japan's northern flank, made a southward advance possible, and gave Japan more leverage in its ongoing negotiations with the United States. But the deteriorating relations between Nazi Germany and the Soviet Union threw Japanese plans into disarray. Retired lieutenant general Baron Ōshima Hiroshi, the Japanese ambassador to Berlin, reported in April the likelihood of a German attack on the Soviet Union. Ōshima's subsequent warnings—especially one of June 5 that recounted a meeting with German Chancellor Adolf Hitler, who told him that war was imminent—prompted a series of inconclusive meetings in mid-June among army, navy, and foreign ministry officials.[70]

If Germany invaded the Soviet Union, Vice Chief of Staff Lt. Gen. Tsukada Osamu and IGHQ's war guidance section wanted to move into southern Indochina, the operations department favored preparations to attack either north or south depending on the situation, and the war ministry's military affairs bureau supported military action against the western powers in East Asia. Fearing that the army would unilaterally attack Siberia, navy leaders stepped up their advocacy of a southern advance to forestall such an eventuality. An emotional Matsuoka demanded an immediate attack on the USSR. Prime Minister Konoe was left with the army's divided estimate, a mercurial foreign minister, and a policy in disarray.[71]

Following the German invasion of the USSR on June 22, 1941, the general staff adopted a wait-and-see attitude, essentially to enter the fighting only if the Soviet Union was in danger of collapse—"falling into Japanese hands like a ripe persimmon," as the staff put it. That time would come when the Soviets pulled one-half their 30 divisions and two-thirds of their 2,800 aircraft from the Far East. According to the general staff's two-stage 22-division contingency plan, the remaining 15 Soviet divisions, judged the equivalent of 11 Japanese divisions, then would be outnumbered two-to-one. Stage one would mobilize 16 divisions to wartime strength; stage two would add 6 more divisions, including 2 from the China front.[72]

The mobilization requirements were staggering. The 12 divisions currently in Manchuria would need 500,000 more troops in addition to their associated animal transport, supplies, and equipment to reach wartime strength. To move those forces to the continent would require at least 800,000 tons of shipping, tie up one-third of Japan's domestic railroad capacity, and monopolize the entire resources of the South Manchurian Railway, Japan's quasi-official rail line in Manchuria, for two months.

The June 25 liaison conference temporized about the Soviet Union while continuing preparations to move north or south. Conferees did, however, agree to use military force if the French refused demands to station Japanese troops in southern Indochina. That same day, IGHQ's operations division laid out a mobilization timeline that required a cabinet decision for war with the Soviets no later than August 10 in order to give the army sufficient time to concentrate the massive forces in their forward assembly areas. The latest the invasion could begin was September 10 because the campaign had to be concluded by mid-October before the harsh Siberian winter closed in and made large-unit operations impossible.[73] The preconditions mandated the classic short, decisive campaign to eliminate the northern threat to Japan.

Hawks on the general staff wanted to strike the USSR immediately, but the war ministry disagreed, fearing the army would be trapped in a protracted war of attrition and lose its strategic flexibility to move south. The war ministry also restricted the troop basis to 16 divisions because of fears that the Kwantung Army, with 22 divisions, might resort to its notorious propensity for unilateral action and drag Japan into war with the Soviet Union.[74] Surely the ghosts of Nomonhan motivated the cautious officers in the war ministry's military affairs branch who advocated moving south.

Germany urged Japan to attack the Soviet Union on June 30 and again on July 2, but the July 2 imperial conference only endorsed the continuation of secret preparations for war against the USSR for the time being. The fateful conference further agreed that in order to achieve its objectives in the southern regions, Japan would not hesitate to fight the United States and Britain. Thus the army was simultaneously preparing for operations in Southeast and Northeast Asia while fighting an open-ended war in China.

Three days later, operations department chief Maj. Gen. Tanaka Shin'ichi convinced Tōjō to deploy two homeland divisions (50,000 men at wartime strength) plus logistical and support troops to Manchuria to sustain the Kwantung Army's buildup. Hirohito approved the mobilization on July 7 despite misgivings that troops were being scattered everywhere without a clear strategic purpose. To preserve secrecy, the call-up was code-named the Kwantung Army Special Maneuvers and army authorities prohibited the usual neighborhood send-offs and public tributes to the recalled reservists. But the disappearance of so many military-age men from the streets and workplace made it impossible to conceal.[75]

By mid-July, the Soviets still had not transferred as many troops to the west as the general staff had expected, and doubts had crept into army thinking about the Germans' ability to wrap up the war by year's end.[76] Amidst this uncertainty over the northern front, the Twenty-fifth Army moved into southern Indochina.

Under the pressure of an ultimatum, on July 21 the French allowed Japanese troops to occupy southern French Indochina. Unlike the earlier occupation of

northern French Indochina, designed to blockade China, the move into southern Indochina signaled Japan's intentions to acquire advance air and staging
bases to wage war against British and Dutch possessions to the south and the
Americans' Philippine colony. The navy insisted on including the Philippines in
order to protect the sea-lanes from the Netherlands East Indies to Japan.

Army Chief of Staff Sugiyama justified the risks to Hirohito because it
would be difficult to settle the China Incident without striking Britain and the
United States. In response to the latest Japanese aggression, on July 26 President
Roosevelt froze all Japanese assets in the United States, and five days later, after
Japanese troops had actually moved into southern Indochina, he embargoed
oil exports to Japan. Although it is often remarked that this forced the navy to
decide on war, it should be remembered that the army had less than two years
of oil stocks for its air, mechanized, and motorized units.[77]

On July 31, Hirohito questioned Sugiyama about canceling the Kwantung
Army mobilization because it had generated international ill will toward Japan,
worsened the nation's strategic position, and likely accounted for the Soviets'
reluctance to redeploy troops to the west. Stopping the mobilization before
the Kwantung Army reached its wartime strength, Sugiyama replied, might
encourage a preemptive Soviet attack. Besides, the mobilized units could serve
as a strategic reserve for contingencies in the southern regions.[78] The next day
Hirohito reluctantly authorized the mobilization to continue.

By early August, however, national policy was shifting, partly in response to
the economic freeze being applied to Japan by western powers, partly because
of the allure of Southeast Asia, and partly because the army was less confident
about the possibility of a German victory over the USSR occurring during
1941. The general staff became more amenable to war ministry proposals to
avoid provocations, remain neutral, and wait until the Soviets were near collapse
before entering the war. Furthermore, the China Expeditionary Army commander, Gen. Hata Shunroku, opposed the withdrawal of any of his divisions
to reinforce the Kwantung Army, and Gen. Anami was still clamoring to attack
Changsha. Accordingly, on August 9 the general staff decided against attacking
the Soviet Union in 1941; instead the sixteen mobilized divisions would remain in a high state of readiness and operations in China would continue. The
general staff would plan a spring 1942 offensive against the Soviet Far East and
concurrently complete preparations for war with Britain and the United States
by the end of November 1941.[79]

The general staff and war ministry well understood the enormous latent
power of the United States, but they expected that it would take the Americans
several years to bring that full potential to bear. During the interval Japan could
secure the territory and resources it needed to fight a protracted war from advantageous forward positions.[80] Because the U.S. military had already started its

buildup (national conscription was approved for one year in September 1940 and later extended, army expansion began in May 1940 with the National Guard federalized that August, and the pace of naval construction sharply increased in June), the sooner Japan acted, the better, because time was on the Americans' side.

Even with the China war steadily draining Japan's military and industrial capability, the September 6 imperial conference decided that for self-defense and national survival the services would complete preparations for war with the United States, Great Britain, and the Netherlands by October. Meanwhile, negotiations would continue on a parallel track, but if diplomacy proved unsuccessful by mid-October, Japan would opt for war. Around the same time opinion makers popularized the idea that the ABCD (American-British-Chinese-Dutch) encirclement of Japan threatened its livelihood and existence. This interpretation refocused popular resentment over shortages of all kinds from the government to sinister foreign conspiracies.[81]

The termination of the Kwantung special exercise also unleashed new operations in China. IGHQ gave Anami the green light to attack Changsha in late August, which four of his divisions captured by late September. When threatened by Chinese counterattacks, they withdrew to their original positions in early October. An aggressive commander, Anami had previously proposed to capture Chongqing, an operation of unquestioned boldness but limited practicality. The Guomindang capital was about 270 miles upriver from the westernmost Japanese outpost on the Yangzi and sheltered by narrow gorges and mountains that made any attack a daunting prospect. Still, IGHQ took the plan under advisement.

The expanded fighting in China was directly linked to Japan's deteriorating relations with the western powers, particularly the United States. At an October 14 cabinet meeting Konoe suggested that diplomacy had to address the issue of Japanese troops in China. Tōjō exploded, angrily denounced American demands that Japan withdraw its troops from China, and asserted that such a policy would wreck any chance for a settlement, endanger Manchukuo, and threaten the security of Korea. He emotionally invoked the spirits of Japan's war dead, their grieving families, and the tens of thousands of wounded soldiers to reject what he termed the diplomacy of surrender. Despite the war minister's bellicosity, when the navy notified the army the same day of its wartime operational schedule, army officers were caught off guard because they had no corresponding plans for ground operations.[82] Four days later, Konoe's third cabinet collapsed.

Hirohito rejected Prince Higashikuni, the army's nominee for prime minister, because he wanted to shield the imperial house from any responsibility should war with the West occur.[83] Instead Tōjō became prime minister, based

Although staged (in the original film a cameraman is standing upright at lower left), this February 1939 photo taken on the Peking-Wuhan rail line conveys the immensity of the Japanese army's task in controlling the vast Chinese countryside. (Courtesy Mainichi shimbun*)*

on the assumption that he could control the army just as he had reasserted discipline after the Indochina crisis. When appointing Tōjō, Hirohito instructed him not to be bound by the September 6 imperial conference decision, allowing the new prime minister a fresh start.

At the November 1 liaison conference, a seventeen-hour marathon, despite reservations from the foreign and finance ministers it was the navy's argument that it was better to go to war sooner rather than later that carried the meeting. The emperor and the navy focused on insuring the empire's survival whereas the army and the government concentrated on establishing a new order in greater East Asia. Preparations for war continued, but if diplomacy succeeded the army could recall troops as late as December 1. Henceforth the army regarded diplomatic talks with the Americans as mere camouflage to mask Japan's final preparations for war.[84]

The November 5 imperial conference formally ratified the liaison conference decision to continue negotiations until December 1, after which Japan would go to war with the West. Adm. Nagano Osami told Hirohito that Japan could fight the Americans and British for two years, but after that he had no guarantees. Sugiyama was confident that if Japan could maintain its maritime line of communication it could build an invincible position. After the session, they presented their respective operational plans to Hirohito, including a detailed account of the Pearl Harbor attack and, with imperial approval, dispatched orders to the responsible commanders.[85]

Occupation policy was decided at a November 20, 1941, IGHQ liaison conference. Military administration in occupied territories would restore security, acquire strategic raw materials, and insure the operational forces' self-sufficiency. A few days later the army took responsibility for Hong Kong, the Philippines, Malaya, Sumatra, Java, British Borneo, and Burma; the navy controlled Dutch Borneo, Celebes, Malacca Islands, the Lesser Sunda Islands, New Guinea, the Bismarck Archipelago, and Guam.[86] Thus the army's focus was primarily continental, the navy's maritime, the inevitable result of the services' chronic inability to agree on a joint strategy.

Military strategy relied on the classic short-term war scenario to seize and quickly eliminate western bases in East Asia while occupying strategic points in the southern region. This in turn would hasten the collapse of Chiang Kai-shek's regime and end the China fighting. Japan would also cooperate with its Axis partners, Germany and Italy, to compel Great Britain to surrender, which would shatter America's will to fight. Although the army was bogged down in a protracted war in China, Sugiyama informed Hirohito on December 1 that Japan had a once-in-a-lifetime chance to break the West's economic embargo and achieve autarky.[87]

Traditional assumptions underpinned this strategy: if Japan could control Southeast Asia's raw materials, the empire probably could achieve self-sufficiency by drawing on those resources to fight a protracted war. Control of the Indian Ocean would cut the line of communication from India to Great Britain, leaving the British short of supplies and raw materials and unable to resist the imminent German invasion. The British capitulation would cause the United States to lose its will to fight, allowing Japan to use neutrals and the Vatican to achieve a favorable negotiated settlement that left the empire in advantageous strategic position.

The army marched off to war against the West with no means to defeat the United States, much less an allied coalition. It never reconciled its traditional dilemma over a short-term or a protracted war, and its overreliance on Nazi Germany to defeat Britain only made an already flawed strategy even weaker. There was no strategic or operational plan after the first six months of hostilities and no thoughtful consideration given to war termination. Trusting in the military prowess of Nazi Germany, army leaders counted on Japan's intangible qualities to overcome a decadent United States. The decisions of late 1941 flowed naturally from the army's past experience, strategic perspective, operational and tactical doctrine, and its carefully cultivated belief in Japanese superiority.

11

The Asia-Pacific War

Japan's war with the West began on December 8, 1941 (Tokyo time), with surprise attacks on British Malaya and Pearl Harbor, Hawaii, preceding a formal declaration of war. Although the tactics seemed to fit a traditional Japanese pattern of preemptive strikes, the opening attacks on Chinese transports in 1894 and against the Russian naval base at Port Arthur in 1905 were integrated parts of a comprehensive diplomatic, political, and military strategy designed to force an early decisive engagement that would lead to a negotiated settlement of hostilities. In the 1941 plans these ingredients were lacking.

The Pearl Harbor raid temporarily neutralized the U.S. Pacific Fleet and allowed the army to conduct amphibious operations against the Netherlands East Indies and the Philippines. The strategic objective was to create a self-sufficient Japan able to fight a protracted war. Initial operational plans included no fixed time limits, except that they should be accomplished within 150 days in order to move either north in the spring against the Soviet Union or defend against a Soviet attack. At the same time, the plans called for Japanese forces to fortify and defend their new and massive southern perimeter until the Allies grew tired of attacking and agreed to a negotiated peace.[1] The strategy acknowledged that the army lacked the means to force a decisive land battle and premised its seize-and-hold strategy on a protracted war of attrition whose end game depended on Germany knocking Britain out of the war. Once Britain surrendered, army leaders hoped the United States would agree to terms.

The navy could bring about a decisive fleet engagement with the Americans in the western Pacific, but it was much less confident about fighting a protracted war of attrition.[2] Furthermore, the naval general staff had aggressively extended the location of the decisive battle, counting on land-based airpower and air bases in the Mandated Islands to project power westward and shield the home islands from enemy reprisals. The navy's requirements for troops to secure its far-flung gains steadily drew the army into the South and Central Pacific regions.

The army originally committed less than half its operational aircraft and one-fifth of its personnel to the opening campaigns, whose purpose was to secure the resources of the southern regions and leverage that success to end the war in China. A December 12 cabinet resolution designated the conflict with the western powers and China the Greater East Asia War, a designation that signified the goal of building a new order in East Asia but not necessarily limiting the war to that geographic area.[3]

On December 8, naval land-based bombers flying from Taiwan surprised and destroyed most of the U.S. Army air units in the Philippines on the ground. Two days later naval land-based bombers operating from bases near Saigon, French Indochina, sank the British battleships *Prince of Wales* and *Repulse*, losing just three aircraft in the attack. During November, army fighters and bombers of the Third Composite Wing (three air divisions) had deployed from southern China to forward bases in Cambodia and southern Indochina. Augmented by the navy's 22d Air Flotilla, the more than 540 aircraft protected the Malaya-bound invasion fleet.[4]

Under Lt. Gen. Yamashita Tomoyuki the Twenty-fifth Army's 18th Division moved south along Malaya's east coast while the 5th Division raced down the west coast. The fast-moving advance—it averaged about 12 miles a day—relied on confiscated allied supplies, especially fuel oil, and the capture of air bases to enable its air umbrella to displace forward to support ground operations. Without air cover, Allied forces were subjected to repeated aerial bombing and strafing that made it almost impossible to concentrate or move entire units effectively. Light and medium tanks led breakthroughs against British Commonwealth forces lacking antitank defenses. In combination with this shock action, Japanese infantrymen relied on their standard envelopment tactics, making shallow hooks into the jungle to outflank and outmaneuver their road-bound enemy.

By the end of January 1942 the Twenty-fifth Army had reached Singapore Island, and on February 15 Yamashita conquered the city and fortress. Two days earlier Japanese troops had overrun the Alexandria Barracks Hospital, bayoneting more than 300 hospital personnel, including wounded patients, in a precursor to the serial atrocities—rape, looting, and murder—that followed Singapore's capitulation. The Japanese occupiers targeted the colony's large Chinese population for reprisals and took about 130,000 British Commonwealth troops into captivity, many of whom were eventually consigned to railroad construction projects in Burma.

Meanwhile, the Fourteenth Army under Lt. Gen. Homma Masaharu landed on Luzon, Philippines, on December 22, 1941, and marched south on Manila. Ambiguous operational directives left Homma unsure whether his objective was the Philippine capital or the destruction of Gen. Douglas MacArthur's

American-Filipino forces. Japanese air superiority again provided an insur-mountable advantage, and MacArthur soon declared Manila an open city. The Fourteenth Army occupied the capital on January 2, 1942, and Homma be-lieved that he had achieved the campaign's objectives.

MacArthur, however, withdrew into the rugged Bataan Peninsula, where Homma's January 9 offensive failed to dislodge him. After this painful setback, a second offensive, launched on April 3, defeated the hungry, sick, and poorly supplied Allies on Bataan. About 12,000 U.S. and 58,000 Filipino personnel were taken prisoner and forced to march about sixty miles to a processing camp. Lacking adequate food, medicine, and water and driven forward by unforgiving Japanese guards, perhaps as many as 600 Americans and 5,000–10,000 Filipinos perished in what became known as the Bataan Death March.[5] It was a foretaste of the treatment the Japanese meted out during their occupation of the Philip-pines. Corregidor Island in Manila Bay held out until May 6, by which time MacArthur was safely in Australia. The Fourteenth Army's handling of the cam-paign, its duration, and the unexpectedly heavy Japanese casualties cost Homma his reputation and command.

Elsewhere, on the night of December 18 the Twenty-third Army attacked Hong Kong, but unexpectedly stubborn British, Canadian, Australian, and Chinese resistance stretched out the fighting a full week before the surrender on Christmas night. Japanese soldiers had raped and murdered westerners and Chinese during the fighting, and afterward the atrocities against the Chinese continued. Thousands of British and Canadian troops went into captivity. In central China, Gen. Anami launched his second Changsha offensive on Decem-ber 24 and entered the city a week later, only to meet fierce Chinese counterat-tacks that cut off two of his divisions in early January 1942. Outnumbered and outmaneuvered, Anami retreated northward.

Naval infantry units captured Guam in the Marianas on December 10; two weeks later, after an initial repulse, naval special landing forces seized Wake Is-land, an important communications center and airfield in the western Pacific. The navy then pushed into the southwest Pacific, justifying this unanticipated expansion as necessary to protect the flank approaches to the Combined Fleet's advance base and anchorage at Truk, Caroline Islands, which fell within range of long-range heavy bombers staging from Rabaul in the Bismarck chain. On January 4, 1942, multifront joint attacks opened against Rabaul, the Solomon Islands, and the northeast New Guinea coast. Joint forces occupied Rabaul by January 23 and subsequently murdered captured Australian personnel. On Feb-ruary 19, navy carrier-based aircraft raided Darwin, Australia. The navy seized bases at Lae and Salamua on the northeast New Guinea coast on March 8. Mi-nor naval construction units also moved to Tulagi, Solomon Islands.

These operations were incidental to the goal of the southern operation, namely the capture of the oil- and resource-rich Netherlands East Indies (NEI). In mid-January 1942 the Sixteenth Army under Lt. Gen. Imamura Hitoshi invaded Borneo, and about 400 naval paratroopers attacked Manado on Celebes. A few hundred army paratroopers dropped on Palembang, Sumatra, on February 14 and seized the NEI's richest oil fields. On the night of February 28–March 1 the Battle of the Java Sea eliminated Allied naval power in the NEI, and on March 1 units of the Sixteenth Army landed in Java, where they quickly occupied Surabaya and the capital, Batavia. Dutch forces surrendered eight days later, and captured military personnel and civilians were placed in internment camps. Although army headquarters in Tokyo regarded Imamura as overly lenient with the Indonesians, tens of thousands of them would later perish while working as forced laborers on Japanese projects throughout Southeast Asia.

Two divisions of the Fifteenth Army invaded Burma on January 20 from staging bases in Thailand. Despite initial—and for China, deeply humiliating—British objections, Chiang Kai-shek sent Chinese troops, including his only mechanized division, to assist in Burma, partly in order to fight alongside his new allies and partly to defend China's one remaining connection with the outside world.[6] The Chinese along with their new British and American allies were routed, mainly because of a lack of air and naval power and ill-equipped and poorly trained infantry. Trucks and tanks left the Allies dependent on roads while the lightly armed Japanese took to the jungle, quickly outflanking and enveloping defenders. Profound disagreements over strategy, including whether to defend Mandalay in northern Burma or counterattack south toward Rangoon, did lasting harm to Allied relations.

By March 8 the Japanese had occupied the capital at Rangoon. Then two more divisions landed near Rangoon in early April to reinforce a two-pronged northward offensive against Mandalay and Laisho. The former would destroy Commonwealth forces, and the latter would seal the Burma Road to cut off supplies to China. Mandalay fell on May 4, and by the end of the month the Fifteenth Army occupied the coast from Ayakab to northern Burma. Once again, air superiority (this time reinforced with army air units from the Philippines) combined with fast-moving infantry enveloping tactics threw the road-bound British-Indian forces into disarray. British suspicion of Chinese fighting effectiveness restricted their deployment to northeastern Burma and limited the Chinese role during the campaign.

In late March the army occupied Andaman and Nicobar islands in the Indian Ocean, and in early April Combined Fleet carrier aircraft bombed Colombo, Ceylon, and the British naval base at Tricomcomlee. Fleet actions sank one light aircraft carrier, two heavy cruisers, and three transports, driving the British Navy from the Indian Ocean.

Although the Imperial General Headquarters had originally planned a strategic defensive, the first stage of operations had progressed so smoothly that the services saw opportunities for further offensives. Neither service had concrete plans nor shared common objectives. The navy, for example, would establish an outer perimeter that reached to Australia, Hawaii, and India. Allied attempts to defend those vital areas would bring about the long-sought climactic fleet engagement. The army, however, was content to defend the current gains and consolidate its forces to repulse enemy counteroffensives anticipated after 1943. In other words, the army wanted to dig in to fight a protracted war of attrition whereas the navy demanded further expansion and the destruction of the U.S. fleet to make a protracted war possible.[7]

In an economy-of-force move, army authorities expected to withdraw sizeable numbers of troops from the southern front to refit, reequip, and modernize them for the long-term struggle. Plans would reduce the 450,000 troops (eleven divisions, seventy-seven air squadrons) to 250,000 personnel (seven divisions, fifty air squadrons) by the end of 1942.[8] The 200,000 recycled troops would reinforce Japan's northern front in anticipation of operations against the Soviet Union beginning in the spring of 1942 and also be available as a strategic reserve to check any Allied counteroffensive in the southern areas, which the high command anticipated would occur sometime after 1943.

At the March 7 liaison conference, the IGHQ accurately identified the Allied forces' priority of defeating Germany first and deduced that this strategic decision would delay any counteroffensive against Japan until after 1943. Attempts would, of course, be made to reopen the Burma Road to aid China, but Japanese agitation of anti-British Indian nationalists would check this move. For the first time the army's strategic planners expressed doubt that Germany could defeat the USSR in 1942, but they held out hope that German occupation of the Caucasus might cause Stalin's regime to collapse.

As for the British and American allies, they were materially powerful but lacked individual fighting spirit. The loss of their advanced bases and colonies had lowered overall Allied morale, and the impending British surrender would be a profound psychological shock to the United States, where societal unrest was likely to develop as the American standard of living declined and wartime sacrifices increased without hope of victory. Based on these encouraging assessments, the liaison conference decided to expand the current gains and create an impregnable strategic defensive perimeter.[9]

Outstanding early successes only concealed Japan's grave structural weakness. The army was already overextended in China, and each new conquest in Asia or the Pacific seemed to demand still another troop commitment to protect the recently acquired territory. Thus the navy needed Rabaul to protect Truk's southern flank, but then needed Port Moresby to protect Rabaul's flank, and then needed northern Australia to protect Moresby. It needed the

Solomons as advance bases for operations against Port Moresby and Australia. And Fiji and Samoa became essential in order to sever the line of communication between Australia and the United States. In China, generals clamored for offensives against Chongqing; in Burma they wanted to drive to India; and in the southern region, admirals dreamed of invading Australia and India.

The imperial navy approved the F-S (Fiji-Samoa) and the Midway operations on April 5. The former would sever the line of communication between the United States and Australia (and thereby deny Australia's use as a forward staging base for the Allied counteroffensive), and the latter would provoke the decisive naval engagement and destruction of the American fleet. It was further decided to occupy the Aleutian Islands to prevent air attacks on Japan from that direction. The Midway operation came as a total surprise to the army, which went along because it was solely a navy operation and there was nothing the army could do about it.[10]

These plans were already in motion when Lt. Col. James Doolittle's U.S. carrier-based medium bombers struck Tokyo and several other Japanese cities in mid-April 1942. The daring raids shocked Japanese authorities, lifted American morale, and were a disaster for China. To prevent future air raids on the homeland, IGHQ ordered the occupation of airfields in eastern China's Zhejiang and Jiangxi provinces that lay within striking range of Japan. Five divisions and three independent mixed brigades of the Thirteenth Army in Shanghai struck southwestward and by mid-May had pushed out from Hangzhou to link up with two divisions from the Eleventh Army at Nanchang.

The Doolittle raid embarrassed the army, which was responsible for air defense of the home islands and was thus persuaded to join the Midway operation to thwart future carrier-based air attacks. Also, to strengthen homeland air defenses, the army withheld several fighter groups previously scheduled to support operations in the Solomons with effects on subsequent fighting there.[11]

By September the Japanese had destroyed the threatening Chinese air bases, some only just constructed, and laid waste to surrounding areas while clearing the 180-mile Hangzhou-Nanchang rail corridor. A neglect of logistics, however, marred the campaign. Shortages of food, ammunition, and transportation left hungry Japanese soldiers mired in the mud during the heaviest rainy season in sixty years. Sickness, especially malnutrition, accounted for three times the number of the 4,000 battle casualties. Thereafter the Eleventh Army at Nanchang secured the vast area running along the north and south banks of the Yangzi. The Doolittle raid also encouraged army planners to attack the Nationalist capital at Chongqing, and by the end of June 1942 the army was once again on the offensive in the South and Southwest Pacific, the Aleutians, and central China.

Around the same time, the North China Area Army tried to broker regional truces by bribing warlords with weapons and money to support the Wang Jing-wei government. The First Army also sought to buy off warlord armies and had some success attracting collaborators. Overall, however, the initiative failed, because the demands of the Pacific theater on Japan's resources left the armies in China without enough weapons, equipment, and money to live up to their promises.[12] In central China planning for the Chongqing operation to deliver the knockout punch to Chinese field armies and destroy the enemy logistic base areas gained momentum in the spring and summer of 1942. Japan was near its military apex, and the China Expeditionary Army assembled sixteen divisions for a five-month offensive to seize Chongqing.

In the Southwest Pacific, the F–S Operation started badly when American carrier aircraft repulsed the imperial navy's approach to Port Moresby, Papua New Guinea, in early May 1942 at the Battle of the Coral Sea. About one month later, U.S. navy aircraft sank four Japanese aircraft carriers during the Battle of Midway, shifting the strategic balance in the Pacific to the Americans. After that strategic disaster, the IGHQ cancelled the F–S Operation in favor of an overland attack on Moresby. The South Seas Detachment (the 144th Infantry Regiment), veterans of Guam and Rabaul, landed at Buna on Papua New Guinea's north coast on July 21 and moved into the mountain ranges towering between Buna and the lights of Moresby. Around the same time, the navy unilaterally dispatched an airfield construction unit to Guadalcanal in the Solomons to build a forward airstrip to support future operations.

The naval general staff's communications intelligence section intercepted radio signals on July 2 that revealed a large American convoy was departing from San Francisco. Subsequent radio traffic in early August indicated that the ships were bound for the east coast of Australia or perhaps Port Moresby. Consequently, on August 4 the navy issued a warning to all units in the area, but low-lying tropical clouds and rainsqualls hampered reconnaissance aircraft searching for the convoy. The U.S. Marine landing on Guadalcanal on August 7 was a complete surprise to the handful of Japanese construction troops on the island, who at first mistook the invasion fleet for a Japanese convoy. It was just as baffling in Tokyo, where army intelligence officers laid out maps on the floor and on their hands and knees searched for Guadalcanal. Only one or two of them even knew that a small navy unit was on the island.

The high command took the American landing lightly, owing partly to its assumption that a major Allied counteroffensive would not begin until late 1943 and partly to faulty intelligence. After the battle of Savo Island, fought during the early-morning hours of August 9, naval reconnaissance pilots reported that the American fleet had vanished and the island seemed deserted. A few days later, the Soviet naval attaché in Tokyo reportedly told informants that the U.S. objective was a reconnaissance-in-force to destroy the airfield and that he expected an imminent withdrawal.[13] Adm. Nagano Osami, naval chief of staff, assured the emperor, who was vacationing at an imperial villa, that there was no need to return to Tokyo over such a trifling affair.

Three days later Col. Ichiki Kiyonao's 600-man detachment landed on Guadalcanal to eject the marines. Believing that he faced a small enemy reconnaissance unit, Ichiki boldly ordered a nighttime frontal assault against what turned out to be a U.S. Marine division. His detachment was almost annihilated and Ichiki killed, yet no responsible army officer or anyone at IGHQ questioned his tactics—and the certainty that cold steel was decisive in battle went unchallenged. Ichiki's disaster was the first in a series of setbacks on Guadalcanal and in eastern New Guinea, whose ramifications rippled throughout the army.

Japanese efforts to defend Guadalcanal diverted priority and resources from New Guinea to that island, halting the drive on Port Moresby and then ordering a withdrawal to Buna-Gona. Likewise, in China the army general staff had approved the CEA's offensive in September, but the need for reinforcements on Guadalcanal drew off units intended for China to the island and forced Anami to abandon his Chongqing campaign. Instead of military force, a December 21, 1942, imperial conference authorized strengthening the Wang Jingwei regime and suspending peace feelers to Chiang's government.

Despite the tough fighting and heavy losses suffered on Guadalcanal, in mid-November the army still believed that it could recapture the island because it would take the United States at least three years to bring its full power to bear. If the army retook Guadalcanal, constructed a series of air bases, and prepared strong defenses in the Solomon Islands, it could offset the future disparity in material strength.[14]

After reverses on Guadalcanal and at Buna-Gona in December, the general staff demanded that the majority of available shipping be given to the army to support current and future operations in the South and Southwest Pacific. The staff's stubborn insistence touched off an emotional confrontation about the allocation of scarce shipping resources, with the war ministry and cabinet on one side and the general staff on the other.

In November 1941 Japan had 6.7 million tons of available shipping, and the Cabinet Economic Planning Board estimated that a minimum of three million tons were needed to sustain the civilian economy. The services, however, required almost four million tons for their initial operations, which would leave the civilian sector short by 10 percent even before any losses. To keep the national economy going, the army promised that it would gradually return 1.1 million tons of shipping to the civilian sector beginning in April 1942 (the expected end of initial operations) and complete the transfer by August. Projected losses of between 800,000 and one million tons of shipping the first year of the war would thereafter decline, and strategic plans envisaged the construction of

1.8 million tons of shipping over the next three years (600,000 tons being the annual maximum capacity for Japan's shipyards).

Although shipping losses were initially lower than expected, the government and war ministry still rejected the general staff's November 1942 demands to divert civilian merchant shipping, insisting that it was needed to move raw materials to Japan for wartime production and finished goods. The chief of the first (operations) department, the volatile Maj. Gen. Tanaka Shin'ichi, who dismissed war ministry adversaries as "courtiers adorned with cherry blossoms," vehemently argued the general staff's position at a December 5 cabinet meeting. When the equally hotheaded Maj. Gen. Satō Kenryō, the war ministry's military affairs bureau chief, angrily rebuffed Tanaka's contentions, the shouting escalated to a fistfight. The next day Tanaka and Tōjō, who was concurrently prime and war minister, engaged in a screaming match that ended abruptly when Tanaka called Tōjō an imbecile. Tanaka was immediately reassigned to the staff of Southern Army Headquarters in Singapore and in March 1943 placed in command of the 18th Division on the faraway Burma front.[15]

Regardless of the emotional fireworks, the fact remained that without additional shipping the army could not recapture Guadalcanal. On December 28 IGHQ alerted the Eighth Area Army on Rabaul, New Britain, to evacuate the island. Learning of this directive, Hirohito requested more information on the army's plans to defeat the Americans and questioned what effect an evacuation might have on military morale. Three days later at an IGHQ imperial conference, the service chiefs acknowledged that shipping shortages made it impossible to move the two divisions required to retake the island. They agreed to abandon Guadalcanal, strengthen defenses in the Central Pacific, and reinforce bases in New Guinea. After reconstitution, the army would launch a counteroffensive to regain any lost territory. IGHQ ordered the evacuation of Guadalcanal on January 4, 1943, but in deference to the field service regulations announced that it was advancing in a different direction![16]

The army's revised Pacific strategy made eastern New Guinea the primary theater and the defense of the northern Solomons secondary. Units would protect strategic points along the New Guinea coast, such as the air and naval bases at Lae and Salamua, and then capture Port Moresby.[17] Attempts to reinforce eastern New Guinea failed when Allied aircraft destroyed much of the 51st Division in transit during the Battle of the Bismarck Sea in early March 1943.

After the attrition of the navy's carrier force at Midway, the joint losses suffered in the Solomons, and the army's Bismarck Sea catastrophe, the March 25, 1943, outline for third stage operations abandoned the concept of aggressively seeking a decisive surface fleet engagement, the navy's traditional doctrine since the late Meiji period, in favor of an active defense organized around an interconnected web of island airbases that in combination with fleet action would destroy the enemy fleet. The war ministry wanted to abandon the overextended South Pacific front and reinforce rear areas, but the operations department of the general staff claimed that a wholesale withdrawal conferred no advantages and would interfere with current operations. The general staff instead offered to withdraw to the northern Solomons, where the army could reconstitute its forces and still defend the resources of the southern region. The navy, however, insisted on holding its gains in the Central Pacific.[18] In short, regardless of losses and shipping shortages, the army remained forward-deployed on an overextended perimeter.

The Allied Counteroffensive

In May 1943 U.S. Army forces invaded Attu Island in the Aleutian chain. IGHQ ordered an evacuation, but the commander of the Northern Army in Hokkaidō decided that the order applied only to the western Aleutians and ignored the beleaguered 2,600-man army garrison on Attu.[19] The badly outnumbered Japanese, isolated from reinforcements and resupply, fought doggedly, but when all hope of rescue was gone the remaining soldiers launched a suicidal attack on May 29. Only twenty-seven survived. Just before leading the final charge, the garrison commander, Col. Yamasaki Yasuyo, radioed IGHQ that he had ordered the able-bodied and wounded alike to fight to the death to avoid the humiliation of capture. An army medical officer executed patients too sick or too seriously wounded to join the final attack in order to preclude any stain on the warrior spirit. The Attu defense force became the first army unit completely destroyed during the war, which earned Yamasaki a posthumous promotion to lieutenant general.

The next day, IGHQ announced the *Attu gyokusai*, a phrase derived from the Chinese classics that conveyed "the transcendent moral quality of such sacrifice." The concept electrified the nation, became a powerful, if ephemeral, propaganda tool, and made fighting to the death acceptable and accepted in the popular consciousness. Retired Maj. Gen. Sakurai, the author of *Human Bullets*, commented in the press that Yamasaki's act had rekindled the army's traditional fighting spirit, which he believed had been weakened by western influences. Interestingly, by early 1944 the army had dropped *gyokusai* in favor of the clumsy phrase "all achieved a heroic death in battle" because touting successive reverses on Tarawa and Makin islands in late 1943 as models of *gyokusai* left the public with the impression that the services were powerless to prevent inevitable defeats.[20]

In June 1943 Tōjō called for increased aircraft production to strengthen the army's military capability and to increase industrial output for the war effort. The services hoped to triple aircraft production to 55,000 planes during 1944, but the Cabinet Planning Board reduced that number to 40,000. The army

opened special air cadet schools to train the pilots needed for the anticipated
air armadas. Recruits from universities entered the air academy, and primary
school graduates enrolled in the youth flying schools. Industrial resources were
diverted from equipping newly activated infantry divisions to manufacturing
aircraft. Army aircraft production almost doubled, to more than 10,000 aircraft,
during 1943 and rose until mid-1944, when shortages of raw materials and
labor hampered production. The tradeoff was obvious; the number of tanks
manufactured annually dropped from about 1,200 in 1942 to 791 in 1943 and
478 in 1944 as production was sacrificed for aircraft.[21]

By the summer of 1943 the war ministry cited the difficulty of resupplying
advance units so distant from Japan as reason to withdraw to the Marianas, where
it could concentrate forces to defend a smaller perimeter organized around a
network of air bases. The general staff refused to abandon New Guinea, and the
navy was unwilling to leave Rabaul because that would imperil Truk, whose
loss would endanger the Marshall Islands. This domino effect would spoil plans
for a decisive fleet engagement near the Marshalls, expose the homeland to
enemy attack, and cut off Japan from natural resources.[22]

A September 30, 1943, imperial conference approved IGHQ's new strategy
to create the absolute defense zone, stretching from the Kurile Islands to the
Ogasawaras and on to the Central Pacific, Western New Guinea, Sumatra, and
Burma. Behind this lengthy defensive perimeter, Japan would marshal its airpower to smash the Allied counteroffensive. IGHQ had finally abandoned the
strategic offensive, and there was no more talk of counteroffensive operations
to regain lost territory.

It would take about a year to complete the new strategy's defensive belt
and reinforce the perimeter and another year to deploy sufficient aircraft to
implement the strategy. The key to success was whether the absolute defense
zone could hold out that long.[23] It was painfully clear that Japan could expect
no help from its German ally, then engaged in a death struggle with the Soviet
Union and facing the likelihood of a second front in Western Europe in the
spring or summer of 1944. Finally, despite the new strategy, the navy insisted on
holding advance bases and outposts in the Gilberts, Bismarcks, and Marshalls,
which lay outside the zone.[24] Likewise, the army approved offensive operations
in eastern New Guinea and deployed troops to defend the Marshalls.

More divisions were needed for the latest strategic shift, and in December
1943 the army lowered the draft age from 20 to 19 years of age, made Koreans
eligible for conscription, extended the military obligation five years to age 45,
and ended student deferments (see Table 11.1). About 170,000 Koreans were
conscripted, but almost all were assigned to labor battalions or rear area service units.[25] Many of the conscripted Japanese students entered pilot training
courses and would account for 45 percent of officer pilots assigned to special

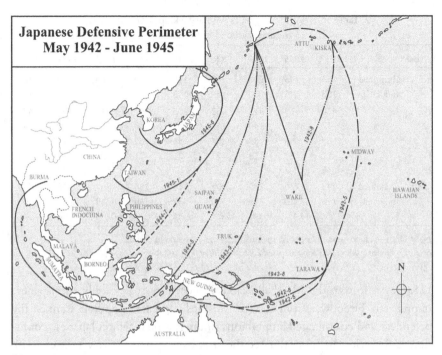

Map 7

attack (suicide) units and 71 percent of those killed in special attacks. The army also relied on higher draft calls achieved by lowering induction standards and recalled more men from the first and second reserves to active duty. The percentage of regulars fell from just over 50 percent in 1941 to 42 percent by 1945 (see Table 11.2).[26]

To meet the need for additional small-unit leaders the army created a special officer cadet system in 1944 that selected graduates of high school, trained them for one year in one of five newly established reserve officers schools, and commissioned them reserve officers. The system ultimately produced 20,000 junior officers, but the vast increase of personnel diluted quality. Grizzled veterans and regular officers derided the newly minted younger reserve officers as "dummy rounds." With weapons and equipment in short supply, many new conscripts were set to work digging fortifications, but even there shortages of cement hindered construction of shoreline fortifications.[27]

In November 1943, U.S. Marines overran Tarawa and several other Gilbert Islands. The defending Japanese naval infantry detachments fought to the death. Of the nearly 4,700-man Japanese garrison, only 17 were taken prisoner (129 Korean laborers were also captured). Although the army's confidential war diary dismissed the battle as having little significance, it was the opening step in the U.S. Navy's offensive across the Central Pacific. The speed and fury of the

Table 11.1. Source of Japan's Military Manpower, 1937–1945
(figures rounded in thousands)

Class		1937	1938	1939	1940	1941	1942	1943	1944	1945
A	Examined	153	195	200	189	195	190	184	310	155
	Inducted	153	195	200	189	195	190	184	310	155
B		470	410	412	402	405	401	412	924	477
		17	125	140	131	135	150	176	690	345
C		89	86	88	84	86	84	85	176	90
D		22	22	22	21	21	21	21	44	23
E		7	7	7	7	7	7	7	14	7
Total	Examined	742	720	729	703	714	703	709	1,468	753
	Inducted	170	320	340	320	330	340	360	1,000	500
	%	22.9%	44.4%	46.6%	45.6%	46.2%	48.3%	50.7%	68.1%	66.4%

Note: Until 1943, 20-year-old cohort; 1944 includes the 19-year-old cohort.
Source: Rikusen gakkai, ed., *Kindai sensōshi gaisetsu Shiryō hen*, 35, table 2-1-8.

U.S. Navy's leap to the Marshall Islands in February 1944 caught the Japanese unprepared. Firepower from surface warships and carrier aircraft stunned the defenders, and coordinated amphibious landings capitalized on Japanese confusion. U.S. carrier aircraft devastated the Truk bastion on February 17, 1944, with reverberations that were felt all the way back to Tokyo.

Four days after the Truk disaster, Tōjō proposed to Hirohito that he assume the concurrent position of chief of staff while Navy Minister Adm. Shimada Shigetarō would take the chief of naval operations portfolio as a means to unify command and control and operational planning. The emperor agreed, describing the consolidation of power as an emergency measure necessary at this critical period of the war. Incumbent Chief of Staff Sugiyama furiously objected to this violation of the army's traditional ironclad rule separating administrative and operational affairs. After a heated argument among the army's big three (Sugiyama, War Minister Tōjō, and the Inspector-General of Military Education, Gen. Yamada Otozō), Tōjō carried the day by stating that he had already explained the change to the emperor. The other two grudgingly agreed with his dual position, but only as a temporary wartime measure. To assist Tōjō and Shimada, two vice chiefs of staff were appointed for each, a senior vice chief and a deputy vice chief. The awkward command arrangements harkened back to the 1880s structure of deputy chief of staffs under Prince Arisugawa and were just as unworkable. Tōjō had added another layer of bureaucracy to a sclerotic decision-making process already encrusted with too many deputies and dependent on cumbersome liaison conferences to coordinate the simplest details of civil-military relationships.

Tōjō's first big decision as army chief of staff under the new system concerned India, which had no place in Japan's coprosperity sphere but posed a

Table 11.2. Regular Army and Reserve Troop Numbers, 1937–1945

Year	Regular Army	Reservists	Total
1937	336,000	594,000	930,000 (63%)
1938	590,400	511,600	1,102,000
1939	804,400	391,600	1,196,000 (32%)
1940	910,000	380,000	1,290,000 (29%)
1941	1,032,500	992,500	2,025,000
1942	1,087,000	1,248,000	1,208,000
1943	1,502,000	2,295,000	2,750,000 (54%)
1944	2,118,400	1,641,600	3,760,000
1945	2,444,000	3,506,000	5,950,000 (58%)

Note: All figures exclude army air force personnel, whose numbers rose from 5,000 in 1937 to 74,500 in 1945. % = percentage of reservists.
Source: Rikusen gakkai, ed., Kindai sensōshi gaisetsu Shiryō hen, 36, table 2-1-9.

threat as a British base for a counteroffensive against Burma and as a supply point for U.S. and Chinese forces operating in China. In August 1942, IGHQ had approved the Fifteenth Army's plans to invade northern Assam and foment an anti-British independence movement. At the time, field commanders, including 18th Division commander Lt. Gen. Mutaguchi Renya, estimated that large ground forces could not penetrate the Arakan mountain range. Tokyo also mistakenly believed that the British had successfully suppressed the India-first nationalist movement and suspended further attempts to destabilize India. After attention shifted to Guadalcanal and the situation in New Guinea worsened, IGHQ postponed the operation indefinitely.

In January 1943, British Brig. Orde Wingate opened a daring four-month campaign behind Japanese lines that proved troops could maneuver in large units regardless of the inhospitable terrain. Two months later, Mutaguchi assumed command of the Fifteenth Army and, impressed by Wingate's feat and a vociferous advocate of the offensive, pressed for an invasion of India to preempt future Allied thrusts by destroying the enemy bases. His superior, Gen. Kawabe Masakazu, commanded the Burma Area Army, and both officers had been involved in the 1937 Marco Polo Bridge Incident. When Kawabe was noncommittal about invading India, Mutaguchi made the emotionally clinching appeal that because they were the combination that had started the Greater East Asia War they should be the ones to end it at Imphal.[28]

Senior staff officers in echelons from the Fifteenth Army to IGHQ opposed Mutaguchi, who reacted by transferring his chief logistician for criticizing the plan. Tōjō considered the whole thing very risky, and the chief of the operations department thought it foolhardy. Nonetheless, on August 7 IGHQ authorized a limited counterattack to occupy key points on the west bank of the Chindwin River, followed by an advance toward Imphal to draw British forces into a battle of attrition. IGHQ issued no detailed guidance, deferring to the custom of not placing excessive restrictions on field commanders. Attached IGHQ liaison officers would provide clarifications, if needed. Mutaguchi ignored these nuances, planned a full-scale offensive to capture Imphal, and found an unlikely ally.

Japanese attempts to organize an Indian National Army (INA) from prisoners of the British Indian Army captured in Malaya and Burma proceeded fitfully until the summer of 1943, when the Indian revolutionary and nationalist Subhas Chandra Bose arrived at Singapore. Appointed commander of the INA, although without military rank, Bose revived the force. Ignorant of the terrible 1943 Bengal famine, a product of British administrative incompetence, Tokyo remained leery of unleashing Bose, but the fiery Indian nationalist convinced Mutaguchi that India was teetering on revolution and that the appearance of his Indian army would tip the balance.[29]

Lt. Gen. Joseph Stilwell, the Deputy Supreme Allied commander in Southeast Asia, was preparing to seize Myitkyina, a strategic road and rail junction in northern Burma halfway between his base at Ledo, India, and Kunming, China, as a first step to reopen the Burma Road. Chinese Central Army forces were also massing along the northeast Burma border, and in September 1943 Mutaguchi dispatched reinforcements to northern Burma.

On Christmas Day 1943 Japanese railroad construction units, using Allied POWs and indigenous forced laborers, had opened a 250-mile stretch of rail line from southwestern Thailand to Moulein in southern Burma, where it connected to the main line running north through Mandalay to Myitkyina. The lives of more than 15,000 Allied prisoners and ultimately 330,000 indigenous workers were taken during construction of the line, which only marginally improved the logistics capacity needed to attack India.[30]

This was of little concern to Mutaguchi, who decreed that the Fifteenth Army would live off the land and captured enemy supplies. For rations the army would herd Burmese cattle and sheep along its route of march; the slow-moving animals quickly ended up in soldiers' cooking pots. Mutaguchi guaranteed a skeptical division commander that the British would surrender after the first Japanese volley. The 5th Air Division, depleted by transfers to New Guinea and the Philippines, was outnumbered four to one, but Mutaguchi assured doubters that air support was not all that necessary. Engineer units that were desperately needed to build roads and repair or build bridges to sustain the army had also been transferred to New Guinea.

After a meeting in late December 1943 with Mutaguchi, the Southern Army sent a senior officer to Tokyo to present the Fifteenth Army's plan. As the officer was preparing to return to the front, he was summoned to the prime minister's official residence where Tōjō, sitting in a steaming bathtub, fired a series of questions that recounted every major objection over the past six months. Assured these were taken care of, Tōjō endorsed the Imphal operation.[31]

In early January 1944 IGHQ ordered the Fifteenth Army's three divisions to destroy British Commonwealth forces near Imphal and occupy strategic points in northeast Burma. Simultaneously, the Thirty-third Army, also three divisions, would drive Chinese forces from northeast Burma and prevent Allied operations from gaining ground in India. The Twenty-eighth Army (two divisions, with another in strategic reserve) would attack farther south on the Ayakab front to draw Allied reserves from Imphal.[32]

Mutaguchi set February 11, 1944 (National Foundation Day), to launch his offensive, which gave him one month to capture Imphal before the rainy season made large-unit movement almost impossible. IGHQ, however, postponed the operation because one division was still en route from China. By the time Mutaguchi began his advance on India on March 8, he was already well behind schedule.

Three days earlier Wingate's glider-borne troops established an airhead in northern Burma that threatened Japanese rear area communications in north and central Burma in support of Stilwell's and Chiang's planned offensives. Mutaguchi was impervious to his commanders' appeals to suspend his offensive until they crushed the expedition. Time was running out, and he pushed ahead—regardless of deteriorating logistics, the daunting terrain, and changing battlefield conditions. Two columns converged on Imphal from the south and the east while one division made a sweeping envelopment to seize Kohima, about 60 miles to the north, a move that would sever the Anglo-Indian line of communication by denying the British Fourteenth Army its main supply base and railhead, located about 30 miles northwest of Kohima.

Complicating the operation was a dysfunctional command. One division commander, Maj. Gen. Yamauchi Masafumi (15th Division), the only Imperial Japanese Army officer to graduate from the U.S. Army staff college at Fort Leavenworth, Kansas, was too westernized and sensitive for Mutaguchi, who labeled him a coward. Mutaguchi detested another division commander (31st Division), the hard-bitten combat veteran Lt. Gen. Satō Kōtoku, who reciprocated, leaving the two barely on speaking terms. A third division commander, Maj. Gen. Yanagida Kenzō (33d Division), a polished staff officer with no combat experience, regarded Mutaguchi as an idiot, and Mutaguchi openly called him a gutless bastard.[33] With a command group that rivaled the worst combinations of the Russo-Japanese War, Mutaguchi set out to conquer India.

Despite the hardships of crossing the Arakan Range, by April 6 advance units of the 31st Division had occupied part of Kohima. Meanwhile, farther south, Yanagida's 33d Division, lacking supplies and air cover, moved too slowly, so

Mutaguchi sacked him and then relieved Yamauchi for reasons of ill health. By that time, the early onset of the rainy season, refined British tactics, and counterattacks ruined any chance to take Imphal. When Mutaguchi could not resupply Satō's division, the fiery general unilaterally withdrew from Kohima on May 31, an unprecedented act by a general officer. Mutaguchi relieved him, but rather than court-martial Satō for desertion in the face of the enemy, which would expose Mutaguchi's incompetence, the Burma Area Army declared Satō mentally unstable and shipped him back to Japan.[34]

By mid-May the general staff knew that Mutaguchi was in trouble, but no one, including Tōjō, would call off the operation. Kawabe was unwilling to act but hoped IGHQ would; years later Mutaguchi admitted that he should have abandoned the Imphal operation, but he could not bring himself to say so. IGHQ finally suspended the operation on July 4, but that was far too late. Soon afterward, Gen. William Slim began pursuit of the retreating, disorganized, and starving Fifteenth Army, having inflicted the worst military defeat the Japanese army ever suffered. The three divisions lost about 40,000 men killed, wounded, or missing. Perhaps another 36,000 support personnel perished during the grim retreat.

Logistics support was poor in all theaters and collapsed completely in some, like Burma. The late military historian Fujiwara Akira asserted that a majority of Japanese military deaths during the Asia-Pacific War resulted from starvation, not hostile action. Put differently, the army's incompetence killed more Japanese soldiers than did the Allies. In China, where Fujiwara served, logistics was left to his infantry battalion rather than specialized construction and transportation units. Although a more conservative recent analysis lowers Fujiwara's percentages, it generally concurs with his estimates.[35]

Besides wasting his army on an ill-considered adventure, Mutaguchi's defeat left the Burma Area Army precariously overextended and vulnerable to Anglo-Indian, American, and Chinese counterthrusts along three fronts. Stillwell's offensive into northwest Burma opened in May 1944 and in August captured Myitkyina. In conjunction with the offensive from the west, in mid-May fourteen Chinese divisions in Yunnan Province attacked from the east along the Burma border; by September they had reopened a portion of the Burma Road.

Japan's southwest front was also crumbling. Minor landings along the New Guinea coast by Australian and American troops forced the Japanese to evacuate Lae in September 1943. The Allies then slowly advanced along the coastline as MacArthur built up and trained the U.S. Sixth Army. In late January 1944 the Sixth Army captured the Admiralty Islands, which isolated New Britain and the 80,000 soldiers and sailors at Rabaul, the major Japanese air and naval base. The general staff activated the Thirty-first Army on February 25 to defend the Carolines, Marianas, Palaus, and Iwo Jima, and reinforced those garrisons as well as forces in western New Guinea. Increasingly effective U.S. submarines mauled several convoys bound for the Marianas, leaving troops there short of equipment, reinforcements, and supplies.[36]

On April 22, MacArthur simultaneously executed three major amphibious landings 200 miles behind the Japanese Eighteenth Army's coastal strongholds in eastern New Guinea. By seizing Hollandia, Netherlands New Guinea, MacArthur split Japanese army forces on New Guinea in two, cutting off the Eighteenth Army in eastern New Guinea and leaving the Second Area Army in western New Guinea waiting for the next blow to fall.

The Loss of the Marianas

Threatened on three fronts—Burma, the Central Pacific, and the Southwest Pacific—IGHQ turned on the main threat, the United States. Wherever the Americans next landed, the Japanese would force a decisive fleet engagement and then destroy the invaders along the beaches. On May 2 the general staff estimated that the Americans' main axis of attack would be the New Guinea–Philippines line. The Marianas were too well defended—a division had just reinforced Saipan, which Tōjō boasted was "impregnable"—for the casualty-averse Americans to assault. The next day the commander of the Combined Fleet ordered the "A" Operation to destroy the U.S. fleet near the Palaus, about halfway between the southern Philippines and the Caroline Islands, a location chosen because it was within the operating radius of the Combined Fleet, then at anchor in the southern Philippines. If the Americans did strike the Marianas, Japanese carrier- and land-based aircraft would destroy them, but a shortage of fleet tankers precluded refueling at sea and hampered any surface fleet operations in the distant islands.[37]

MacArthur's invasion of Biak, Schouten Islands, in late May became the focus of the *Kon* (All) Operation, a joint effort to reinforce the garrison, destroy American shipping, and isolate the invading ground forces. After two unsuccessful sorties, by early June *Kon*, backed by Japan's two super battleships, was ready to destroy the Biak lodgment. Then intelligence reports reached IGHQ that imminent landings were expected in the Marianas. The navy immediately ordered the "A" Operation because the loss of the island chain would put Tokyo within range of American long-range bombers.

Carrier- and land-based aircraft flying from Guam, Tinian, and the Carolines engaged the U.S. invasion fleet on June 19–20, costing about 400 aircraft and three aircraft carriers but inflicting little damage in return. Two U.S. Marine divisions had assaulted Saipan on June 15, 1944, and, supported by a U.S. Army division, in bloody fighting with heavy casualties on both sides secured the island. The fall of the supposedly impregnable bastion forced the IGHQ war diarist to concede that Japan had lost the initiative; the nation would slowly descend into ruin unless a decisive battle reversed the situation by breaking the Americans' will to fight. Lacking that, the only course was for all Japanese to emulate the Attu garrison's example and fight to the death.[38] The battle's signature event, however, was a last-ditch suicide attack, launched in the early morning hours of July 7, that included perhaps 3,000 soldiers from various decimated units and some Japanese civilian settlers.

There were about 22,000 Japanese civilians on Saipan; many expected no mercy from the American invaders, and perhaps several hundred had committed suicide during and after the battle. Sensational propaganda, however, made it appear that thousands had chosen self-immolation over the humiliation of capture, but at least 15,000 civilians survived the fighting, and many of those killed were lost during the pre-invasion bombardment.[39] Authorities made much of the civilians' supposedly enthusiastic cooperation with the army to defend Saipan. This was obviously crude propaganda, but its underlying purpose was chilling: to convince Japanese civilians that they too were expected to fight to the bitter end to protect the homeland. In short, the army had imposed its standard of no surrender onto the civilian population to legitimize the notion of death before dishonor and collective suicide for all Japanese.

Saipan's fall as well as the first B-29 air raid against the Japanese home islands on June 15 caused the collapse of Tōjō's cabinet. Retired Gen. Koiso Kuniaki became the new prime minister and in early August replaced the liaison conference with the Supreme Council for the Direction of the War.[40] Despite the grandiloquent title, the council was unable to provide strategic direction because the military refused to discuss operational matters in the presence of civilians, denied the prime minister information, and ignored Koiso's recommendations.

Changing Operational and Tactical Doctrine

Defeats on the borders of India, the Marianas, and the Southwest Pacific ended the absolute defensive zone strategy. In its place, on July 24 IGHQ issued the Shō (Victory) plan to cover four contingencies—the defense of (1) the Philippines, (2) Taiwan and the Ryukyu Islands, (3) southern and central Japan, and (4) northern Japan and the Kurile Islands. Should the enemy attack any one of these sectors, the imperial army and navy would hurl their entire might against the invaders in a decisive battle. The next day Sugiyama and Umezu hedged that commitment by agreeing that the army would commit 70 percent of its resources against the Americans during 1944 to win a decisive battle, but retain 30 percent as the cadre to rebuild for a protracted war.[41]

The first meeting of the Supreme Council for the Direction of the War convened on August 19 in the emperor's presence and authorized the Shō plans.

Emperor Hirohito (center) presides over the inaugural meeting of the Supreme Council for the Direction of the War on August 19, 1944. Seated to his right are the service chiefs of staff and their deputies. Prime Minister Koiso Kunaki is second on the emperor's left. Others include War Minister Sugiyama Hajime (fifth from left) and Military Affairs Bureau chief Major General Satō Kenryō, last on the left. (Copyright © 2008 The Yomiuri Shimbun)

Strategic guidance declared that no matter what Germany's fate after the Normandy landings in June 1944 and the Soviet summer offensive, the Japanese military intended to defend the homeland and prosecute war to the bitter end. The Allies' desire to end war sooner rather than later in order to minimize their casualties and greater disruption of their national economies indicated weakness; and by marshaling available resources, preparing civilian morale for the impending air attacks from the Marianas and China, and using diplomacy—possibly enlisting the Soviet Union as an intermediary—Tokyo could reverse its unfavorable international situation.[42]

The army also reconsidered its counteramphibious doctrine. Prewar planners had never expected to be defending small Pacific atolls or islands, and the army subsequently adapted its standard tactical doctrine for the defense of a riverline as counteramphibious doctrine for island fighting. Units would defend along the waterline, weaken the invaders, and then destroy the survivors with a counterattack. Yamasaki's charge at Attu and the fighting on Saipan exemplified the waterline defense.

The army continually analyzed its battlefield performance in the Pacific campaigns and distributed lessons learned to field units, but it remained preoccupied with its traditional Soviet opponent and assumed that the navy would handle the Americans. Not until September 1943 did the inspector-general of military education direct army schools to switch curricula from tactics, training, and education for war with the Soviet Union and give top priority to instruction on countering American operations.[43] School commandants protested, citing a lack of suitable materials and curricula on U.S. tactics and no curriculum available for instructors. One frustrated instructor announced the change to his class, remarking that he didn't know a damn thing about American tactics.[44]

During the first half of 1944, circumstances had prevented units from conducting the waterline defense and gave the Americans a conflicting sense of evolving Japanese tactics. At Biak in May and June 1944 the counterattack against the American lodgment foundered, not from any reluctance to execute the assault but because the rough terrain and distance from the main Japanese positions to the invasion beaches made coordinated, concentrated attacks impossible. After piecemeal attacks failed, the battered defenders retreated and then fought a tenacious delaying action from the numerous caves that pockmarked the island. At Peleliu in September 1944 the failure of the tank-infantry assault to split the U.S. Marine invaders on the invasion beaches—the original battle plan—forced the garrison into a protracted defense from the island's coral caves. The saw-toothed terrain canalized American attacks and enhanced the defense, and a two- or three-day campaign turned into a two-month nightmare.[45] It appeared to the United States that the Japanese army was adjusting tactics to engage in protracted fighting.

It was not until mid-August 1944, however, that IGHQ issued "Essentials of Island Defense" (the first completely new tactical manual since 1928), which instructed units to organize hardened positions for a protracted defense, including a last-stand fight to the death. The new doctrine was not a simple static defense but instead preached a mobile defense organized around fortifications and strongpoints that would serve as launching points to counterattack the invaders. Counteramphibious warfare doctrine now stressed improved fortifications, greater unit dispersal, successful concealment, and—of course—fighting spirit.[46]

In October the draft counteramphibious landing doctrine superseded "Essentials of Island Defense." Based on practical combat experience and lessons learned, the army officially abandoned defense at the water's edge and called for inland defenses in depth. Time and materiel, however, were unavailable to construct the multipositional defenses the manual advised. More important, at the military academy and staff college, officers had absorbed the message that the offensive pressed home with cold steel won battles and wars and that imbedded offensive doctrine could not be changed overnight.[47] As late as April 1945, for example, even the emperor would question the Okinawa garrison's reasons for abandoning the water's edge defense and giving up the island's airfields without a fight, a sentiment shared by IGHQ, other major headquarters, and probably most line-unit commanders on Okinawa.

The long-sought-after *Shō* operation came at Leyte, Philippines, after MacArthur's October 20 landing there. The navy threw its remaining capital ships into an ambitious, complex, and daring three-pronged attack on the beachhead that nearly succeeded, but finally ended with the loss of thirteen capital ships, three light cruisers, eight destroyers, and six submarines without achieving their objectives. As for the army, it had initially expected to fight the main ground battle on Luzon, but IGHQ and the general staff uncritically accepted the navy's exaggerated battle claims that its pilots had destroyed several American aircraft carriers during the October 12–15 Battle of the Taiwan Sea.

Believing that U.S. air and surface elements had been eliminated during the subsequent surface naval engagements in the central Philippines, the army general staff thought that MacArthur was trapped in his beachhead. Ignoring the advice of Lt. Gen. Yamashita Tomoyuki, the commander of the Fourteenth Area Army who wanted to fight the critical battle on Luzon, IGHQ ordered ground reinforcements to Leyte, expecting that they would formally accept MacArthur's surrender. Eventually elements of seven divisions were thrown into the Leyte campaign, where all were lost in the fighting. Furthermore, stripping the strategic reserve from Luzon fatally compromised Yamashita's overall strategy to defend the Philippines.[48]

China-Burma-India

By 1943 IGHQ was routinely transferring first-line divisions from China to shore up hard-pressed Japanese forces in the Pacific and southwest Asia theaters. To replace them, the army upgraded brigades to division status, but the new divisions lacked mobility and artillery support. These ersatz formations took over security in the occupied zones of China while the remaining first- and second-line divisions conducted limited offensives along wide frontages that employed converging columns to seize objectives. In North China the army wreaked as much havoc as possible to disrupt the Chinese military plans and sow domestic civilian disorder. Unable to garrison more conquered territory, the Japanese invariably withdrew, and the Chinese Communist or Central Government troops slowly reclaimed the devastated region.

The final major operation of 1943 against Changde (November–December) was the most ambitious that year and involved six divisions. The newly established Chinese-American Composite Wing and U.S. Army Air Forces delivered effective air support that forced the Japanese ground troops to assemble and move only at night. Since 1942 the Japanese Army Air Force had taken responsibility for air operations on the continent, but the appearance of American airpower in China forced it onto the defensive. In mid-December 1943 army bombers successfully struck Chinese airfields and air bases in southwestern China, but they could not prevent Chinese forces from retaking Changde on December 9.

In April 1944 U.S.-trained and -equipped Chinese divisions in Burma (the X-Force) and smaller American units tried to reopen the Burma Road leading into China as part of a limited Allied counteroffensive in north Burma. The combined forces reached Myitkyina in mid-May, causing the Thirty-third Army to abandon north Burma. The stubborn Japanese garrison at Myitkyina held out until early August against three Chinese divisions, giving the Japanese time to prepare another defensive line farther south.

During the Myitkyina siege, the fighting around Imphal-Kohima crested, menacing the Allied supply line—including that of the X-Force. Meanwhile, in early May, the Chinese 20th Army Group (sixteen divisions) in Yunnan (Kunming), known as the Y-Force, crossed the Salween River on a broad front about 100 miles east of Myitkyina, attempting to open the Burma route from the northeast by ejecting the Japanese 56th Division from Longling and ultimately linking up with the X-Force at Bhamo, Burma.

On June 1, the Chinese 11th Army Group joined the fighting on the southern flank, threatening to isolate the Japanese mountain strongholds. Because the Japanese still held Myitkyina, Chiang could not reinforce the Y-Force; consequently, Japanese counterattacks against Chinese river crossing points, skillful use of the jungle-covered mountain ranges to slow the Chinese drive, the onset of the monsoon season, and a successful counterstroke against the southern arm of the Chinese pincer halted the advance in late June. Further counterattacks to drive the Chinese west of the Salween ended in failure in mid-September. By this time the catastrophic defeat of the Japanese Fifteenth Army along the Burma-India border relegated the Thirty-third Army to the strategic defensive. Simultaneously, the growing Chinese awareness of the actual scope of the *Ichigō* (Number One) operation diverted its attention from north Burma.

The *Ichigō* offensive undertaken by the China Expeditionary Army between mid-April 1944 and early February 1945 was the largest military operation in the army's history, using approximately 500,000 troops (twenty divisions)—about 80 percent of the CEA's forces—supported by almost 800 tanks, more than 1,500 artillery guns, over 15,500 vehicles, and 240 aircraft. It aimed to destroy the American B-29 air bases in China within range of the Japanese mainland and to force open an overland route from Pusan, Korea, to French Indochina. Beginning around April 1944, replacements for *Ichigō* were brought from Korea and Manchuria to central China, but many were poorly equipped, sharing rifles until they could arm themselves with discarded Chinese weapons.[49]

Ichigō's first phase (mid-April to late May 1944) involved a north-south pincer to clear the southern portion of the Peking-Wuhan Railway and occupy Luoyang. The second stage (May to December 1944) consisted of massive sequenced offensives as the Eleventh Army pushed south, captured Changsha and Hengyang (which was desperately defended), and with the Twenty-third Army seized several American air bases. The Twenty-first Army then moved from northern Indochina to meet these forces, opening an overland line of communication running the length of China.

To secure the Indochina rear area, in early March 1945 the Japanese army preempted a suspected coup by attacking the French garrisons in Indochina (about 50,000 strong) and, after bitter fighting in the north, driving the French into southern China. They then removed French administrators and encouraged the Vietnamese to take control. "Liberation" was costly because the Japanese army confiscated Vietnam's rice crop and disrupted the food distribution system to create a famine that claimed perhaps 200,000 Vietnamese lives. All this suffering mattered little in the larger conflict because by this time the Asia-Pacific War had turned decisively against Japan.

In Burma the Chinese had made good progress since mid-October uncovering the Thirty-third Army's left flank by advancing south from Myitkyina. Three divisions linked up at Bhamo and then struck southwest, pushing back the weakened Japanese, who had retreated to the east side of the Shwell River by December.[50] Although the *Ichigō* offensive did divert Chinese troops from Burma, the remaining units continued their two-pronged offensive in northern Burma, linking up in late January 1945, reopening the entire Burma Road in February, and reaching Lashio in mid-March. These actions broke the five-year-long Japanese blockade of China and culminated in a decisive land campaign in Burma.

The Japanese army still held most Chinese cities and huge swaths of territory, but it was incapable of further offensive operations. During the eight-year China war, Japan suffered 410,000 killed (230,000 after December 1941) and 920,000 wounded. Although no reliable figures are available for Chinese losses, perhaps as many as ten million Chinese soldiers died during the fighting, and civilian casualties certainly surpassed that number. The protracted fighting also dislocated tens of millions of Chinese, who took to the roads in search of survival.[51] If the army had gone to war with the West in 1941 to break the stalemate in China, four years later the China theater was still stalemated, but with a major difference: Japan now confronted a mortal danger from the American counteroffensive.

On January 20, 1945, the services approved the first joint operational plan of the war, indeed the first in Japan's modern military history. Operation *Tengō* (Heaven) relied on special attack or suicide tactics, counting on elite air units to shatter the American offensive. Operation *Ketsu-gō* (Decisive) would prepare homeland defenses against invasion. The Fourteenth Area Army would continue fighting on Luzon to divert Allied strength while the army and navy strengthened the Ogasawaras (Iwo Jima) and Okinawa against enemy attack as part of *Ten-gō*. The army regarded the latter two islands as outpost battles and preliminaries to the decisive battle of the war—the American invasion of Japan. Perhaps more accurately, all three were homeland battles, because during the fighting on Iwo Jima and Okinawa, the home islands fell under U.S. heavy bomber attacks of growing savagery, an increasingly effective naval blockade, and naval carrier air and surface ship attacks.[52]

IGHQ's mid-February strategic estimate conceded the overwhelming material superiority of the United States, anticipated that the Americans would use their British and Chinese allies to wear down Japan's continental defenses, and presumed that the United States would pressure the Soviet Union to enter the war against Japan. But the Americans were operating on extended lines of communication vulnerable to attack. They were averse to heavy casualties, and if Japan adopted a *shūkketsu* (bleeding) strategy to defend the Ogasawaras and Okinawa, the army could buy time to build up homeland defenses for the war's climactic battle and make the Americans think twice about the consequences of invading the home islands.[53]

The small volcanic island of Iwo Jima, midway between Tokyo and Saipan, was the first *shūkketsu* battle. The roughly 11-square-mile island restricted maneuver and was ideal for defense. Lt. Gen. Kuribayashi Tadamichi had worked since June 1944 to transform it into a killing ground. Kuribayashi's plan was simple; he intended to hold out as long as possible, overriding objections from offensive-minded officers who advocated the traditional waterline defense. On February 19, three U.S. Marine divisions stormed Kuribayashi's honeycomb of cave and underground fighting positions in one of the most ferocious land battles of the Pacific War. Kuribayashi's final message transmitted to IGHQ on March 16 conceded the American victory, but he pledged to return as a spirit to witness the imperial army turn defeat into victory.[54] The fighting claimed 21,000 Japanese dead and more than 26,000 U.S. Marine casualties, including almost 7,000 killed. For the first time in the Pacific counteroffensive, the American attackers had suffered higher casualties than the Japanese defenders. The *shūkketsu* strategy had made a point.

For all the bloodshed, however, Iwo Jima was a prelude to Okinawa, where a large civilian population made for an entirely different campaign. Army commanders ruthlessly co-opted civilians to support their determination to hold the island regardless of cost. Shortly after the American landing on Saipan, on June 28, 1944, the war ministry and the cabinet approved the evacuation of noncombatants from Okinawa and other threatened islands. The army supported relocation for tactical, not humanitarian, reasons. The Thirty-second Army Chief of Staff, Lt. Gen. Chō Isamu, minced no words with the Okinawa legislature, telling it that combat units could maneuver more freely with fewer civilians in the way.[55]

The evacuation of Okinawa began in tragedy. In mid-August 1944 a U.S. submarine torpedoed a transport packed with refugees, and more than 700 schoolchildren perished. Fearful of more submarine attacks and not fully convinced the Americans would invade, Okinawans resisted evacuation—but prefectural authorities used schoolteachers, neighborhood associations, and village councils to pressure people to leave. As it turned out, the first ship was the only one lost during an evacuation that lasted into mid-March 1945, involved 187 vessels, and removed about 60,000 children to Japan and 20,000 civilians to Taiwan.[56] The army also ordered a mass evacuation of 60,000 elderly and children from southern Okinawa, the anticipated battleground, to the desolate northern end of the island. Any lingering doubts about the army's regard for the Okinawans disappeared after Chō's newspaper editorial in January 1945 declared the army's intention to confiscate all food once the enemy landed. The army's mission, he wrote, was to win, and it would not allow itself to be defeated by helping starving civilians.[57]

Yet the army ordered civilians to do its bidding. The Thirty-second Army conscripted or recalled to active duty 25,000 Okinawans between the ages of 17 and 45 and deployed them in poorly equipped self-defense or volunteer units. Scores of middle school students were conscripted and organized into special student units. Young girls from middle and high schools formed the female students' field force, worked as nurses in field hospitals, and carried rations and ammunition to fighting units.[58] During the battle, soldiers murdered civilians who got in their way. They confiscated food from starving women and children. They executed islanders speaking in the local dialect as spies. On smaller outlying islands, fanatical junior officers imposed draconian measures, executing scores of Okinawans as alleged spies or for disobeying army orders. The most notorious crime occurred on Tokashiki, where an army captain allegedly executed dozens of villagers and coerced more than 300 survivors into committing collective suicide.[59]

The Thirty-second Army's defense of Okinawa was also controversial. Unsure of the Americans' next objective, IGHQ transferred Okinawa's strongest division to Taiwan and refused to replace it, citing the danger from U.S. submarines as justification for holding a division in Japan rather than sacrificing the unit at sea. This decision affected the navy's Ten-gō plan, which called for a series of concentrated special-attack kamikaze aircraft to destroy the enemy at sea while ground forces repulsed them on the beaches. To execute the strategy,

IGHQ and the Tenth Area Army on Taiwan ordered Okinawa's airfields held at all costs to support the kamikaze operations. But the Thirty-second Army considered airpower a secondary factor and felt betrayed by IGHQ's refusal to send reinforcements to defend airfields. As a consequence, the Thirty-second Army unilaterally abandoned the airstrips to contract its defensive perimeter.[60] U.S. Army and Marine landings on April 1, 1945, met little resistance, quickly overran the airfields, and moved inland, where they eventually confronted the main Japanese defensive belts in a grim war of attrition.

Two days later, the emperor questioned the decision to abandon the airfields; IGHQ and the Tenth Area Army then ordered a counterattack to retake them and destroy the invaders at the waterline. Disagreement among the Thirty-second Army's senior staff officers nullified that order, and thereafter the ground battle degenerated into a brutal slugging match. U.S. losses in the two months of back-and-forth fighting totaled more than 65,000 casualties (26,000 nonbattle losses). According to Japanese sources, military losses were 65,000 killed, but 100,000 civilians died in the battle, including approximately 24,000 Okinawans impressed into service and thrown into battle with little training or equipment.[61] The staggering civilian losses suggest the savagery of the fighting and the Japanese army's indifference to their fate.

The prolonged fighting also pinned the U.S. fleet and supply transports to Okinawan waters, where they were targets of repeated large-scale suicide attacks by army and navy kamikaze flyers. Between April 1 and June 30, 1945, about 2,500 special attack aircraft sank 36 American ships and damaged more than ten times that number. Almost 5,000 U.S. sailors perished, and another 5,000 were wounded. American casualties of this magnitude were, as one historian put it, "an extremely ominous indicator amid preparations for an invasion of Japan."[62]

What made Okinawa even more frightening was the Thirty-second Army's belief that the terrible suffering of the island's civilian population was worthwhile because each day that Okinawa held out was another day to prepare for the decisive battle of the homeland. Though the deeply rooted main island prejudice against Okinawans likely contributed to the army's harsh treatment of civilians, it is unlikely that the army would have been more considerate of civilians on Kyūshū. After all, as early as February 1945 the war diary noted that civilians would have to subsist on minimum rations as determined by the army.[63] Transformed from a backwater to the scene of the bloodiest Pacific campaign, Okinawa bore the trademarks of an army that was not defending Japanese citizens or protecting their lives but was buying time for the defense of the mainland against Allied invasion. Okinawa and its inhabitants were sacrificed to prepare homeland defenses and to make the point that a similar determination to die was expected of Japanese in the home islands.

Finale

The day after the American landings on Okinawa, the operations department chief informed Prime Minister Koiso (who would resign within a week) that the occupation of Okinawa made an invasion of the home islands inevitable.[64] Preparations for that eventuality had been under way since January 1945, when the army began large-scale mobilizations of new divisions. At that time, IGHQ anticipated an American-led invasion occurring in June or July, continuing British pressure on the Burma front and landings in Malaya in the spring, the reopened Burma Road strengthening Chiang's forces, and the Soviets likely to give the required one-year's notice to abrogate the neutrality pact when it came due for renewal in April 1946. If Moscow judged the Japanese weak, the Soviets might enter the war regardless of the pact. Nevertheless, the joint service appreciation concluded that the military was determined to fight to the bitter end to achieve victory. According to army authorities, there was "an urgency to the German and Japanese war situation," but they were convinced that Japan's enemies were also suffering and that the global war had reached the stage of an endurance contest.

On April 8 IGHQ unveiled its homeland defense plans, which relied heavily on suicide attacks to destroy enemy transports at the main landing beaches. A handful of senior Japanese leaders simultaneously sought the Soviet Union's mediation to end the war before the decisive battle. To preserve secrecy, the so-called Big Six—the prime, foreign, war, and navy ministers along with the two service chiefs of staff—agreed on May 11 to float a Soviet peace feeler. Their goal was twofold; to prevent the Soviets from entering the current war by engaging them in diplomacy, and to have the Soviets mediate an end to war. But it was not until June 3 that the foreign minister approached the Soviet ambassador to Japan with the offer.[65]

By that time the approaching fall of Okinawa caused IGHQ to present a revised strategy at the June 8 imperial conference. Documents prepared for the meeting noted the tremendous American losses suffered on Okinawa (half the U.S. aircraft carriers were believed lost to special air attacks), and IGHQ concluded that the Okinawa fighting had delayed the forecast enemy invasion of Kyūshū until late August. At that time the Americans' objective would be to capture air bases in Kyūshū to support a follow-on invasion of the Tokyo plain in the early fall. The accompanying army analysis was bleak. Japan's line of communication had been disrupted by Allied air and submarine attacks that endangered the nation's food supply. Heavy bomber raids by B-29s flying from the Marianas had significantly reduced industrial output, and the firebombing of some sixty Japanese cities coupled with the loss of Okinawa had shaken public morale. People were losing confidence in their leaders, and inflation added to their discontent. Shortages in all areas—shipbuilding, steel, food—were compounded by incessant air and naval attacks on rolling stock that had disrupted domestic railroad lines, the implication being that even if one could produce war materiel, there was no way to move it.[66]

War Minister Gen. Anami Korechika still insisted that if Japan could hold out through 1945, the toll taken on the Americans during the Kyūshū invasion would break U.S. morale and will to continue the war. After all, a 5.2 million-man army still controlled large areas of China. Between April and early August 1945 the army had reinforced Kyūshū with twelve divisions and 450,000 personnel, who were deployed along the major landing beaches. Planning for the decisive battle of the homeland was well advanced, and though army leaders understood that they could not defeat the American invasion, they intended to inflict such painful losses that the United States would agree to a negotiated settlement along Japan's terms. Consequently, the army would commit everything it had and fight to the bitter end to preserve *kokutai* (defined as the national structure of Japan under the unbroken imperial line) and defend the home islands. The generals acknowledged that widespread starvation was likely during the winter of 1945–1946 and that by the spring of 1946 Japan would be incapable of further military action.[67] Emperor Hirohito reconvened an imperial conference on June 22 to address the contradictions. He told the Big Six to cooperate to end the war; despite the sovereign's instructions, Anami urged caution, for to appear overanxious to end the war at any price would only expose weakness and encourage the Soviets to enter the war. Hirohito insisted that the negotiations go forward.

After IGHQ approved the *Ichigō* offensive in January 1944, the army had stopped sending divisions from China to the Pacific fronts. Instead, the Kwantung Army in Manchuria became the source of reinforcements for the Pacific, and by January 1945 IGHQ had pulled out eleven of its first-line divisions. Concurrent with the loss of Okinawa, on June 4 Chief of Staff Gen. Umezu Yoshijirō notified the Kwantung Army and the China Expeditionary Army commanders that homeland defense had top priority, so they could expect neither reinforcements nor support from Japan. Since May the Kwantung Army had been mobilizing reservists throughout Manchuria to reconstitute its forces, and by July it had assembled about 700,000 troops, most poorly armed and equipped. Its new strategy called for a series of phased withdrawals to a redoubt on the Manchurian-Korean border, where it would make a final stand. Throughout the spring and early summer months of 1945 army intelligence reported that an extensive military buildup in the Soviet Far East was underway but concluded that the Soviets would wait until the spring of 1946 to invade Manchuria.[68]

After the Atomic Bombs

The atomic destruction of Hiroshima on August 6, the Soviet entry into the war three days later, and the atomic bombing of Nagasaki the same morning brought the war to an abrupt and unexpectedly sudden end. The atomic weapons were of course unprecedented, but the Soviet offensive in Manchuria, despite the army's monitoring of the Russian military buildup, achieved operational surprise. Unprepared, poorly trained, and ill-equipped Japanese units were outgunned and outmaneuvered by fast-moving Soviet tank and mechanized columns. They quickly fell apart, and the phased withdrawal turned into a rout, as evidenced by the Soviets' capturing more than 600,000 Japanese. Within eight days the Soviets had overrun most of Manchuria and landed forces in northern Korea. About 26,000 Japanese troops were killed along with as many as 170,000 of the 1.5 million Japanese residents in Manchuria. An estimated 130,000 prisoners died in Soviet captivity, and between 300,000 and 500,000 Japanese remain unaccounted for.[69]

The popular military historian Hando Kazutoshi observed that the Soviet entry into the war ended the possibility of a negotiated settlement for civilian leaders and diplomats because there was no one left to serve as a mediator in truce discussions. For the army leaders, the atomic bomb was the greater shock because, lacking a military countermeasure, they could no longer continue to fight in expectation of gaining more advantageous conditions to end the war.[70]

News of the second atomic bomb that destroyed the city of Nagasaki, with threats of more to follow, arrived during an August 9 emergency imperial conference. Even after these unprecedented disasters, Anami insisted that the army deserved to fight its last battle and still demanded conditions as its price for negotiations. *Kokutai* must be preserved; the Japanese, not the Allies, would try alleged war criminals; the military would repatriate its overseas forces; and there would be no occupation. Everyone else at the meeting knew it was over. Six days of indecision, attempted compromises, and dashed hopes ended on August 14 when Hirohito broke a deadlocked conference by declaring that Japan would accept the American terms.

IGHQ, the general staff, and the war ministry transmitted orders to the far-flung armies to lay down their arms. Although some units questioned the order and threatened resistance, army authorities quelled large-scale disobedience by invoking imperial authority. The same appeal to the throne that seventy-seven years earlier had established the modern army was now used to disband it.

Japan's Pacific War went through five easily discernable stages. First was the offensive from December 1941 until the reverses at Coral Sea and particularly

Midway in June 1942. Next came a period of attrition as Japan tried to hold or regain territory. By November 1943 Japan was on the strategic defensive and suffered a series of heavy defeats through August 1944. In an effort to reverse the Allied momentum, in the fall of 1944 Tokyo sought a decisive battle, but the crushing air, ground, and naval losses in the Philippines left no alternative except to endure. This final stage lasted from January 1945 until the atomic destruction of two Japanese cities. On the battlefields of Iwo Jima and Okinawa the army inflicted heavy losses on the advancing Americans, but the United States retaliated by inflicting untold suffering on Japanese civilians through a strategy of indiscriminate aerial bombardment, unrestricted submarine warfare, naval blockade and mining, and ultimately atomic bombs. Perhaps the ghastliness of it all made the Pacific phase of the war so clear-cut—Japan lost, the United States won.

But throughout the rest of Asia conditions were far more clouded. Manchuria and northern Korea fell under Soviet control temporarily, but the massive Japanese army in China, although officially ordered to lay down their weapons, remained armed, kept local order, and allied with the Guomindang Central Army to fight the Chinese Communists.[71] Japanese troops controlled Indochina, Malaya, and Singapore. They controlled the Netherlands East Indies, where they sponsored independence movements. This is not to say the indigenous peoples liked their brutal Japanese occupiers—quite the opposite; but it does help explain the volatility on the Asian continent during the immediate postwar period. Japan did not just destroy and discredit the western colonial forms imposed on Asians. Tokyo's own brand of tyranny had left wide swaths of the continent more or less ungovernable, susceptible to rebellion and revolution. Japanese occupation policies only convinced fellow Asians that the way to independence would never be led by Japan. Instead, resistance leaders across the continent took command and fashioned a decade of anticolonial wars.[72]

12

Epilogue

On August 16, 1945, Maj. Sugi Shigeru led about 100 young soldiers from the army's air signal training school in Ibaraki prefecture to Tokyo in order to protect the emperor from the imminent allied occupation. The Guard Division, which was responsible for defending the palace, shooed them away, but the group congregated at Ueno Park, eventually occupying the art museum. More arrivals from the school swelled their numbers to around 400 armed and emotional young men. Sugi ignored senior officers' orders to disband, and the next day Maj. Ishihara Sadakichi, a Guard Division officer and friend of Sugi's, was sent to convince him to leave. While the two were talking, a second lieutenant assigned to the training school walked up and shot Ishihara to death. Sugi in turn shot and killed the lieutenant. The murders broke the spell of an imperial rescue mission, and the disillusioned troops drifted away. That night Sugi and three other junior officers committed suicide.[1] The scene of the army's decisive victory in 1868 over supporters of the Tokugawa shogunate became the backdrop for the imperial army's violent curtain call in 1945.

Radical young reformers had created the new army of 1868 and forged intensely personal relationships as young men at war bonded by danger. Their personal ties created a web of informal connections that transcended the emerging political, military, and bureaucratic institutions. The first generation of leaders not only held the various levers of state power but also knew how to use them. They also possessed a self-assertiveness that attracted adherents and repelled opponents.

The army's formative experiences left it riven with competing internal factions dominated by strong contending personalities who held diametrically opposing visions of a future army. Reaction to the Chōshū-Satsuma domination of senior military ranks produced anti-Yamagata stalwarts like Miura and Soga who simultaneously represented a French faction that opposed Yamagata's and Katsura's Prussian clique. Arguments about the merits of differing force structures and the functions of a general staff consumed most of the 1880s. Though the army successfully adapted division formations and staff organizations, it failed to institutionalize the highest decision-making process and formalize command and control arrangements.

Lacking that apparatus, army leaders had to rely on the emperor to resolve disagreements and authorize policy. From beginning to end, the army depended on its relationship with the throne for authority as well as legitimacy and enshrined its unique connection to the emperor in the Meiji Constitution. Although the army steadily increased its power, it still remained one of many government institutions (which were simultaneously expanding their influence) competing for imperial certification. Initially, army leaders used the symbols of the throne to promote nationalism or a sense of nationhood, but by the early 1900s they were manipulating the imperial institution to secure larger force structures and budgets. By the 1930s they used appeals to the throne to justify illegal acts at home and aggression overseas.

The formative period realized its immediate goal, which was the preservation of domestic order. Had Japan fallen into civil chaos during the 1870s or 1880s, the nation might have shared a fate similar to China's. By quelling civil disturbances and crushing armed insurrections, the army guaranteed domestic order and became the bedrock of the oligarchic government. Thereafter a series of midrange objectives carried Japan through two limited regional wars. In each the army initially sought to protect previously acquired gains on the Asian continent, and successive victories brought in new acquisitions that in turn required protection and ever-larger military forces.

Between 1868 and 1905 the army played a significant role in achieving the nebulous but shared national strategic goal of creating "a rich country and a strong army." At the least, the slogan suggested a general approach to modernize Japan in order to fend off potential enemies. The well-ordered colonial world of nineteenth-century western imperialism fit the conservative approach of Japan's oligarchs and military leaders, who were often the same individuals. Working in a well-defined international system, men like Yamagata cautiously developed the army's strategy in reaction to events.

Successors built on Yamagata's foundation, modified the army's institutions to meet new requirements, and institutionalized doctrine, training, and professional military education. The steadily expanding conscription system indoctrinated youths, who in turn transmitted military values to their communities, as the army became an accepted part of the larger society. But the second generation of leadership faced the problem of perpetuating the oligarch consensus, an impossible task because of the emergence of other strong competing elites— the bureaucracy, political parties, big business—whose demands for their shares of power and influence inevitably shifted national priorities and international policies.

Furthermore, once the nation had achieved the goals of the Meiji Restoration, a new strategic consensus was required. It never materialized. The army responded with strategic plans that reflected narrow service interests, not national ones. Army culture increasingly protected the military institution at the expense of the nation. One might say the army had always put itself first, but after 1905 the tendency was exacerbated by the absence of an agreed-upon common opponent, a strategic axis of advance, and force structure requirements.

Until the Russo-Japanese War fierce debates raged within the army about Japan's future. Should the government be satisfied to be a minor power defended by a small territorial army, or should Japan, undergirded by an expanded army and navy, aspire to a dominant role in Asia?[2] Imperial sanction for the 1907 imperial defense policy set Japan on the latter course because of fears of a Russian war of revenge, rising anti-Japanese sentiment in the United States, and an obsession to preserve continental interests acquired at great cost in blood and treasure. International pressures helped to shape the army, but perhaps the internal debate, division, and dissension were decisive in its overall evolution. In other words, the formulation of strategy, doctrine, and internal army policy decided the army's and the nation's fate.

Japan's post-1905 aspirations for regional security enlarged the army's responsibilities to encompass garrison and pacification duties in Korea and the railroad zone in Manchuria. The army's emphasis in the 1907 imperial defense policy aimed to protect those newly acquired interests by conducting offensive operations against a resurgent Russia. The navy, intent on expanding south, identified the United States as its potential opponent. Military objectives were not focused, and the formulation of long-term military strategy foundered as the army compromised internally on force structure issues and externally with the navy over budget shares and the strategic axis of advance.

Too often after 1907 long-term strategic planning was sacrificed for short-term service-specific goals to protect budgets and resolve internal doctrinal and philosophical differences. Formalized strategic planning reflected parochial service interests, not national ones, and military strategy habitually depended on unrealistic plans that the nation could not afford. Military strategy was never integrated into a comprehensive national strategy and never fully coordinated from the top. The last cabinet consensus was for war with Russia in 1904, but even then there was no service agreement on how to fight the campaign. Decision-making had less to do with national unanimity than with the absence of an agreed-upon national strategy.

Unable and unwilling to resolve fundamental differences, the services went their separate strategic ways and produced operational and force structure requirements whose implementation would have bankrupted the nation. Recognizing this, the Diet and political parties consistently rejected the army's more radical proposals for higher appropriations into the early 1920s. At a time of unprecedented global flux, internal fissures plagued army planning and operations while external friction with the legislature, the imperial court, and the public disrupted hopes for service expansion.

Economic austerity intensified the bitter factional disputes over strategy and force structure that erupted between Tanaka Giichi, Ugaki Kazushige, and Uehara Yūsaku. These were not idle disagreements about abstract numbers of divisions but fundamental expressions of substantially different approaches to future warfare. Put differently, the army had moved from its personality-based cliques of the nineteenth century to professionally based groups led by officers holding competing and incompatible visions of future warfare. Traditionalists argued there was no need to match the technology of the West because Japan's next war would be in northeast Asia, not Western Europe. Excessive reliance on technology would detract from traditional martial values and fighting spirit. And the divergent proposals became zero-sum choices; the army either funded personnel or modernization.

Major international realignments after World War I, particularly in Northeast Asia, reinvigorated the army's mission. Under the revised postwar international structure, Japan confronted a growing Chinese nationalism, a resurgent Soviet Union in North Asia, and a weakening of the western grip on Asia. New ideologies of communism, democracy, and national self-determination threatened the army's core values by questioning the legitimacy of the imperial throne. During and after World War I, changing requirements for national security rewrote the rules governing international relations. Alliances that had been the basis of international stability were suspect. Treaties to reduce armaments or guarantee commercial opportunity appeared anti-Japanese. Most of all, modern warfare meant total war—whose preparations had to extend beyond national borders, making it impossible to pursue a conservative foreign policy in a well-ordered international framework and simultaneously achieve military goals of self-sufficiency required to wage total war.

Japan's new theorists of warfare deemed the acquisition of China's resources vital national interests and thereby elevated China to a central place in army strategy. Army officers became more aggressive and assertive toward China and made radical, often unilateral, decisions about national security that converted a traditionally defensive strategy into an aggressive, acquisitive one. This decisive strategic alteration set Japan on a course that challenged the postwar international order. Unilateral action by army officers failed in China in 1927 and 1928, but the army's stunning "Conspiracy at Mukden" in 1931 rendered Manchuria and North China essential national interests. Instead of the army serving the interests of the state, the state came to serve the army.[3]

Senior army leaders, however, were unable to agree on the limits of continental expansion or the type of army required for the changing ways of warfare. The bitter clashes between Araki and Nagata about the timing for war with the Soviet Union and army modernization were not resolved, only carried forward as disputes between Ishiwara and Umezu over China policy, rearmament, and a short-war or long-war strategy. Likewise, the war ministry and general staff often found themselves at odds over strategic decisions during the Siberian Expedition, the China Incident, and the 1941 decision for war with the Soviet Union. They continued to argue about strategy during the Asia-Pacific War, disagreeing about the merits of holding an extended defensive perimeter, Burma operations, and homeland defense, among others. The internal bickering was masked by a united front adopted against the navy, the Diet, political parties, and the foreign ministry. As much as army leaders disliked it, even in wartime they had to deal with these competing elites, compromise with them, and bargain to gain their ends.

Between 1916 and 1945, six army generals served as prime minister. Only one, Tōjō Hideki, displayed an ability to control subordinates and administer the cabinet, but his attempt to consolidate control made powerful enemies within the army who collaborated to assure his downfall. A dominant war minister like Terauchi Masatake fell victim to the rice riot mobs, Tanaka Giichi resigned after the Zhang Zuolin fiasco, and Hayashi Senjūrō quit so soon after taking the premiership that pundits nicknamed it the "eat-and-run" cabinet. Abe Nobuyuki served briefly with little distinction, and Koiso Kuniaki resigned after the defeats in the Philippines and Iwo Jima, unable to coordinate military and national strategy.

The outbreak of full-scale warfare in China in 1937 ended the army's ambitious modernization and rearmament plans. But the army did not prepare for the last war. It planned well for the next war, only against the wrong opponent. Japan could not afford to prepare simultaneously for the army to fight the Soviet Union in Manchuria and the navy to fight the United States in the Pacific. Stated differently, the services consistently produced a military strategy that the nation could not afford. Only the United States had the resources and industrial capacity to underwrite a global maritime and continental military strategy. Japan went to war against the one opponent it could never defeat. Appeals to warrior spirit to offset American material superiority pitted merciless men against impersonal machines in a savage war that ended in atomic destruction.

Suicide tactics, fighting to the last man, and brutality during the Asia-Pacific War became the legacy of Japan's first modern army. Yet the concept of literally fighting to the death did not gain popular acceptance until the late 1930s and was not institutionalized until 1941. After the Boshin Civil War and the Satsuma

Rebellion there were no mass suicides by the defeated rebels. The collective suicides by sixteen members of the White Tiger Brigade during the Boshin War represented a tragedy of such unusual proportions that the event became enshrined in popular memory. It is true that the Meiji leaders meted out cruel punishments to high-ranking rebels and instigators, but the new government took pains to reintegrate most of the former insurgents into society. Government propaganda and the deification of wartime heroes during the Russo-Japanese War intersected with a popular reaction to western values that revived derivative samurai ideals as somehow representative of true Japanese spirit to create new standards for battlefield conduct. This attitudinal change eventually metastasized into tactical and operational doctrine that prohibited surrender, coerced soldiers to fight to the death, and ultimately endorsed the desperation kamikaze tactics of 1944–1945.

Ordinary soldiers did not fight ruthlessly to the bitter end because of a common samurai gene pool or military heritage. The great paradox is that the only samurai the new Meiji leaders ever trusted were themselves. Appeals to a mythical warrior ethos were government and army devices to promote the morale of a conscript force that neither the civil nor military leaders held in much regard.

In macro terms, soldiers fought because the educational system inculcated a sense of national identity and responsibility to the state, patriotism, and reverence for imperial values that the army in turn capitalized on to indoctrinate pliable conscripts with idealized military values. At the micro level, they continued to fight when all hope was gone for various institutional and personal reasons. Army psychologists identified tough training, solid organization, army indoctrination, and small-unit leadership as factors in sustaining unit cohesion in extremis.[4] Personal reactions were as varied as the conscripts. Some fought to uphold family honor (usually sons of veterans), others simply to survive one more day, and most to support others. Based on recent, preliminary research, it appears that the vertical solidarity between junior leaders (lieutenants and senior sergeants) and the conscripts they led played a more significant role in combat motivation than in western armies.[5]

Any generalizations about the army's Asia-Pacific wartime performance require caveats. Battles or campaigns that ended in the almost total destruction of army units usually occurred when they were surrounded, as happened at Nomonhan, or defending isolated atolls such as Peleliu and smaller islands like Attu, Saipan, and Iwo Jima, where retreat was impossible. Conversely, on Guadalcanal, New Guinea, Luzon, and China, large Japanese army forces conducted tactical and operational retreats to preserve unit integrity. True, those armies suffered heavy losses, but most occurred after their logistics systems collapsed. There were also times such as at Leyte when withdrawal was an option but senior commanders' stubbornness and ordinary soldiers' docility had predictable disastrous results. Mutaguchi's Burma campaign is probably the most notorious example, but even his battered army did not fight to the last man.

An assessment of the Japanese army must address its brutality. The army's conduct in the Boshin War, the Satsuma Rebellion, and the Taiwan Expedition was at times reprehensible and reflected a combination of traditional Japanese military practices of the samurai class and late nineteenth-century western colonial pacification policies against indigenous peoples. In 1894, however, the Second Army's massacre of Chinese at Port Arthur went beyond accepted international standards, and the army reacted by protecting its interests, not punishing the perpetrators. Just a few years later, during the Boxer Expedition, Japanese soldiers were models of good behavior, operating under draconian discipline designed to impress the western allies with the nation's enlightened and civilized military forces. If nothing else, the experience suggests that the army could enforce strict field discipline when it found it to its advantage. The army's conduct during the Russo-Japanese War was likewise exemplary; prisoners of war were well treated, European residents of Port Arthur were not harmed, and international rules of land warfare were observed. A decade later, German prisoners taken at Tsingtao were similarly well treated. The army's conduct during the Siberian intervention was at times atrocious, but perhaps comprehensible, as the consequence of fighting a nasty guerrilla war in the wasteland.

A sea change in attitudes about civilians and prisoners seems to date from the 1920s. Notions of total war made civilians an essential component of an enemy's overall war-making capability and therefore legitimate targets to one degree or another by all major military powers. The army's hardening attitude during the 1930s about being captured complemented a growing contempt for enemies who surrendered. The permissible violence that unofficially suffused the barracks drew on concepts of superiority to toughen the conscripts while the gradual militarization of Japanese society, abetted by a national educational system that glorified martial values, contributed to a sense of moral and racial superiority. Popular stereotypes of devious Chinese[6] made their way into field manuals, and when full-scale warfare broke out in China in 1937, officers at all levels condoned or connived at murder, rape, arson, and looting.

War crimes may afflict all armies, but the scope of Japan's atrocities was so excessive and the punishments so disproportionate that no appeal to moral equivalency can excuse their barbarity. Between July 1937 and November 1944 in China, for instance, the army court-martialed about 9,000 soldiers for assorted offenses, most involving either crimes against superior officers or desertion, indicating that internal discipline mattered more to the army than external brutality.[7]

By the late 1930s the Japanese army relied on violence to terrorize Chinese opponents and civilians into submission. The army was as ruthless with Japanese citizens (Okinawa being the case in point) as it was with indigenous populations under its occupation because it placed the institution's prestige first and justified illegal acts to protect it. First readily observable after the Port Arthur massacre, the trend accelerated in the late 1920s with field insubordination (1927 Shandong), assassination (1928 Zhang Zuolin), criminal conspiracies (1931 Manchuria, 1932 Shanghai, and 1936 Inner Mongolia), and the sack of China, which began in July 1937 and continued into August 1945. The government, the army, and the navy ignored reports of mistreatment of Allied POWs and crimes against civilians to perpetuate the institution, not the nation.

Violence was idiosyncratic, depending on commanders' attitudes and orders. Too often senior Japanese officers ordered the execution of prisoners and civilians, the destruction of villages and cities, and condoned or encouraged plunder and rape. Junior officers followed orders (or acted secure in the knowledge that no punishment awaited them), and the enlisted ranks followed the permissive lead and took out their frustration and anger on the helpless. Not all Japanese soldiers participated in war crimes, and those who did cannot be absolved because they were following orders or doing what everyone else in their unit was. They were the "ordinary men" in extraordinary circumstances who became capable of the worst.[8]

Between the cease-fire of August 15 and Japan's formal surrender on September 2, the cabinet ordered all ministries to destroy their records—orders that were soon extended to local government offices throughout Japan. The imperial army tried to conceal its past, particularly its long record of atrocities throughout Asia. A week-long bonfire consumed the war ministry's and general staff's most sensitive, and likely most incriminating, documents. Imperial general headquarters also transmitted burn-after-reading messages to overseas units ordering them to destroy records related to the mistreatment of Allied prisoners of war, transform comfort women into army nurses, and burn anything "detrimental to Jap[anese] interests."[9] Finally, former army officers concealed significant materials from the occupying American authorities so that they could write an "unbiased" account of what they called the Greater East Asia War after the occupation ended.

Throughout the war, the army had routinely starved and beaten prisoners and had murdered tens of thousands of Caucasian prisoners and hundreds of thousands of Asian captives. Disturbed by the postwar outpouring of such revelations, in mid-September Foreign Minister Shigemitsu Mamoru conveyed his thinking on the matter to Japanese diplomats in neutral European nations. "Since the Americans have recently been raising an uproar about the question of our mistreatment of prisoners, I think we should make every effort to exploit the atomic bomb question in our propaganda."[10] Instead of confronting the issue of war crimes, Shigemitsu tried to shift attention from it, a precedent the Japanese government has followed ever since.

The Allies' dragnet for Japanese war criminals covered most of East Asia and identified and punished Japanese for war crimes committed throughout the area of Japanese conquest. Besides the twenty-eight leaders designated Class A war criminals (a number that included fourteen army generals) for plotting aggressive war, 5,700 Japanese subjects were tried as Class B and C war criminals for conventional crimes, violations of the laws of war, rape, murder, mistreatment of prisoners of war, and so forth. About 4,300 were convicted, almost 1,000 sentenced to death, and hundreds given life imprisonment.[11]

Others escaped justice. The most notorious example was Unit 731, a biological warfare unit in Manchuria that conducted human experiments on prisoners to test the lethality of the pathogens they manufactured. At war's end the unit destroyed its headquarters and germ-warfare facilities as its commander, Lt. Gen. Ishii Shirō, and his senior officers escaped the advancing Soviet armies and made their way back to Japan. Ishii later traded his cache of documents to Supreme Commander Allied Forces (SCAP), Japan, in exchange for immunity from prosecution as a war criminal.[12]

For all the bluster about one's responsibility to emulate samurai values, only about 600 officers committed suicide to atone for their roles in bringing Japan to defeat and disaster. That number included just 22 of the army's 1,501 army generals.[13] Other general officers disarmed their troops throughout Asia and the Pacific in accordance with Tokyo's August 17 notification to major commands that surrendering soldiers were not to be considered prisoners of war and that unit order and discipline would be maintained.[14]

The immediate military problems were the repatriation of overseas Japanese and the dissolution of the army. Even with Japanese cooperation, these were staggering tasks. More than 6.6 million Japanese were outside home islands (more than half of them soldiers and sailors), and there were one million Chinese and Koreans brought to Japan as forced laborers during the war who had to be returned home. About two million Japanese were in Manchuria, one million in Korea and Taiwan, and about one-and-a-half million in China. Others were scattered across Southeast Asia, the Southwest and Central Pacific, and the Philippines.[15] The enormous mass migration was carried out between 1945 and 1947, using U.S. Navy and Japanese ships, many crewed by Japanese seamen. Repatriation and demobilization went smoothly, and Gerhard Weinberg has noted the paradox between the turmoil in Asia that followed Japan's defeat and, notwithstanding the desperate conditions, the relative tranquility in Japan itself.[16]

In mid-September 1945 SCAP dissolved the imperial general headquarters and made the war and navy ministries responsible for demobilization of the armed forces. By December 1945 the ministries had disbanded all military forces in the Japanese home islands. SCAP then converted the ministries into demobilization boards that continued to muster out returning overseas veterans until October 1947, when the boards too were inactivated. After a generation of insubordination, conspiracy, and iniquity, in one of the great surprises of World War II Japanese officers obeyed orders and presided over the dissolution of their army. Perhaps nothing befitted the army so much as its self-administered demise.

The rapid rise of Japan's first modern army was a remarkable accomplishment that succeeded against long odds. Army leaders faced difficult options whose outcomes were never certain. Their choices set the army on a course whose direction was buffeted by foreign threats, altered by personalities, and changed by domestic developments. What continues to define the army, however, is its fall, a descent into ruthlessness and barbarity during the 1930s whose repercussions are still felt today through much of Asia. That legacy will forever haunt the old army.

Appendix 1
War Ministers and Army Chiefs of Staff

Army Ministers under the Council of State
Military Department

Ōmura Masujirō	July 1869–September 1869
Maebara Issei	December 1869–September 1870
Vacant	
Lt. Gen. Yamagata Aritomo	July 1871–February 1873

Army Ministry

Vacant	
Lt. Gen. Yamagata Aritomo	June 1873–February 1874
Vacant	
Maj. Gen. Tsuda Izuru	April 1874–June 1874 (acting)
Lt. Gen. Yamagata Aritomo	June 1874–December 1878
Lt. Gen. Saigō Tsugumichi	February 1877–November 1877 (acting)
Lt. Gen. Saigō Tsugumichi	September 1878–November 1878 (acting)
Lt. Gen. Saigō Tsugumichi	December 1878–February 1880
Lt. Gen. Ōyama Iwao	February 1880–December 1885

Installation Dates of Prime Ministers, War Ministers, and Army Chiefs of Staff under the Cabinet System, 1885–1945

Prime Minister	*War Minister*	*Army Chief of Staff*
Itō Hirobumi	Lt. Gen. Ōyama Iwao	Prince Arisugawa Taruhito
December 1885	December 1885	March 1886
Kuroda Kiyotaka		Lt. Gen. Ōzawa Takeo
April 1888		May 1889
Yamagata Aritomo		Prince Arisugawa Taruhito
December 1889		March 1890

Installation Dates of Prime Ministers, War Ministers, and Army Chiefs of Staff under the
Cabinet System, 1885–1945 *continued*

Prime Minister	*War Minister*	*Army Chief of Staff*
Matsukata Masayoshi May 1891	Lt. Gen. Takashima Tomonosuke May 1891	Prince Komatsu Akihito January 1895
Itō Hirobumi August 1892	Gen. Ōyama Iwao August 1892	
Matsukata Masayoshi September 1896	Gen. Saigō Tsugumichi (acting) October 1894	
	Yamagata Aritomo March 1895	
	Adm. Saigō Tsugumichi (acting) April 1895	
	Gen. Ōyama Iwao May 1895	
	Lt. Gen. Takashima Tomonosuke September 1896	
Itō Hirobumi January 1898	Gen. Katsura Tarō January 1898	Lt. Gen. Kawakami Sōroku January 1898
Ōkuma Shigenobu June 1898		
Yamagata Aritomo November 1898	Lt. Gen. Kodama Gentarō December 1900	Gen. Ōyama Iwao May 1899
Itō Hirobumi October 1900		
Katsura Tarō June 1901	Gen. Terauchi Masatake March 1902	Yamagata Aritomo June 1904
Saionji Kinmochi January 1906		Gen. Kodama Gentarō April 1906
Katsura Tarō July 1908		Gen. Oku Yasukata July 1906
Saionji Kinmochi August 1911	Lt. Gen. Ishimoto Shinroku August 1911	Gen. Hasegawa Yoshimichi January 1912
Katsura Tarō December 1912	Lt. Gen. Uehara Yūsaku April 1912	
Yamamoto Gonbei February 1913	Lt. Gen. Kigoshi Yasutsuna January 1912	
	Lt. Gen. Kusunose Sachihiko June 1913	

Installation Dates of Prime Ministers, War Ministers, and Army Chiefs of Staff under the Cabinet System, 1885–1945 *continued*

Prime Minister	War Minister	Army Chief of Staff
Ōkuma Shigenobu April 1914	Lt. Gen. Oka Ichinotsuke April 1914	Gen. Uehara Yūsaku December 1915
Terauchi Masatake October 1916	Lt. Gen. Ōshima Kenichi August 1915	
Hara Kei September 1918	Lt. Gen. Tanaka Giichi September 1918	
Takahashi Korekiyo November 1921	Lt. Gen. Yamanashi Kenzō June 1921	
Katō Tomosaburō June 1922	Gen. Tanaka Giichi September 1923	Gen. Kaai Misao March 1924
Yamamoto Gonbei September 1923	Lt. Gen. Ugaki Kazushige January 1924	
Kiyoura Keigo January 1924		
Katō Kōmei June 1925		
Wakatsuki Reijirō January 1926	Gen. Shirakawa Yoshinori April 1927	Gen. Suzuki Sōroku March 1926
Tanaka Giichi April 1927		
Hamaguchi Osachi July 1929	Gen. Ugaki Kazushige July 1929	Gen. Kanaya Kenzō February 1930
Watatsuki Reijirō April 1931	Lt. Gen. Abe Nobuyuki June 1930 (acting)	
	Gen. Minami Jirō April 1931	
Inukai Tsuyoshi December 1931	Lt. Gen. Araki Sadao December 1931	Prince Kan'in Kotohito December 1931
Saitō Makoto May 1932	Gen. Hayashi Senjurō September 1934	
Okada Keisuke July 1934	Gen. Kawashima Yoshiyuki September 1935	
Hirota Kōki March 1936	Gen. Terauchi Hisaichi March 1936	
Hayashi Senjurō February 1937	Lt. Gen. Nakamura Kōtarō February 1937	

Installation Dates of Prime Ministers, War Ministers, and Army Chiefs of Staff under the Cabinet System, 1885–1945 *continued*

Prime Minister	*War Minister*	*Army Chief of Staff*
Konoe Fumimaro June 1937	Gen. Sugiyama Hajime February 1937	
Hiranuma Kiichirō January 1939	Gen. Itagaki Seishirō June 1938	
Abe Nobuyuki August 1939	Gen. Hata Shunroku August 1939	
Yonai Mitsumasa January 1940		
Konoe Fumimaro July 1940	Gen. Tōjō Hideki July 1940	Gen. Sugiyama Hajime October 1940
Konoe Fumimaro July 1941		
Gen. Tōjō Hideki October 1941		Gen. Tōjō Hideki February 1944
		Gen. Umezu Yoshijirō July 1944
Koiso Kuniaki July 1944	Gen. Sugiyama Hajime July 1944	
Suzuki Kantarō April 1945	Gen. Anami Korechika April 1945	
Prince Higashikuni Naruhiko August 1945	Prince Higashikuni Naruhiko August 1945 (acting)	
Shidehara Kijurō October 1945	Gen. Shimomura Sadamu August 1945	

Appendix 2

Japanese Field Army Headquarters in China, 1937–1939

Date	Headquarters
August 26, 1937	China Garrison Army inactivated; North China Area Army activated
August 15, 1937	Shanghai Expeditionary Army activated (inactivated March 14, 1938)
August 26, 1937	North China Area Army activated
November 7, 1937	IGHQ organized Central China Area Army (Provisional) with Shanghai Expeditionary Army and 10th Army as main force; this becomes Central China Expeditionary Army (officially activated on December 1, 1937)
September 19, 1938	IGHQ activated 21st Army for south China operations
December 15, 1938	Organic units of 2d Army assigned to 11th Army; 2d Army inactivated upon return to Japan
September 23, 1939	Central China Expeditionary Army inactivated and same day China Expeditionary Army (September 12, 1939) activated along with 13th Army
September 23, 1939	North China Army activated
November 1939	China Expeditionary Army

China Expeditionary Army
  North China Area Army (all garrison units)
          First Army
          Twelfth Army
          Mongolia Garrison Army
          3 divisions attached directly to Area Army
  Directly attached to China Expeditionary Army
          Eleventh Army
          Thirteenth Army
          Twenty-First Army
          3d Air Group

Appendix 2
Japanese Field Army
Headquarters in China
1937-1939

Notes

Chapter 1. Prelude to Imperial Restoration

1. I have omitted macrons in the case of major Japanese cities. Unless otherwise noted, all Japanese-language secondary sources were published in Tokyo.

2. Fujiwara Akira, *Nihon gendaishi taikei* [An outline of contemporary Japanese history], *Gunjishi* [Military history] (Tōyō keizai shinpōsha, 1961), 6–8.

3. Hōya Tōru, *Sensō no Nishonshi* [Warfare in Japanese history] 18, *Boshin sensō* [The Boshin war] (Yoshikawa kōbunkan, 2007), 44; Kaneko Tsunenori, *Heiki to senjutsu no Nihonshi* [A history of weapons and tactics in Japan] (Hara shobō, 1982), 142–143.

4. Japan adopted the Julian calendar in 1873. I have converted earlier dates from the Japanese lunar calendar to the Julian calendar according to the table in appendix 3 of Rekishigaku kenkyūkai, ed., *Nihonshi nenpyō* [A chronological table of Japanese history] (Iwanami shinsho, 1966).

5. Konishi Shirō, *Nihon no rekishi* [A history of Japan] 19, *Kaikoku to jōi* [Open the country and expel the barbarians] (Chūō kōron, 1966), 274–276, 283–286.

6. Kaneko, *Heiki to senjutsu*, 142.

7. See Noguchi Takehiko, *Chōshū sensō* [The Chōshū wars] (Chūkō shinsho, 2006), 44; Sun Tzu, *The Art of War*, translated by Samuel B. Griffith (London: Oxford University Press, 1963), 91 and n1.

8. Noguchi, *Chōshū sensō*, 74–76.

9. Fujiwara, *Gunjishi*, 12.

10. Ibid., 10; Roger F. Hackett, *Yamagata Aritomo in the Rise of Modern Japan, 1838–1922* (Cambridge, Mass.: Harvard University Press, 1971), 38, 40–41.

11. Noguchi, *Chōshū sensō*, 187.

12. Ibid., 204–215.

13. Ibid., 167–168; Konishi, *Kaikoku to jōi*, 414.

14. Kaneko, *Heiki to senjutsu*, 144–145.

15. Hata Ikuhiko, *Tōsuiken to teikoku rikukaigun no jidai* [Supreme command in the age of the imperial army and navy] (Heibonsha shinsho, 2006), 101; Takemoto Tomoyuki, "Ōmura Masujirō ni okeru Yōshiki heihōron no keisei" [Western-style warfare in Ōmura Masujirō's formulations], *Gunji shigaku* 38:2 (September 2002), 22–23, 31–32.

16. Hōya, *Boshin sensō*, 46–47. Rumors persisted that Kōmei was poisoned to make way for the more pliable boy-emperor Meiji. In 1990, however, definitive evidence appeared that Kōmei suffered from purpura and died from hemorrhaging associated with the disease.

17. Inoue Kiyoshi, *Nihon no rekishi* [A history of Japan] 20, *Meiji ishin* [The Meiji

restoration] (Chūō kōronsha, 1966), 54; Hoshikawa Takeo, gen. ed., *Rekishi gunzō shirizū tōkubetsu genshū* [Illustrated historical series special edition], *Kettai han, zusetsu bakumatsu Boshin Seinan sensō* [The definitive volume, the illustrated account of the bakumatsu, Boshin, and Satsuma wars] (Gakken kenkyūsha, 2006), 98–103; Fujioka Kenjirō, ed., *Nihon rekishi chimei jiten* [Geographical dictionary of Japanese history] (Tokyoto shuppan, 1981), 357.

18. Hirao Michio, *Boshin sensōshi* [A history of the Boshin war] (Misaki shobō, 1971), 11; Charles D. Sheldon, "The Politics of the Civil War of 1868," in W. G. Beasley, ed., *Modern Japan: Aspects of History, Literature, and Society* (Rutland, VT: Charles E. Tuttle, 1976), 35; Sasaki Suguru, *Boshin sensō* [The Boshin war] (Chūkō shinsho, 1977), 24.

19. Hoshikawa, *Kettai han, zusetsu bakumatsu Boshin Seinan sensō*, 102–103; Hirao, *Boshin sensōshi*, 11; Sheldon, "Civil War," 35.

20. Hōya, *Boshin sensō*, 62, 67; Inoue, *Meiji Ishin*, 58; Sheldon, "Civil War," 35. On possession of the emperor's person, see John Whitney Hall, "A Monarch for Modern Japan," in Robert E. Ward, ed., *Political Development in Modern Japan* (Princeton, NJ: Princeton University Press, 1968), 44.

21. Hōya, *Boshin sensō*, 68. Ninnaji was born as Prince Yoshiaki but entered the Buddhist priesthood at age 12, taking the title Ninnaji no miya. He returned to secular life in 1867 as a junior councilor at the court. He was the nephew of Prince Arisugawa.

22. Sasaki, *Boshin sensō*, 28; Inoue, *Meiji ishin*, 54–59; Sheldon, "Civil War," 37–39; Hirao, *Boshin sensōshi*, 20; Fujiwara, *Gunjishi*, 17; Hoshikawa, *Kettai han, zusetsu bakumatsu Boshin Seinan sensō*, 102–103; Hōya, *Boshin sensō*, 80, 287.

Chapter 2. Civil War and the New Army

1. Kumagai Tadasu [Kumagai Mikahisa], *Teikoku rikukaigun no kisō chishiki* [A basic knowledge of the imperial army and navy] (Kōjinsha NF bunko, 2007), 156; Hackett, *Yamagata*, 56.

2. Ikuda Makoto, *Nihon rikugunshi* [A history of Japan's army] (Kyōikusha, 1980), 20–21.

3. One *koku* equaled about five U.S. bushels. Fujiwara, *Gunjishi*, 24–25; Kumagai Mikahisa, *Nihongun to jinteki seidō to mondai ten no kenkyū* [Research about the personnel system of the Japanese military and problem areas] (Kokusho kyōin, 1995), 24; Ichisaka Tarō, *Chōshū kiheitai* [The Chōshū kiheitai] (Chūkō shinsho, 2002), 195–197.

4. Bōeicho bōei senshishitsu, ed. [Japan, defense agency, military history department], *Senshi sōsho* [Official military history] 8, *Daihon'ei rikugunbu* [Imperial general headquarters, army department] (Asagumo shimbunsha, 1967), part 1, 4; Fujiwara, *Gunjishi*, 19.

5. Hōya, *Boshin sensō*, 127, 171. One *ryō* was the equivalent of one U.S. dollar. In June 1871 the Japanese government announced the New Currency Ordinance that created the yen, which was equivalent to US$1. Toshiki Tomita, "Government Bonds in the Meiji Restoration Period," Nōmura Research Institute, NHI Papers No. 87, March 1, 2005, 5. The yen steadily depreciated to $0.50 by 1894 and stabilized there until 1932, when it sunk to $0.28; by 1941 it was worth $0.23. Kyoto daigaku bungakubu, kokushi kenkyūshitsu, ed., *Nihon kindaishi jiten* [*Dictionary of modern Japanese history*] (Tōyō keizai shinpōsha, 1976 ed.), table 49, 899.

6. Hōya, *Boshin sensō*, 46–47; Sheldon, "Civil War," 47.

7. Hōya, *Boshin sensō*, 235, 257; Sasaki, *Boshin sensō*, 147.

8. See Ivan Morris, *The Nobility of Failure: Tragic Heroes in the History of Japan* (New York: Holt, Rinehart, and Winston, 1975), 229–230.

9. Sasaki Suguru, *Boshin sensō*, 60; Hōya, *Boshin sensō*, 164–166; M. William Steele, "The

Rise and Fall of the Shōgitai: A Social Drama," in Tetsuo Najita and J. Victor Koschmann, eds., *Conflict in Modern Japanese History: The Neglected Tradition* (Princeton, NJ: Princeton University Press, 1982), 133, 137.

10. Sasaki, *Boshin sensō*, 62.

11. Fujiwara, *Gunjishi*, 20; Hirao, *Boshin sensōshi*, 57–58; Hoshikawa, gen. ed., *Zusetsu bakumatsu Boshin Seinan sensō*, 112–115.

12. Sasaki, *Boshin sensō*, 63; Hirao, *Boshin sensōshi*, 60, 62.

13. Inoue, *Meiji ishin*, 110–111; Steele, "Rise and Fall of the Shōgitai," 141, 144; Sheldon, "Civil War," 44.

14. Sasaki, *Boshin sensō*, 108. The league was later joined by six other domains and allied itself with Aizu.

15. Harold Bolitho, "The Eichigo War, 1868," *Monumentica Nipponica* 34:3 (Autumn 1979), 262, 265; Kaneko, *Heiki to senjutsu*, 149–152.

16. Bolitho, "Eichigo War," 264.

17. Hirao, *Boshin sensōshi*, 129.

18. Hata, *Tōsuiken to teikoku*, 101; Hirao, *Boshin sensōshi*, 123; Hoshikawa, *Zusetsu bakumatsu Boshin Seinan sensō*, 126–127.

19. Bolitho, "Eichigo War," 265; Hirao, *Boshin sensōshi*, 159.

20. Inoue, *Meiji ishin*, 112–113; Hirao, *Boshin sensōshi*, 167.

21. Hōya, *Boshin sensō*, 226–230.

22. Suzuki Akira, *Shiba Ryōtarō to mitsu no sensō* [Shiba Ryōtarō and three wars] (Asahi shimbunsha, 2004), 22–23; Ōe Shinobu, *Yasukuni jinja* [The Yasukuni shrine] (Iwanami shoten, 1984), 118–119; Hōya, *Boshin sensō*, 226; Ichisaka, *Chōshū kiheitai*, 180.

23. Hara Kiyoshi, *Boshin sensō* [The Boshin war] (Hanawa shobō, 1963), 52–53.

24. Ibid., map 184; Matsushita Yoshio, *Meiji no guntai* [The military of the Meiji era] (Shibundō, 1963), 42–45. Kuroda was a wife beater, and in March 1878 during a drunken rage he stabbed his wife to death. Home Minister Ōkubo declared that Kuroda was not that type of person, and a subsequent police investigation exhumed the corpse only to conclude that there was insufficient evidence of murder. The case was buried in silence. Irogawa Daisuke, *Nihon no rekishi* [A history of Japan] 21, *Kindai kokka no shuppatsu* [The starting point of the modern nation] (Chūō kōronsha, 1966), 13–14.

25. Asakawa Michio, "Ishin kengunki ni okeru Nihon rikugun no yōhei shisō" [Strategic and tactical thought in the Japanese army during the restoration] *Gunji shigaku* 38:2 (September 2002), 11.

26. Mōri Toshihiko, *Taiwan shuppei* [The Taiwan expedition] (Chūkō shinsho, 1996), 157; Rikusen gakkai, eds., *Kindai sensōshi gaisetsu* [An overview of modern war history] jo (Rikusen gakkai, 1984), 12.

27. Ikuda, *Nihon rikugunshi*, 21–22.

28. Wagatsuma Hideki, ed., *Nihon seiji saiban shiroku, Meij—zen* [A historical record of Japan's political trials—the early Meiji period] (Dai ichi hōki shuppan kabushiki kaisha, 1968), 102–110.

29. Wagatsuma, *Nihon seiji saiban shiroku*, 102–110.

30. Hata, *Tōsuiken to teikoku*, 104–105.

31. Headed by Iwakura Tomomi, the most important court noble in the Meiji government, the mission returned in September 1873.

32. Hata, *Tōsuiken to teikoku*, 114; Ikuda, *Nihon rikugunshi*, 15.

33. Yui Masaomi, "Meiji shoki no kengun kōsō" [Plans for building the army during the

early Meiji period], in Yui Masaomi, Fujiwara Akira, and Yoshida Yutaka, eds., *Nihon kindai shisō taikei* 4 [An outline of modern Japanese thought], *Guntai to heishi* [The military and the soldiery] (Iwanami shoten, 1989), 426.

34. Inoue, *Meiji ishin*, 176–177.

35. Yui, "Meiji shoki," 436; Inoue, *Meiji ishin*, 168; Kumagai Tadasu, *Teikokurikukaigun kisō chishiki*, 113, 157; Kumagai Mikahisa, *Nihongun to jinteki seidō to mondai ten no kenkyū*, 24–25; Fujiwara, *Gunjishi*, 24.

36. Ikuda, *Nihon rikugunshi*, 26–27; Matsushita, *Meiji no guntai*, 12.

37. Hara Takeshi, *Meijiki kokudo bōeishi* [A history of homeland defense during the Meiji period] (Kinseisha, 2002), 26; Fujiwara, *Gunjishi*, 23–25; Matsushita, *Meiji no guntai*, 12; Ikuda, *Nihon rikugunshi*, 26; Tobe Ryōichi, *Nihon no kindai* [A history of modern Japan] 9, *Gyakusetsu no guntai* [The military paradox] (Chūō kōronsha, 1998), 34.

38. Ikuda, *Nihon rikugunshi*, 27; *Daihon'ei rikugunbu* part 1, 5, 9.

39. Yui, "Meiji shoki," 452–454.

40. Hara Takeshi, *Meijiki kokudo*, 16.

41. Kumagai Tadasu, *Teikokurikukaigun kisō chishiki*, 114; Yoshida Yutaka, *Nihon no guntai* [The Japanese military] (Iwanami shinsho, 2002), 36–37, 46; Stewart Lone, *Army, Empire and Politics in Meiji Japan* (London: St. Martin's, 2000), 16; Kumagai Mikahisa, *Nihongun to jinteki seidō*, 24–25.

42. Ikuda, *Nihon rikugunshi*, 23–25; Kumagai Mikahisa, *Nihongun to jinteki seidō*, 30, 40; Nishioka Koshoku, "Kanbu kyōiku seidō no sōsetsu to hatten" [The establishment and development of the officer education system], in Okumura Fusao and Kuwada Etsu, eds., *Kindai Nihon sensōshi* [A history of modern Japan's wars] 1, *Nisshin Nichi-Ro sensō* [The Sino-Japanese and the Russo-Japanese wars] (Dōdai keizai konwakai, 1996), 61.

43. Nishioka, "Kanbu kyōiku seidō," 58.

44. Rikusen gakkai, *Kindai sensōshi gaisetsu*, 12. The army abolished the NCO academy in 1899.

45. Nishioka, "Kanbu kyōiku seidō," 60; Ikuda, *Nihon rikugunshi*, 24; Endō Yoshinobu, *Kindai Nihon guntai kyōikushi kenkyū* [A study of the history of modern Japanese military education] (Aoki shoten, 1994), table 314, 92–93; Tobe, *Gyakusetsu*, 31.

46. Tobe, *Gyakusetsu*, 56; Yoshida Yutaka, *Nihon no guntai*, 36–37, 46; Lone, *Army, Empire*, 16.

47. Yoshida Yutaka, *Nihon no guntai*, 20.

48. Nishioka, "Kanbu kyōiku seidō," 57; Tanaka Keimi, *Rikugun jinji seidō gaisetsu, zenkan* [An outline of the army's personnel system, pt. 1], *Bōeicho bōei senshibu kenkyū shiryō* 80 RO–1H [Japan, self-defense agency, self-defense military history department, research document 80-1H], mimeo, 1981, 62.

49. Richard Sims, *French Policy towards the Bakufu and Meiji Japan, 1854–95* (Surrey: Curzon, 1998), 241–242; Nishioka, "Kanbu kyōiku seidō," 64; Kumagai Mikahisa, *Nihongun no jinjiteki seidō*, 57. The academy would move to Zama, about 25 miles southwest of Tokyo, in 1937.

50. Kumagai Tadasu, *Kisō chishiki*, 214; Tobe, *Gyakusetsu*, 91–92.

51. Kumagai Tadasu, *Kisō chishiki*, 126–127, 248. The three generals were Tanaka Giichi, who also became prime minister; Yamanishi Hanzō; and Mutō Shingi.

52. Endō, *Kindai Nihon guntai kyōikushi kenkyū*, 92–93; see also Ernst L. Presseisen, *Before Aggression: Europeans Prepare the Japanese Army* (Tucson: University of Arizona Press, 1965), 67; Sims, *French Policy towards the Bakufu*, 195.

53. Kumagai Mikahisa, *Nihongun no jinjiteki seidō*, 56, 65–66.

54. Asakawa, "Ishin kengunki," 5.

55. Kumagai Mikahisa, *Nihongun to jinteki seidō*, 40–41; Ikuda, *Nihon rikugunshi*, 53.

56. Heiyama Kanki, "Nihon rikugun ni okeru sakusen jō no yōkyū to kenkyū kaihatsu no kankei: yasenhō wo shūtai toshite" [The relationship of developmental research and operational requirements in the Japanese army, mainly for artillery], *Bōeicho bōei senshibu kenkyū shiryō*, 85 RO-2H, mimeo, 1985, 3–4, 6.

57. Janet E. Hunter, *The Emergence of Modern Japan: An Introductory History since 1853* (London: Longman Group UK, 1989), 111; Mikiso Hane, *Modern Japan: A Historical Survey* (Boulder, CO: Westview, 1986), 141–142.

58. Kumagai Mikahisa, *Nihongun to jinteki seidō*, 55–56; Yui, "Meiji shoki no kengun kōsō," 439–440.

59. Yui, "Meiji shoki no kengun kōsō," 440; Ikuda, *Nihon rikugunshi*, 27.

60. Hackett, *Yamagata*, 66. The standard work is Katō Yōko, *Chōheisei to kindai Nihon 1868–1945* [The conscription system and modern Japan, 1868–1945] (Yoshikawa Kōbunkan, 1996); Rikusen gakkai, *Kindai sensōshi gaisetsu*, 6.

61. Tobe, *Gyakusetsu*, 46; see also Hackett, *Yamagata*, 66.

62. Ikuda, *Nihon rikugunshi*, 28; Yui, "Meiji shoki no kengun kōsō," 459; Tobe, *Gyakusetsu*, 108.

63. Fujiwara, *Gunjishi*, chart 34; Kawano Hitoshi, *"Gyōkusai" no guntai—"seikan" no guntai* [An annihilated army—an army returning alive] (Kōdansha, 2001), 28–29.

64. Tobe, *Gyakusetsu*, 41–42, 45–46; Hackett, *Yamagata*, 67.

65. Hara Takeshi, *Meijiki kokudo bōeishi*, 45; Tobe, *Gyakusetsu*, 42–43, 50.

66. Mikiso Hane, *Peasants, Rebels, and Outcasts: The Underside of Modern Japan* (New York: Pantheon, 1982),18; Kumagai Tadasu, *Kisō chishiki*, 26–27; Hara Takeshi, *Meijiki kokudo*, 16; Hackett, *Yamagata*, 62; Tobe, *Gyakusetsu*, 31; Hata, *Tōsuiken to teikoku*, 105–106. Yamada would return to active duty in 1877 to command a brigade with distinction during the Satsuma Rebellion and later would found Nihon University.

67. Takamae Eiji, *The Allied Occupation of Japan* (New York: Continuum International Publishing Group, 2002), 372; Tobe, *Gyakusetsu*, 58.

68. Tobe, *Gyakusetsu* 140; Kurono Taeru, *Sanbō honbu to rikugun daigaku* [The general staff and the army staff college] (Kōdansha, 2004), 21; Yui, "Meiji shoki no kengun kōsō," 497.

69. Nishioka, "Kanbu kyōiku seidō," 67; Matsushita, *Meiji no guntai*, 109; Fujiwara, *Gunjishi*, 71.

70. Asakawa, "Ishin kengunki," 7; Endō, *Kindai Nihon guntai kyōikushi kenkyū*, 59; Presseisen, *Before Aggression*, 30; Tobe, *Gyakusetsu*, 58.

71. Kumagai Tadasu, *Kisō chishiki*, 116, 119; Asakawa Michio, "Shinbi chōhei ni kansuru hitotsu kenkyū" [Research concerning the 1871 conscription act] *Gunji shigaku* 32:1 (June 1996), 30–32.

72. Kitaoka Shin'ichi, "The Army as Bureaucracy: Japanese Militarism Revisited," *Journal of Military History*, Special Issue, 57:5 (October 1993), 70.

Chapter 3. Dealing with the Samurai

1. Tobe, *Gyakusetsu*, 10.

2. Hackett, *Yamagata*, 70–71.

3. Mōri, *Taiwan shuppei*, 118–119; Tobe, *Gyakusetsu*, 54, 57.

4. Inoue, *Meiji ishin*, 398.

5. Wagatsuma, *Nihon seiji saibanshi roku*, 339; Ogawara Masamichi, *Seinan sensō: Saigō Takamori to Nihon saigō no naisen* [The southwest war: Saigō Takamori and Japan's final civil war] (Chūkō shinsho, 2007), 8.

6. Mōri, *Taiwan shuppei*, 124–129. Since the early seventeenth century the Satsuma domain had claimed the Ryūkyūs as a vassal, and the government used this pretext for intervention.

7. Kaneko, *Heiki to senjutsu*, 160; Kojima Keizou, *Boshin sensō kara seinan sensō e* [From the Boshin war to the southwest war] (Chūkō shinsho, 1996), 210–211; Ogawara, *Seinan sensō*, 11.

8. Ōe Shinobu, *Nihon no sanbō honbu* [Japan's general staff headquarters] (Chūkō shinsho, 1985), 23.

9. Hata, *Tōsuiken to teikoku*, 107.

10. Hara, *Meijiki kokudo bōeishi*, 45–48; Tobe, *Gyakusetsu*, 50; Matsushita, *Meiji no guntai*, 47.

11. Ogawara, *Seinan sensō*, 8, 17.

12. Ibid, 40, 50. Ikai Toshiaki, *Seinan sensō: sensō no taigi to dōin sareru minshu* [The southwest war: duty and mobilization of the populace for the war] (Yoshikawa kōbunkan, 2008), 7.

13. Kaneko, *Heiki to senjutsu*, 163; Morris, *Nobility of Failure*, 263; James H. Buck, "The Satsuma Rebellion of 1877: From Kagoshima through the Siege of Kumamoto Castle," *Monumenta Nipponica* 28:4 (Winter 1973), 431; Ogawara, *Seinan sensō*, 239.

14. Kaneko, *Heiki to senjutsu*, 167.

15. Kuwada Etsu, "Taigai rikugun gunbi no kakuchō" [The expansion of the army's military preparations for overseas (operations)], in Okumura and Kuwada, eds., *Kindai Nihon sensōshi*, 140; Presseisen, *Before Aggression*, 55; Kurono, *Sanbō honbu to rikugun daigaku*, 25; Ogawara, *Seinan sensō*, 65, 68.

16. Ogawara, *Seinan sensō*, 81–83; Buck, "Satsuma Rebellion of 1877," 437.

17. Ōe, *Sanbō*, 27.

18. On Tani's suspicions see Ikai, *Seinan sensō*, 46.

19. Kaneko, *Heiki to senjutsu*, 168, 177.

20. Tobe, *Gyakusetsu*, 74; Ōe, *Sanbō*, 25; Kurono, *Sanbō honbu to rikugun daigaku*, 25; Hata, *Tōsuiken to teokoku*, 71.

21. Hashimoto Masaki, "Tabaruzaka-gunki sōshitsu zenya" [The battle of Tabaruzaka—on the eve of the loss of the military colors], pt. 1, *Rekishi to jimbutsu* (October 1971), 243–245. During the fighting at Kumamoto, the garrison's chief of staff was seriously wounded. Maj. Kodama Gentarō replaced him and believed that Nogi should have committed suicide to atone for losing his colors. The colors were recovered in January 1879, and that May, Kodama ordered Nogi confined to quarters for three days as punishment for the lost standard. Rikusenshi kenkyū fūkyūkai, ed., *Rikusen shishu* [Collected land warfare history], vol. 11, *Ryōjun yōsai kōrakusen* [The reduction of the Port Arthur fortress]. Hara shobō, 1969, 205–206. Ōe, *Sanbō*, 30. Nogi's later rehabilitation seemed to hinge on his pre-Satsuma Rebellion service as Yamagata's confidential agent in Kyūshū. Nogi and his wife committed ritual suicide in September 1912 to follow Emperor Meiji in death. His last will and testament stated that the loss of his regimental standard was the reason for his suicide. Yamamuro Kentoku, *Gunshin* [War gods] (Chūko shinsho, 2007), 108.

22. Ogawara, *Seinan sensō*, 88.

23. Ibid., 121–122.

24. Yamamoto Daisei, *Shōhai no kōzō: Nichi-Ro senshi o kagaku suru* [The structure of victory and defeat: thinking scientifically about the Russo-Japanese war] (Hara shobō, 1981), 13; Heiyama, "Nihon rikugun ni okeru sakusenjō," 6. Apparently an April 11, 1877, dispatch by Inukai Ki, a future prime minister, to the *Yūbin hōchi* newspaper first mentioned the three characteristics. See Ogawara, *Seinan sensō*, 125.

25. Inoue, *Meiji ishin*, 448; Hata Ikuhiko, *Nihon no horyo* [Japanese prisoners of war] jō (Hara shobō, 1998), vol. 1, 20; Ogawara, *Seinan sensō*, 226.

26. Tobe, *Gyakusetsu*, 60.

27. Ikuda, *Nihon rikugunshi*, 38.

28. Heiyama, "Nihon rikugun ni oekru sakusenjō," 4; Kurono, *Sanbō honbu to rikugun daigaku*, 24; Yokoyama Hisayuki, "Military Technological Strategy and Armaments Concepts of [the] Japanese Imperial Army—Around the Post-WWI Period," National Institute for Defense Studies (NIDS), *NIDS Security Reports*, No. 2 (March 2001), 118–119.

Chapter 4. The Army of Meiji

1. Wagatsuma, *Meiji zen*, 441.

2. Tobe, *Gyakusetsu*, 53; Kuwada, "Nisshin sensō mae," 8.

3. Matsushita, *Meiji no guntai*, 67; Kaneko, *Heiki to senjutsu*, 180.

4. Matsushita, *Meiji no guntai*, 67; Ikuda, *Nihon rikugunshi*, 42; Yui Masaomi, "Meiji shoki no kengun kōsō," in *Guntai heishi*, 484–485. Several Japanese military historians claim that Yamagata also intended to stifle military participation in the popular rights movement. Hata Ikuhiko, however, points out there is no supporting documentary evidence for such an interpretation (Hata, *Tōsuiken*, 97), which in any case seems premature in 1878, a time well before the popular movement peaked in the early 1880s.

5. Kurono, *Sanbō honbu to rikugun daigaku*, 6, 27, 29–30.

6. Katsura followed Ōmura Masujirō's advice to learn about foreign military institutions by studying abroad. Kurono Taeru, *Teikoku rikugun no "kaikaku to teikō"* [Reform and resistance in the imperial army] (Kōdansha, 2006), 52.

7. Ōe, *Sanbō*, 31, 34–35; Presseisen, *Before Aggression*, 62, 64; Morimatsu Toshio, *Daihon'ei* [Imperial general headquarters] (Kyōikusha rekishi shinsho, 1980), 31.

8. Ōe, *Sanbō*, 35–36.

9. Morimatsu, *Daihon'ei*, 31–33; Kurono, *Kaikaku to teikō*, 29–30; Fujiwara, *Gunjishi*, 77.

10. Tobe, *Gyakusetsu*, 97; Kumagai Mikahisa, "Kyūrikukaigun shōkō no senbetsu to kyōiku" [Officer selection and education in the former army and navy], *Bōeicho bōei senshibu kenkyū shiryō* 80 RO-12H [Japan, self-defense agency, self-defense military history department, research document 80-12H], mimeo, 1980, 60–61; Maebara Toshio, "Nihon rikugun no 'kōbō' ni kakawaru riron to kyōgi" [The Japanese army's theory and doctrine for offensive and defensive operations], *Bōeichō bōei senshibu kenkyū shiryō* 86 RO-5H, mimeo, 1986, 45. The number of prize-winning graduates varied between six and ten students, depending on class size.

11. Suzuki, *Shiba Ryōtarō to mitsu no sensō*, 22–23; Ikuda, *Nihon rikugunshi*, 43; Harada Keiichi, *Kokumingun no shinwa* [The myth of the people's army] (Yoshikawa Kōbunkan, 2001), 213.

12. John K. Fairbank, Edwin O. Reischauer, and Albert M. Craig, *East Asia: The Modern Transformation* (Boston: Houghton Mifflin, 1965), 299; Andrew Gordon, *A Modern History of Japan from Tokugawa Times to the Present* (New York: Oxford University Press, 2003), 87–88.

13. Ōshima Akiko, "Iwayuru Takebashi jihen no 'yoha' ni tsuite" [Concerning the after-effects of the so-called Takebashi incident], *Gunji shigaku* 32:3 (December 1996), 34–35, 42, 44.

14. Rikusen gakkai, *Kindai . . . gaisetsu*, 6; Tobe, *Gyakusetsu*, 56; Katō, *Chōheisei to kindai Nihon*, table 46–47.

15. Tobe, *Gyakusetsu*, 65. Lt. Gen. Torio Koyata commanded the Imperial Guard in 1881 and became the cabinet statistics institute director. Lt. Gen. Tani Tateki was the commandant of the military academy and concurrently the Toyama school commandant. He later became agriculture and commerce minister and retired from the army in 1889. Lt. Gen. Miura Gorō commanded the western army district and between 1882 and 1884 was the military academy

commandant. In 1884 he was placed on the inactive list; he retired from the army in August 1886. Maj. Gen. Soga Sukenori was the acting central army director in 1881. The next year he became vice chief of staff, and in 1885 he commanded the Sendai garrison. He retired in 1886.

16. Tobe, *Gyakusetsu*, 71; Hackett, *Yamagata*, 86; Carol Gluck, *Japan's Modern Myths: Ideology in the Late Meiji Period* (Princeton, NJ: Princeton University Press, 1985), 53–54.

17. Fujiwara, *Gunjishi*, 68.

18. Yamagata Aritomo, "Shinrinpō heibi ryakuhyō" [Memorial to the throne on the military advances in neighboring China], November 13, 1881, in *Guntai-heishi*, 279–287; Kuwada Etsu, "Nisshin sensō" [The Sino-Japanese war], *Gunjishi gaku* 119 (December 1994), 8; Kuwada, "Taigai rikugun gunbi no kōchō," 143.

19. Kurono Taeru, *Dai Nihon teikoku no seizon senryaku* [The imperial Japanese empire's strategy for survival] (Kōdansha, 2004), 20.

20. Ibid., 21, 23–24.

21. Kuwada, "Nisshin sensō," 9.

22. Kurono, *Daigaku*, 37–38; Kuwada, "Nisshin sensō," 9; Morimatsu, *Daihon'ei*, 38; Kuwada, "Taigai rikugun gunbi no kōchō," 145; Kurono, *Dai Nihon teikoku no seizon senryaku*, 21–22.

23. Morimatsu, *Daihon'ei*, 35; Hara, *Meijiki kokudo bōeishi*, 187; Kuwada, "Taigai rikugun gunbi no kōchō," 147–148.

24. Katō, *Chōheisei to kindai Nihon*, 46–48; Kumagai Tadasu, *Kisō chishiki*, 120–121.

25. Tobe, *Gyakusetsu*, 109. The personnel strength figures are from Rikusen gakkai, ed., *Kindai sensōshi gaisetsu, shiryō hen* [An outline of modern war history: documents appendix] table 2-1-2, 39.

26. Treaties signed with the United States and Great Britain by the *bakufu* in 1858 surrendered tariff autonomy, among other humiliating concessions that made Japan economically subordinate to foreign governments.

27. Kurono, *Kaikaku*, 53; Fujiwara, *Gunjishi*, 78; Kurono, *Daigaku*, 43.

28. Kurono, *Dai Nihon teikoku no seizon senryaku*, 27–28.

29. Gordon, *Japan*, 91. Tani continued to criticize the government and was seconded to the reserves the following year. Further talks on treaty revision occurred in 1890 and 1894. In July 1894 Britain agreed to end extraterritoriality in 1899 and customs control in 1911. Other western powers followed the British lead.

30. Tobe, *Gyakusetsu*, 109.

31. Kuwada, "Nisshin sensō," 10; Morimatsu, *Daihon'ei*, 38; Hara, *Meijiki kokudo*, 110–113.

32. Kurono, *Kaikaku*, 85; Kurono, *Daigaku*, 48; Kurono, *Teikoku*, 25.

33. Ikuda, *Nihon rikugunshi*, 55; Kuwada Etsu and Maebara Toshio, *Nihon no sensō zūkai to dēta* [The wars of Japan—maps and data] (Hara shobō, 1982), plate 5 on type divisions.

34. Yui, "Meiji shoki no kengun kōsō, 499; Hara, *Meijiki kokudo bōeishi*, 8.

35. Kuwada, "Nisshin sensō," 13.

36. Kurono, *Daigaku*, 59, 61–65; Endō, *Kindai Nihon guntai kyōiku*, 92, 98–99; Kumagai Mikahisa, *Nihongun no jinteki seidō*, 58–59; Ikuda, *Nihon rikugunshi*, 52–53.

37. Presseisen, *Before Aggression*, 104–105; Kurono, *Daigaku*, 39–41; Kumagai Tadasu, *Kisō chishiki*, 31.

38. Presseisen, *Before Aggression*, 112.

39. Kumagai Tadasu, *Kisō chishiki*, 65–66. The surge in employing foreign military professionals occurred between 1872 and 1877 when the Japanese hired French personnel exclusively; twenty-five in 1872, twenty-four in 1873, thirty-seven in 1874, forty-three in 1875,

thirty-eight in 1876, thirty in 1876, and thirteen in 1877; ibid., 74–75. Japanese officers regarded the French army superior to the German in artillery, musketry, and engineering technical instruction and veterinary sciences while Germany was preeminent in medicine and accounting. Ibid., 67.

40. Tobe, *Gyakusetsu*, 94; Kurono, *Daigaku*, 76–77. Meckel's views reflected a growing trend in mainstream European military thought to emphasize morale as the key ingredient on the battlefield. See Robert A. Doughty, *Pyrrhic Victory: French Strategy and Operations in the Great War* (Cambridge, MA: Belknap Press of Harvard University Press, 2005), 25–27; and Eric Dorn Brose, *The Kaiser's Army: The Politics of Military Technology in Germany during the Machine Age, 1870–1918* (New York: Oxford University Press, 2001), 70–74.

41. Kurono, *Daigaku*, 75; Kumagai Mikahisa, "Kyūrikukaigun shōkō no senbetsu," 63.

42. Endō, *Guntai kyōiku*, 60–62.

43. Presseisen, *Before Aggression*, 125–126, 148.

44. Ōe Shinobu, *Shōwa no rekishi* [A history of the Shōwa era] 3, *Tennō no guntai* [The emperor's army] (Shogakkan, 1982), 95; Kurono, *Daigaku*, 61–66; Kumagai Mikahisa, "Kyūrikukaigun shōkō no senbetsu," 63; Yamaguchi Muneyuki, *Rikugun to kaigun—rikukaigun shōkōshū no kenkyū* [The army and the navy—research on army and navy officers] (Kiyōbundo shuppan kabushiki kaisha, 2000), 16–22.

45. Nishioka, "Kanbu kyōiku seidō no sōsetsu to hatten," 70; Yamada Ichirō, "Nisshin sensō ni okeru iryō—eisei," in Okumura Fusao and Kuwada Etsu, eds., *Kindai Nihon sensōshi* [A history of modern Japan's wars] vol. 1, *Nisshin Nichi-Ro sensō* [The Sino-Japanese and Russo-Japanese wars] (Dōdai keizai kodankai, 1995), 233.

46. Kumagai Tadasu, *Kisō chishiki*, 218; Itō Takashi and Momose Takaji, eds., *Jiten Shōwa senzenki no Nihon seidō to jittai* [Dictionary of Japan's prewar Shōwa period system and essence] (Yoshikawa Kōbunkan, 1990), 319.

47. Tobe, *Gyakusetsu*, 95; Kumagai Tadasu, *Kisō chishiki*, 80–81.

48. Tobe, *Gyakusetsu*, 112.

49. Kurono, *Daigaku*, 45–46; see also Kurono, *Kaikaku*, 70–71. The 1874 regulation as revised in 1881 stipulated the wartime service criterion.

50. Kurono, *Kaikaku*, 56–57; Presseisen, *Before Aggression*, 117–119.

51. Presseisen, *Before Aggression*, 117; Kurono, *Kaikaku*, 58; Stewart Lone, *Army, Empire, and Politics in Meiji Japan* (London: St. Martin's, 2000), 16, 19; Hara, *Meijiki kokudo bōeishi*, 154.

52. Presseisen, *Before Aggression*, 117–118; Kurono, *Kaikaku*, 71.

53. Kurono, *Kaikaku*, 73; Hata, *Tōsuiken*, 113.

54. Kurono, *Kaikaku*, 74–75.

55. Matsushita, *Meiji no guntai*, 50–51.

56. Endō, *Guntai kyōikushi kenkyū*, 59, 64; Kurono, *Daigaku*, 45–46; Tanaka, *Rikugun jinji seidō gaisetsu, zenkan*, 80 RO-1H, 181.

57. Morimatsu, *Daihon'ei*, 41.

58. Ikuda, *Nihon rikugunshi*, 52.

59. Yui, "Meiji shoki no kengun kōsō," 490–492; Morimatsu, *Daihon'ei*, 45.

60. Morimatsu, *Daihon'ei*, 46–47.

61. Ibid.; Tobe, *Gyakusetsu*, 75–76.

62. Morimatsu, *Daihon'ei*, 43, 45, 47–52; Ōe Shinobu, *Gozen kaigi* [The imperial conferences] (Chūkō shinsho, 1991), 139–140.

63. Fujiwara, *Gunjishi*, 77. In 1889, of forty-two general officers, sixteen were from Chōshū (Yamagata's clique) and eight from Satsuma (Ōyama's clique), or 57 percent of the total. Of twenty navy admirals, one was from Chōshū and nine from Satsuma. Hata, *Tōsuiken*, 114.

64. Endō, *Guntai kyōiku*, 109; Kumaga, *Kisō chishiki*, 109; Yui, "Meiji shoki no kengun kōsō," 473–474. The figures do not total 100 percent because of rounding. The percentage of conscripts from agriculture was 81.5 in 1882, 80.8 in 1884, and 79.5 in 1888. The percentage distribution of labor in agriculture was 71.2 in 1882, 67.9 in 1890, 65 in 1900, 64.3 in 1910, 53.6 in 1920, 49.4 in 1930, and 44 in 1940.

65. Yui, "Meiji shoki no kengun kōsō," 468–469; Tobe, *Gyakusetsu*, 119.

66. Harada, *Kokumingun no shinwa*, 53–60.

67. Kumagai Tadasu, *Kisō chishiki*, 74–75, 122; Yui, "Meiji shoki no kengun kōsō," 474.

68. Yui, "Meiji shoki no kengun kōsō," 467–469.

69. Harada, *Kokumingun*, 56, 58; Morimatsu, *Daihon'ei*, 38.

70. Katō, *Chōheisei to Kindai Nihon*, 46–48; Kumagai Tadasu, *Kisō chishiki*, 120–121.

71. Rikusen gakkai, *Kindai sensōshi gaisetsu*, 6, 33; Kumagai Tadasu, *Kisō chishiki*, 120, 139; Iguchi Kazuki, *Nichi-Ro sensō no jidai* [The Russo-Japanese war era] (Yoshikawa Kōbunkan, 1998), 22; Kawashima [?], "Gundōin no seidō to jissai" [The military mobilization system and its reality], *Bōeicho bōei senshibu kenkyū shiryō* 95 RO-4H, mimeo, 1980, 12, 15.

72. Ichinose Toshiya, *Meiji, Taishō, Shōwa guntai manyūaru* [Military pamphlets of the Meiji, Taishō, and Shōwa periods] (Kōbunsha, 2004), 81; Yui, "Meiji shoki no kengun kōsō," 482; Kumagai Tadasu, *Teikoku rikukaigun*, 251–253; Toshio Iritani, *Group Psychology of the Japanese in Wartime* (London: Kegan Paul, 1991), 98.

Chapter 5. To Asia: The Sino-Japanese War

1. Since the 1870s Yamagata had occupied a succession of key posts in the army and civil government and other ministerial-level posts; war minister (1873–1874, 1874–1878) and concurrently chief general staff bureau (1874–1876), chief of the general staff (1878–1882), home minister and concurrently chief of staff (1883–1885), *kangun* (1887–1889), and prime minister (1889–1891, 1898–1900).

2. Matsushita, *Nihon kokubō no higeki* [The tragedy of Japan's national defense] (Fūyō shobō, 1975), 34–36.

3. Kurono, *Kaikaku*, 41–43.

4. Yamagata Aritomo, "Gunji ikensho" [Opinions on the military] in *Guntai heishi*, 299–306; Kuwada, "Nisshin sensō," 10–11.

5. Lone, *Army, Empire*, 22–23; Fujiwara, *Gunjishi*, 68.

6. Gordon, *Modern History of Japan*, 91; Yui, "Meiji shoki no kengun kōsō," 461; Ōe, *Sanbō*, 47; Kurono, *Daigaku*, 45–47; Presseisen, *Before Aggression*, 118–119.

7. Fujiwara, *Gunjishi*, 79; Tobe, *Gyakusetsu*, 128–130.

8. Ōe, *Sanbō*, 50. In August 1892 the emperor dissolved the Diet as part of Itō's plan to elect pro-government politicians who would pass the cabinet's legislative program. Massive police interference and violence marred the second Diet election campaign of 1892, but the opposition parties still returned with a majority of seats.

9. Hara, *Meijiki kokudo bōeishi*, 156, 195; Saitō Seiji, *Nisshin sensō no gunji senryaku* [Military strategy for the Sino-Japanese war] (Fūyō shobō, 2003), 25, 138–139. A narrow-gauge rail needed 75–76 cars to transport a division whereas a standard-gauge rail required about half that number.

10. Presseisen, *Before Aggression*, 122; Hara, *Meijiki kokudo bōeishi*, 251; Saitō, *Nisshin sensō no gunji senryaku*, 24–25.

11. Saitō, *Nisshin sensō no gunji senryaku*, 20–25; Kyū sanbō honbu hensan [Former headquarters general staff], eds., *Nisshin sensō* [The Sino-Japanese war] (Tokuma shoten, 1995), 425.

12. Yui, "Meiji shoki no kengun kōsō," 473–474; Nobutaka Ike, "War and Moderniza-tion," in Robert E. Ward, ed., *Political Development in Modern Japan* (Princeton, NJ: Princeton University Press, 1968), 196. On the question of literacy, see Richard Rubinger, "Who Can't Read and Write: Illiteracy in Meiji Japan," *Monumenta Nipponica*, 55:2 (2000), 163–198; and P. F. Kornicki, "Literacy Revisited: Some Reflections on Richard Rubinger's Findings," *Monu-menta Nipponica*, 56:3 (2001), 381–395.

13. Harada Keiichi, *Shirizū Nihon kingendaishi* [The history of Japanese modern and con-temporary history] 3, *Nisshin Nichi-Ro sensō* [The Sino-Japanese and Russo-Japanese wars] (Iwanami shinsho, 2007), 182–183.

14. Yoshida Yutaka, *Nihon no guntai*, 100, 103, 114; Kumagai Mikahisa, "Nihongun no jinji," 116.

15. Ichinose Toshiya, *Meiji, Taishō, Shōwa guntai manyuaru*, 37, 48.

16. Heiyama, "Nihon rikugun sakusenjō no yōkyō," 85 RO-2H, 7, 11, 33; Lone, *Army, Empire*, 28–29; Saitō, *Nisshin sensō no gunji senryaku*, 32.

17. Rikusen gakkai, ed., *Kindai sensōshi gaisetsu*, 22; Yoshida, *Nihon no guntai*, 183.

18. Harada, *Kokumin no shinwa*, 125, 141, 153.

19. Hackett, *Yamagata*, 138; Harada, *Nisshin Nichi-Ro sensō*, 27.

20. Kuwada, "Nisshin sensō mae," 16; Hackett, *Yamagata*, 138.

21. Saitō, *Nisshin sensō no gunji senryaku*, 17; Presseisen, *Before Aggression*, 133; Tobe, *Gyaku-setsu*, 110; Kumagai Tadasu, *Kisō chishiki*, 225. Meiji's first appearance in a naval uniform came in 1905 after the navy's victory over the Russian fleet in the Tsushima Strait. Yoshida, *Nihon no guntai*, 36.

22. Saitō, *Nisshin sensō no gunji senryaku*, 18, 29, 32; Hara Takeshi, "Nisshin sensō ni okeru hondo bōei" [Homeland defense during the Sino-Japanese war], *Gunji shigaku*, 30:3 (De-cember 1994), 36. The army had partially mobilized its reserves in 1882 in response to an outbreak of anti-Japanese violence in Korea and again in 1885 for field exercises.

23. Endō, *Kindai Nihon guntai kyōiku*, 99; Rikusen gakkai, ed., *Kindai sensōshi gaisetsu*, 22. The original understrength division became the 7th Division, based in Hokkaidō beginning in 1894 although not formally reorganized until after the Sino-Japanese War (1894–1895).

24. Harada, *Kokumingun no shinwa*, 52. A total of 74,880 draft resisters or deserters were recorded during the period.

25. Endō, *Kindai Nihon guntai kyōiku*, 61, 99–102.

26. Morimatsu, *Daihon'ei*, 53–55; Toyama Saburō, *Nihon kaigunshi* [A history of the Japa-nese navy] (Kyōikusha, 1980), 46.

27. Kurono, *Daigaku*, 82; Morimatsu, *Daihon'ei*, 61–63; Saitō, *Nisshin sensō no gunji senry-aku*, 34.

28. Morimatsu, *Daihon'ei*, 63; Ikuda, *Nihon rikugunshi*, 52; Matsushita, *Meiji no guntai*, 96.

29. Kurono, *Teikoku kokubō*, 29; Kuwada Etsu, "Taigai rikugun gunbi no kochō" [Exag-gerated army preparations for overseas (operations)], in Okumura and Kuwada, eds., *Kindai Nihon sensōshi*, 151–152.

30. Hara Takeshi, "Nisshin sensō ni okeru hondo bōei," 35–37; Saitō, *Nisshin sensō no gunji senryaku*, 39.

31. Kurono, *Dai Nihon teikoku*, 40; Saitō, *Nisshin sensō no gunji senryaku*, 36–37.

32. Kuwada, "Taigai rikugun gunbi no kochō," 152; Kurono, *Dai Nihon teikoku*, 40; Kurono, *Daigaku*, 88.

33. Michael A. Barnhart, *Japan and the World since 1868* (London: Edward Arnold, 1995), 15; Saitō, *Nisshin sensō no gunji senryaku*, 52.

34. Mutsu Munemitsu, *Kekkenroku: A Diplomatic Record of the Sino-Japanese War, 1894–1895,*

trans. Gordon Berger (Princeton, NJ: Princeton University Press, 1982), 7, 258–259 n 10; Fujimura Michio, *Nisshin sensō* [The Sino-Japanese war] (Iwanami shinsho, 1973), 66–67.

35. Hackett, *Yamagata*, 160–161; Stewart Lone, *Japan's First Modern War: Army and Society in the Conflict with China, 1894–95* (London: St. Martin's Press, 1994), 26–27.

36. Morimatsu, *Daihon'ei*, 63, 76–77.

37. Toyama, *Nihon kaigunshi*, 69–70; Kurono, *Daigaku*, 90–91.

38. Saitō, *Nisshin sensō no gunji senryaku*, 58; Kurono, *Dai Nihon teikoku*, 40–41.

39. Saitō, *Nisshin sensō no gunji senryaku*, 63, 77 n 62; Charles J. Schencking, *Making Waves: Politics, Propaganda, and the Emergence of the Imperial Japanese Navy, 1868–1922* (Stanford, CA: Stanford University Press, 2005), 91–92.

40. Harada Keiichi, *Nisshin Nichi-Ro sensō*, 70; Kurono, *Daigaku*, 89.

41. Morimatsu, *Daihon'ei*, 81; Tobe, *Gyakusetsu*, 139–140.

42. Saitō, *Nisshin sensō no gunji senryaku*, 173; Harada, *Nisshin Ni-Ro sensō*, 70; Morimatsu, *Daihon'ei*, 76–77, 79; Lone, *Japan's First Modern War*, 32–33.

43. Hara, "Nisshin sensō ni okeru hondo bōei," 40–42; Kyū sanbō honbu hensan, eds., *Nisshin sensō*, 422–423; Saitō, *Nisshin sensō no gunji senryaku*, 223.

44. Ōe Shinobu, *Nichi-Ro sensō gunjishiteki kenkyū* [A military history study of the Russo-Japanese war] (Iwanami shoten, 1976), 6–7; Kawashima, "Gundōin no seidō to jissai," 95 RO-4H, 139; Ōe Shinobu, *Nichi-Ro sensō to Nihon guntai* [The Russo-Japanese war and the Japanese military] (Rippū shoten, 1987), 261. The exceptions were Maj. Gen. Nozu Michitsura, commander 5th Division and subsequently commander 2d Army, and his successor as division commander, Maj. Gen. Mutsu Yasukata.

45. Kyū sanbō honbu hensan, *Nisshin sensō*, 155.

46. Rikusen gakkai, *Kindai sensōshi gaisetsu*, 25.

47. Harada, *Nisshin Nichi-Ro sensō*, 81.

48. Kuwada, "Nisshin sensō ni okeru yusō-hokyū," in Okumura and Kuwada, eds., *Nisshin Nichi-Ro sensō*, 251–252.

49. Kuwada, "Nisshin sensō," 5; Kyū sanbō honbu hensan, *Nisshin sensō*, 425, 401. To lift one division required about 65,000 tons of shipping, roughly fifty vessels.

50. Kyū sanbō honbu hensan, *Nisshin sensō*, 400–402.

51. Harada, *Nisshin Nichi-Ro*, 77–80.

52. Kuwada, "Nisshin sensō," 6.

53. Ibid., 252.

54. Yamamoto, *Shōhai no kōzō*, 33.

55. Ibid., 239; Yamada, "Nisshin sensō ni okeru iryō-eisei," 235, 248.

56. Endō, *Kindai Nihon guntai kyōiku*, 104–106; Ikuda, *Nihon rikugunshi*, 74.

57. Presseisen, *Before Aggression*, 142; Ōe, *Nichi-Ro sensō Nihon guntai*, 57. Thirty-eight civilians attached to the army were also killed.

58. Hata, *Nihonjin no horyo*, vol. 1, 7–9. Hata believes this was the genesis of the infamous *Senjinkun* (code of battlefield conduct) of 1941.

59. Mutsu, *Kekkenroku*, 73; Harada, *Nisshin Nichi-Ro sensō*, 76.

60. Tobe, *Gyakusetsu*, 145–146; Lone, *First Modern War*, 156–157; Fujimura, *Nisshin sensō*, 132–133.

61. Lone, *Army, Empire*, 31.

62. Ōe Shinobu, *Heishitachi no Nichi-Ro sensō* [The soldiers of the Russo-Japanese war] (Asahi sensho, 1988), 58; Hara Takeshi, "Nichi-Ro sensō no eikyō" [Legacies of the Russo-Japanese war], *Gunji shigaku* 36:3–4, (March 2001), 14; Harada, *Nisshin Nichi-Ro sensō*, 72–73.

63. Tobe, *Gyakusetsu*, 144–145, 146, but see also the contradictory figures in Lone, *First Modern War*, 152–153.

64. Lone, *First Modern War*, 98–99; Harada, *Nisshin Nichi-Ro sensō*, 158–163.

65. Kyū sanbō honbu hensan, *Nisshin sensō*, 296.

66. Lone, *First Modern War*, 40.

67. Saitō, *Nisshin sensō no gunji senryaku*, 163.

68. Actual Japanese losses were 40 killed, 241 wounded, and 7 missing.

69. Kurono, *Daigaku*, 95; Lone, *First Modern War*, 154; Ōe, *Sanbō honbu*, 71; Saitō, *Nisshin sensō no gunji senryaku*, 164–165.

70. Saitō, *Nisshin sensō no gunji senryaku*, 158; Kurono, *Daigaku*; Fujimura, *Nisshin sensō*, 129; Kuwada, "Nisshin sensō," 258–259.

71. Saitō, *Nisshin sensō no gunji senryaku*, 163–164; Fujimura, *Nisshin sensō*, 129–131; Lone, *First Modern War*, 40–43; Kyū sanbō honbu hensan, *Nisshin sensō*, 307–308.

72. Kyū sanbō honbu hensan, *Nisshin sensō*, 296–308; Yoshida, *Nihon no guntai*, 50. In the Sino-Japanese War frostbite accounted for 7,226 hospital admissions, slightly over 6 percent of all patients; see Ōe, *Nichi-Ro gunjiteki kenkyū*, table 2-14, 170. During the Russo-Japanese war frostbite accounted for 1 percent of all hospital admissions and only 2,538 cases. Ibid., table 2-16, 172.

73. Lone, *First Modern Army*, 42; Harada, *Nisshin Nichi-Ro sensō*, 81.

74. Shumpei Okamoto, *The Japanese Oligarchy and the Russo-Japanese War* (New York: Columbia University Press, 1970), 47–48.

75. Ōe, *Nichi-Ro sensō to Nihon guntai*, 45–46.

76. Hillary Conroy, *The Japanese Seizure of Korea, 1868–1910* (Philadelphia: University of Pennsylvania Press, 1960), 314–318; Sumiya Misao, *Nihon no reikishi*, 22, *Dai Nihon teikoku no shiren* [The trials of the great Japanese empire] (Chūō kōron, 1966), 52.

77. Tanaka Tokihiko, "Min pi satsugai jihen" [The murder of Queen Min], in Wagamatsu Sakai, ed., *Nihon seiji saiban shiroku Meiji—go* (Dai ichi hōki shuppan kabushiki kaisha, 1969), 217, 221–223, 229; Conroy, *The Japanese Seizure of Korea*, 306–307, 310–323; Peter Duus, *The Abacus and the Sword: The Japanese Penetration of Korea, 1895–1910* (Berkeley: University of California Press, 1995), 108–112. In November the Justice Ministry indicted Miura and forty-seven other Japanese, who ranged from top advisers to the Korean government to unemployed thugs and adventurers. The verdict, delivered the following January, declared them not guilty by virtue of insufficient evidence of criminal action.

78. Barnhart, *Japan and the World*, 25; Iguchi, *Nichi-Ro sensō no jidai*, 51, 101.

79. Conroy, *The Japanese Seizure of Korea*, 327; Denis and Peggy Warner, *The Tide at Sunrise: A History of the Russo-Japanese War, 1904–1905* (New York: Charterhouse, 1974), 122–123.

80. Fujiwara, *Gunjishi*, 103–104; Ōe, *Nichi-Ro gunjishiteki kenkyū*, 9.

81. Ōe, *Nichi-Ro gunjishiteki kenkyū*, 10–11.

82. Kurono, *Teikoku kokubō*, 37; Ikuda, *Nihon rikugunshi*, 69; Fujiwara, *Gunjishi*, 105; Iguchi, *Nichi-Ro sensō no jidai*, 18–20.

83. Ikuda, *Nihon rikugunshi*, 72; Tanaka, *Rikugun jinji seidō gaisetsu*, RO 80-1H, 62–63, 66.

84. Ōe, *Nichi-Ro sensō to Nihon guntai*, 195; Ikuda, *Nihon rikugunshi*, 72–73.

85. Fujiwara, *Gunjishi*, 98; Ikuda, *Nihon rikugunshi*, 70.

86. Fujiwara, *Gunjishi*, 105; Heiyama, "Nihon rikugun sakusen jō no yōkyū, 85 RO-2H, 19.

87. Ōe, *Nichi-Ro sensō to Nihon guntai*, 243.

88. Tobe, *Gyakusetsu*, 137–138; Ono Keishi, "Nisshin sensō ato keieiki no gunji shishutsu to zaisei seikaku" [The management of military expenditures and financial policies after the

Sino-Japanese War], *Gunji shigaku* 40:2–3 December 2004), 45, 49. The navy figures are from Schencking, *Making Waves*, table 3, 104.

89. Barnhart, *Japan and the World*, 29; Ono, "Nisshin sensō ato keieiki," 49–50, 55.

Chapter 6. Back to the Continent: The Russo-Japanese War

1. Ian Nish, "Japan's Indecision during the Boxer Disturbances," *Journal of Asian Studies* 20:4 (August 1961), 449; Ōe, *Sanbō honbu*, 84. As a 16-year-old, Fukushima had fought in the Boshin War; later, as an English-language translator and newspaper reporter during the Satsuma Rebellion, he found his way to Yamagata's headquarters. Yamagata appointed him his intelligence chief in 1878 and launched Fukushima's military career. Fukushima became a national hero during 1892–1893 when he returned from attaché duty in Berlin via Vladivostok by making an epic fourteen-month solitary crossing of Siberia by horseback. Without ever commanding a troop unit, his intelligence work carried him to the general staff and service in the Boxer Expedition.

2. Kawano Koaki, "Hoku Shin jiken" [The north China incident], in Okumura and Kuwada, *Nisshin Nichi-Ro sensō*, 377–378, 385.

3. Ibid., 386.

4. Kuwada and Maebara, *Nihon no sensō zukai to dēta*, plate 2. Subsequent reinforcements from British India, France, Russia, and Germany, including Vietnamese, Indian, and Chinese soldiers, to pacify the region brought the overall expedition to 70,000 personnel.

5. Shimanuki Shigeyoshi, *Senryaku: Nichi-Ro sensō (jō)* [The strategy of the Russo-Japanese war, 1] (Hara shobō, 1980), 103.

6. Kuwada and Maebara, *Nihon no sensō zukai to dēta*, plate 2. The quote on polite looting is cited in Meirion and Susie Harries, *Soldiers of the Sun* (New York: Random House, 1992), 72–73; Ōe, *Yasukuni jinja*, 16.

7. Matsuzaki Shoichi, "Shina chūtonshin zōkyō mondai" *(jō)* [The problem of the reinforcement of the China garrison army, part 1], *Kokugakuin zasshi* 96:2 (February 1995), 28.

8. Kurono Taeru, *Teikoku kokubō hoshin no kenkyū* [Researching the course of imperial defense policy] (Sōwasha, 2000), 69–70; Tani Hisao, *Kimitsu Nichi-Ro senshi* [The classified history of the Russo-Japanese war] *Meiji hyakunenshi sōsho* [The Meiji centennial series] vol. 3 (Hara shobō, 1971), 94; Bōeichō, *Daihon'ei rikugunbu (1)*, 91.

9. Morimatsu, *Daihon'ei*, 98–99.

10. Mark R. Peattie and David C. Evans, *Kaigun* (Annapolis, MD: Naval Institute Press, 1997), 49–50; Morimatsu, *Daihon'ei*, 105–108.

11. Ōe, *Sanbō honbu*, 82.

12. Okamoto, *Oligarchy*, 71–72; Tani, *Kimitsu Nichi-Ro senshi*, 82; Ōe, *Sanbō honbu*, 84.

13. Kurono, *Daigaku*, 115; Kurogawa Yuzō, *Kindai Nihon no gunji senryaku gaisetsu* [An overview of modern Japan's military strategy] (Fūyō shobō, 2003), 50; see also Okamoto, *Oligarchy*, 76–77.

14. Ōe, *Sanbō honbu*, 82; Inoki Masamichi, *Gunkoku Nihon no kōbō* [The rise and fall of militarist Japan] (Chūkō shinsho, 1995), 30–31.

15. Kodama was home minister and concurrently education minister. In June 1904 he was promoted to general when he left the position to become chief of staff for Ōyama's Manchurian Army.

16. Inoki, *Gunkoku Nihon no kōbō*, 36; Ikuda, *Nihon rikugunshi*, 80; Tani, *Kimitsu Nichi-Ro senshi*, 82, 94–95; Kurokawa, *Kindai Nihon no gunji senryaku gaishi*, 50–51; Kurono, *Teikoku kokubō*, 40–43.

17. Warner, *Tide*, 189–190; Tani, *Kimitsu Nichi-Ro senshi*, 44–48; Kasahara Hidehiko, *Meiji tennō* [The Meiji emperor] (Chūkō shinsho, 2006), ii, 265.

18. Furuya Tetsuō, *Nichi-Ro sensō* [The Russo-Japanese war] (Chūkō shinsho, 1966), 96–98.

19. Kurono, *Daigaku*, 126; Hata, *Tōsuiken*, 81; Okamoto, *Japanese Oligarchy*, 36.

20. Sumiya, *Dai Nihon teikoku no shien*, 257.

21. Inoki, *Gunkoku Nihon no kōbō*, 39; see also Warner, *Tide*, 287; Furuya, *Nichi-Ro sensō*, 103.

22. Yoshihisa Tak Matsusaka, "Human Bullets, General Nogi, and the Myth of Port Arthur," in John W. Steinberg, et al., eds., *The Russo-Japanese War in Global Perspective*, 1 (Leiden, Netherlands: Brill, 2005), 179.

23. Furuya, *Nichi-Ro sensō*, 103.

24. Sumiya, *Dai Nihon teikoku no shien*, 263 (quote); Ōe, *Nichi-Ro gunjiteki kenkyū*, 330.

25. Hosaka Masayasu, *Shōwa rikugun no kenkyū* [Research about the army of the Shōwa period, 1] (Asahi bunko, 2006), 43.

26. Kurono, *Daigaku*, 124–125.

27. Warner, *Tide*, 236.

28. Sumiya, *Dai Nihon teikoku no shien*, 263; Warner, *Tide*, 390.

29. Ōe, *Nichi-Ro gunjiteki kenkyū*, 335; Furuya, *Nichi-Ro sensō*, 126–127; Ōe, *Nichi-Ro to Nihon guntai*, 169; Yamamura, *Gunshin*, 51.

30. Furuya, *Nichi-Ro sensō*, 125. The 14th Division was mobilized June 13; the 15th and 16th divisions were mobilized on August 8.

31. The army used the special term *minikui*, meaning "shameful, ugly," as a modifier preceding the word for *surrender*. Ichinose, *Meiji, Taishō, Shōwa guntai manyūaru*, 95.

32. Warner, *Tide*, 304–305; Furuya, *Nichi-Ro sensō*, 106.

33. Furuya, *Nichi-Ro sensō*, 123–124; Hosaka, *Shōwa rikugun no kenkyū* (1), 45.

34. Furuya, *Nichi-Ro sensō*, 122–124, 128–129.

35. Okamoto, *Oligarchy*, 110.

36. Ibid., 111.

37. Harada, *Nisshin Nichi-Ro sensō*, 214–218; Okamoto, *Oligarchy*, 116; Bōeichō, *Daihon'ei rikugunbu* (1), 118–123.

38. Ichinose, *Meiji, Taishō, Shōwa guntai manyūaru*, 28–34, 41, 67–69.

39. Kurono, *Daigaku*, 67, 111.

40. Nogi had retired in 1901 because he believed allegations about officers from his regiment for looting during the Boxer Rebellion had tarnished his reputation. Robert Jay Lifton, Shuichi Kato, and Michael R. Reich, *Six Lives Six Deaths* (New Haven, CT: Yale University Press, 1977), 50.

41. Warner, *Tide*, 322; Tani, *Kimitsu Nichi-Ro sensō*, 167–168.

42. Warner, *Tide*, 335.

43. Ibid., 268; Ōe, *Nichi-Ro sensō gunjiteki kenkyū*, 321–324.

44. Ōe, *Sanbō honbu*, 104; Kurono, *Daigaku*, 129.

45. Kurono, *Daigaku*, 135–136.

46. Ibid., 136; Ōe, *Sanbō honbu*, 108.

47. Furuya, *Nichi-Ro sensō*, 156–157; Ōe, *Sanbō honbu*, 109.

48. Hosaka, *Shōwa rikugun no kenkyū* (1), 44; Bōeicho, *Daihon'ei rikugunbu* (1), 106; Lone, *Army, Empire*, 106; Kurono, *Daigaku*, 126; Hata, *Tōsuiken*, 81.

49. Kurono, *Daigaku*, 127; Furuya, *Nichi-Ro sensō*, 110; Ōe, *Sanbō honbu*, 93, 97.

50. Sumiya, *Dai Nihon teikoku no shien,* 259; Tani, *Kimitsu Nichi-Ro senshi,* 196; Furuya, *Nichi-Ro sensō,* 100.

51. See Tani, *Kimitsu Nichi-Ro senshi,* 166; Warner, *Tide,* 237.

52. Warner, *Tide,* 368; Furuya, *Nichi-Ro sensō,* 108; Shimanuki Shigeyoshi, *Senryaku Nichi-Ro sensō (ge)* [Strategy: The Russo-Japanese war, 2] (Hara shobō, 1980), 402.

53. Warner, *Tide,* 375.

54. Ōe, *Nichi-Ro gunjiteki kenkyū,* 329. Of 1,260 field grade infantry officers (majors and lieutenant colonels), almost 21 percent (263) were killed in action and 15 percent (1,453) of the 9,694 junior grade infantry officers (captains and lieutenants) were also killed. The army did not normally promote NCOs to regular commissioned officers, but it was forced to promote more than 2,200 to fill the losses. Ōe, *Nichi-Ro sensō to Nihon guntai,* 236.

55. Okamoto, *Oligarchy,* 126; Ōe, *Nichi-Ro sensō to Nihon guntai,* 163–164.

56. Ichinose, *Meiji, Taishō, Shōwa guntai manyuaru,* 87; Furuya, *Nichi-Ro sensō,* 119–120; Iguchi, *Nichi-Ro sensō no jidai,* 149.

57. Lifton, Kato, and Reich, *Six Lives Six Deaths,* 51; Furuya, *Nichi-Ro sensō,* 120; Rikusen-shi kenkyū fukyūkai, *Ryōjun yōsai kōrakusen,* 122.

58. Ōe, *Sanbō honbu,* 99. Lt. Col. Arita Jō, an instructor at the military staff college, would become chief of staff of the Second Army's logistics section, and Lt. Col. Kakizaki Tomus-aburō, an instructor at the Toyama School, would become chief of staff for the First Army logistics section (Ōe, *Sanbō honbu,* 99–100). Lt. Col. Fujii Kōtsuchi, known for his prewar staff study of road networks in Korea, became chief of staff of logistics for the Third Army.

59. Yamaguchi, *Rikugun to kaigun,* 81; Ōe, *Sanbō honbu,* 99.

60. Ichinose, *Meiji, Taishō, Shōwa guntai manyuaru,* 97; Ōe, *Nichi-Ro sensō gunjiteki,* 550, 552.

61. Furuya, *Nichi-Ro sensō,* 109, 161; Ōe, *Nichi-Ro sensō gunjiteki,* 335.

62. Ōe, *Nichi-Ro sensō gunjiteki,* 335.

63. Harada, *Kokumin no shinwa,* 141.

64. Yamamoto, *Shōhai no kōzō,* 85.

65. Furuya, *Nichi-Ro sensō,* 122, 131; Okamoto, *Oligarchy,* 106.

66. Furuya, *Nichi-Ro sensō,* 157.

67. Yamamoto, *Shōhai no kōzō,* 154.

68. Shimanuki, *Senryaku Nichi-Ro sensō* 2: 394–395.

69. Tokyo placed Taiwan under martial law so its garrison was unavailable to reinforce the Manchurian armies.

70. Furuya, *Nichi-Ro sensō,* 133–134.

71. Tatsuno Shino, "Meiji tennō to sono shūi" [Emperor Meiji in those circumstances], in Suzuki Tsutome, gen ed., *Nihon rekishi shiri-zu* [Japanese history series] 19, *Nisshin-Nichi-Ro sensō* [The Sino-Japanese and Russo-Japanese wars] (Sekai bunkasha, 1970), 77; Warner, *Tide,* 458–459; Matsusaka, "Human Bullets," 194.

72. Warner, *Tide,* 464–465; Furuya, *Nichi-Ro sensō,* 134–137.

73. Sumiya, *Dai Nihon teikoku no shien,* 267; Shimanuki, *Senryaku Nichi-Ro sensō,* 2: 426–428. Nogi's chief of staff, Ijichi, was appointed chairman of the newly established Port Arthur readjustment committee, in effect firing him.

74. Furuya, *Nichi-Ro sensō,* 159.

75. Kyūsanbō honbu, *Nichi-Ro sensō* [The Russo-Japanese war] *(ge)* (Tokuma Bunkō, 1994), 2: 332; Ōe, *Nichi-Ro sensō gunjiteki,* table 2-16, 172; table 2-2, 130; table 2-3, 131. Hara Takeshi, "Hohei chūshin no hakuhei shūgi no keisei" [The evolution of close-quarter infantry doctrine] *Nichi-Ro sensō* (II) [The Russo-Japanese war, part II], Special Issue, *Gunji shigaku* 41:1 and 2 (June 2005), table 2, 273, gives a total of 173,151 killed or wounded (14.6

percent of the 1,183,470 engaged). Adding deaths due to illness (21,424) yields a more accurate figure of around 200,000 personnel losses.

76. Hara Takeshi, "Nichi-Ro sensō no eikyō," 14.

77. Ichinose, *Meiji, Taishō, Shōwa guntai manyūaru*, 97, 115–117.

78. They were punished for surviving the sinking of the *Kinshu Maru* when almost all their comrades chose suicide or certain death rather than surrender.

79. Ōe, *Nichi-Ro sensō gunjiteki kenkyū*, 378 and n129, 399–400.

80. Ōe, *Sanbō honbu*, 110–111; Hata, *Nihonji horyo*, 1: 10, 12, 21.

81. Hata, *Nihonjin no horyo* 1: 9–10.

82. Despite Japanese claims, similar ideas of offensive spirit, masculinity, and intangible qualities permeated European armies as well and may account for the popularity of Sakurai's book with western audiences.

83. Yamamuro, *Gunshin*, xii, 23, 35, 82–83.

84. Naoko Shimazu, "The Myth of the 'Patriotic Soldier': Japanese Attitudes towards Death in the Russo-Japanese War," *War & Society* 19:2 (October 2001), 71, 77, 81.

85. Ōe, *Sanbō honbu*, 78; Iguchi, *Nichi-Ro sensō no jidai*, 162–166.

86. Ōe, *Sanbō honbu*, 113; Iguchi, *Nichi-Ro sensō no jidai*, 166–167.

87. Ōe, *Nichi-Ro sensō to Nihon guntai*, 187–190. See also Tani, *Kimitsu Nichi-Ro senshi*, 3, introduction.

88. Iguchi, *Nichi-Ro sensō no jidai*, 168.

89. Hata, *Tōsuiken*, 149. Maj. Gen. Asada Nobuaki kept his promise by receiving a barony in 1907 and later rose to the rank of full general.

Chapter 7. Institutionalizing National Military Strategy

1. Tobe, *Gyakusetsu*, 163.

2. Kurono Taeru, *Nihon o horoboshita kokubō hōshin* [The national defense policies that ruined Japan] (Bungei shinsho, 2002), 22–24.

3. This included sixteen mobilized reserve brigades, the equivalent of eight divisions.

4. Kurono, *Nihon o horoboshita*, 38–41; Kurono, *Daigaku*, 145; Kurogawa, *Gunji senryaku gaisetsu*, 82. Kodama's proposals would field nineteen active divisions. Excluding the Guards Division, he would form six corps of three divisions each from the remaining eighteen divisions.

5. Kurono, *Daigaku*, 146–148; Kurogawa, *Gunji senryaku gaisetsu*, 66; Kurono, *Nihon o horoboshita*, 29; Schencking, *Making Waves*, 123.

6. Kurono Taeru, *Teikoku kokubō hōshin ni kenkyū: riku-kaigun kokubō shisō no tenkaito tokuchō* [A study of imperial national defense policy: the development and characteristics of the army and the navy's ideas on national defense] (Sōwashi, 2000), 8–9, 85–86, 105. In May 1887 the council of state established the Board of Military Councilors, best thought of as a liaison and advisory function for army and navy coordination, to provide pros and cons of military matters. Members included service chiefs, service ministers, and inspector-generals who reported directly to the emperor (Matsushita, *Meiji no guntai*, 95; Morimatsu, *Daihon'ei*, 46).

7. Kurogawa, *Gunji senryaku gaisetsu*, 64; Kurono, *Nihon o horoboshita*, 29–33; Kurono, *Teikoku kokubō*, 98; Yoshida Yutaka, "Nihon no guntai" [The Japanese army], in Ōe Shinobu et al. eds., *Iwanami Koza, Nihon no tsūshi*, 17 [Iwanami's lectures on common Japanese history, vol. 17], *kindai* [modern], part 2 (Iwanami shoten, 1994), 154.

8. Kurogawa, *Gunji senryaku gaisetsu*, 75.

9. Ibid., 73.

10. Matsushita, *Kokubō higeki*, 78–83; see also Kurokawa, *Gunji senryaku gaisetsu*, 74–78; Kurono, *Teikoku kokubō*, 105–109; Kurono, *Nihon o horoboshita*, 34.

11. Kurono, *Nihon o horoboshita,* 35–37.

12. Schencking, *Making Waves,* 127–128; Kurono, *Nihon o horoboshita,* 32–33.

13. Hata, *Tōsuiken,* 154, 156–157; Tobe, *Gyakusetsu,* 157.

14. Tobe, *Gyakusetsu,* 156.

15. Hata, *Tōsuiken,* 154–155; Kurono, *Daigaku,* 153–154; Tobe, *Gyakusetsu,* 158.

16. Kurono Taeru, "'Teikoku kokubō hōshin' senryaku sakusen yōhei kō" [Strategy and Tactics of the (1907) "imperial defense policy"] *Gunji shigaku* 31:4 (March 1996), 10; Kurono, *Teikoku kokubō,* 156–157.

17. Leonard A. Humphreys, *The Way of the Heavenly Sword: The Japanese Army in the 1920s* (Stanford, CA: Stanford University Press, 1995), 18. Terauchi had been wounded in the Satsuma Rebellion and invalided with a disabled right arm.

18. Ibid., 18–19 and quote, 65; Kurono, *Daigaku,* 44.

19. Hata, *Tōsuiken,* 154–156; Humphreys, *Heavenly Sword,* 22.

20. Ichinose, *Meiji, Taishō, Shōwa guntai manyūaru,* 113.

21. Kurogawa, *Kindai gunji senryaku,* 53–54.

22. Hara Takeshi, "Hohei chūshin," 274–275.

23. Ibid., 273–274.

24. Yokoyama, "Military Technological Strategy and Armaments," 123–126; Kaneko, *Heiki to senjutsu no Nihonshi,* 185.

25. Kuzuhara Kazumi, "'Sentō kōyō' no kyōgi no keisei to kōchokuka" [The structure of principles of command and its ossification] *Gunji shigaku* 40:1 (June 2004), 20; Hara Takeshi, "Hohei chūshin," 276, 279–280.

26. Hara Takeshi, "Hohei chūshin," 282 and table 6, page 285.

27. Endō, *Kindai Nihon guntai kyōikushi kenkyū,* 126–127; Hata, *Nihon horyo,* 2: 20; Hara Takeshi, "Hohei chūshin," 282.

28. Hara Takeshi, "Hohei chūshin," 282.

29. Endō, *Kindai Nihon guntai kyōikushi kenkyū,* 196–197.

30. Yoshida Yutaka, "Nihon no guntai," 169–170, 152; Endō, *Kindai Nihon guntai kyōikushi kenkyū,* 138–139.

31. Endō, *Kindai Nihon guntai kyōikushi kenkyū,* 194. In 1909 the national rate was 1.85 suicides per 10,000.

32. Ibid., 15.

33. Yoshida Yutaka, "Nihon no guntai," 163, 170.

34. Ibid., 163, 170–171.

35. Endō, *Kindai Nihon guntai kyōikushi kenkyū,* 18, 139.

36. Ibid., 34; Yoshida Yutaka, *Nihon no guntai,* 11; Yoshida Yutaka, "Nihon no guntai," 174.

37. Yoshida Yutaka, "Nihon no guntai," 163, 172; Richard J. Smethurst, *A Social Basis for Prewar Japanese Militarism: The Army and the Rural Community* (Berkeley: University of California Press, 1974), xiv–xv.

38. Smethurst, *A Social Basis for Prewar Japanese Militarism,* 9, 15, 18, 20, 71–72.

39. Ibid., 25–28.

40. Kurono, *Daigaku,* 163–164.

41. Kobayashi Hiroharu, *Sensō no Nihonshi* [Warfare in Japanese history] 21, *Sōryokusen to demokurashi* [Total war and democracy] (Yoshikawa Kōbunsha, 2008), 83, 125.

42. Kurono, *Daigaku,* 173, 176.

43. Ibid., 167, 170–171; Kurono, *Teikoku rikugun no kaikaku to teikō,* 101; Kurono, *Teikoku kokubō,* 161–162.

44. Kurono, *Teikoku kokubō,* 158–161.

45. Kurokawa, *Kindai gunji senryaku*, 105–106.

46. Kurono, *Nihon o horoboshita*, 58.

47. Koiso's study was titled "Teikoku kokubō shigen" [Natural resources for imperial defense]. Kurogawa, *Kindai gunji senryaku*, 103; Kurono, *Teikoku kokubō*, 171.

48. Kurono, *Teikoku kokubō*, 170–171. The study group chaired by Tanaka Giichi drafted "Waga kokugunbi to Shina to no kankei" [China's relationship to our nation's military preparations] in May 1917 and "Zenkoku dōin keikaku hitsuyō no gi" [Essential principals for a national mobilization plan] in September 1917.

49. Kurono, *Teikoku kokubō*, 173; Kurokawa, *Kindai gunji senryaku*, 94.

50. Kurono, *Nihon o horoboshita*, 66. The army burned the extant copy of the 1918 revision of imperial defense in August 1945. The contents were later deduced from draft papers and the recollections of former staff officers who participated in the process.

51. Kurono, *Nihon o horoboshita*, 70–71; Kurono, *Teikoku kokubō*, 168, 163, citing Ugaki Kazushige's diary.

52. Kurogawa, *Kindai gunji senryaku*, 115, 117.

53. Kurono, *Teikoku kokubō*, 153, 182; Tobe, *Gyakusetsu*, 224; see Rikusen gakkai, eds., *Kindai sensō, shiryō*, 170 for differing figures. Schencking, *Making Waves*, 217 agrees with Tobe's numbers.

54. Kurono, *Nihon o horoboshita*, 75; Kurono, *Teikoku kokubō*, 183.

55. Kurono, *Daigaku*, 163–168.

56. Ibid., 170–171,175; James William Morley, *The Japanese Thrust into Siberia, 1918* (New York: Columbia University Press, 1957), 102.

57. Kobayashi, *Sōryokusen to demokurashi*, 225; Humphreys, *Heavenly Sword*, 26.

58. Ōuchi Tsutomu, *Nihon no rekishi* [A history of Japan] 23, *Taishō demokurashi* [Taishō democracy] (Chūō kōronsha, 1966), 159–162. Kobayashi, *Sōryokusen*, 242.

59. Humphreys, *Heavenly Sword*, 27.

60. Hackett, *Yamagata*, 329; Tobe, *Gyakusetsu*, 180–181; Humphreys, *Heavenly Sword*, 25–29; Ōe, *Sanbō honbu*, 134.

61. Kobayashi, *Sōryokusen*, 244–245.

62. Ibid., 258–261.

63. Humphreys, *Heavenly Sword*, 28–29.

64. Ibid., 45–46.

Chapter 8. Short War or Total War?

1. Kurono, *Daigaku*, 184.

2. Ibid., 179.

3. Kurono, *Nihon o horoboshita*, 108, 115–116.

4. Ibid., 98.

5. Kurokawa, *Kindai Nihon gunji senryaku*, 132, 139–141.

6. Katogawa Kōtarō, *Teikoku rikugun kikōbutai* [The imperial army's mechanized corps] (Hara shobō, 1981 rev. ed.), 43–44; Kurokawa, *Kindai Nihon gunji senryaku*, 132.

7. Humphreys, *Heavenly Sword*, 62; Kurono, *Teikoku kokubō*, 226; Katogawa Kōtarō, *Rikugun no hanshō* [Reflections on the army] (*ge*) (Bunkyō shuppan, 1996), 26.

8. Sayama Jirō, *Taihō nyūmon* [A guide to artillery weapons] (Kōjinsha NF bunko, 1999), 108; Katogawa, *Hanshō*, 19; Kuzuhara, "'Sentō kōyō' no kyōgi," 25–26.

9. Katogawa, *Teikoku rikugun kikōbutai*, 43, 72; Katogawa, *Hanshō*, 16.

10. Kurono, *Nihon o horoboshita*, 102.

11. Kurono, *Daigaku*, 179–180.

12. Humphreys, *Heavenly Sword*, 65; Kurono, *Teikoku rikugun kaikaku to teikō*, 120.

13. See Humphreys, *Heavenly Sword*, 64–72, for a detailed account.

14. Kurono, *Teikoku rikugun kaikaku to teikō*, 120.

15. Kurono, *Teikoku kokubō*, 9.

16. Ibid., 211.

17. Kurono, *Nihon o horoboshita*, 112–115; Kurono, *Teikoku kokubō*, 234; Matsushita, *Nihon kokubō higeki*, 92.

18. Kurono, *Teikoku kokubō*, 238. Ugaki wanted to reduce the number of active divisions to seventeen, and this would become a bone of contention in the 1925 reorganization plan.

19. Kurono, *Nihon o horoboshita*, 115; Kurokawa, *Kindai gunji senryaku*, 143–144, 148.

20. Kurokawa, *Kindai gunji senryaku*, 139–141, 147; Kurono, *Teikoku rikugun kaikaku to teikō*, 112–118.

21. Kurono, *Daigaku*, 181; Kurono, *Teikoku kokubō*, 224–225. Fukuda was the commander of the Taiwan Army and in August 1923 became a member of the Board of Military Councilors.

22. Kurono, *Nihon o horoboshita*, 102–103.

23. Ibid.

24. Kurono, *Teikoku kokubō*, 231.

25. Kitaoka Shinichi, *Nihon no kindai* [Modern Japan] 5, *Seitō kara gunbu e, 1924–1941* [From political parties to military (control), 1924–1941] (Chūō kōronsha, 1999), 145–147. In 1909 the army had created a Joint Provisional Military Balloon Research Committee for aerial observation, and six years later the war ministry formed the army air force as an independent branch to support ground operations. During World War I, a few army and navy aircraft reconnoitered or bombed the German fortress at Qingdao. The army also activated its first air squadron in Japan. Ōe, *Tennō no guntai*, 224–225.

26. Ikuda, *Nihon rikugunshi*, 113–114.

27. Yoshida, *Nihon no guntai*, 5, 8.

28. Kurono, *Nihon o horoboshita*, 106.

29. Smethurst, *Social Basis*, 39; Yoshida, *Nihon guntai*, 143; Kawashima, "Gun dōin no seidō," 95 RO-4H, 85–87, 93.

30. Watanabe Yukio, *Ugaki Kazushige* (Chūkō shinsho, 1993), 17 (chart).

31. Takahashi Masae, *Shōwa no gunbatsu* [The military cliques of the Shōwa period] (Chūkō shinsho, 1969), 54.

32. See Humphreys, *Heavenly Sword*, 111–116.

33. For example, see Yamaguchi Muneyuki, *Rikugun to kaigun—rikukaigun shōkōshi no kenkyū* [Army and navy—research about the army's and navy's officers] (Osaka: Seibundō, 2000), 45.

34. Humphreys, *Heavenly Sword*, 40; Hori Shigeru, "'Chōbatsu' no sūchiteki jittai ni kansuru hitotsu kyōsai" [Considerations concerning the actual numbers of the Chōshū clique] *Gunji Shigaku* 43:1 (June 2007), 23–25, 29, 31. See also Tobe, *Gyakusetsu*, 267.

35. Kurokawa, *Kindai gunji senryaku*, 113.

36. Maebara, "Nihon rikugun no 'kōbō,'" 86 RO-5H, 147, 203; Kurogawa, *Kindai gunji senryaku*, 113–114.

37. Maebara, "Nihon rikugun no 'kōbō,'" 86 RO-5H, 201–206, 257; Humphreys, *Heavenly Sword*, viii; Bōeicho bōei kenshūjō, senshishitsu, ed., *Senshi sōsho* [Official military history] 27, *Kantōgun* [The Kwantung army] part 1 (Asagumo shimbunsha, 1969), 25–27. I am indebted to Stanford University Press for permission to use material in this section that will

appear in the forthcoming publication *The Battle for China: Essays on the Military History of the Sino-Japanese War.*

38. Bōeicho, *Kantōgun*, 25–27; Ōe, *Tennō no guntai*, 218 (quote).

39. Kuzuhara, "'Sentō kōyō' no kyōgi," 19.

40. Ibid., 21.

41. Endō, *Kindai Nihon guntai kyōikushi kenkyū*, 165–166; Rikugunshō [War ministry], *Sentō kōryō*, [Combat principles], February 6, 1929 (Ikeda shoten, reprint 1977), 12, 65, 69, 128; Maebara, "Nihon rikugun," 220, 226.

42. Kuzuhara, "'Sentō kōyō,'" 23, 27; Kyōiku sōkanbu [Inspector-general of military education], "Hohei sōten sōan hensan riyūsho" [Reasons for the revisions to the draft infantry manual], 1928, 9, para 3, Japan Defense Agency Archives (hereafter JDA).

43. For other possible reasons, see Ulrich Straus, *The Anguish of Surrender* (Seattle: University of Washington Press, 2003), 21.

44. Endō, *Kindai Nihon guntai kyōikushi kenkyū*, 176.

45. Kuzuhara, "'Sentō kōyō,'" 27–28.

46. Ibid.; Sanbō sōchō [Chief of staff, army], "TaiSō sentōhō yōkō" [Summary of combat methods against the Soviets], May 6, 1933, JDA.

47. Yoshida, *Nihon no guntai*, 156–158; Tobe, *Gyakusetsu*, 258 and 259 (chart); Fujiwara Akira, *Nihon gunjishi (jō)* [Japanese military history] (Nihon hyōronsha, 1987), 191–192. The number of graduates varied; between 1910 and 1915 they averaged about 720 per class but thereafter declined to less than half that number by the early 1920s.

48. Tanaka Keishi, "Rikugun jinji seidō gaisetsu" (*kōban*) [An overview of the army personnel system] part 2, in Bōeichō bōei kenshōjō senshibu, *Kenkyū shiryō*, 80 RO-1H, mimeo, 1980, 34–35; Kumagai Tadasu, *Kisō chishiki*, 141–144. It cost an estimated 210 yen annually for food and clothing at a time when an average white-collar worker's yearly salary was about 950–1,000 yen. Kumagai, *Kisō chishiki*, 144.

49. Yoshida, *Nihon no guntai*, 73; Kumagai Mikahisa, "Kyūriku kaigun shōkō no senbatsu to kyōiku," *Kenkyū shiryō*, 80 R-12H, 129.

50. Tanaka, "Rikugun jinji," 113; Yoshida, *Nihon no guntai*, 88, 91.

51. Yoshida, *Nihon no guntai*, 103, 159–160; Kumagai Mikahisa, *Nihongun no jinteki seidō to mondaiten no kenkyū*, 109; Itō and Momose, *Jiten*, 372.

52. Ishige Shin'ichi, "Chū kō itchi ni okeru guntai shisō to kyōiku shisō" [The military's concept of loyalty and filial piety as seen in educational concepts] *Gunji shigaku* 37:4 (March 2002), 15.

53. Tobe, *Gyakusetsu*, 197 (chart).

54. Endō, *Kindai Nihon guntai kyōikushi kenkyū*, 80, 258–259; Yoshida, *Nihon no guntai*, 168–169, 190.

55. Yoshida, *Nihon no guntai*, 161–164.

56. Fujiwara Akira, *Uejinishita eiyūtachi* [Starving heroes] (Aoki shoten, 2001), 186–187; Edward J. Drea, "In the Army Barracks of Imperial Japan," *Armed Forces and Society* 15:3 (1989); Humphreys, *Heavenly Sword*, 80, 106, and 171; Yoshida, "*Nihon no guntai*," 169–170; Yoshida, *Nihon no guntai*, 182.

Chapter 9. Conspiracies, Coups, and Reshaping the Army

1. Yamagata, Katsura, and Terauchi were still active-duty general officers when serving as prime minister.

2. Tobe Ryōichi, *Nihon rikugun to Chūgoku* [The Japanese army and China] (Kōdansha,

1999), 143; Marius B. Jansen, "Introduction," in James William Morley, ed., *Japan's Road to the Pacific War: Japan Erupts: The London Naval Conference and the Manchurian Incident, 1928–1932; Selected Translations from Taiheiyō sensō e no michi: kaisen gaiko shi* (New York: Columbia University Press, 1984), 128–129.

3. Tobe, *Nihon rikugun*, 147.

4. Jansen, "Introduction," 129.

5. Tobe, *Nihon rikugun*, 86.

6. Ibid., 84–85, 87; Kitaoka, *Seitō kara gunbu e*, 80–81.

7. Masumi Junnosuke, *Shōwa tennō to sono jidai* [The Shōwa emperor and that era] (Yamakawa shuppansha, 1998), 95; Kojima Noboru, *Tennō* [The emperor] 2 (Bungei shūnjū, 1974), 40–41; Humphreys, *Heavenly Sword*, 165 n 82, 225.

8. Hirohito was 26 years old when he became emperor in December 1926. He selected Shōwa (Enlightened Peace) for his reign name. Japanese emperors are referred to posthumously by the era name of the reign, i.e., Hirohito is now known as the Shōwa emperor.

9. Handō Kuzutoshi, *Shōwashi, 1926–1945* [Shōwa history from 1926 to 1945] (Heibonsha, 2004), 31–32; Masumi, *Shōwa tennō*, 95; Kojima, *Tennō*, 43, 45. Saionji had learned the details of the plot in late August.

10. Nihon kokusai seiji gakkai, eds., *Taiheiyō sensō e no michi* [The road to the Pacific war] 1, *Manshū jihen zenya* [The eve of the Manchurian incident] (Asahi shimbunsha, 1963), 316; Humphreys, *Heavenly Sword*, 166.

11. Masumi, *Shōwa tennō*, 101; Kojima, *Tennō*, 61.

12. Nara Takeji, "Nara Takeji jijiūbukanchō nikki" (shō), [Selections from imperial aide-de-camp General Nara Takeji's diary], *Chūō kōron* (September 1990), 327, 330; Humphries, *Heavenly Sword*, 169; Masumi, *Shōwa tennō*, 107.

13. Mark R. Peattie, *Ishiwara Kanji and Japan's Confrontation with the West* (Princeton, NJ: Princeton University Press, 1975), 110–122; Takehiko Yoshihashi, *Conspiracy at Mukden: The Rise of the Japanese Military* (New Haven, CT: Yale University Press, 1963), 145–165.

14. Yoshihisa Nakamura and Ryōichi Tobe, "The Imperial Japanese Army and Politics," *Armed Forces and Society* 14:4 (Summer 1988), 521.

15. Watanabe Yukio, *Ugaki Kazushige* (Chūkō shinsho, 1993), 62–63, 66–67; Hata Ikuhiko, *Gun fashizumu undōshi* [A history of the military fascist movement] (Kawade shobō shinsha, 1962), 26.

16. Watanabe, *Ugaki*, 55–57. Ugaki remained as war minister until April 1931. In June he went on the reserve list and became governor-general of Korea, a post he held for the next five years.

17. Tobe, *Gyakusetsu*, 254; Watanabe, *Ugaki*, 72; James B. Crowley, *Japan's Quest for Autonomy* (Princeton, NJ: Princeton University Press, 1968), 99–100; Kitaoka, *Seitō kara gunbu e*, 221.

18. Kitaoka, *Seitō kara gunbu e*, 156–157; Nakamura and Tobe, "Imperial Japanese Army and Politics," 522; Hata, *Tōsuiken*, 192.

19. Shiraishi Hiroshi, "Manshū jiken ni okeru Kantōgun no kōyū ninmu to sono kaiwaku-unyō mondai" [The Kwantung army's basic mission during the Manchurian incident and an interpretation of the problem of operational movement of troops], in *Saikō: Manshū jiken* [Reconsiderations of the Manchurian incident] *Gunji shigaku* 37:2 and 3 (October 2001), 196–197; Hata Ikuhiko, "Manshū ryōyū no shisoteki genryū" [The ideological background of the occupation of Manchuria] in ibid., 43; Nara, "Nara Takeji jijiūbukanchō nikki," 338.

20. Usui Katsumi, *Manshū jihen* [The Manchurian incident] (Chūkō shinsho, 1974), 45, 48–49. Vice Chief of Staff Lt. Gen. Ninomiya Harushige initially refused to send reinforcements and instructed Honjō to handle the incident with the minimum necessary force.

Although unwilling to send reinforcements, the next day Ninomiya, along with Lt. Gen. Araki, the inspector-general of military education; and Lt. Gen. Sugiyama Hajime, the vice war minister agreed that the army would have to bring down the government if it interfered with current operations in Manchuria.

21. Kitaoka, *Seitō kara gunbu e*, 160; Nara, "Nara Takeji jijiūbukanchō nikki," 340–341.

22. Usui, *Manshū jiken*, 41; Ikō Toshiya, *Sensō no Nihonshi* [Warfare in Japanese history] 22, *Manshū jihen kara Nitchū zenmen sensō e* [From the Manchurian incident to the total war in China] (Yoshikawa Kōbunkan, 2007), 21–22.

23. Takahashi, *Shōwa no gunbatsu*, 125; Hashimoto Kingoro, "Hashimoto taisa no shuki" [Colonel Hashimoto's notes], in Nakano Hideo, *Shōwashi no genten* [The source of Shōwa history] 2, *Manshū jihen to Jūgatsu jiken* [The Manchurian incident and the October incident] (Kōdansha, 1973), 252.

24. Takahashi, *Shōwa no gunbatsu*, 129; Tobe, *Gyakusetsu*, 255. Tatekawa assumed the post in August.

25. Hata, *Gun fashizumu*, 35–36; Kitaoka, *Seitō kara gunbu e*, 221–222; Tobe, *Gyakusetsu*, 255.

26. Takahashi, *Shōwa no gunbatsu*, 116; Hata, *Gun fashimzumu*, 48–49 n 4; Nakano Hideo, *Shōwashi no genten* [The origins of Shōwa history] 3, *Go ichi go jihen, Kisareta shinjitsu* [The vanished truth of the May 15 incident] (Kōdansha, 1974), 104.

27. Ben-Ami Shillony, *Revolt in Japan* (Princeton, NJ: Princeton University Press, 1973), 29.

28. Troops moved on Harbin on January 27 and captured it in early February 1932. On March 1, the Japanese government announced the creation of the new state of Manchukuo.

29. Handō, *Shōwashi*, 92; Donald A. Jordan, *China's Trial by Fire: The Shanghai War of 1932* (Ann Arbor: University of Michigan Press, 2001), 11–12. There are doubts about Tanaka's direct involvement in the attack (the chanting procession took a wrong turn and ended up near the factory), but no doubt that he was an agent provocateur. See Kojima Noboru, *Nitchū sensō* [The Sino-Japanese war] 2 (Bunshūn bunkō, 1988), 176.

30. Jordan, *China's Trial*, 87.

31. Kojima Noboru, *Nitchū sensō*, 221.

32. Ibid., 252.

33. A more critical version states an officer threatened to shoot them if they did not advance. *Yukan Fuji*, August 27, 1970. See also *Asahi shimbun*, June 13, 2007.

34. Hillis Lory, *Japan's Military Masters* (New York: Viking, 1943), 44; Katō Hidetoshi, "Bidan no genkei" [The origins of a legend], in *Asahi jyanaru*, ed., *Shōwashi no shunkan* [Dramatic moments in Shōwa history] (*jō*), *Asahi sensho* 11 (Asahi shimbunsha, 1974), 128; *Japan Weekly Chronicle*, March 24, 1932. For an extended analysis of the *bakudan sanyūshi*, see Yamamuro, *Gunshin*, 189–260.

35. Yamamuro, *Gunshin*, 225–228, 234, 237, 260.

36. Katō, "Bidan no genkei," 127; Furikawa Seisuke, ed., *Nikudan sanyūshi dōzō kensetsukai hōkoku* [Report of the construction committee for the human bullet three brave heroes statue] (privately published, 1936), 8.

37. Hata, *Nihonjin horyu*, 33–39.

38. Terasaki Hidenari and Mariko Terasaki Miller, eds., *Shōwa tennō Dokuhakuroku—Terasaki Hidenari goyōgakari nikki* [The Shōwa emperor's soliloquy—unattached court official Terasaki Hidenari's diary] (Bungei shūnjū, 1991), 28; Kuwada and Maebara, *Nihon no sensō*, plate 15. Also see Jordan, *China's Trial*, 187–190.

39. Ōuchi, *Fashizumu e no dori*, 310.

40. Stephen S. Large, "Nationalist Extremism in Early Shōwa Japan: Inoue Nissho and the 'Blood-Pledge Corps Incident,' 1932," *Modern Asian Studies* 35:3 (2001), 535, 544; Nakano,

Go ichi go jiken, 123–124; Hata, *Gun fashizumu*, 46–48. The lengthy and sensational Blood Brotherhood trial began in late June 1933 but was prorogued in August by a defense motion to censure the presiding judge. When the court reconvened in late March 1934, Inoue turned it into a political theater that generated enormous public sympathy, including thousands of petitions for clemency on the grounds that the murderers had acted sincerely from noble motives. After a two-and-one-half-year trial, judges sentenced Inoue and his two triggermen to life in prison and other members to various prison terms. All were paroled in a general amnesty of 1940.

41. Shillony, *Revolt in Japan*, 36.

42. Humphreys, *Heavenly Sword*, 61; Bōeichō, Bōeikenshūjō, senshibu, *Daihon'ei rikugunbu*, 402; Bōeichō, Bōeikenshūjō, senshibu, *Senshi sōsho* [Official military history] vol. 27, *Kantōgun* (1) [The Kwantung Army, part 1] (Asagumo shimbunsha, 1969), 145.

43. Kurono, *Teikoku kokubō*, 249.

44. Ibid., 254–255.

45. Humphreys, *Heavenly Sword*, 178; Kurono, *Horoboshita*, 130; Kurono, *Teikoku kokubō*, 264.

46. Kurono, *Horoboshita*, 128.

47. Shillony, *Revolt in Japan*, 31–32; Yoshida, *Nihon no guntai*, 190.

48. Yoshida, *Nihon no guntai*, 183–184.

49. Kurono, *Horoboshita*, 122–125, 128, 130–134; Kurono, *Teikoku kokubō*, 251, 262; Obata was promoted to colonel in July 1937 and to major general in April 1932.

50. Michael Barnhart, *Japan Prepares for Total War: The Search for Economic Security, 1919–1941* (Ithaca, NY: Cornell University Press, 1987), 34–35; Kitaoka, *Seitō kara gunbu e*, 176. In 1933 Prime Minister Saitō Makoto established the five-ministers conference composed of the premier and foreign, finance, army, and navy ministers to coordinate revisions to Japan's diplomatic, financial, and defense policies. Kitaoka, *Seitō kara gunbu e*, 184.

51. Kurono, *Teikoku kokubō*, 258–259; Bōeichō, Bōeikenshūjō, senshibu, *Daihon'ei rikugunbu*, 347–348; Kitaoka, *Seitō kara gunbu e*, 216.

52. Tobe, *Gyakusetsu*, 275–276. First Lt. Kurihara Yasuhide, "Seinen shōkō undō to wa nani ka" [What is the young (army) officers' movement?], in Takahashi Masae, ed., *Gendaishi shiryō* [Documents of contemporary history] 5, *Kokkashugi undō* [The nationalist movement] (Misuzu shobō, 1964), 764–774. Wada Hidekichi, a member of the editorial board of Tokyo's *Jiji* newspaper, interviewed Kurihara and Capt. Ōkura Eiichi, an activist stationed outside of Tokyo, for the article. See Wada Hidekichi, "Ni ni roku jihen zenya" [The eve of the 2-26 incident], in *Asahi shimbunsha*, eds., *Kataritsugu Shōwashi* [Shōwa history handed down from one generation to the next] 2 (*Asahi shimbun*, 1976), 10–13.

53. Shillony, *Revolt in Japan*, 45–46; Kitaoka, *Seitō kara gunbu e*, 228–229.

54. *Emperor Hirohito and His Chief Aide-de-Camp: The Honjō Diary, 1933–36*, translated by Mikiso Hane (Tokyo: University of Tokyo Press, 1982), 151–152, entry for July 16, 1935.

55. Shillony, *Revolt in Japan*, 47, 53; Kurihara, "Seinen shōkō undō," 765; Crowley, *Japan's Quest*, 267.

56. Takahashi Masae, *Ni ni roku jiken* [The 2-26 incident] (Chūkō shinsho, 1994, rev. ed.), 229–230.

57. Shillony, *Revolt in Japan*, 169–170.

58. Shillony, *Revolt in Japan*, 169–170, 201; Takahashi, *Ni ni roku*, 179, 227. Two other rebel officers had previously committed suicide.

59. Hayashi Shigeru, *Nihon no rekishi* [A history of Japan] 25, *Taiheiyō sensō* [The Pacific war] (Chūō kōronsha, 1967), 17; Fujiwara, *Gunjishi*, 175; Ōe, *Tennō no guntai*, 211–212.

60. Kitaoka, *Seitō kara gunbu e*, 240–241.

61. Takahashi, *Ni ni roku*, 2–26, 244–245.

62. Kurono, *Horoboshita*, 159–160, 167; Kurono, *Teikoku kokubō*, 315; Kurokawa, *Gunji senryaku*, 187, 189. This discussion of national defense policy is adapted from my essay in the forthcoming Stanford University Press volume *The Battle for China: Essays on the Military History of the Sino-Japanese War.*

63. Kurogawa, *Gunji senryaku*, 189; Kurono, *Horoboshita*, 169.

64. Kurono, *Horoboshita*, 163–164.

65. Matsushita, *Nihon kokubō no higeki*, 77; Hata, *Tōsuiken*, 179; Yoshida, *Nihon no guntai*, 129; Kido Kōichi kenkyūkai, eds., *Kido Kōichi nikki (jō)* [The diary of Kido Kōichi] (Tokyo daigaku shuppansha, 1966), 494, entry for May 13, 1936.

66. Stephen E. Pelz, *Race to Pearl Harbor* (Cambridge, MA: Harvard University Press, 1974), 173–174; Saburō Shiroyama, *War Criminal: The Life and Death of Hirota Kōki*, translated by John Bester (Kōdansha, 1977), 145; Momose Takashi and Itō Takashi, *Jiten Shōwa senzenki no Nihon* [Dictionary of Japan's prewar Shōwa period] (Tokyo: Yoshikawa Kōbunkan), 277; *Kido nikki*, 489; Kurono, *Teikoku kokubō*, 316; Kageyama, "Shina jiken," 42; Kurono, *Horoboshita*, 161.

67. Kurogawa, *Gunji senryaku*, 193.

68. Kurono, *Teikoku kokubō*, 321.

69. Sanbō honbu dai ni ka (second section, army general staff), "Kokubō kokusaku teikō" [Principles of national defense and national policy], in Nihon kokusai seiji gakkai, eds., *Taiheiyō sensō e no michi* [The road to the Pacific war] 8, *bekkan shiryō hen* [documentary appendix] (Asahi shibunsha, 1963), 224.

70. Kurono, *Teikoku kokubō*, 316–317.

71. Ibid.; Kurogawa, *Gunji senryaku*, 186; "Teikoku gaikō hōshin" [Imperial foreign policy], August 7, 1936, in Gaimushō [Foreign ministry], ed., *Nihon gaikō nenpyō narabi ni shuyō bunsho* [A chronology of Japanse diplomacy and important documents], *Meiji hyakunenshi sōsho*, 2 (Hara shobō, 1965), 345–347; Parks Coble, *Facing Japan: Chinese Politics and Japanese Imperialism, 1931–1937* (Cambridge, MA: Harvard University Press, 1991), 334. The Anti-Comintern Pact with Germany was signed that October and approved by the Privy Council on November 25, 1936.

72. Kurono, *Horoboshita*, 173; Hata Ikuhiko, *Rokōkyō jihen no kenkyū* [An inquiry into the Marco Polo bridge incident] (Tokyo daigaku shuppansha, 1996), 46; Barnhart, *Japan Prepares for Total War*, 44.

73. Peattie, *Ishiwara Kanji*, 201; Shimada Toshihiko, "Designs of North China, 1933–1937," translated by James B. Crowley, in Morley, *China Quagmire*, 199–200; Kaigun chūōbu [Naval headquarters], "Kokusaku kōryō" [General principles of national policy], draft April 1936, in Shimada Toshihiko and Inaba Masao, eds., *Gendaishi shiryō*, 8, *Nitchū sensō* (1) [The Sino-Japanese war, part 1] (Misuzu shobō, 1964), 354–355; Sanbō honbu, dai 2 ka, "Kokubō kokusaku teikō" [Outline for state policy for national defense], June 30, 1936, *Taiheiyō sensō e no michi, bekkan*, 224.

74. Kurono, *Horoboshita*, 175, 185; Kurokawa, *Gunji senryaku*, 195–197.

75. Bōeichō, *Daihon'ei rikugunbu*, 402–404; Bōeichō, *Kantōgun*, 145, 167.

76. Ikuda, *Nihon rikugunshi*, 153–154, 157; Mark R. Peattie and David Evans, *Kaigun: Strategy, Tactics, and Technology in the Imperial Japanese Navy, 1887–1941* (Annapolis, MD: Naval Institute Press, 1997), 334; Kitaoka, *Seitō kara gunbu e*, 268–269.

77. Crowley, *Japan's Quest*, 311; Fujiwara Akira, *Shōwa no rekishi* [A history of the Shōwa reign] 3, *Nitchū zenmen sensō* [Total war between Japan and China] (Shogakkan, 1982), 24–25; Kitaoka, *Seitō kara gunbu e*, 271–272.

78. Kurono, *Horoboshita*, 182–183.

79. Katogawa Kōtarō, *Rikugun no hansei (jō)* [Reflections on the army] (Bunkyō shuppan, 1996), 19. Three divisions, the 5th, 11th, and 12th, had amphibious assault missions and were equipped with the lighter and more easily transportable mountain artillery.

80. Bōeichō, *Kantōgun*, 559; Rikujō bakuryō, ed., "Nomonhan jiken no hōheisen" [Artillery battles during the Nomonhan incident] mimeo, 1965, 53–59, Japan Defense Agency (JDA); Wada Kazuo, "Nihon rikugun heiki gyōsei seidōshi no kenkyū" *(ge)* [Research on the administrative and organizational history of the Japanese army's weaponry], Bōeichō Bōei kenshūjō senshibu, Kenkyū shiryō, 83 RO-4H, mimeo, 1983, 14.

81. Bōeichō Bōei kenshūjō senshishitsu, *Senshi sōsho* [Official military history] 86, *Shina jihen rikugun sakusen* [Army operations during the China incident] 1, *Shōwa jūsannen ichigatsu made* [To January 1938] (Asagumo shimbunsha, 1982), 96; Katogawa, *Teikoku rikugun kikōbutai*, 43, 72, 77, 94, 197, and 239; Lt. Col. Kobayashi, IJA, "Tai sensha yōhō (senhō) no hensen sūsei" [Trends and changes in antitank operations (tactical)], mimeo, circa 1940, in *Nissō senshi jumbi shiryō* [Background historical materials for the history of the Japanese-Soviet fighting], mimeo, n.d., JDA. These concepts are discussed further in Edward Drea, "The Imperial Japanese Army (1868–1945): Origins, Evolution, Legacy," in Jeremy Black, ed., *War in the Modern World since 1815* (London: Routledge, 2003), 89–91.

82. Rikugun gakkai, ed., *Kindai sensōshi gaisetsu shiryō hen* [An outline of modern warfare—documentary appendix] (Rikusen gakkai, 1984), 39.

Chapter 10. The Pivotal Years, 1937–1941

1. Hata, *Rokōkyō*, 9.

2. Bōeichō, *Daihon'ei rikugunbu*, 412–413; Hata, *Rokōkyō*, 47; Shimanuki Takeji, "Dai 1 ji sekai daisen igo no kokubō hōshin, shoyō heiryoku, yōhei kōryō no hensen" [Changes to national defense policy, matters of force structure, and operational employment of troops after the First World War] *(ge) Gunjishi gaku* 9:1 (June 1973), 74; Usui Katsumi, *Shinhan Nitchū sensō* [The Sino-Japanese war, new, rev. ed.] (Chūkō shinsho, 2000), 52.

3. James Boyd, "In Pursuit of an Obsession: Japan in Inner Mongolia in the 1930s," *Japanese Studies* 22:3 (2002), 296.

4. Cited in Bōeichō, *Shina Jiken Rikugun Sakusen*, 91; Bōeichō, *Daihon'ei rikugunbu*, 418–419.

5. Yamada Akira, *Daigensui Shōwa tennō* [Generalissimo—the Shōwa emperor] (Shin Nihon shuppansha, 1994), 62–63; Miller, *Shōwa tennō dokuhakuroku*, 35–36.

6. Morimatsu, *Daihon'ei*, 193.

7. Ibid., 194.

8. Ibid.

9. Yamada, *Daigensui*, 70–72.

10. David Anson Titus, *Palace and Politics in Prewar Japan* (New York: Columbia University Press, 1974), 263; Yamada, *Daigensui*, 70–72.

11. Yoshida Akira and Mori Shigeki, *Sensō no Nihonshi* [A history of Japan's wars] 23, *Ajia Taiheiyō sensō* [The Asia-Pacific war] (Yoshikawa Kōbunkan, 2007), 34–42, 274–275.

12. Morimatsu, *Daihon'ei*, 198–199; Bōeichō, *Shina jiken rikugun sakusen*, 414–416.

13. Morimatsu, *Daihon'ei*, 200; Itō and Momoe, *Jiten Shōwa senzenki*, 15–16; Kurono, *Daigaku*, 235.

14. Miller, *Shōwa tennō dokuhakuroku*, 37; Yamada, *Daigensui*, 66; Bōeichō, *Shina jihen rikugun saksusen*, 283.

15. Hata Ikuhiko, *Nankin jiken* [The Nanjing incident] (Chūō kōronsha, 1986), 65–66.

16. Ibid., 71.

17. Cited in Masahiro Yamamoto, *Nanking: Anatomy of an Atrocity* (Westport, CT: Praeger, 2000), 93.

18. Daqing Yang, "Documentary Evidence and Studies of Japanese War Crimes: An Interium Assessment," in Nazi War Crimes and Japanese Imperial Government Records Interagency Working Group, *Researching Japanese War Crimes: Introductory Essays* (Washington, DC: National Archives and Records Administration, 2006), 30.

19. Hata, *Nankin jihen*, 93. The issue is controversial. See Daqing Yang, "Atrocities at Nanjing: Searching for Explanations," in Diana Lary and Stephen MacKinnon, eds., *Scars of War: The Impact of Warfare on Modern China* (Vancouver: University of British Columbia Press, 2001), 78–79.

20. Hata Ikuhiko, *Nitchū sensō* [The Sino-Japanese war] (Kawade shobō, 1972), 156, 287.

21. Fujiwara, *Nitchū zenmen sensō*, 226; Ōe, *Tennō no guntai*, foldout.

22. Yoshida, *Nihon no guntai*, 207–210; Fujiwara Akira, *Chūgoku sensen jūgunki* [A record of wartime service on the China front] (Ōtsuki shoten, 2002), 28; Yoshida Yutaka, *Ajia Taiheiyō sensō* [The Asia Pacific war] (Iwanami shinsho, 2007), 95–96.

23. Furuya Tetsuo, *Nitchū sensō* [The Sino-Japanese war] (Iwanami shinsho, 1985), 154.

24. Yamada, *Daigensui*, 83; John Hunter Boyle, *China and Japan at War, 1937–1945: The Politics of Collaboration* (Stanford, CA: Stanford University Press, 1972), 76–77.

25. Yamada, *Daigensui*, 97.

26. The navy's construction program that commenced in 1935 is included in the percentage.

27. Hayashi, *Taiheiyō sensō*, 86–87; Gordon M. Berger, *Parties out of Power in Japan, 1931–1941* (Princeton, NJ: Princeton University Press, 1977), 156; Barnhart, *Japan and the World*, 115.

28. Hata, *Nitchū sensō*, 288. Between February 20 and May 10 the 5th Division lost about 6,600 men; the 10th Division recorded around 5,000 casualties from March 14 through May 12. The majority of the losses occurred during the Taierzhuang operation. Chinese losses were approximately 20,000 troops. Bōeichō bōei senshishitsu, eds., *Senshi sōsho*, 89, *Shina jihen rijugun sakusen* [Army operations during the China incident] 2, *Shōwa 14 nen 9 gatsu made* [To September 1939] (Asagumo shimbunsha, 1976), 41; Kojima Noboru, *Nitchū sensō* [The Sino-Japanese war] 4 (Bunshun bunko, 1988), 329.

29. Diana Lary, "Drowned Earth: The Strategic Breaching of the Yellow River Dyke, 1938," *War and History* 8:2 (2001), 198–202; Diana Lary, "A Ravaged Place: The Devastation of the Xuzhou Region, 1938," in Lary and MacKinnon, *Scars of War*, 112 table 4.3.

30. Hata Ikuhiko, "The Japanese-Soviet Confrontation, 1935–1939," translated by Alvin D. Coox, in James William Morley, ed., *Japan's Road to the Pacific War, Deterrent Diplomacy: Japan, Germany, and the USSR 1935–1940* (New York: Columbia University Press, 1976), 131; Itō and Momoe, *Jiten Shōwa senzenki*, 311; Rikusen gakkai, *Kindai sensōshi gaisetsu*, 62.

31. Yamada, *Daigensui*, 98; Alvin D. Coox, *The Anatomy of a Small War: The Soviet-Japanese Struggle for Changkuofeng/Khasan, 1938* (Westport, CT: Greenwood, 1977), 54, 61–65; Alvin D. Coox, *Nomonhan: Japan against Russia, 1939*, 1 (Stanford, CA: Stanford University Press, 1985), 120, 130, 134.

32. For example, Obata's influential "TaiSo sentōhō yōkō" of May 1933.

33. Furuya, *Nitchū sensō*, 172; Stephen MacKinnon, "The Tragedy of Wuhan, 1938," *Modern Asian Studies* 30:4 (1986), 932.

34. Handō Kazutoshi, *Nomonhan no natsu* [Nomonhan summer] (Bungei shūnjū, 1998), 12.

35. Boyle, *China and Japan at War*, 215–217.

36. Katogawa, *Teikoku rikugun kikōbutai*, 211; Handō, *Nomonhan*, 167.

37. See among other reports, Lt. Col. Konuma Haruo, "Nomonhan jiken yori kansatsu seru tai 'Sō' kindaisen no jissō" [The realities of modern warfare against the Soviet Union based on the Nomonhan incident], February 1940; Daihon'ei rikugunbu, Nomonhan jiken kenkyū iinkai dai 1 kenkyū iinkai [Imperial general headquarters, first research subcommittee of the subcommittee to investigate the Nomonhan incident], "Nomonhan jiken kenkyū hōkoku" [Nomonhan incident research report], January 10, 1940; and Col. Terada Masao, "Nomonhan jiken ni kansuru shōken" [Opinions concerning the Nomonhan incident], October 13, 1939, all JDA.

38. See Handō Kazutoshi, *Nomonhan*, 332–344; Hata, *Nihonjin furyo*, 67; Alvin D. Coox, *Nomonhan: Japan against Russia, 1939*, 2 (Stanford, CA: Stanford University Press, 1985), 928–940.

39. Hata, *Nihonjin furyo*, 72–73; Gomikawa Jumpei, *Nomonhan*, 2 (Bunshun būnkō, 1978), 241, 244–245.

40. Ikō, *Manshū jihen kara*, 163–165.

41. Kisaka Junichirō, *Shōwa no rekishi* [A history of the Shōwa era] 7, *Taiheiyō senso* [The Pacific war] (Shogakkan, 1989), 235.

42. Usui, *Nitchū senso*, 106; Inaba Masao and Usui Katsumi, eds., *Gendaishi shiryō* [Documents of contemporary history] 9, *Nitchū sensō* 2 [The Sino-Japanese war, part 2] (Misuzu shobō, 1964), xxxiv; Dai jū-ichi gun sanbō [Eleventh Army staff], "Shōwa jūyonnen toki sakusen sakusen keika no gaiyō" [An overview of the 1939 winter season operation and the course of operations], March 5, 1940, *Gendaishi shiryō* 9: 440.

43. "Shōwa jūyonnen toki sakusen sakusen," 440.

44. Imaoka Tōuomi [?], "Shōwa 14 nen aki kara 15 nen zenhan ni okeru rikugun chūōbu no hataraki" [Working in army central headquarters from the fall of 1939 to the middle of 1940], in Dōdai kurabu kōenshu, ed., *Shōwa gunji hiwa (chū)* [Secret tales of the Shōwa military] (Dōdai keizai kōndankai, 1997), 140–142.

45. Fujiwara, *Nitchū zenmen senso*, 288–289.

46. Ibid., 249; Kurono, *Nihon o horoboshita*, 196.

47. Fujiwara, *Nitchū zenmen senso*, 249; Boyle, *China and Japan at War*, 292–293.

48. Fujiwara, *Nitchū zenmen senso*, 247 quote; Daihon'ei rikugunbu, "Sekai jōsei no sui-i ni tomonau jikyoku shōri yōryō" [Outline for management of the situation attendant to changing world conditions], July 3, 1940, in Bōeichō Bōeikenshūjō, *Senshi sōsho*, 20, *Daihon'ei rikugunbu*, part 2 (Asagumo shimbunsha, 1968), 20: 49–50.

49. Fujiwara, *Nitchū zenmen senso*, 250–251.

50. Bōeichō, Bōeikenshūjō, *Daihon'ei rikugunbu*, part 2, 48; Fujiwara, *Nitchū zenmen senso*, 254–255.

51. Kitaoka, *Seitō kara gunbu e*, 343; Gomikawa Junpei, *Gozen kaigi* [The imperial conferences] (Bunshun bunko, 1984), 16–17; Ōe Shinobu, *Gozen kaigi* [The imperial conferences] (Chūkō shinsho, 1991), 23.

52. Kitaoka, *Seitō kara gunbu e*, 344–345; Usui, *Nitchū senso*, 114.

53. Kitaoka, *Seitō kara gunbu e*, 346–347.

54. Kurono, *Nihon o horoboshita*, 198.

55. Kurono, *Daigaku*, 228; Kurono, *Nihon o horoboshita*, 199.

56. Hata Ikuhiko, "The Army's Move into Northern Indochina," translated by Robert A. Scalapino, in James William Morley, ed., *Japan's Road to the Pacific War: The Fateful Choice: Japan's Advance into Southeast Asia, 1939–1941* (New York: Columbia University Press, 1980), 193–203.

57. Kitaoka, *Seitō kara gunbu e*, 349; Kurono, *Dai Nihon teikoku no zonzai senrykau*, 218; Hosoya Chihiro, "Britain and the U.S. in Japan's View of the International System, 1937–41," in Ian Nish, ed., *Anglo-Japanese Alienation, 1919–1952: Papers of the Anglo-Japanese Conference on the History of the Second World War* (Cambridge, UK: Cambridge University Press, 1982), 66; Gerhard Weinberg, *A World at Arms: A Global History of World War II* (Cambridge, UK: Cambridge University Press, 1994), 247 and 999 n276.

58. Hata, "The Army's Move," 206–207.

59. Kisaka, *Taiheiyō sensō*, 181; Karl Friday, "Bushido or Bull? A Medieval Historian's Perspective," *The History Teacher* 27:3 (May 1994), 346–347.

60. Nobutaka Ike, *Japan's Decision for War: Records of the 1941 Policy Conferences* (Stanford, CA: Stanford University Press, 1967), 13.

61. Miller, *Shōwa tennō dokuhakuroku*, 70.

62. Lyman P. Van Slyke, "The Battle of the Hundred Regiments: Problems of Coordination and Control during the Sino-Japanese War," *Modern Asian Studies* 30:4 (October 1996), 979–1005.

63. Yoshida, *Ajia Taiheiyō sensō*, 114; Ikō, *Manshū jihen kara*, 169–171.

64. Ikō, *Manshū jihen kara*, 171–178.

65. Mainichi shimbunsha, eds., *Ichiokunin no Shōwashi* [One hundred millions' Shōwa history] 6, *Nitchū sensō* [The Sino-Japanese war] 4 (December 1979), 81; Fujiwara Akira, *Taiheiyō sensōron* [A theory of the Pacific war] (Aoki shoten, 1982), 124–125.

66. Kisaka, *Taiheiyō sensō*, 55.

67. Pelz, *Race to Pearl Harbor*, 222.

68. Thomas R. H. Havens, *Valley of Darkness: The Japanese People and World War Two* (New York: W. W. Norton, 1978), 15; Ikuda, *Nihon rikugunshi*, 182.

69. Gomikawa, *Gozen*, 32; Kitaoka, *Seitō kara gunbu e*, 355–356.

70. Follow-up messages from Japanese diplomats in Berlin and Vienna in late April, early May, and June suggested an attack might occur in June. There were also contradictory messages from the Japanese ambassador in Moscow. Shimada, *Kantōgun*, 153–154; U.S. Department of Defense, *The "Magic" Background of Pearl Harbor (Feb. 14, 1941–May 12, 1941)* (Washington, DC: U.S. Government Printing Office, 1977), 48–50; Msg. Berlin to Tokyo, No. 366, April 16, 1941; No. 370, April 24, 1941; No. 377, May 6, 1941; and msg. Vienna to Tokyo, No. 378, May 9, 1941, A-189–96; Hosoya Chihiro, "The Japanese-Soviet Neutrality Pact," translated by Peter A. Berton, in Morley, *Japan's Road to the Pacific War: The Fateful Choice: Japan's Advance into Southeast Asia, 1939–41* (New York: Columbia University Press, 1980), 91; Pelz, *Race to Pearl Harbor*, 223.

71. Kurono, *Dai Nihon teikoku no sonzai senryku*, 220; Daihon'ei rikugunbu, sensō shidō han [Imperial general headquarters, army division, war guidance section] eds., *Kimitsu sensō nisshi* [Confidential war diary] (Kinseisha, 1998 reprint), 111–121; Shimada, *Kantōgun*, 155; Coox, *Nomonhan*, 1035.

72. Hosoya, "Japanese-Soviet Neutrality Pact," 96, 102; Coox, *Nomonhan*, 1035, 1037, 1042–1043. Twelve divisions would come from the Kwantung Army, two from the Korea Army, and two from the homeland reserve.

73. See Ike, *Japan's Decision for War*, 61–62; Bōeichō Bōeikenshūjō, *Senshi sōsho*, 73, *Kantō-gun (2)* [The Kwantung army, part 2] (Asagumo shinbunsha, 1974), 20–23; Shimada, *Kantōgun*, 156, 158; Coox, *Nomonhan*, 1037; but see Kurono, *Nihon o horoboshita*, 210.

74. "Rokugatsu jūroku nichi dai sanjūichikai renraku kōndaikai" [The June 16 (1941) 31st liaison roundtable], in Sanbō honbu, ed., *Sugiyama memo (jō)* [General Sugiyama Hajime's memoranda, part 1] *Meiji hyakunenshi sōsho* [The Meiji centennial series] 16, (Hara shobō, 1967), 224; Ikuda, *Nihon rikugunshi*, 185; Hosoya, "Japanese-Soviet Neutrality Pact," 103–104; Coox, *Nomonhan*, 1040, Kurono, *Nihon no horoboshita*, 209.

75. Coox, *Nomonhan*, 1041–1042; Shimada, *Kantōgun*, 163–164; Ikuda, *Nihon rikugunshi*, 187; Hosoya, "Japanese-Soviet Neutrality Pact," 104.

76. *Kimitsu sensō nisshi*, 136, 138, July 22 and 30 entries, respectively.

77. Weinberg, *World at Arms*, 252; Usui, *Nitchū sensō*, 123; Ikuda, *Nihon rikugunshi*, 187.

78. Shimada, *Kantōgun*, 167; *Sugiyama memo*, 284; see Yamada Akira, *Shōwa tennō no gunji shisō to senryaku* [The Shōwa emperor's military thought and strategy] (Kōkura shobō, 2002), 150.

79. Ike, *Japan's Decision*, 112–113; Coox, *Nomonhan*, 1048–1059; Ikuda, *Nihon rikugunshi*, 188; Shimada, *Kantōgun*, 175.

80. Tobe, *Gyakusetsu*, 307, quoting Hatano Sumio.

81. Ikuda, *Nihon rikugunshi*, 193.

82. Usui, *Nitchū sensō*, 129; Yoshida, *Ajia Taiheiyō sensō*, 12; Ōe, *Sanbō honbu*, 200.

83. Miller, *Shōwa tennō dokuhakuroku*, 69.

84. Ike, *Japan's Decision*, 200; "Jūichi gatsu tsuitachi renraku kaigi jōkyō" [Circumstances of the November 1 (1941) liaison conference] in *Sugiyama memo*, 1: 385; *Daihon'ei kimitsu nisshi*, 351.

85. Ike, *Japan's Decision*, 208–239; Ikuda, *Nihon rikugunshi*, 193; Suekuni Masao and Koike I'ichi, eds., *Kaigunshi jiten* [Historical dictionary of the Japanese navy] (Kokusho kankōkai, 1985), 62.

86. Kisaka, *Taiheiyō sensō*, 218–220.

87. *Sugiyama memo*, 1: 544.

Chapter 11. The Asia-Pacific War

1. I am indebted to Dr. Stanley L. Falk for these observations.

2. Yoshida Yutaka, *Ajia Taiheiyō sensō* [The Asia-Pacific war] (Iwanami shinsho, 2007), 86.

3. Yoshida Yutaka and Mori Shigeki *Sensō no Nihonshi* [Warfare in Japanese history] 23, *Ajia Taiheiyō sensō* [The Asia-Pacific war] (Yoshikawa kūbunkan, 2007), 109; Ikuda, *Nihon rikugunshi*, 199. In December 1941 the Japanese army had fifty-one divisions; twenty-seven were engaged in China operations, thirteen were stationed in Manchuria to deter the USSR, and the remaining eleven were homeland strategic reserve, including those positioned in Korea. Five of the strategic reserve units were newly organized and not rated combat ready.

4. Douglas Gillison, *Australia in the War of 1939–1945*, series 3, vol. 1, *Royal Australian Air Force 1939–1942* (Canberra: Australian War Memorial, 1962), 224; Kimata Shirō, *Rikugun kōkū senshi: Mare sakusen kara Okinawa tokkō made* [A history of the army air force: From the Malaya operation to the Okinawa special attack corps] (Keizai ōraisha, 1982), 10–11.

5. See Stanley L. Falk, *March of Death* (New York: W. W. Norton, 1962) for an excellent account of the Japanese treatment of prisoners of war captured in the Philippines in early 1942. I am again indebted to Dr. Falk for his comments on this section.

6. Northern Burma had also continued a formal relation of allegiance to China even after the British had colonized the country.

7. Kurogawa, *Gunji senryaku*, 213.

8. Ikuda, *Nihon rikugunshi*, 201.

9. Morimatsu, *Daihon'ei*, 227–229.

10. Kisaka, *Taiheiyō sensō*, 123.

11. I am again grateful to Dr. Falk for these insights.

12. Usui, *Nitchū sensō*, 144–146.

13. Hata, *Taiheiyō sensō roku daikessen (jō)* [Six decisive battles of the Pacific war], *Sakugo no senjō* [Mistaken battlegrounds] (Chūkō bunko, 1998), 93.

14. Daihon'ei seifu renraku kaigi [Imperial general headquarters and government liaison conference], "Sekai jōsei handan" [Estimate of the world situation], November 7, 1942, in Sanbō honbu, ed., *Sugiyama memo, ge* [General Sugiyama Hajime's memoranda, 2] *Meiji hyakunenshi sōsho* [Official history of the Meiji centennial] 17, (Hara shobō, 1967), 161.

15. Kisaka, *Taiheiyō sensō*, 157–158; Hata, *Tōsuiken*, 174.

16. Hata, *Sakugo*, 118; Sugiyama Hajime and Nagano Osamu, "Yōhei jikō ni kanshi sōjō" [Report to the throne on operational troop matters], December 31, 1942, in Yamada Akira, *Sensō shidō*, 249–251; see also ibid., 121, 124.

17. Kurogawa, *Gunji senryaku*, 218.

18. Ibid., 216–219.

19. Ōe, *Tennō no guntai*, 293; Kojima Noboru, *Taiheiyō sensō (ge)* [The Pacific war, 2] (Chūkō shinsho, 1966), 35.

20. John W. Dower, *War without Mercy: Race and Power in the Pacific War* (New York: Pantheon, 1986), 231 quote; Yoshida, *Ajia Taiheiyō sensō*, 137; Yamamuro, *Gunshin*, 322.

21. Kojima, *Taiheiyō sensō*, 59; Rikusen gakkai, *Kindai sensōshi gaisetsu, shiryō hen*, 172, table 5-3-3; Ikuda, *Nihon rikugunshi*, 210, 213.

22. Kurogawa, *Gunji senryaku*, 223.

23. Ikuda, *Nihon rikugunshi*, 213.

24. Kurogawa, *Gunji senryaku*, 224.

25. Yoshida, *Ajia Taiheiyō sensō*, 112.

26. Kisaka, *Taiheiyō sensō*, 368; Tobe, *Gyakusetsu*, 328. As for the officer corps, 35 percent were regulars in 1939, and 19 percent were regulars in 1945. By 1945 the army was running short of officers, especially captains. It had an overall officer shortfall of around 25 percent. *Kindai sensōshi gaisetsu*, 38.

27. Ikuda, *Nihon rikugunshi*, 215, 229; Yamaguchi, *Rikugun to kaigun*, 118.

28. Kojima, *Taiheiyō sensō*, 119.

29. Joyce C. Lebra, *Japanese-Trained Armies in Southeast Asia* (New York: Columbia University Press, 1977), 24–36.

30. Kojima, *Taiheiyō sensō*, 131–132; Arthur Swinson, *Four Samurai* (London: Hutchinson, 1968), 121.

31. Swinson, *Four Samurai*, 125–126; Louis Allen, *Burma: The Longest War 1941–45* (New York: St. Martin's Press, 1984), 166.

32. Kojima, *Taiheiyō sensō*, 117.

33. Allen, *Burma*, 164 and n1.

34. Yamauchi died of tuberculosis two months after his relief. Yanagida was retired then recalled to command the Port Arthur fortress. A court-martial declared Satō mentally unstable and seconded him to the reserves. Mutaguchi was seconded to the reserves but during Japan's final mobilization was recalled to command the military preparatory academy. Kawabe was transferred to Tokyo, promoted general, and made commander of the combined air forces.

35. Fujiwara Akira, *Uejini shita eiyūtachi* [Starving heroes] (Aoki shoten, 2001), 3, 121; Hata Ikuhiko, "Dai niji seikai taisen no Nihonjin senbotsusha zō" [An image of the Japanese war dead in the second world war] *Gunji shigaku* 42:2 (September 2006), 11.

36. Kojima, *Taiheiyō sensō*, 179–180.

37. Ibid., 182–183; Kurogawa, *Gunji senryaku*, 227.

38. Daihon'ei rikugunbu sensō shidō han [Imperial general headquarters, army department, war guidance section], *Kimitsu sensō nisshi (ge)* [Confidential war diary, 2] (Kinseisha, 1998), 552, entry for July 1, 1944.

39. Haruko Taya Cook, "The Myth of the Saipan Suicides," *MHQ* 7:3 (Spring 1995), 12–19.

40. Morimatsu, *Daihon'ei*, 233–238.

41. Kojima, *Taiheiyō sensō*, 230, 233.

42. Saikō sensō shidō kaigi [Supreme council for the direction of the war], "Sekai jōsei handan," August 19, 1944; and "Kongō toru beki sensō shidō no teikō" [Outline for the future course of war guidance], August 19, 1944: both Sanbō honbu, ed., *Haisen no kiroku* [Record of defeat] *Meiji hyakunenshi sōsho* [Official history of the Meiji centennial] 38 (Hara shobō, 1979), 49–52 and 55–57, respectively. See also Kojima, *Taiheiyō sensō*, 237.

43. Mori and Yoshida, *Ajia Taiheiyō sensō*, 73; Shirai Akio, *Nihon rikugun kunren no kenkyū* [A study of the Japanese army's doctrine] (Fūyō shobō, 2003), 149–150.

44. Kobe Tatsu, "Nanpō sakusen ni okeru rikugun no kyōiku kunren" [Army education and doctrine for southern region operations], *Kenkyū shiryō*, 85 RO-3H mimeo, 1985, 63; Hata Ikuhiko, "Taiheiyō sensō makki ni okeru Nihon rikugun no tai Bei sempō—mizugiwa ka kikyu ka" [The Japanese army's tactics against the Americans in the latter stages of the Pacific war—waterline defense or attrition?] *Nihon hōgaku* 73:2 (December 2007), 703–704.

45. Tamura Yōzō, *Gyokusai Biaku shima* [Annihilation at Biak island] (Kōjinsha, 2004), 133, 186–187; Takahashi Fumio, *Dai jūyoun shidan shi* [History of the 14th division] (Utsunomiya: Shimano shimbunsha, 1990), 325–328, 350.

46. Kondō Shintsuke, "Taiheiyō sensō ni okeru Nihon rikugun taijōriku sakusen shisō," *Kenkyū shiryō*, 92 RO-4H, mimeo, 1992, 131. A first draft was completed in November 1943. Shirai, *Nihon rikugun 'senkun' no kenkyū*, 215. A fifth edition of the infantry manual was issued in 1940.

47. Kondō, "Taiheiyō sensō ni okeru Nihon rikugun taijōriku," 135.

48. For definitive accounts of the Leyte campaign see Stanley L. Falk, *Decision at Leyte* (New York: W. W. Norton, 1966), and Ōoka Shōhei, *Reite sakusen* [Military record of the Leyte operation] (Chūō kōronsha, 1966).

49. Yoshida and Mori, *Ajia Taiheiyō sensō*, 202; Usui, *Nitchū sensō*, 163.

50. IGHQ had ordered the transfer of the 2d Division from Burma to Saigon because of continuing defeats in the Pacific and southern Burma.

51. Kuroha Kiyotaka, *Nitchū jūgonen sensō (ge)* [The fifteen-year Sino-Japanese war, 3] (Kyōikusha, 1979), 266; Hsi-sheng Ch'i, "The Military Dimension, 1942–1945," in James C. Hsiung and Steven I. Levine, eds., *China's Bitter Victory: The War with Japan, 1937–1945* (M. E. Sharpe, 1992), 180, table 3.

52. Daihon'ei rikukaigunbu [Imperial general headquarters, army and navy departments], "Teikoku rikukaigun sakusen tairyō" [Outline of imperial army and navy operations], January 20, 1945, in Takagi Sōkichi, *Taiheiyō kaisenshi* [A history of the naval war in the Pacific, rev. ed.] (Iwanami shinsho, 1977), document appendix no. 24, 231–233.

53. Saikō sensō shido kaigi hōkoku, "Sekai jōsei handan" [Estimate of the world situation], February 15, 1945, in Sanbō honbu, *Haisen no Kiroku*, 230–232.

54. Cited in Kumiko Kakehashi, *So Sad to Fall in Battle* (New York: Presidio, 2007), 186.

55. Hara Takeshi, "Okinawasen ni okeru kenmin no kengai sōkai" [The wartime evacuation of Okinawans], in Gunjishi gakkai, ed., *Dai ni ji sekai taisen* (3), 131.

56. Ibid., 124–125.

57. Kisaka, *Taiheiyō sensō*, 378.

58. Kojima Noboru, *Shikkan (jō)* [The commanders, 1] (Bunshun būnkō, 1974), 129; Kisaka, *Taiheiyō sensō*, 378.

59. In August 2005 an 88-year-old former army major who commanded the garrison on one island and the 77-year-old younger brother of a deceased army captain who commanded the Tokashiki garrison filed suit, claiming that they issued no such orders and their actions had been intentionally misrepresented. A court rejected their defamation lawsuit in March 2008.

60. Tobe Ryōichi, et al., *Shippai no honshitsu* [The essence of defeat] (Chūkō bunko, 1991), 236, 242.

61. Maeda and Kuwada, *Chizu to dēta*, plate 62.

62. Richard B. Frank, *Downfall: The End of the Imperial Japanese Empire* (New York: Random House, 1999), 71 quote; Thomas M. Huber, *Japan's Battle of Okinawa, April–June 1945*, Leavenworth Paper No. 18 (Washington, DC: U.S. Government Printing Office, 1990), 120.

63. Handō Kazutoshi, *Shikkikan to Sanbō* [Commanders and staff officers] (Bungei shūnjū, 1992), 249; *Kimitsu sensō nisshi*, 671, entry for February 20, 1945.

64. *Kimitsu sensō nisshi (ge)*, 696, entry for April 4, 1945.

65. Daihon'ei rikukaigunbu, "Daihon'ei ni okeru hondo sakusen jumbi keishō" [Imperial general headquarters' plans for preparations for homeland defense], April 8, 1945, in Takagi, *Taiheiyō kaisenshi*, document appendix No. 26, 236–239; Frank, *Downfall*, 110–113.

66. Gozen kaigi [Imperial conference], "Kongō torubeki sensō shidō no konpon tairyō" [Fundamental outline of future wartime guidance], June 8, 1945; "Seikai jōsei handan," June 8, 1945; and "Kokuryoku no genjō" [The present state of national power], June 8, 1945; all in Sanbō honbu, *Haisen no kiroku*, 266–270.

67. Frank, *Downfall*, chapters 11, 12, and 13, has a thorough discussion of the Japanese buildup and expectations.

68. Yoshida, *Ajia Taiheiyō sensō*, 139; Coox, *Nomonhan*, 1059; Gomikawa Shumpei, *Shinwa no hōkai* [The collapse of a myth] (Bungei bunko, 1991), 235; Edward J. Drea, "Missing Intentions: Japanese Intelligence and the Soviet Invasion of Manchuria, 1945," *Military Affairs* (April 1984), 66–70.

69. Takamae Eiji, *The Allied Occupation of Japan* (New York: Continuum, 2002), 111.

70. Hata Ikuhiko, Handō Kazutoshi, Hosaka Masayuki, and Sakamoto Takao, *Shōwashi no ronten* [Disputed points of Shōwa history] (Bunshun shinsho, 2000), 201.

71. Donald G. Gillin and Charles Etter, "Staying on: Japanese Soldiers and Civilians in China, 1945–1949," *Journal of Asian Studies* 42:3 (May 1983), 497–500.

72. See Ronald H. Spector, *In the Ruins of Empire: The Japanese Surrender and the Battle for Postwar Asia* (New York: Random House, 2007).

Chapter 12. Epilogue

1. Ōtani Keijirō, *Shōwa kempeishi* [A history of the military police during the Showa era] (Tokyo: Misuzu shobō, 1966), 532. Major Ishiwara had participated in the murder of the 1st Division commander on the night of August 14–15.

2. Hata, *Tōsuiken*, 178.

3. I am indebted to Dr. Robert H. Berlin for this insight. My reference is to Takehiko

Yoshihashi, *Conspiracy at Mukden: The Rise of the Japanese Military* (New Haven, CT: Yale University Press, 1963).

4. Senjō shinri chōsa hōkoku [Report of the investigation of battlefield psychology], "Senjō shinri chōsa ni motozuku shōken" [Opinions based on the study of battlefield psychology], 1939, JDA; Kawano Hitoshi, "*Gyokusai" no guntai, "senhen" no guntai* [An army for annihilation; an army for returning alive] (Kōdansha sensho mechiya, 2001), 174–175.

5. Kawano Hitoshi, "Nitchū sensō ni okeru sentō no rekishishakaigakuteki kōsatsu" [A historical sociology of combat in the Sino-Japanese war: combat morale in the 37th division], Gunjishi Gakkai, ed., *Nitchū sensō no shosō* [Various aspects of the Sino-Japanese war] special issue of *Gunjishi* 33:2–3, 197–216.

6. Rikugun hohei gakkō [Army infantry school], *Tai-Shinagun sentōhō no kenkyū* [A study of tactical principles against the Chinese army], January 1933, JDA.

7. Tobe, *Gyakusetsu*, 334, table; Ōhama Tetsuya and Ozawa Ikurou, *Teikoku rikukaigun jiten* [A dictionary of the imperial army and navy] (Dōdaisha, 1984), 19–20, tables 8 and 9.

8. Christopher R. Browning, *Ordinary Men: Reserve Police Battalion 101 and the Final Solution in Poland* (New York: HarperPerennial, 1993), 188–189.

9. Cited in Robert Hanyok, "Wartime COMINT Records in the National Archives about Japanese War Crimes in the Asia and Pacific Theaters, 1978–1997," in Nazi War Crimes and Japanese Imperial Government Records Interagency Working Group, ed., *Researching Japanese War Crimes* (Washington, DC: National Archives and Records Administration, 2006), 135.

10. War Dept. ACS, G-2, "MAGIC"—Diplomatic Summary, No. 1269, September 15, 1945, 11.

11. Edward J. Drea, "Introduction," in *Researching Japanese War Crimes*, 7. Among the B and C class war criminals were 173 Taiwanese and 148 Koreans.

12. In late 1949 the Soviet Union tried several members of Unit 731 that had been captured during the Manchurian campaign in August 1945.

13. *Kindai sensōshi gaisetsu, shiryō hen*, 38; Ōe, *Tennō no guntai*, 51. Five navy admirals also committed suicide.

14. GHQ, USAFP, MIS, GS, ULTRA Intelligence Summary, No. 128, Aug 19/20, 1945.

15. Takemae, *Allied Occupation of Japan*, 110; Hosaka, *Shōwa rikugun no kenkyū*, 463; Maeda and Kuwada, *Chizu to dēta*, plate 67.

16. Weinberg, *A World at Arms*, 894.

Selected Bibliography

Japanese-Language Books (all published in Tokyo, Japan)

Amemiya Shoichi. *Kindai Nihon no sensō shidō* [Modern Japan's wartime leadership]. Yoshikawa Kōbunkan, 1997.

Bōeichō, Bōeikenshūjō, senshibu, ed. *Senshi sōsho* [Official military history].Vol. 8, *Daihon'ei rikugunbu* [Imperial general headquarters], part 1. Asagumo shimbunsha, 1967.

———.Vol. 27, *Kantōgun* [The Kwantung army], part 1. Asagumo shimbunsha, 1969.

———.Vol. 51, *Hondo kessen jumbi* [Preparations for the defense of the homeland], part 1. Asagumo shimbunsha, 1971.

———.Vol. 57, *Hondo kessen jumbi* [Preparations for the defense of the homeland], part 2. Asagumo shimbunsha, 1972.

———.Vol. 73, *Kantōgun* [The Kwantung army], part 2. Asagumo shimbunsha, 1974.

———.Vol. 86, *Shina jihen rikugun sakusen* [Army operations during the China incident], part 1. Asagumo shimbunsha, 1975.

———.Vol. 89, *Shina jihen rikugun sakusen* [Army operations during the China incident], part 2. Asagumo shimbunsha, 1976.

———.Vol. 102, *Rikukaigun nenpyō* [A chronology of the army and navy]. Asagumo shimbunsha, 1980.

Dōdai kurabu kōenshu, ed. *Shōwa gunji hiwa* [Secret tales of the Shōwa military]. 3 vols. Dōdai keizai kōndankai, 1997.

Endō Yoshinobu. *Kindai Nihon guntai kyōikushi kenkyū* [A study of modern Japan's military education history]. Aoki shoten, 1994.

Fujimura Michio. *Nisshin sensō* [The Sino-Japanese war]. Iwanami shinsho, 1973.

Fujioka Kenjirō, ed. *Nihon rekishi chimei jiten* [Geographical dictionary of Japanese history]. Tokyotō shuppan, 1981.

Fujiwara Akira. *Chūgoku sensen jūgunki* [Record of wartime service on the China front]. Ōtsuki shoten, 2002.

———. *Nihon gendaishi taikei* [Systematized Japanese contemporary history]. *Gunjishi* [Military history]. Tōyō keizai shinpōsha, 1961.

———. *Nihon gunjishi* [A military history of Japan]. 2 vols. Nihon hyōronsha, 1987.

———. *Shōwa no rekishi* [A history of the Shōwa reign].Vol. 5, *Nitchū zenmen sensō* [Japan and China's total war]. Shogakkan, 1982.

———. *Uejini shita eiyūtachi* [Starving heroes]. Aoki shoten, 2001.

Furuya Tetsuo. *Nichi-Ro sensō* [The Russo-Japanese war]. Chūkō shinsho, 1966.

———. *Nitchū sensō* [The Sino-Japanese war]. Iwanami shinsho, 1989.

Gaimusho, ed. *Nihon gaikō nenpyō narabi ni shuyō bunsho* [A chronology of Japan's diplomacy, with major documents]. *Meiji hyakunenshi sōsho* [Official history of the Meiji centennial], vols. 1 and 2. Hara shobō, 1965.

Gomikawa Junpei. *Gozen kaigi* [The imperial conferences]. Bunshun bunkō, 1984.

———. *Nomonhan* [Nomonhan]. 2 vols. Bunshun bunko, 1978.

———. *Shinwa no hōkai* [The collapse of a myth]. Bungei bunko, 1991.

Gunjishi gakkai, ed. *Kimitsu sensō nisshi* [Confidential war diary of imperial general headquarters]. 2 vols. Kinseisha, 1998.

———. *Nichi-Ro sensō* [The Russo-Japanese war]. 2 vols. Kinseisha, 2005.

Handō Kazutoshi. *Nomonhan no natsu* [Nomonhan summer]. Bungei shunjū, 1998.

———. *Shikkan to sanbō* [Commanders and staff officers]. Bunshun bunko, 1992.

———. *Shōwashi, 1926–1945* [A history of the Shōwa reign, 1926–1945]. Heibonsha, 2004.

Hara Kiyoshi. *Boshin sensō* [The Boshin war]. Hanawa shobō, 1963.

Hara Takeshi. *Meijiki kokudo bōeishi* [A history of homeland defense during the Meiji period]. Kinseisha, 2002.

———. "Okinawasen ni okeru kenmin no kengai sōkai" [Forced evacuation of civilians from Okinawa]. *Gunjishi gakkai*, ed., *Dai ni ji sekai taisen: shūsen*, vol. 3. Kinseisha, 1995.

Harada Keiichi. *Kokumingun no shinwa* [The myth of the people's army]. Yoshikawa Kōbunkan, 2001.

———. *Nisshin Nichi-Ro sensō* [The Sino-Japanese and Russo-Japanese wars]. Vol. 3, *Shirizū Nihon kingendaishi* [Japan's modern and contemporary history series]. Iwanami shinsho, 2007.

Hata Ikuhiko. *Gun fashizumu undō shi* [The military fascist movement]. Kawade shobō shinsha, 1972.

———. *Nankyō jiken* [The Nanjing incident]. Chūkō shinsho, 1986.

———. *Nihon no horyo* [Japan's prisoners of war]. 2 vols. Hara shobō, 1998.

———. *Nihon rikukaigun sōgō jiten* [A comprehensive dictionary of Japan's army and navy]. Tokyo daigaku shuppansha, 1991.

———. *Nitchū sensōshi* [A history of the Sino-Japanese war]. Kawade shobō shinsha, 1972.

———. *Rokōkyō jihen no kenkyū* [Research about the Marco Polo bridge incident]. Tokyo daigaku shuppansha, 1996.

———. *Shōwashi no gunjintachi* [Military men of Shōwa history]. Bungei shunjū, 1982.

———. *Taiheiyō sensō roku daikessen* [Six major decisions during the Pacific war]. 2 vols. Chūkō bunko, 1998.

———. *Tōsuiken to teikoku rikukaigun no jidai* [The age of the prerogative of supreme command and the imperial army and navy]. Heibonsha shinsho, 2006.

Hayashi Shigeru. *Nihon no rekishi* [A history of Japan]. Vol. 25, *Taiheiyō sensō* [The Pacific war]. Chūō kōronsha, 1967.

Heiyama Kanki. "Nihon rikugun ni okeru sakusen jō no yōkyū to kenkyū kaihatsu no kankei: yasenhō wo shutai toshite" [The relationship between the Japanese army's operational requirements and developmental research—on the subject of field artillery]. *Bōeichō bōei senshibu kenkyū shiryō*, 85 RO-2H, mimeo, 1985.

Hirao Michio. *Boshin sensōshi* [A history of the Boshin war]. Misaki shobō, 1971.

Hosaka Masayasu. *Shōwa rikugun no kenkyū* [Research about the Shōwa army]. 2 vols. Asahi bunko, 2006.

Hoshikawa Takeo, ed. *Rekishi gunzō shirizū tōkubetsu henshi* [Special edition—military group history]. "Kettei han" Zusetsu Bakumatsu Boshin Seinan sensō* [Definitive edition—Illustrated account of the bakumatsu, Boshin, and Satsuma wars]. Gakushu kenkyūsha, 2006.

Hōya Tōru. *Sensō no Nishonshi* [Warfare in Japanese history].Vol. 18, *Boshin sensō* [The Boshin war].Yoshikawa Kōbunkan, 2007.

Ichinose Toshiya. *Kindai Nihon no chōheisei to shakai* [Conscription and society in modern Japan].Yoshikawa Kōbunkan, 2004.

————. *Meiji Taishō Shōwa guntai manyūaru* [Military pamphlets of the Meiji, Taishō, and Shōwa periods]. Kōbunsha shinsho, 2004.

Ichisaka Tarō. *Chōshū kiheitai* [The Chōshū kiheitai]. Chūkō shinsho, 2002.

Iguchi Kazuki. *Nichi-Ro sensō no jidai* [The age of the Russo-Japanese war]. Yoshikawa Kōbunkan, 1998.

Ikai Toshiaki. *Seinan sensō: sensō no taigi to dōin sareru minshu* [The Satsuma war:A just war and the masses who were mobilized].Yoshikawa Kōbunkan, 2008.

Ikō Toshiya. *Sensō Nihonshi* [Warfare in Japanese history].Vol. 22, *Manshū jihen kara Nitchū zenmen sensō e* [From the Manchurian incident to a full-scale Sino-Japanese war].Yoshikawa Kōbunkan, 2007.

Ikuda Makoto. *Nihon rikugunshi* [A history of Japan's army]. Kyōikusha rekishi shinsho, 1980.

Inoki Masamichi. *Gunkoku Nihon no kōbō* [The rise and fall of militarist Japan]. Chūkō shinsho, 1995.

Inoue Kiyoshi. *Nihon no rekishi* [A history of Japan].Vol. 20, *Meiji ishin* [The Meiji restoration]. Chūō kōronsha, 1966.

Itō Takashi. *Nihon no rekishi* [A history of Japan].Vol. 30, *Jūgonen sensō* [The fifteen years war]. Shogakkan, 1976.

Itō Takashi and Momose Takashi. *Jiten: Shōwa senzen no Nihon* [A dictionary of prewar Shōwa Japan].Yoshikawa Kōbunkan, 1990.

Kaneko Tsunenori. *Heiki to senjutsu no Nihonshi* [A history of Japanese weapons and tactics]. Hara shobō, 1982.

Kasahara Hidehiko. *Meiji tennō* [The Meiji emperor]. Chūkō shinsho, 2006.

Katō Yōko. *Chōheisei to kindai Nihon, 1868–1945* [The conscription system and modern Japan, 1868–1945].Yoshikawa Kōbunkan, 1996.

Katogawa Kōtarō. *Rikugun no hanshō* [Reflections on the army]. 2 vols. Kenpakusha, 1996.

————. *Sanjūpachi hoheiju* [The type-38 infantry rifle]. Shirogane shobō, 1975.

————. *Teikoku rikugun kikōbutai* [The imperial army's armored units]. Rev. ed. Hara shobō, 1981.

Kawano Hitoshi. *"Gyokusai" no guntai—"seikan" no guntai* [An annihilated army—an army returning alive]. Kōdansha, 2001.

Kawashima [?]. *"Gundōin no seidō to jissai"* [The military mobilization system and its reality]. *Bōeichō bōei senshibu kenkyū shiryō* 95 RO-4H, mimeo, 1980.

Kido Kōichi kenkyūkai, eds. *Kido Kōichi nikki* [*Kido Kōichi* diary]. 2 vols. Tokyo daigaku shuppansha, 1966.

Kisaka Junichirō. *Shōwa no rekishi* [A history of the Shōwa reign].Vol. 7, *Taiheiyō sensō* [The Pacific war]. Shogakkan, 1989.

Kita Hiroaki. *Nitchū kaisen* [The beginning of the Sino-Japanese war]. Chūkō shinsho, 1994.

Kitaoka Shinichi. *Nihon no kindai* [Modern Japan].Vol. 5, *Seitō kara gunbu e 1924–1941* [From political parties to military cliques, 1924–1941]. Chūō kōronsha, 1999.

Kobayashi Hiroharu. *Sensō no Nihonshi.* [Warfare in Japanese history].Vol. 21, *Sōryokusen to demokurashi* [Total war and democracy]. Yoshikawa Kōbunsha, 2008.

Kobe Tatsu. "Nanpō sakusen ni okeru rikugun no kyōiku kunren" [Army education and training for southern area operations]. *Bōeichō bōei senshibu kenkyū shiryō*, 85 RO-3H, mimeo, 1985.

Kojima Keizō. *Boshin sensō kara Seinan sensō e* [From the Boshin war to the Satsuma war]. Chūkō shinsho, 1996.

Kojima Noboru. *Nitchu sensō* [The Sino-Japanese war]. 5 vols. Bunshūn bunkō, 1988.

———. *Sanbō* [The staff officers]. 2 vols. Bunshūn bunko, 1975.

———. *Shikkikan* [The commanders]. 2 vols. Bunshūn bunko, 1974.

———. *Taiheiyō sensō* [The Pacific war]. 2 vols. Chūkō shinsho, 1966.

———. *Tennō* [The emperor]. 5 vols. Bungei shūnjū, 1974.

Kōketsu Atsushi. *Nihon kaigun no shūsen kōsaku* [The Japanese navy's war termination stratagems]. Chūkō shinsho, 1996.

Kondō Shintsuke. "Taiheiyō sensō ni okeru Nihon rikugun taijōriku sakusen shisō" [The Japanese army's thinking on counter-amphibious operations during the Pacific war]. *Bōeichō bōei senshibu kenkyu shiryō*, 92 RO-4H, mimeo, 1992.

Konishi Shirō. *Nihon no rekishi* [A history of Japan].Vol. 19, *Kaikoku to jōi* [Open the country and expel the barbarians]. Chūō kōron, 1966.

Kumagai Mikahisa. "Kyū rikukaigun shōkō no senbetsu to kyōiku" [The selection and education of officers in the former army and navy]. *Bōeichō bōei senshibu kenkyū shiryō* 80 RO-12H, mimeo, 1980.

———. *Nihongun no jinteki seidō to mondaiten no kenkyū* [The Japanese military's personnel system and research about its problem areas]. Kokusho kankōkai, 1995.

Kumagai Tadasu [Mikahisa]. *Teikoku rikukaigun no kisō chishiki* [A basic knowledge of the imperial army and navy]. Kōjinsha NF bunko, 2007.

Kurogawa Yuzō. *Kindai Nihon no gunji senryaku gaisetsu* [An outline of modern Japan's military strategy]. Fūyō shobō, 2003.

Kuroha Kiyotaka. *Nitchū 15 nen sensō* [The 15-year Sino-Japanese war]. 3 vols. Kyōikusha rekishi shinsho, 1977–1979.

Kurono Taeru. *Dai Nihon teikoku no seizon senryaku* [The greater Japanese empire's survival strategy]. Kōdansha, 2004.

———. *Nihon o horoboshita kokubō hōshin* [National defense policies that destroyed Japan]. Bungei shinsho, 2002.

———. *Sanbō honbu to rikugun daigaku* [The general staff and the army general staff school]. Kōdansha gendai shinsho, 2004.

———. *Teikoku kokubō hōshin no kenkyū* [Research about imperial defense policy]. Sowasha, 2000.

———. *Teikoku rikugun no "kaikaku to teikō"* [Reform and opposition in the imperial army]. Kōdansha gendai shinsho, 2006.

Kurosawa Fumitaka. *Daisen kanki no Nihon rikugun* [The period of the great war and the Japanese army]. Misuzu shobō, 2000.

Kuwada Etsu and Maebara Toshio. *Nihon no sensō zukai to dēta* [Japan's wars—maps and data]. Hara shobō, 1982.

Kyū sanbō honbu hensan, eds. *Nichi-Ro sensō* [The Russo-Japanese war]. 2 vols. Tokuma shoten, 1994.

———. *Nisshin sensō* [The Sino-Japanese war].Tokuma shoten, 1995.

Maebara Toshio. "Nihon rikugun no 'kōbō' ni kakawaru riron to kyōgi" [Theories and deliberations concerning the Japanese army's offensive and defensive]. *Bōeicho bōei senshibu kenkyū shiryō* 86 RO-5H, mimeo, 1986.

Mainichi shimbunsha, eds. *Ichiokunin no Shōwashi: Nihon no sensō* [100 millions' Shōwa history:The wars of Japan]. 6 vols. Mainichi shimbunsha, 1978.

Maruyama Shigeo. *Inparu sakusen jūgunki* [Diary of a military correspondent on the Imphal operation]. Iwanami shinsho, 1984.

Masumi Junnosuke. *Shōwa tennō to sono jidai* [The Shōwa emperor and that age].Yamakawa shuppansha, 1998.

MatsushitaYoshio. *Meiji no guntai* [The Meiji military]. Shibundō, 1963.

———. *Nihon kokubō no higeki* [The tragedy of Japan's national defense]. Fūyō shobō, 1976.

Miller, Terasaki Mariko. *Shōwa tennō dokuhakuroku Terasaki Hidenari Goyōgakari nikki* [The Shōwa emperor's soliloquy: unattached court official Terasaki Hidenari's diary]. Bungei shūnjū, 1991.

MōriToshihiko. *Taiwan shuppei* [The Taiwan expedition]. Chūkō shinsho, 1996.

Morimatsu Toshio. *Daihon'ei* [Imperial general headquarters]. Kyōikusha rekishi shinsho, 1980.

Nakano Hideo. *Shōwashi no genten* [The origins of Shōwa history]. 4 vols. Kōdansha, 1973–1975.

Nihon kokusai seiji gakkai, eds. *Taiheiyō sensō e no michi* [The road to the Pacific war]. 8 vols. Asahi shibunsha, 1963.

NoguchiTakehiko. *Chōshū sensō* [The Chōshū wars]. Chūkō shinsho, 2006.

Ōe Shinobu. *Chō Saku Rin bakusatsu* [The assassination of Zhang Zuolin]. Chūkō shinsho, 1989.

———. *Gozen kaigi* [The imperial conference]. Chūkō shinsho, 1991.

———. *Heishitachi no Nichi-Ro sensō* [The soldiers of the Russo-Japanese war].Asahi shimbunsha, 1988.

———. *Nichi-Ro sensō no gunjishiteki kenkyū* [The Russo-Japanese war and military research]. Iwanami shoten, 1976.

———. *Nichi-Ro sensō to Nihon guntai* [The Russo-Japanese war and the Japanese military]. Rippu shobō, 1987.

———. *Nihon no sanbō honbu* [Japan's general staff]. Chūkō shinsho, 1985.

———. *Shōwa no rekishi* [A history of the Shōwa reign]. Vol. 3, *Tennō no guntai* [The emperor's army]. Shogakkan, 1982.

———. *Yasukuni jinja* [TheYasukuni shrine]. Iwanami shinsho, 1984.

Ogawara Masamichi. *Seinan sensō: Saigō Takamori to Nihon saigō no naisen* [The Satsuma war: Saigō Takamori and Japan's final civil war]. Chūkō shinsho, 2007.

Ōhama Tetsuya and Ozawa Ikurou. *Teikoku rikukaigun jiten* [A dictionary of the imperial army and navy]. Dōseisha, 1984.

Okumura Fusao and Kuwada Etsu, eds. *Kindai Nihon sensōshi* [A history of modern Japan's wars].Vol. 1, *Nisshin Nichi-Ro sensō* [The Sino-Japanese and Russo-Japanese wars]. Dōdai keizai kōdankai, 1996.

Ōoka Shōhei. *Reite sakusen* [Military record of the Leyte operation]. Chūō kōronsha, 1966.

Ōsugi Kazuo. *Nitchū jūgonen sensōshi* [A history of the fifteen years war]. Chūkō shinsho, 1996.

Ōtani Keijirō. *Shōwa kempeishi* [A history of the military police during the Shōwa era]. Misuzu shobō, 1966.

Ōuchi Tsutomu. *Nihon no rekishi* [A history of Japan].Vol. 23, *Taishō demokurashi* [Taishō democracy]. Chūō kōronsha, 1966.

Rekishigaku kenkyūkai, ed. *Nihonshi nenpyō* [Chronology of Japanese history]. Iwanami shoten, 1966.

Rikusen gakkai, ed. *Kindai sensō gaisetsu* [An outline of modern warfare]. 2 vols. Rikusen gakkai, 1984.

———. *Kindai sensōshi gaisetsu shiryō hen* [An outline of modern warfare—Documentary appendix]. Rikusen gakkai, 1984.

Rikusenshi kenkyū fūkyūkai, ed. *Rikusen shishū* [Collected land warfare history]. Vol. 11, *Ryōjun yōsai kōrakusen* [The reduction of the Port Arthur fortress]. Hara shobō, 1969.

Saitō Seiji. *Nisshin sensō no gunji senryaku* [The military strategy of the Sino-Japanese war]. Fūyō shobō, 2003.

Sanbō honbu, ed. *Haisen no kiroku* [Record of a lost war]. Vol. 38, *Meiji hyakunenshi sōsho* [Official history of the Meiji centennial]. Hara shobō, 1979.

___. Sugiyama memo (General Sugiyama Hajime's notes). 2 parts. *Meiji hyakunenshi sōsho* [Official history of the Meiji centennial], vols. 16 and 17. Hara shobō, 1967.

Sasaki Suguru. *Boshin sensō* [The Boshin war]. Chūkō shinsho, 1990.

Sayama Jirō. *Taihō nyūmon* [Introduction to artillery weapons]. Kōjinsha NF bunko, 1999.

Shimada Toshihiko. *Kantōgun* [The Kwantung army]. Chūkō shinsho, 1965.

Shimanuki Shigeyoshi. *Senryaku: Nichi-Ro sensō* [Strategy: The Russo-Japanese war]. 2 vols. Hara shobō, 1980.

Shirai Akio. *Nihon rikugun kunren no kenkyū* [Research concerning the Japanese army training]. Fūyō shobō, 2003.

Suekuni Masao and Koike I'ichi, eds. *Kaigunshi jiten* [Dictionary of naval history]. Kokusho kankōkai, 1985.

Suzuki Akira. *Shiba Ryōtarō to mitsu no sensō* [Shiba Ryōtarō and three wars]. Asahi shimbunsha, 2004.

Takahashi Masae. *Ni ni roku jiken* [The 2-26 incident]. Rev. ed. Chūkō shinsho, 1994.

———. *Shōwa no gunbatsu* [The military cliques of the Shōwa reign]. Chūkō shinsho, 1969.

Takaki Sōkichi. *Taiheiyō sensōshi* [A history of the Pacific war]. Rev. ed. Iwanami shinsho, 1977.

Tamura Yōzō. *Biaku shima gyokusai* [Annihilation at Biak island]. Kōjinsha NF bunko, 2004.

Tanaka Keimi. *Rikugun jinji seidō gaisetsu* [An outline of the army's personnel system, pt. 1] *Bōeichō bōei senshibu kenkyū shiryō* 80 RO-1H [Japan, self-defense agency, self-defense military history department, research document 80-1H] mimeo, 1981.

Tanaka Ryūkichi. *Nihon gunbatsu antōshi* [Japan's military cliques' secret feuds]. Chūkō bunko, 1988.

Tani Hisao. *Kimitsu Nichi-Ro senshi* [Confidential history of the Russo-Japanese war]. Vol. 3, *Meiji hyakunenshi sōsho* [Official history of the Meiji centennial]. Hara shobō, 1971.

Tobe Ryōichi. *Nihon no kindai* [Modern Japan]. Vol. 9, *Gyakusetsu no guntai* [The military paradox]. Chūō kōronsha, 1998.

———. *Nihon rikugun to Chūgoku* [The Japanese army and China]. Kōdansha, 1999.

Tobe Ryōichi et al. *Shippai no honshitsu* [The essence of defeat]. Chūkō bunko, 1991.

Toyama Saburō. *Nihon kaigunshi* [A history of the Japanese navy]. Kyōikusha rekishi shinsho, 1980.

Toyama Shigeki and Adachi Yoshiko, eds. *Kindai Nihon seijishi hikkei* [A handbook of modern Japan's political history]. Iwanami shoten, 1961.

Toyoda Jō. *Kaigun gunreibu* [The naval general staff]. Kōdansha bunko, 1993.

Usui Katsumi. *Manshū jihen* [The Manchurian incident]. Chūkō shinsho, 1974.

———. *Nitchū sensō* [The Sino-Japanese war]. 1967. Rev. ed., Chūkō shinsho, 2000.

Wagamatsu Sakai, ed. *Nihon seiji saiban shiroku, Meiji—zen* [A documentary account of Japan's political trials—the first half of the Meiji period]. Dai ichi hōki shuppan kabushiki kaisha, 1968.

———. *Nihon seiji saiban shiroku Meiji—go* [A documentary account of Japan's political trials—the second half of the Meiji period]. Dai ichi hōki shuppan kabushiki kaisha, 1969.

Watanabe Yukio. *Ugaki Kazushige* [Ugaki Kazushige]. Chūkō shinsho, 1993.

Yamada Akira. *Daigensui Shōwa tennō* [Generalissimo Shōwa emperor]. Shin Nihon shuppansha, 1994.

———. *Shōwa tennō no gunji shisō to senryaku* [The Shōwa emperor's ideas and military strategy]. Kokura shobō, 2002.

Yamaguchi Muneyuki. *Rikugun to kaigun—rikukaigun shōkōshi no kenkyū* [Army and navy—research about the army's and navy's officers]. Seibundō, 2000.

Yamamoto Daisei. *Shōhai no kōzō: Nichi-Ro senshi o kagaku suru* [The structure of victory or defeat: A scientific approach to the Russo-Japanese war]. Hara shobō, 1981.

Yamamuro Kentoku. *Gunshin* [War gods]. Chūō shinsho, 2007.

Yoshida Toshio. *Nihon rikukaigun no shōgai* [The lifetime of Japan's army and navy]. Bunshūn bunko, 2001.

Yoshida Yutaka. *Ajia Taiheiyō senso* [The Asia-Pacific war]. Iwanami shinsho, 2007.

———. *Nihon no guntai* [The Japanese military]. Iwanami shinsho, 2002.

———. "Nihon no guntai" [The Japanese military]. In Ōe Shinobu et al., eds., *Iwanami kōza Nihon tsushi* [Iwanami's lectures on common Japanese history]. Vol. 17, *Kindai 2* [The modern period]. Iwanami shoten, 1994.

———. *Shōwa tennō no shūsenshi* [A history of the Shōwa emperor's war termination]. Iwanami shinsho, 1992.

Yoshida Yutaka and Mori Shigeki. *Senso no Nihonshi* [Warfare in Japanese history]. Vol. 23, *Ajia Taiheiyō senso* [The Asia-Pacific war]. Yoshikawa kōbunkan, 2007.

Yui Masaomi, Fujiwara Akira, and Yoshida Yutaka, eds. *Nihon kindai shishō taikei* [An outline of modern Japanese thought]—Vol. 4, *Guntai heishi* [The military and the soldiery]. Iwanami shoten, 1989.

Japanese-Language Periodicals

Asakawa Michio. "Ishin kengunki ni okeru Nihon rikugun no yōhei shisō" [Strategic and tactical thought in the Japanese army in its formative period]. *Gunji shigaku* 38:2 (September 2002), 4–19.

———. "Shinbi chōhei ni kansuru hitotsu kenkyū" [Research concerning the 1871 conscription ordinance]. *Gunji shigaku* 32:1 (June 1996), 20–37.

Hara Takeshi. "Nisshin senso ni okeru hondo bōei" [Homeland defense during the Sino-Japanese war]. *Gunji shigaku* 30:3 (December 1994), 35–46.

———. "Hohei chūshin no hakuhei shūgi no keisei" [The evolution of hand-to-hand combat as the basis of infantry tactics]. Special Issue, *Gunji shigaku* 41:1–2 (June 2005), 271–287.

Hashimoto Masaki. "Tabaruzaka-gunki soshitsu zenya" [The battle of Tabaruzaka on the eve of the loss of the regimental colors], part 1. *Rekishi to jimbutsu* (October 1971), 227–245.

Hata Ikuhiko. "Dai niji sekai taisen no Nihonjin sembotsusha zō" [A study of the numbers of Japanese war dead during the Second World War]. *Gunji shigaku* 42:2 (September 2006), 4–27.

Hori Shigeru. "'Chōbatsu' no sūchiteki jittai ni kansuru hitotsu kyōsai" [A statistical study of the Chōshu clique]. *Gunji shigaku* 43:1 (June 2007), 20–35.

Ishige Shin'ichi. "Chū ko itchi ni okeru guntai shisō to kyōiku shisō" [Military thought and educational thought regarding loyalty and filial piety]. *Gunji shigaku* 37:4 (March 2002), 4–17.

Kikegawa Hiromasa. "Boshin senso kenkyū no seikō to kadai" [A reassessment of Japanese scholarship on the Boshin war]. *Gunji shigaku* 32:1 (June 1996), 38–57.

Kurono Taeru. "'Teikoku kokubō hōshin' senryaku sakusen yōheikō" [Strategic and operational considerations for the 1907 "imperial defense policy"]. *Gunji shigaku* 31:4 (March 1996), 4–18.

Kuwada Etsu. "Nisshin sensō mae no Nihongun no tairiku shinkō junbi setsu ni tsuite" [The Japanese military's invasion preparations before the Sino-Japanese war]. *Gunji shigaku* 30:3 (December 1994), 4–18.

Kuzuhara Kazumi. "'Sentō kōyō' no kyōgi no keisei to kōchiku ka" [Principles of Combat: From formation to ossification]. *Gunji shigaku* 40:1 (June 2004), 19–37.

Muranaka Tomoyuki. "Yamagata Aritomo no 'riekisen' gainen [Yamagata Aritomo's line of interests]. *Gunji shigaku* 42:1 (June 2006), 76–92.

Nara Takeji. "Nara Takeji Jijūbukancho nikki (shō)" [Imperial aide-de-camp Nara Takeiji's diary]. *Chūō koron* (September 1990), 324–360.

Ono Keishi. "Nisshin sensō ato keieiki no gunji shishutsu to zaisei seikaku" [The management of military expenditures and financial policies after the Sino-Japanese War]. *Gunji shigaku* 40:2–3 (December 2004), 45–60.

Ōshima Akiko. "Iwayuru Takebashi jihen no 'yōha' ni tsuite" [Concerning the after-effects of the so-called Takebashi incident]. *Gunji shigaku* 32:3 (December 1996), 34–47.

Ōyama Hiroshi. "Kyū Nagoyaken Shōshū no Tokyo chindaihei ni kansuru jitsotsu kyōsai" [Conscripts from the former Nagoya prefecture serving in the Tokyo garrison]. *Gunji shigaku* 32:1 (June 1996), 58–70.

Shimanuki Takeji. "Dai 1 ji sekai daisen igo no kokubō hōshin, shoyō heiryoku, yōhei kōryō no hensen" [National defense policy, force structure, and operational research in the post–World War I period], part 2. *Gunjishi gaku* 9:1 (June 1973), 65–75.

Shonohara Masato. "Meiji rikugun to Tamura Iyozō" [The Meiji army and Tamura Iyozō]. *Gunji shigaku* 32:2 (September 1996), 30–44.

Takemoto Tomoyuki. "Ōmura Masajirō ni okeru Yōshiki heihyōnron no keisei" [Ōmura Masajirō 's formulation of western-style military theories]. *Gunji shigaku* 38:2 (September 2002), 20–34.

———. "Ōmura Masajirō no kengun kōsō" [Ōmura Masajirō's ideas on military construction]. *Gunji shigaku* 42:1 (June 2006), 22–40.

English-Language Books

Allen, Louis. *Burma: The Longest War, 1941–45*. New York: St. Martin's, 1984.

———. *The End of the War in Asia*. New York: Beekman/Esanu, 1976.

Barnhart, Michael A. *Japan Prepares for Total War: The Search for Economic Security, 1919–1941*. Ithaca, NY: Cornell University Press, 1987.

———. *Japan and the World since 1868*. London: Edward Arnold, 1995.

Bergamini, David. *Japan's Imperial Conspiracy*. New York: Pocket Books, 1972.

Berger, Gordon M. *Parties out of Power in Japan, 1931–1941*. Princeton, NJ: Princeton University Press, 1977.

Bix, Herbert P. *Hirohito and the Making of Modern Japan*. New York: HarperCollins, 2000.

Boyle, John Hunter. *China and Japan at War, 1937–1945*. Stanford, CA: Stanford University Press, 1974.

Browning, Christopher R. *Ordinary Men: Reserve Police Battalion 101 and the Final Solution in Poland*. New York: HarperPerennial, 1993.

Butow, Robert J. C. *Tojo and the Coming of the War*. Stanford, CA: Stanford University Press, 1960.

Coble, Parks. *Facing Japan: Chinese Politics and Japanese Imperialism, 1931–1937*. Cambridge, MA: Harvard University Press, 1991.

Conroy, Hillary. *The Japanese Seizure of Korea, 1868–1910*. Philadelphia: University of Pennsylvania Press, 1960.

Cook, Haruko Taya, and Theodore Cook. *Japan at War: An Oral History*. New York: New Press, 1992.

Coox, Alvin D. *The Anatomy of a Small War: The Soviet-Japanese Struggle for Changkuofeng/Khasan, 1938*. Westport, CT: Greenwood, 1977.

———. *Nomonhan: Japan against Russia*. 2 vols. Stanford, CA: Stanford University Press, 1985.

Crowley, James B. *Japan's Quest for Autonomy*. Princeton, NJ: Princeton University Press, 1968.

Dower, John W. *War without Mercy: Race and Power in the Pacific War*. New York: Pantheon, 1986.

Drea, Edward J. *In The Service of the Emperor: Essays on the Imperial Japanese Army*. Lincoln: University of Nebraska Press, 1998.

Dreyer, Edward L. *China at War, 1901–1949*. New York: Longman, 1995.

Duus, Peter. *The Abacus and the Sword: The Japanese Penetration of Korea, 1895–1910*. Berkeley: University of California Press, 1995.

Fairbank, John K., Edwin O. Reischauer, and Albert M. Craig. *East Asia: The Modern Transformation*. Boston: Houghton Mifflin, 1965.

Falk, Stanley L. *Bataan: The March of Death*. New York: W. W. Norton, 1962.

———. *Decision at Leyte*. New York: W. W. Norton, 1966.

———. *Seventy Days to Singapore*. New York: Putnam, 1975.

Frank, Richard B. *Downfall*. New York: Random House, 1999.

Gluck, Carol. *Japan's Modern Myths*. Princeton, NJ: Princeton University Press, 1985.

Gordon, Andrew. *A Modern History of Japan from Tokugawa Times to the Present*. New York: Oxford University Press, 2003.

Hackett, Roger F. *Yamagata Aritomo in the Rise of Modern Japan, 1838–1922*. Cambridge, MA: Harvard University Press, 1971.

Hall, John Whitney. "A Monarch for Modern Japan," in Robert E. Ward, ed., *Political Development in Modern Japan*. Princeton, NJ: Princeton University Press, 1968.

Hane, Mikiso. *Peasants, Rebels, and Outcasts: The Underside of Modern Japan*. New York: Pantheon, 1982.

Harries, Meirion, and Susie Meirion. *Soldiers of the Sun*. New York: Random House, 1992.

Havens, Thomas. *Valley of Darkness*. New York: W. W. Norton, 1978.

Hayashi, Saburo. *Kogun: The Japanese Army in the Pacific War*. Westport, CT: Greenwood, 1978.

Honjo, Shigeru. *Emperor Hirohito and His Chief Aide-de-Camp: The Honjo Diary, 1933–36*. Translated by Mikiso Hane. Tokyo: University of Tokyo Press, 1982.

Hsiung, James C., and Steven I. Levine, eds. *China's Bitter Victory: The War with Japan, 1937–1945*. New York: M. E. Sharpe, 1992.

Huber, Thomas M. *Japan's Battle of Okinawa, April–June 1945*. Leavenworth Papers No. 18. Washington, DC: U.S. Government Printing Office, 1990.

Humphreys, Leonard A. *The Way of the Heavenly Sword: The Japanese Army in the 1920s*. Stanford, CA: Stanford University Press, 1995.

Hunter, Janet E. *The Emergence of Modern Japan: An Introductory History since 1853*. London: Longman Group UK, 1989.

Ienaga, Saburo. *The Pacific War*. New York: Pantheon, 1978.

Ike, Nobutaka. *Japan's Decision for War*. Stanford, CA: Stanford University Press, 1967.

———. "War and Modernization," in Robert E. Ward, ed., *Political Development in Modern Japan*. Princeton, NJ: Princeton University Press, 1968.

Jordan, Donald A. *China's Trial by Fire: The Shanghai War of 1932*. Ann Arbor: University of Michigan Press, 2001.

Kakehashi, Kumiko. *So Sad to Fall in Battle*. New York: Presidio, 2007.

Large, Stephen S. *Emperor Hirohito and Shōwa Japan: A Political Biography*. London and New York: Routledge, 1992.

Lary, Diana, and Stephen MacKinnon, eds. *Scars of War: The Impact of Warfare on Modern China*. Vancouver: UBC Press, 2001.

Lebra, Joyce C. *Japanese-Trained Armies in Southeast Asia*. New York: Columbia University Press, 1977.

Lifton, Robert Jay, Shuichi Kato, and Michael R. Reich. *Six Lives Six Deaths*. New Haven, CT: Yale University Press, 1977.

Lone, Stewart. *Army, Empire, and Politics in Meiji Japan*. London: St. Martin's, 2000.

———. *Japan's First Modern War*. London: St. Martin's, 1994.

Lory, Hills. *Japan's Military Masters*. New York: Viking, 1943.

Matsusaka, Yoshihisa Tak. "Human Bullets, General Nogi, and the Myth of Port Arthur," in John W. Steinberg, et al., eds., *The Russo-Japanese War in Global Perspective*. Leiden, Netherlands: Brill, 2005.

Maxon, Yale Candee. *Control of Japanese Foreign Policy: A Study of Civil-Military Rivalry, 1930–1945*. Berkeley and Los Angeles: University of California Press, 1957.

Morley, James William, ed. *The China Quagmire*. New York: Columbia University Press, 1983.

———. *The Fateful Choice*. New York: Columbia University Press, 1980.

———. *Japan Erupts*. New York: Columbia University Press, 1984.

———. *The Japanese Thrust into Siberia, 1918*. New York: Columbia University Press, 1957.

Morris, Ivan. *The Nobility of Failure: Tragic Heroes in the History of Japan*. New York: Holt, Reinhart, and Winston, 1975.

Mutsu, Munemitsu. *Kenkenroku*. Edited and translated by Gordon M. Berger. Princeton, NJ: Princeton University Press, 1982.

Nish, Ian, ed. *Anglo-Japanese Alienation, 1919–1952: Papers of the Anglo-Japanese Conference on the History of the Second World War*. Cambridge, UK: Cambridge University Press, 1982.

Okamoto, Shumpei. *The Japanese Oligarchy and the Russo-Japanese War*. New York: Columbia University Press, 1970.

Paine, S. C. M. *The Sino-Japanese War of 1894–1895*. Cambridge, UK: Cambridge University Press, 2003.

Peattie, Mark R. *Ishiwara Kanji and Japan's Confrontation with the West*. Princeton, NJ: Princeton University Press, 1975.

Peattie, Mark R., and David Evans. *Kaigun*. Annapolis, MD: Naval Institute Press, 1997.

Pelz, Stephen E. *Race to Pearl Harbor*. Cambridge, MA: Harvard University Press, 1974.

Presseisen, Ernst L. *Before Aggression: Europeans Prepare the Japanese Army*. Tucson: University of Arizona Press, 1965.

Schencking, Charles J. *Making Waves: Politics, Propaganda, and the Emergence of the Imperial Japanese Navy, 1868–1922*. Stanford, CA: Stanford University Press, 2005.

Sheldon, Charles D. "The Politics of the Civil War of 1868," in W. G. Beasley, ed., *Modern Japan: Aspects of History, Literature, and Society*. Rutledge, VT: Charles E. Tuttle, 1976.

Shillony, Ben-Ami. *Politics and Culture in Wartime Japan*. Oxford: Clarendon, 1981.

———. *Revolt in Japan*. Princeton, NJ: Princeton University Press, 1973.

Shiroyama, Saburō. *War Criminal: The Life and Death of Hirota Kōki.* Translated by John Bester. Tokyo: Kōdansha, 1977.

Sims, Richard. *French Policy towards the Bakufu and Meiji Japan, 1854–95. Meiji Japan Series 3.* Surrey, UK: Curzon, 1998.

Smethurst, Richard J. *A Social Basis for Prewar Japanese Militarism: The Army and the Rural Community.* Berkeley, CA: University of California Press, 1974.

Spector, Ronald H. *Eagle against the Sun.* New York: Free Press, 1985.

Steele, William M. "The Rise and Fall of the Shogitai: A Social Drama," in Tetsuo Najita and J. Victor Koschmann, eds., *Conflict in Modern Japanese History.* Princeton, NJ: Princeton University Press, 1982.

Steinberg, John W., Bruce W. Menning, David Schimmelpennick van der Oye, David Wolff, and Shinji Yokote, eds. *The Russo-Japanese War in Global Perspective.* 2 vols. Leiden, Netherlands: Brill, 2005, 2007.

Straus, Ulrich. *The Anguish of Surrender.* Seattle: University of Washington Press, 2003.

Supreme Commander for the Allied Powers. *Reports of General MacArthur,* vol. 1 and *Supplement,* vol. 2, parts 1 and 2. Washington, DC: SCAP, 1966.

Swinson, Arthur. *Four Samurai.* London: Hutchinson, 1968.

Takamae, Eiji. *The Allied Occupation of Japan.* New York: Continuum, 2002.

Titus, David Anson. *Palace and Politics in Prewar Japan.* New York: Columbia University Press, 1974.

Tohmatsu, Haruo, and H. P. Willmott. *A Gathering Darkness: The Coming of War to the Far East and the Pacific, 1921–1942.* Lanham, MD: SR Books, 2005.

Toland, John. *The Rising Sun.* New York: Random House, 1970.

Tsuji, Masanobu. *Japan's Greatest Victory, Britain's Worst Defeat.* Translated by Margaret E. Lake. New York: Sarpedon, 1993.

Warner, Denis, and Peggy Warner. *The Tide at Sunrise: A History of the Russo-Japanese War, 1904–1905.* New York: Charterhouse, 1974.

Weinberg, Gerhard. *A World at Arms.* Cambridge, UK: Cambridge University Press, 1994.

Wells, David, and Sandra Wilson, eds. *The Russo-Japanese War in Cultural Perspective, 1904–05.* New York: St. Martin's, 1999.

Yamamoto, Masahiro. *Nanking: Anatomy of an Atrocity.* Westport, CT: Praeger, 2000.

Yoshihashi, Takehiko. *Conspiracy at Mukden.* New Haven, CT: Yale University Press, 1963.

English-Language Periodicals

Bolitho, Harold. "The Eichigo War, 1868." *Monumenta Nipponica* 34:3 (Autumn 1979), 259–277.

Boyd, James. "In Pursuit of an Obsession: Japan in Inner Mongolia in the 1930s." *Japanese Studies* 22:3 (2002), 289–303.

Buck, James H. "The Satsuma Rebellion of 1877: From Kagoshima through the Siege of Kumamoto Castle." *Monumenta Nipponica* 28:4 (Winter 1973), 427–446.

Cook, Haruko Taya. "The Myth of the Saipan Suicides." *MHQ* 7:3 (Spring 1995), 12–19.

Drea, Edward J. "In the Army Barracks of Imperial Japan." *Armed Forces and Society* 15:3 (1989), 329–348.

———. "Missing Intentions: Japanese Intelligence and the Soviet Invasion of Manchuria, 1945." *Military Affairs* (April 1984), 66–70.

Friday, Karl F. "Bushidō or Bull? A Medieval Historian's Perspective on the Imperial Army and the Japanese Warrior Tradition." *History Teacher* 27:3 (May 1994), 339–349.

Gillin, Donald G., and Charles Etter. "Staying on: Japanese Soldiers and Civilians in China, 1945–1949." *Journal of Asian Studies,* 42:3 (May 1983), 497–517.

Humphreys, Leonard A. "Crisis and Reaction: The Japanese Army in the 'Liberal' Twenties." *Armed Forces and Society* 5:1 (Fall 1978), 73–92.

Kitaoka, Shin'ichi. "The Army as Bureaucracy: Japanese Militarism Revisited." *Journal of Military History,* Special Issue, 57:5 (October 1993).

Large, Stephen S. "Nationalist Extremism in Early Shōwa Japan: Inoue Nissho and the 'Blood-Pledge Corps Incident,' 1932." *Modern Asian Studies* 35:3 (2001), 533–564.

Lary, Diana. "Drowned Earth: The Strategic Breaching of the Yellow River Dyke, 1938." *War in History* 8:2 (2001), 191–207.

Lone, Stewart. "Between Bushidō and Black Humor." *History Today* 55:9 (September 2005), 20–27.

———. "The Sino-Japanese War, 1894–95, and the Evolution of the Japanese Monarchy." *Japan and China: Miscellaneous Papers.* Suntory-Toyota International Centre for Economics and Relate Disciplines, London School of Economics and Political Science, 1993.

MacKinnon, Stephen. "The Tragedy of Wuhan, 1938." *Modern Asian Studies* 30:4 (1966), 931–943.

Nakamura, Yoshihisa, and Ryoichi Tobe. "The Imperial Japanese Army and Politics." *Armed Forces and Society* 14:4 (Summer 1988), 511–525.

Nish, Ian. "Japan's Indecision during the Boxer Disturbances." *Journal of Asian Studies* 20:4 (August 1961), 449–461.

Shimazu, Naoko. "The Myth of the 'Patriotic Soldier': Japanese Attitudes Towards Death in the Russo-Japanese War." *War & Society* 19:2 (October 2001), 69–89.

Van Slyke, Lyman P. "The Battle of the Hundred Regiments: Problems of Coordination and Control during the Sino-Japanese War." *Modern Asian Studies* 30:4 (October 1996), 979–1005.

Yokoyama, Hisayuki. "Military Technological Strategy and Armaments Concepts of [the] Japanese Imperial Army—Around the Post-WWI Period." National Institute for Defense Studies (NIDS), *NIDS Security Reports,* No. 2 (March 2001).

Index